Everyday Ethics for the
Criminal Justice Professional

Everyday Ethics for the Criminal Justice Professional

Second Edition

Kelly Cheeseman

Claudia San Miguel

Durant Frantzen

Lisa Nored

CAROLINA ACADEMIC PRESS
Durham, North Carolina

Library of Congress Cataloging-in-Publication Data

Cheeseman, Kelly.
 Everyday ethics for the criminal justice professional / Kelly Cheeseman,
Claudia San Miguel, Durant Frantzen, and Lisa Nored. -- Second Edition.
   pages cm
 Includes bibliographical references and index.
 ISBN 978-1-61163-414-3 (alk. paper)
 1. Criminal justice, Administration of--Moral and ethical aspects. 2. Law
enforcement--Moral and ethical aspects. 3. Criminal justice personnel--Profes-
sional ethics. I. San Miguel, Claudia. II. Title.

 HV7419.C4784 2015
 174'.3--dc23

                          2015034432

                CAROLINA ACADEMIC PRESS
                      700 Kent Street
               Durham, North Carolina 27701
                Telephone (919) 489-7486
                   Fax (919) 493-5668
                   www.cap-press.com

            Printed in the United States of America
                      2018 Printing

In Memoriam: Kelly Cheeseman

Dr. Kelly Cheeseman will be fondly remembered as an energetic champion of criminal justice. Kelly was devoted to her discipline and her students. She was a talented classroom instructor, avid researcher and faithful colleague. She was always sensitive to the bridge between the academy and the profession and sought to find the appropriate balance between the two in her research, teaching and service. Kelly is missed dearly among those of us who were fortunate enough to work with her. This book was one of her cherished projects, and we are honored to continue with a new edition in her memory.

Contents

Acknowledgments

Lisa S. Nored would like to thank her co-authors for their hard work and the opportunity to collaborate on this project with such talented scholars. She would also like to thank her husband, Deron, and her children, Hunter, Holden, Hayden, and Hayes for their continued patience and support.

Claudia San Miguel would like to thank her husband, Fructuoso San Miguel, III for his patience, love, encouragement, and continued support.

Durant Frantzen would like to thank his wife, Lana Frantzen, and his two sons—Cole and Chad—for giving him the inspiration, love, and fortitude to achieve his goals.

Everyday Ethics for the Criminal Justice Professional

1

An Introduction to Everyday Ethics in Criminal Justice

Chapter Objectives

- The student will understand the meaning of ethics
- The student will understand how ethics relates to the criminal justice system
- The student will learn to define the word *ethics*
- The student will differentiate between the words ethics and morality
- The student will understand the importance of ethics for criminal justice professionals

Introduction

Before beginning our quest to understand ethics in criminal justice, we must start by talking about ethics in general, in broad terms. As noted by Braswell, McCarthy and McCarthy (2008) the study of ethics must be viewed as a journey or as an exploration. We face ethical dilemmas and decisions that have moral implications on a daily basis, whether in our profession or in our personal lives. Exploring ethics may, in some cases, mean that core beliefs and assumptions that we hold about life, justice, fairness, equity and morality will be challenged or changed. The process of becoming an ethical person is a never-ending progression in which self-evaluation and reflection should become commonplace. Reading this book should help you to think about ethics as it relates not only to criminal justice and its various careers, but also how you approach daily interactions and circumstances. Simply put, how to make ethics a part of your everyday life. Consider the following news stories and the implications of each situation:

- February 2014—Several Air Force officers, including lieutenants and captains in charge of handling the country's nuclear reactors, were found to have cheated on monthly proficiency exams. Some officers cheated with answers they received by text message from another missile officer.

Others knew about the cheating incident but failed to report it to supervisors. All officers involved in the cheating incident were relieved of their duties of handling nuclear missiles and ordered to undergo re-training and re-testing.

- May 2014—A Mississippi elementary school principal convened a meeting with teachers, a week before a national assessment test was administered to students, on how to help students cheat on the exam. The principal also bubbled-in answers for students who left questions unanswered.
- June 2013—A Grapeland, Texas, police officer, in attendance at a weekend party during his off-duty hours, was terminated for allowing a female party-goer to wear his duty belt. The belt held the officer's weapon, Taser, and ammunition. Pictures of the incident were posted on social media and the officer was quickly terminated.
- May 2015—A Prince George's County police officer, who was plotting to kill his ex-wife and mother of his children, was arrested and charged with murder in connection to a double shooting at a McDonald's restaurant parking lot. The officer killed one man and injured his ex-wife.

All of the situations above point to people violating laws or policies. The consequences of their actions vary in seriousness, although they can all be considered to be a violation of ethics. Careful consideration of these and other ethical dilemmas are an important part of forming an ethical basis from which to operate. Braswell et al. (2008, p. 8) discuss five goals that should be included in examining crime, justice and ethics.

1. Become aware of and be open to ethical issues in their entirety, both the small (telling a lie) and the grandiose (stealing millions of dollars from clients).

Look at them equally as equal to each other

2. Begin developing analytical skills that will help to critically examine the why and how of what we do in the criminal justice system.
3. Grow in our ability to become more personally responsible (accountable for our actions).
4. Appreciate the coercive nature of the criminal justice system (many interactions in criminal justice are making people do things they do not want to do, such as going to prison).
5. Develop wholesight. This means exploring things from both a mind and heart perspective, appreciating all the costs involved in the criminal justice system.

Ethics in criminal justice is ever-present. It is found everywhere, from laws enforced by local, state, and federal police, to decisions made by defense and prosecuting attorneys, to the choices made in jails and prisons by correctional administrators. Ethics is so interwoven in the justice system that sometimes it is simply overlooked as an integral element that preserves fundamental rights outlined by our forefathers in the U.S. Constitution. It is also, at times, overlooked as the driving force that guides policies, practices, operations, and procedures of the criminal justice system. In a sense, ethics filters through the most mundane and routine activities of the police to the most dangerous and life-threatening situations that require the use of deadly force. It permeates the courtroom environment during arraignments, grand juries, and trials, the latter of which may involve sentencing a defendant to death. Ethics also seeps into the everyday operations of jails and prisons whose staff is charged with safeguarding the due process rights of those convicted of crimes while also having discretion to use reasonable force to maintain order in an environment ripe for violence. Finally, ethics guides research in criminal justice; it ensures that empirical investigators do not violate the basic rights of human subjects as they search for answers to society's crime problems.

Arguably, there are very few organizations that are more ethically charged than those that compose the criminal justice system. While some describe the actions of police as "morally dangerous" (Braswell et al., 2008), all other components of the system are equally susceptible to the hazards of unethical decision-making. For example, in the case of *Kingsley v. Hendrickson* (2015), jail staff members smashed a pretrial detainee's head against a concrete bunk and tased him for noncompliance. While the U.S. Supreme Court will rule on this case, a state jury found the jail staff members not guilty of violating the detainee's due process rights under the Fourteenth Amendment.

According to Wright (1999), it is only natural for the criminal justice system to sometimes succumb to inappropriate, illegal, and unethical behavior. After all, he says, "part of the problem is simply the fallibility of human beings" (p. 2). Another argument for the ethically-dangerous environment that seemingly characterizes the criminal justice system is the ability of its personnel to use discretion. Discretion, while defined by most as a necessary evil, allows actors of the system to be swayed by circumstances and/or situations outside the realm of the law (Roberg, Novak, & Cordner, 2005). That is, it allows them to weigh factors not necessarily relevant to fulfilling their duty as ethical public servants. They may begin to abide by the *spirit of the law* as opposed to the *letter of the law.*

This book is an introduction to the various ethical dilemmas and issues found within the criminal justice system. It will examine moral pitfalls found in the fields of policing, courts, and corrections as well as for researchers who examine factors that effect crime and justice. It will help you realize the importance of ethics for actors of the criminal justice system and those who occupy their time researching cause and effect relationships between variables. While this book may highlight the many ethical traps in criminal justice, it is never too late to begin practicing ethical decision-making.

Thinking Questions

1. What are some of the ethical decisions you make on daily basis?
2. What are Braswell et al.'s (2008) 5 goals in understanding ethics in criminal justice?
3. Describe what you believe to be the biggest ethical concern in criminal justice today.

What Is Ethics?

Ethics is a word that invokes the sensitivities of people especially when it involves the actions of professionals working in the criminal justice system. It can be a divisive word because it tends to elicit strong reactions and a word whose meaning is influenced by our upbringing, personal and work experiences, religious beliefs, moral philosophy, friends, co-workers, the U.S. Constitution, and the many laws that exist at the state and federal levels (Braswell et al., 2008; Souryal, 2010; Roberg et al., 2005). It is, therefore, a word whose meaning can be highly subjective, although ancient philosophers such as Socrates, Aristotle, and Plato would tend to disagree on the subjective nature of the word (Souryal, 2010). Ethics, in many ways, can be an elusive term with various meanings depending on the situation and circumstance. But, the most common way to define the term is to say that it is a set of moral principles that guides human behavior (Close & Meier, 1995). Some have defined ethics as the science of moral conduct, duty, and the responsibility to do the right thing (Braswell et al., 2008). So, what is the difference between the words *ethics* and *morality*? The definitions for the terms ethics and morality are very similar because they share the same root meaning. The Greek word *ethos* means character or conduct while the Latin word *moralis* pertains to custom or character (Close & Meier, 1995). While some would argue, however, that ethics and morality are distinct and mutually exclusive words, most are of the opinion that ethics is "a branch of philosophy that is concerned with the study of what is morally right and wrong, good and bad" (Souryal, 2010, p. 58). That is, ethics involves the study of the everyday application of moral principles. Box 1.1 provides an overview of some general practical applications of ethical and moral principles.

Box 1.1 General Ethical Principles (Perry, 2000)

- Compassion: concern for the well-being of others.
- Nonmaleficence: avoiding inflicting suffering and hardship on others.
- Beneficence: preventing and alleviating others' suffering; meeting the needs of the most vulnerable; promoting others' happiness (strongest toward our family and friends).
- Fairness: treating people the way they deserve to be treated; as having equal rights unless merit or need justifies special treatment.
- Courage in opposing injustice.
- Respect for the Constitution and other laws enacted by legitimate governing bodies.
- Honesty: not deceiving anyone who deserves to know the truth.
- Not making promises that we don't intend to keep.
- Keeping promises that we made freely.
- Integrity: upholding our obligations in spite of personal inconvenience.

Some specific obligations of public officials:

- Use impartial judgment in the service of all constituents.
- Avoid conflicts of interest that could undermine your objective judgment.
- Don't show favoritism toward family and friends in hiring.
- Don't solicit or accept bribes from people seeking to influence your official decisions.

Criminal justice employees each have unique aspects to their jobs. According to Pollock (2010), there are four common ethical elements that each criminal justice professional encounters.

1. *Discretion*—The power to make a decision or act in a manner that the individual feels is right or correct (which may differ from what another individual believes to be the right decision).
2. *The duty to enforce the law*—Service to the law is part of every criminal justice career and is also expected even if the individual disagrees with the law itself.
3. *The duty to uphold constitutional protections*—Fundamental to the Constitution are the concepts of due process and equal protection. As citizens, we grant the government and its agents the ability to catch and punish individuals for wrongdoing. The Constitution lays out ground rules that we must follow so that we do not abuse that power. Fundamental constitutional amendments that have direct implications for criminal justice professionals include:

Amendment IV

The right of the people to be secure in their persons, houses, papers, and effects, against unreasonable searches and seizures, shall not be violated, and no warrants shall issue, but upon probable cause, supported by oath or affirmation, and particularly describing the place to be searched, and the persons or things to be seized.

Amendment V

No person shall be held to answer for a capital, or otherwise infamous crime, unless on a presentment or indictment of a grand jury, except in cases arising in the land or naval forces, or in the militia, when in actual service in time of war or public danger; nor shall any person be subject for the same offense to be twice put in jeopardy of life or limb; nor shall be compelled in any criminal case to be a witness against himself, nor be deprived of life, liberty, or property, without due process of law; nor shall private property be taken for public use, without just compensation.

Amendment VI

In all criminal prosecutions, the accused shall enjoy the right to a speedy and public trial, by an impartial jury of the state and district wherein the crime shall have been committed, which district shall have been previously ascertained by law, and to be informed of the nature and cause of the accusation; to be confronted with the witnesses against him; to have compulsory process for obtaining witnesses in his favor, and to have the assistance of counsel for his defense.

Amendment VIII

Excessive bail shall not be required, nor excessive fines imposed, nor cruel and unusual punishments inflicted.

Amendment XIV

All persons born or naturalized in the United States, and subject to the jurisdiction thereof, are citizens of the United States and of the State wherein they reside. No State shall make or enforce any law which shall abridge the privileges or immunities of citizens of the United States; nor shall any State deprive any person of life, liberty, or property, without due process of law; nor deny to any person within its jurisdiction the equal protection of the laws.

These core principles apply to all citizens and bias in application of laws should not occur.

4. *They are public servants*—The job of those in criminal justice is to serve the best interest of the citizens and to hold themselves accountable to the public, because so much trust and power is bestowed upon

them. Because of the nature of the work, they are held to a higher standard than the average citizen regardless of whether they desire to have this standard applied to them. Fundamentally, they work for and their salaries are paid for by the public.

The everyday application of moral principles by professionals in the system can be complicated by many factors, situations, and circumstances, including one's interpretation of the Constitution. Consider the case of *Atwater v. City of Lago Vista* (2001). Driving home after her children's soccer practice, Gail Atwater was arrested for failing to place seatbelts on her small children, and herself, as she drove through the city of Lago Vista. Under Texas law, the failure for any front-seat passengers to wear a seatbelt is a misdemeanor, punishable by a fine of $50. Officer Turek noticed that Atwater and her children, all front-seat passengers, were in violation of the law. He proceeded to conduct a traffic stop that resulted in Atwater's arrest for failure to secure all passengers with seatbelts. Before taken into custody, Turek yelled at her for not caring about the welfare of her 3-year-old son and 5-year-old daughter. After repeated pleas to lower his voice because it was frightening her two children and pleas to allow her to take her children to a friend's house before going to the police station, Turek continued the verbal tirade and rejected her idea for childcare. Atwater's friends eventually arrived and removed the children from the scene but not before she was handcuffed and placed in the backseat of the patrol car without a seatbelt.

Atwater spent one hour in jail before posting bail. A few months after the incident, she filed suit under 42 U.S.C. § 1983 claiming that her Fourth Amendment right to "be secure against unreasonable searches and seizures" was violated when Officer Turek arrested her for a crime whose punishment should only have been a fine. The U.S. Supreme Court, in balancing individual rights versus public safety, ruled that Officer Turek, while having the discretion not to take Atwater into custody, acted within the scope of the framers of the Constitution when arresting Atwater, despite also conducting a warrantless roadside arrest. The court said

> Atwater's arrest satisfied constitutional requirements. It is undisputed that Turek had probable cause to believe that Atwater committed a crime in his presence. Because she admits that neither she nor her children were wearing seat belts, Turek was authorized (though not required) to make a custodial arrest without balancing costs and benefits or determining whether Atwater's arrest was in some sense necessary. Nor was the arrest made in an extraordinary manner, unusually harmful to her privacy or physical interests. At-

water's arrest and subsequent booking, though surely humiliating, were no more harmful to her interests than the normal custodial arrest. (pp. 33–34)

However, Justice O'Connor, writing the dissenting opinion in *Atwater*, noted that:

> Arresting Atwater was nothing short of counterproductive. Atwater's children witnessed Officer Turek yell at their mother and threaten to take them all into custody. Ultimately, they were forced to leave her behind with Turek, knowing that she was being taken to jail. Understandably, the 3-year-old boy was "very, very, very traumatized." After the incident, he had to see a child psychologist regularly, who reported that the boy "felt very guilty that he couldn't stop this horrible thing … he was powerless to help his mother or sister." Both of Atwater's children are now terrified at the sight of any police car. (pp. 393–395)

So although Atwater was in the right it still had a (-) effect

This case raises everyday ethical dilemmas faced by police. Officer Turek could have issued a citation for failure to wear a seatbelt and allowed Atwater to pay a fine—the punishment originally intended by the City of Lago Vista to deter people from breaking the law. Instead, he decided to use his discretion and arrest her. Did Officer Turek act unethically or was he simply trying to teach her a lesson about the dangers of not wearing a seatbelt? Did he go too far in fulfilling his responsibility and duty as a public servant? In fact, court documents indicate he had pulled her over a few months before and during this most recent incident told her "we've met before … this time you're going to jail." What about his ethical duty to protect her children from harm? Was it not harmful for them to see their mom arrested? Was it not harmful to see her belittled and berated by an officer of the law? Is it possible that Officer Turek acted ethically with respect to her arrest but not when he scared the children?

All of the questions above are examples of how ethics filters through the actions of professionals in the criminal justice system. Sometimes, however, applying ethics to everyday situations is easier said than done. Every area of criminal justice has large amounts of power over others. Consider the overwhelming amount of discretionary power given to prosecutors and judges. Prosecutors (district attorneys) decide which cases have merit. If they feel a case does not have enough evidence they have to choice not to prosecute or pursue charges. In states that have capital punishment, prosecutors choose whether or not they want to seek a capital conviction. They have the power to seek plea agreements and police officers may make choices based on prosecutorial preferences. Judges also have great amounts of discretion and power. Judges give juries instruction, make decisions about sentencing, can either accept or reject plea bargains and also make decisions about what evidence is admissible in a trial. Legal and judicial ethics will be discussed at length in Chapters 5 and 6.

Police in their own right have a great amount of discretion in their daily decision making. Police officers have the power to detain a person as well as search his or her vehicle if they have probable cause. Police officers can choose to issue a ticket or allow an individual to go free with just a warning. Police detectives have the power to interrogate suspects or individuals they believe have something to do with a crime. Additionally, detectives have the power to decide which persons are suspects and which people do not merit further investigation. Police personnel are also in close contact with valuables at crimes scenes as well as drugs or money that is confiscated. Opportunities exist for the police to engage in many forms of corruption. Ethics and police work will be discussed in Chapters 3 and 4.

Correctional personnel also have discretion and opportunities to engage in corruption. Correctional officers make decisions about offenders' daily living and can control access to things such as visitation, access to medical treatment or the commissary. Officers also have the ability to write offense reports which could result in the loss of "good time." Prison administration and supervisors might also place someone into administrative segregation or transfer them to another facility. Probation officers make recommendations to judges in pre-sentence investigation reports and also have the power to file violation reports which could send an offender to jail or prison. Parole officers also have the ability to file violation reports and return offenders to prison. The ethics of working in corrections will be discussed in Chapters 7 and 8.

Special attention should also be given to people who work in loss prevention and/or security. In dealing with potential shoplifters there is the need to ensure that an individual is not detained or searched illegally. Additionally, in many instances the individuals employed in loss prevention are not public employees but work for private corporations or security firms. Chapter 9 will focus special attention on this unique sector of criminal justice. Another area of criminal justice that has increased in popularity is that of forensics. Forensics can include latent fingerprint examination, toxicology, DNA testing, forensic anthropology, and blood splatter analysis. Because of the great influence that forensic evidence has on jurors and the court of public opinion, the ethical handling and treatment of forensic evidence is paramount. Also, how forensic lab technicians testify about evidence is another area of ethical concern. See Box 1.2 for an article involving a problem with the FBI's and New York State Police's crime labs.

Box 1.2 Scandals in the Crime Labs

Timesunion.com — Posted on April 23, 2015 | By TU Editorial Board

We don't yet know the full extent of the damage caused by scandals in the FBI's and New York State Police's crime labs. But if those agencies hope to restore public faith in the role of forensic science in the criminal justice system, it is essential that they find out what went wrong and why, and explain how they will try to prevent this from happening again.

What has come out so far is shocking, especially when one considers that these are two of the nation's premier forensic labs.

Amid an investigation that is already into its third year, the FBI and U.S. Justice Department have acknowledged that 26 of the 28 examiners in the FBI lab's microscopic hair comparison unit gave flawed testimony in almost all the criminal cases in which they provided evidence over two decades. Some 2,500 cases are under review, reports The Washington Post, covering 46 states, including six in New York, as well as the District of Columbia.

Thirty-two of those were death penalty cases. Nine people have since been executed.

How many of those cases resulted in wrongful convictions is yet to be determined. But out of seven cases in Washington, D.C., five people have so far been exonerated.

New York State Police, meanwhile, seeks to fire 15 forensic scientists implicated in an alleged cheating scandal at the DNA lab in Albany. All were suspended without pay this week and issued termination notices.

The action follows a six-month internal investigation. Nearly half the lab's DNA analysts have been relieved of their crime lab duties.

In this instance, the scientists are suspected of cheating on a qualification test for a controversial new type of DNA analysis that the state has planned to implement, although top officials are said to be leery of it.

Ethics in forensic science will be looked at in depth in Chapter 13.

For all criminal justice personnel there will be opportunities to be unethical. As noted by Pollock (2010) there are steps that can be taken when determining what course of action someone should take when faced with an ethical dilemma:

1. Examine all possible resolutions to the situation and examine all the possible costs and effects of each possibility. Each situation has short

and long term ramifications although not every individual is able to see the implications of every decision. In some cases the pressure to get out of the situation may cause a person to find any answer to be plausible, even if it is not.

2. Determine if any of the possible results of the situation would be viewed as unreasonable if other people were made aware of the situation or if it were to be made public. If the results of a decision would cause embarrassment if they were known to individuals outside of the organization the decision made should be brought into question. People who are acting unethically or are on the ethical slippery slope generally like to keep their behavior a secret. Individuals and agencies that are unwilling to make their actions public could or should face scrutiny.

3. A criminal justice professional must be able to justify the decision based on his or her own set of values and beliefs. If a person has to make a difficult choice about a situation he or she also has to ensure that the decision made is in line with his or her own values and morals and one in which he or she can take responsibility for (Pollock, 2010).

Becoming an ethical person is a journey in which one must evaluate his or her own morals and values and also face everyday choices that will have a lasting effect on themselves, their co-workers, the citizens they serve and the offenders in the criminal justice system. Due to the positions of public trust that are held by members of the criminal justice profession careful examination of how law enforcement, lawyers, judges, correctional officers, community supervision officers (probation and parole), private security personnel, loss prevention employees, forensic scientists and criminal justice researchers carry out their duties is paramount in any discussion of ethics.

If we examine the decisions we make with honesty and wholesight, caring about all members of the community we can begin to become moral and ethical criminal justice professionals (Braswell et al., 2008). The remaining pages of this book are designed to help you become aware of ethical situations around you, not only in the criminal justice profession but also in everyday life.

References

Braswell, M.C., McCarthy, B.R., & McCarthy, B.J. (2008). *Justice, crime, and ethics*. Newark, NJ: Anderson Publishing.

Close, D., & Meier, N. (1995). *Morality in criminal justice: An introduction to ethics*. New York: Wadsworth Publishing Company.

Perry, D. (2000). Ethics in Public Service. Retrieved October 2, 2010. http://www.scu.edu/ethics/publications/submitted/Perry/service.html.

Pollock, J. (2010). *Ethical Dilemmas and Decisions in Criminal Justice.* Florence, KY: Wadsworth Publishing.

Roberg, R., Novak, K., & Cordner, G. (2005). *Police and society.* Los Angeles, California: Roxbury.

Souryal, S.S. (2010). *Ethics in criminal justice.* Cincinnati, OH: Anderson Publishing.

Wright, K.N. (1999). Leadership is the key to ethical practice in criminal justice agencies. *Criminal Justice Ethics*, 18, 68–69.

Cases Cited

Atwater v. City of Lago Vista, 532 U.S. 318 (2001).

Kingsley v. Hendrickson, _____ (2015)

2

The Theory Behind the Practice
The Origins of Thought on Ethics and Its Relationship to the CJ Professional

Chapter Objectives

- The student will become aware of normative ethics
- The student will be introduced to utilitarianism and teleological ethics
- The student will be exposed to deontological ethics
- The student will understand the unique features of criminal justice ethics
- The student will become aware of foundations of punishment to include: deterrence, rehabilitation, retribution, incapacitation and restorative justice

Introduction

Ethical considerations are common in most professional occupations, including fields such as medicine, business, pharmaceutical research, as well as in criminal justice. Criminal justice professionals are faced with challenging situations and some of them are unique to the profession. For example, police officers are given broad discretion to arrest or detain subjects. Lawyers, judges and juries in the criminal court system make decisions about sentences and, in some cases, whether or not someone receives a sentence of life or death. Probation and parole officers have wide discretion on terms of an offender's probation or parole. Institutional corrections personnel hold the power of granting "good time" (days in which a sentence is reduced, normally for good behavior and a clean prison record) and other conditions of confinement such as access to commissary, visitation, whom they are celled with and how often they have recreation time. Criminal justice professionals are enmeshed in a "culture of force," in which decisions they make involve using force or determining how much force to use to gain compliance. Consequently, discussing morality and ethics cannot be overlooked in a discussion of how the criminal justice system operates and function.

Before beginning an in-depth discussion on ethical practices among criminal justice practitioners, we must first examine the foundations of ethical thinking in general and examine how the theoretical purpose and origins of ethical thinking have impacted the American criminal justice system.

A Glimpse at Ethical Perspectives

It is important to understand different points of view before being able to understand and assess the ethical quality, or lack thereof, of everyday incidents in the criminal justice system. Theoretical perspectives in ethics fall into two main categories: teleological theories and deontological theories. Teleological theories are sometimes referred to as those that tend to favor a consequentialist point of view while deontological theories are sometimes called nonconsequentialist. Let's take a look at the main differences between these two perspectives.

The word teleological originates in the Greek root, *telos*, which means *ends* or *consequences of actions*. Thus, this group of theories measures the ethical value of a decision or action based on its consequences (Closer & Meier, 1995). But, since they are generally measured on the notion of *utilitarianism*, consequences are deemed ethical, moral, or right based on the "greatest happiness" doctrine (Souryal, 2010). That is, did the decision or action produce the greatest amount of happiness for as many people as possible? Consider the *Atwater* case, did Officer Turek's actions comport with the notion of utilitarianism? Was her arrest ethically justifiable because it served a greater good to society?

Jeremy Bentham (1748–1832) and John Stuart Mill (1979) are the two individuals best associated with explaining utilitarianism (Souryal, 2010). Bentham is usually placed alongside Cesare Beccaria in discussions of classical criminology. He was a person who believed that individuals are rational beings, capable of considering the consequences of their actions (Akers, 2000). He also proposed the panopticon prison design: a design intended to make inmates think they were being watched at all times (Seiter, 2004). Again, his proposed prison design underscores a rational component to human action. He supposed that if inmates are tricked into believing they are being watched at all times, they may be deterred from engaging in criminal behavior.

Bentham was an English philosopher and lawyer during the Age of Enlightenment which was a period marked by significant changes in legal, political, economic, and moral philosophy (Banks, 2008). Although he never practiced law, he wrote a book entitled *Introduction to the Principles of Morals and Legislation* in 1789. In his book, he explained that nature has placed mankind under the governance of two sovereign masters, *pain* and *pleasure*. It is for them alone to point out what we ought to do, as well as to determine what we shall do. On the one hand is the standard of right and wrong, while on the other is the chain of causes and effects. They govern us in all we do, in all we say, and in all we think.

For Bentham, the two sovereign masters, pain and pleasure, guide all of our actions and because of it, the consequences of our actions may be unethical or immoral if we do not also consider that succumbing to pleasure may cause pain for others or to ourselves. He, therefore, believed that humans were not only rational beings but guided by hedonism. We are seekers of pleasure and avoiders of pain (Souryal, 2010). Because humans, by nature, wanted to avoid pain, Bentham proposed a hedonistic calculus that weighs the proportion of pleasure and painful consequences of our actions. In essence, he believed that we could compute the amount of pleasure or happiness of any given action and therefore help us determine if we were on an ethical path.

Let's take a closer look at the hedonistic calculus. The calculus consisted of seven elements:

1. the intensity of pleasure or pain
2. the duration of pleasure and pain
3. the certainty of pleasure or pain
4. the purity of pleasure or pain
5. the extent of pleasure or pain
6. the propinquity (nearness or remoteness) of pleasure or pain, and
7. the fecundity of pleasure or pain

In more simple terms, Bentham was essentially saying:

1. One should engage in actions that produce intense pleasure as opposed to mild, moderate, or minimal pleasure.
2. Long-lasting pleasure as opposed to transient pleasure is preferable.
3. One should also engage in actions that are certain to produce happiness as opposed to only a small probability that it will produce happiness.
4. An act that produces only pleasure or happiness is better than one that also results in a little pain.
5. An act that produces the greatest amount of happiness for the greatest number of people is better than one that produces only happiness one person, or happiness to only a fraction of society.
6. It is better to engage in actions that one knows will produce happiness either instantaneously or in the near future.

7. Actions that produce happiness multiple times are better than those that have only a one-time effect; also, actions that produce happiness at first but later cause pain should be avoided.

So, based on the calculus, an action is deemed ethical or morally superior if it produces a long-term pleasurable or happy outcome for the individual as well as for others. If actions produce nominal happiness to the individual but also caused pain to others, then the action is not worth pursuing. Also, if the action resulted in happiness for only the individual and not for others, Bentham would consider it morally incorrect. Remember, he believed in the utility of actions that produced the greatest good for the greatest number of people. Thus, before pursuing a course of action, the individual must weigh the probability that the action will result in a happy ending for him and others. As you can see, this is a lot for an individual to consider. Sometimes, calculating the duration, long-term consequences, and probability that an action will produce pleasure or pain may take years (Close & Meier, 1995).

Close and Meier (1995) indicate several practical problems with utilitarianism. First, it is virtually impossible for us to either quantify the amount of happiness or pain of any given action and it is also difficult to assess its intrinsic value. Second, definitions of happiness and pain vary from person to person. So, what makes one person happy or sad may be entirely different from another person's notions of pleasure and pain. Third, it is impossible to know at all times the consequences of our actions.

John Stuart Mill (1806–1873) was aware of these flaws during the nineteenth century. He was an English philosopher as well, and a proponent of utilitarianism but disagreed with Bentham's hedonistic calculus (Souryal, 2010). Mill believed that instead of trying to quantify the pleasure or pain of an action, we should use a qualitative approach. In other words, he argued that it is impossible to aggregate the consequences of actions and instead favored looking at its intrinsic or intended value of actions. He also believed that actions can be deemed ethically or morally superior even if they do not produce happiness for every human. As long as it produced a beneficial effect for those existing in our immediate environment, the act can be deemed ethical (Close & Meier, 1995).

Deontological theories, on the other hand, are not so much concerned with the consequences of actions. The word deontological originates in the Greek word *deon*, which means binding. This group of theories judge the ethical value of actions based on one's duty or responsibility to act (Close & Meier, 1995). Essentially, this group of theories is known as duty-based theories. German philosopher Immanuel Kant (1724–1804) is recognized for his clarification of deontological theories.

Kant first explained that individuals have an innate motivation to do what is right. We have a natural tendency to help others, to perform selfless good deeds, and to strive to be an ethical or moral person. While he believed that there were varying degrees of selfless motivation, Kant argued that it was difficult to assess the ethical value of an action if it was motivated by this natural and instinctive predisposition to do what is right (Banks, 2008). He proposed to assess the ethical quality of an act based on duty or responsibility. In other words, if an individual already has a tendency to do what's right, then the action was motivated by impulse and not by free will. An action cannot be judged as ethically correct if it is guided by impulse alone. It must be judged, according to Kant, on one's free will to abide, or not to abide, by societies rules regarding moral duty or responsibility. So, the act, and not its consequences, is what must be judged (Dreisbach, 2008).

In his books *Groundworks of the Metaphysic of Morals* (1785), *Critique of Practical Reason* (1788) and *Metaphysics of Morals* (1797), Kant describes his idea of a categorical imperative, which is an unconditional rule. Mainly, he argued that actions are deemed morally superior if they are driven first by rational choice and then by a duty or responsibility to adhere to societal rules, regardless of the outcome (Banks, 2008). He also said that when we are unsure what the ethically correct action to take is, we must ask ourselves—what would the majority of society or reasonable person do in this situation? If my actions were to suddenly become a universal rule, would society agree that it was morally correct?

Let's consider this easy practical example regarding the saying, "*honesty is always the best policy*." Telling someone the truth may cause them to become sad or angry. It may even produce feelings of anxiety for the truth-teller. But, Kant would argue that those who tell the truth, regardless of the pain or outcome it will likely produce for the individual (and ourselves), engage in ethical conduct. Because of the pain it may cause, truth-telling is not instinctual, but rather a rational choice to do what's right; a choice that conforms with what the majority of society or reasonable person would do in the same situation regardless of the consequences. While not codified in any legal document, it is a rule adhered to by the majority of society.

To summarize, Kant said:

1. "Every rational being must so act as if he were through his maxim always a legislating member in the universal kingdom of ends."
2. "Act in such a way that you treat humanity, whether in your own person or in the person of any other, always at the same time as an end and never merely as a means to an end."

3. "Act only according to that maxim whereby you can at the same time will that it should become a universal law without contradiction."

In simple terms, this is what he means:

1. Actions are ethically superior if others in society, in a similar circumstance, would also take the same course of action.
2. Conduct is ethical when it is motivated by a duty to act as opposed to the pain or pleasure it will produce for others and/or us.
3. If we can imagine our act someday becoming universally accepted, then it is the right things to do.

In a sense, the U.S. Supreme Court tends to take a deontological approach when deciding cases. As with the *Atwater* case, the majority of the Supreme Court decided in favor of Officer Turek. They were not swayed by the emotional and psychological pain the arrest may have caused Ms. Atwater and her children. Rather, they were sided with their duty to uphold the fundamental tenets of the U.S. Constitution. They examined the intent of the framers of the Bill of Rights and asked themselves if their decision, and Turek's actions, would comport with the original meaning of the Fourth Amendment. The justices, writing the majority opinion, were simply following the amendment's rules.

It is not uncommon for the Court to use the "reasonable person" test when deciding cases. For instance, there have been several cases where the Court has been asked to determine what constituted an arrest. In almost every case, the Court has emphasized that "when taking into account all of the circumstances surround the encounter [between an individual and police], the police conduct would have communicated to a reasonable person that he was not at liberty to ignore the police presence and go about his business" (*Kaupp v. Texas*, 2003). In other words, the Court undergoes a thought process where they ask themselves, "What would a reasonable person do, think, and/or respond in this situation?" The Court has applied this test in stop-and-frisk cases as well (del Carmen, 2007).

Thinking Questions

1. Compare and contrast the teleological and deontological ethical paradigms.
2. What are the elements of the hedonistic calculus?
3. What is the categorical imperative? How does it apply to ethics in criminal justice?

Father teaches Authority
Mother teaches Relationship

Basis of Ethical Principles in Criminal Justice

Braswell, McCarthy, and McCarthy (2008) explain that ethics, particularly for criminal justice practitioners, is shaped by three main frameworks: 1) a personal sense of justice, 2) the social context of justice, and 3) the criminal justice sense of justice. The first framework is shaped by our parents, our upbringing, and life experiences. The lessons of right and wrong instilled in us by our parents or caregivers at an early age influence how we behave as adults. The second framework that shapes our notions of ethical conduct is influenced by our experiences, particularly as adults, by our friends, co-workers, or individuals we tend to associate with quite often. In this case, we succumb to the influences of others and may surrender our ethical principles to the group's will. The final framework focuses on principles of justice and fairness as professionals in the criminal justice field.

Inevitably, your point of view on what is or is not ethical is shaped by everyday experiences on the job. Constant reminders that criminals try to manipulate the system in such a way that they are set free or receive minimal punishment, can eventually shape your view of justice. Caldero and Crank (2004) clarify that ethics, especially for criminal justice professionals, is tied to what they refer to as "the noble cause"—trying to make the world a safer place by arresting and locking up criminals. Sometimes the noble cause can put the right people behind bars for a long time but it may involve "bending the rules" a little and perhaps even circumventing ethical principles found in the U.S. Constitution. We'll talk about the noble cause in another chapter.

This is how everyone has an understanding of justice as a virtue

The U.S. Constitution

The Social Compact

Our Constitution, especially the Bill of Rights, embodies the ethical contract between the government and its populace (Souryal, 2010; Albanese, 2007). It contains provisions to safeguard individual and property rights, but also serves as a guide for the way individuals should be treated by justice professionals. It outlines the limits of government authority and the procedures to be taken when infringements on individual rights are necessary to preserve peace and tranquility.

Read the following amendments. They are the cornerstone of ethical guidelines for criminal justice professionals.

- Fourth Amendment—Protection from unreasonable search and seizure. *The right of the people to be secure in their persons, houses, papers, and effects, against unreasonable searches and seizures, shall not be violated, and no Warrants shall issue, but upon probable cause, supported by Oath or af-*

firmation, and particularly describing the place to be searched, and the persons or things to be seized.

- Fifth Amendment—Due process, double jeopardy, self-incrimination, eminent domain.

  No person shall be held to answer for any capital, or otherwise infamous crime, unless on a presentment or indictment of a Grand Jury, except in cases arising in the land or naval forces, or in the Militia, when in actual service in time of War or public danger; nor shall any person be subject for the same offence to be twice put in jeopardy of life or limb; nor shall be compelled in any criminal case to be a witness against himself, nor be deprived of life, liberty, or property, without due process of law; nor shall private property be taken for public use, without just compensation.

- Sixth Amendment—Trial by jury and rights of the accused; Confrontation Clause, speedy trial, public trial, right to counsel.

  In all criminal prosecutions, the accused shall enjoy the right to a speedy and public trial, by an impartial jury of the State and district where in the crime shall have been committed, which district shall have been previously ascertained by law, and to be informed of the nature and cause of the accusation; to be confronted with the witnesses against him; to have compulsory process for obtaining witnesses in his favor, and to have the Assistance of Counsel for his defense.

- Eighth Amendment—Prohibition of excessive bail and cruel and unusual punishment.

  Excessive bail shall not be required, nor excessive fines imposed, nor cruel and unusual punishments inflicted.

The other amendments of the Bill of Rights contain individual freedoms of religion, speech, press, and assembly which are important to our democracy (Albanese, 2007). However, the amendments above help differentiate between ethical and unethical conduct by justice professionals. They help us decide what is just or unjust; what is fair and not fair; what is arbitrary and what is necessary.

Souryal (1998) cautions, however, that the Constitution itself contains elements that "have not always been successful in preserving the principles of justice and goodness" (p. 97). For example, the institution of slavery was once a well-protected element of the Constitution. He argues that because the constitution is a living document, subject to the interpretation of justices, its principles can be manipulated to support unethical conduct such as the internment of Japanese-Americans during the Second World War. More recently, critics have pointed to the slanted use of the Fourth Amendment to help fight the

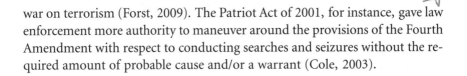

war on terrorism (Forst, 2009). The Patriot Act of 2001, for instance, gave law enforcement more authority to maneuver around the provisions of the Fourth Amendment with respect to conducting searches and seizures without the required amount of probable cause and/or a warrant (Cole, 2003).

Ethical Codes

Every organization or agency of the criminal justice system maintains an ethical code of conduct. An ethical code of conduct spells out basic and commonsensical rules of behavior. Usually, practitioners swear an oath at the commencement of their employment to abide by the rules. For the most part, codes of ethics underscore impartiality when applying the laws of the country, state, or municipality. They also call attention to the ethically-charged nature of their work. While ethical codes will be discussed in upcoming chapters, let's take a quick look at the code of ethics in law enforcement. It says:

> As a Law Enforcement Officer, my fundamental duty is to serve mankind; to safeguard lives and property; to protect the innocent against deception, the weak against oppression or intimidation, and the peaceful against violence or disorder; and to respect the Constitutional rights of all men to liberty, equality and justice. I will keep my private life unsullied as an example to all; maintain courageous calm in the face of danger, scorn, or ridicule; develop self-restraint; and be constantly mindful of the welfare of others. Honest in thought and deed in both my personal and official life, I will be exemplary in obeying the laws of the land and the regulations of my department. Whatever I see or hear of a confidential nature or that is confided in me in my official capacity will be kept ever secret unless revelation is necessary in the performance of my duty.
>
> I will never act officiously or permit personal feelings, prejudices, animosities or friendships to influence my decisions. With no compromise for crime and the relentless prosecution of criminals, I will enforce the law courteously and appropriately without fear of favor, malice or ill will, never employing unnecessary force or violence and never accepting gratuities.
>
> I recognize the badge of my office as a symbol of public faith, and I accept it as a public trust to be held so long as I am true to the ethics of the police service. I will constantly strive to achieve these objectives and ideals, dedicating myself before God to my chosen profession ... law enforcement.

The American Bar Association also has a code of conduct for attorneys that emphasizes impartiality in fulfilling their duties. The American Correctional Association also encourages correctional personnel to put biases and prejudices aside when administering punishment. Codes of ethics are promulgated to enhance professionalism and a duty for public service (Souryal, 2010). When individuals in the criminal justice system follow the dictates set forth in their respective codes, the result is a work environment that encourages professionalism. The code provides them with a general framework to decipher right and wrong; just and unjust behavior; and ethical and unethical conduct. The code may also foster a sense of pride in being a public servant which only enhances professionalism.

But, what good are codes if, as Braswell et al. (2008) noted, our moral compass is influenced by what our co-workers think of us? What good is a code if our behavior, including ethical conduct, is affected by socialization occurring at one's place of employment? Also, codes of ethics are only successful if members of the organization take them seriously. Wright (1999) notes that ethical conduct in criminal justice agencies is compromised by an organizational climate that is indifferent to rule-breaking. He also says that ethical leadership is the key to practicing everyday ethics.

While the U.S. Constitution and codes of ethics are instruments that help guide ethical behavior, they are not the sole basis for ethics in criminal justice. As you will see in the chapters to come, ethics is influenced by many factors, legal and extra-legal. Sometimes it is based on group affiliation, indifference by supervisors, or a belief that violating the law is necessary to protect people from harm. Sometimes unethical behavior is justified as necessary for the greater good of society.

Thinking Questions

1. What are the three ethical frameworks outlined by Braswell et al. (2008)?
2. What the constitutional amendments that provide ethical principle for criminal justice professionals?
3. What are the ethical codes of law enforcement personnel? The ABA?

Punishment and Ethics: How Our Personal Philosophy Impacts Our Daily Practice

While punishment is generally considered to be a part of corrections, all criminal justice personnel are stakeholders in punishment and how these philosophical reasons by which we choose to punish law violators impacts ourselves, the criminals and society. This section will focus on examining theories and rationales for punishment such as deterrence, rehabilitation, retribution, incapacitation and the more recent idea of restorative justice. Interestingly, the criminal justice system pursues a combination of purposes, which can be in conflict with one another. For instance, is it possible to punish an offender while also pursuing the goal of rehabilitation? Will we change offender behavior by using the "eye for an eye" retributive mentality? Can American society agree on how it wants offenders to be treated?

Punishment can be used to describe anything that causes pain or is a consequence of doing something "wrong." Punishment is also defined in some cases as a grueling process or endeavor (i.e., I have been enduring a punishing workout routine to train for a marathon). However, punishment as a criminal sanction must be examined in a different way. According to Flew (1954), punishment for criminal offenses must consist of five elements:

1. It must involve an unpleasantness to the victim.
2. It must be for an offense, actual or supposed.
3. It must be of an offender, actual or supposed.
4. It must be the work of personal agencies; in other words, it must not be the natural consequence of an action.
5. It must be imposed by an authority or an institution against whose rules the offense has been committed. If this is not the case, then the act is not one of punishment but is simply a hostile act. Similarly, direct action by a person who has no special authority is not properly called punishment, and is more likely to be an act of hostility.

Clearly, if an offense is committed and the matter is handled by a private citizen, it is merely personal revenge, not a punitive sanction or formal punishment. Citizens give the government authority to carry out penalties for criminal offenses. Another key element is the fact that it must be a legitimate and legally defined offense. For instance, an offender cannot be punished by the criminal justice system for a perceived infraction that has not been enacted into a law. Corrections cannot punish individuals for things that have not been deemed offensive by legal statutes, county or city ordinances, or judicial precedent. Punishment carried out by the criminal justice system follows rules, guidelines and restrictions. Creativity in punishments, influenced by feelings or anger, is not meant to play a role in modern day American criminal punishment.

Historically, types and proportions of punishment were arbitrary and left in the hands of the local nobles or dignitaries who delegated their authority to punishers. Many criminal offenses were handled by using the death penalty or other forms of corporal punishment. This model follows most closely with retributive ideologies.

Retribution

Deterrence is a proactive policy, in that it aims to prevent future offenses. Conversely, retribution is reactive, seeking out revenge for a past act. The idea of retaliation can be traced to the Old Testament as well as the Code of Hammurabi.

Box 2.1 Examples of Laws from the Code of Hammurabi

- If a son strikes his father, his hands shall be hewn off.
- If any one is committing a robbery and is caught, then he shall be put to death.
- If he breaks another man's bone, his bone shall be broken.
- If conspirators meet in the house of a tavern-keeper, and these conspirators are not captured and delivered to the court, the tavern-keeper shall be put to death.
- If the "finger is pointed" at a man's wife about another man, but she is not caught sleeping with the other man, she shall jump into the river for her husband.
- If a man be guilty of incest with his daughter, he shall be driven from the place (exiled).
- If a man knock out the teeth of his equal, his teeth shall be knocked out.

Often known as "lex talionis" (the law of retaliation), this form of punishment was aimed at taking away an equal portion of what you, as an offender, had taken. Historically, punishment was brutal and often excessive in proportion to the crime committed. Punishments ranged from beatings, mutilation, being boiled in oil, drawing and quartering, death by disembowelment, and other forms of execution (hanging, being burned at the stake). For example, stealing might invoke a penalty of having one's hand cut off. Punishment at this time was directed primarily at the physical body.

Retribution in modern American criminal justice is not nearly as harsh or violent as earlier versions. While previous forms of retribution were seen as more focused on revenge, retribution, as applied today, is more impersonal as it is administered by a neutral party through the legal system. What remains the same is the belief that offenders need to feel the pain of their action whether it be literally or symbolically through incarceration. One of the fundamental questions of retribution is how much punishment equals the amount of harm done to the victim? Many proponents of "get tough" policies advocate for harsher punishments and argue that incarceration has become too "easy" for offenders. Additionally, some individuals see capital punishment as a way in which to achieve retribution, believing that if you take a person's life you should have your life taken away.

Restitution can also include monetary payments in the form of fines. Community service and additional ways of paying back the community are other forms of retribution. When possible, offenders who are able can provide payments in cases where material possessions or money have been lost as a result of criminal actions. (This is most common with property crimes such as burglary or larceny.) In the case of some criminal activities, communities may choose to have the offender work off their offense by serving time on an offender work crew cleaning graffiti or working on city, town or county work projects. In some cases, this could also include working on a chain gang for Florida Sheriff Wayne Ivey.

Box 2.2 Florida Sheriff Reintroduces Chain Gang

Brevard County, Florida (Florida Today) — May, 2013

The sheriff in this county of beaches and spaceships has launched a very visible anti-crime campaign that civil-rights activists are questioning.

For the past few weeks, a small band of convicted inmates from Brevard County Jail has been working on a chain gang. First-year Sheriff Wayne Ivey says he launched the project as a sort of living and breathing public service announcement, choosing black-and-white striped costumes harkening to a bygone era; black boots with chains around the ankles; and bold, bright signage aimed at making the chain gang as visible as possible.

"Not a new concept, but certainly an effective one," Ivey said.

Not everyone agrees. Civil rights activists and others have doubts about whether shackled inmates on county roadsides is the appropriate way to get across an anti-crime message and wonder if the concept itself is outdated or even unconstitutional.

"Given the connotations of slavery and forced labor that a chain gang brings up, it is not ideal," said spokesman Baylor Johnson of the American Civil Liberties Union of Florida, who noted the U.S. Supreme Court in 1996 found some kinds of chain gangs violated the U.S. Constitution's protection against cruel and unusual punishment.

Ivey stressed that his chain gangs are not shackled to one another and each man is a volunteer. It's not a forced assignment. And it doesn't include inmates who are a danger to the community.

Controversial Sheriff Joe Arpaio in Arizona's Maricopa County, known for his tough law-and-order stance, has had male chain gangs since 1995, female chain gangs since 1996 and chain gangs for juveniles convicted as adults since 2004. Those inmates, who work eight hours a day six days a week, also are volunteers who want to get outside even if it means weeding, clearing brush or picking up litter in the hot sun.

Other sheriff's departments across the country—including Bristol County, Mass.; Butler County, Ohio; and Clallam County, Wash.,—have volunteer chain gangs, some since the late 1990s though Bristol County Sheriff Thomas Hodgson prefers to call his inmates tandem work crews. Prisons in several states including Arizona and Iowa also have shackled inmate crews that do landscaping or cleanup outside prison grounds.

A few sheriff's departments have tried and abandoned the idea, including Johnson County, Ind., which had too small a staff to keep up with the program's popularity.

The Brevard County Sheriff's Office operates about five inmate work details outside the jail on any given day, but this new work-crew is the only one outfitted in bold, black and white stripes and locked up in chains. The sheriff hopes the new look will send a message.

"I remember growing up as a small kid, looking out the window of our home at members of the chain gang working in a ditch and thinking to myself: That's not a place I would ever want to be," Ivey said. "I've said from the very beginning that I'm going to put emphasis on crime prevention, and this is a component of that. Not wanting to go to jail is a form of crime prevention."

Ivey said the chain gang instills a strong work ethic in the inmates, which can be part of their rehabilitation, while also acting as a high-profile deterrent to passersby.

Under state law, only inmates convicted of a crime can participate on a work detail. They must qualify for "trustee" status, meaning their criminal history is neither extensive nor violent and they have demonstrated good behavior in jail.

Thirty-five men volunteered for the eight positions on the chain gang.

"Once they're sentenced, we're allowed to work them X number of hours per day," Ivey said, adding that he chose volunteers for the chain gang because he wanted to make sure all inmates on the detail bought into its mission of being an anti-crime public relations campaign.

The sheriff said all jail work details save taxpayers money because the inmates do manual labor that the county otherwise would have to pay others to do.

Some work in the jail's cafeteria. Some refurbish bicycles. Some train dogs in shelters. The Sheriff's Department estimates that all of the work programs provide about $10 million worth of labor each year.

The new, all-male chain gang is working in cooperation with the Brevard County Public Works Department. Lately, they've been cleaning up trash along the roads.

Ivey said the work assignment gives the convicts a chance to enjoy sunshine and fresh air.

"It's got its perks for them, as well," Ivey said.

Ivey said he wasn't aware of another chain gang in Florida. Spokeswoman Ann Howard for the Florida Department of Corrections said her department doesn't use them.

Traditional chain gangs, in which inmates are shackled together, were challenged as violating the U.S. Constitution's protection against cruel and unusual punishment in a 1996 lawsuit in Alabama, according to the American Civil Liberties Union of Florida. The U.S. Supreme Court also found it unconstitutional to shackle an inmate to a post.

In Ivey's iteration of the chain gang, inmates ankles are shackled, but inmates are not chained to one another.

"It's hard to say whether a modified chain gang in which prisoners are individually chained for security purposes would pass constitutional muster," the ACLU of Florida's Johnson said.

Ivey said the county had no additional costs to put the program in place compared to the cost of unchained work crews. The inmates wear black and white striped uniforms, which differ from clothing worn by other inmates on work crews.

Ivey said he chose the outfits because they're consistent with a common, historical image of inmates on chain gangs.

"You have the old scared straight program," Ivey said. "To some degree, this is part of that."

Larry Lawton, a former convict turned life coach, is opposed to the chain gang idea.

"Chain gangs send a bad message about our county," said Lawton, who is based in Palm Bay, Fla. "I don't think people want to come to this county as a tourist or a beach person and see people in chains."

A campaign to help inmates with drug addiction, which is a contributing factor in criminal activity, is a more productive use of the department's time and resources, Lawton said.

Ivey said the inmates were receptive to the idea when he presented it.

"Before I even got through talking about the program, I had people volunteering," he said.

Jeffrey Alan Rhoades volunteered. He was arrested for stealing his aunt's purse in July 2012. He was convicted and sentenced to probation but tested positive for drugs in December and was sentenced to serve 270 days in jail.

"We're just here today to clean up the park, help out, you know, make sure everything's clean for the community and set an example for little kids," he said recently, standing in the parking lot at the Pineda Causeway Boat Ramp, wearing an orange hat and a fluorescent green vest over his black and white stripes.

He and seven other men walked around the park, picking bits of plastic from the vegetation near the river.

> Spirits seemed high. Some men smiled as they worked. Sometimes, the men sang in call-and-response chorus: "We are the chain gang, the mighty Ivey chain gang."

Retribution is often popular rhetoric and Sheriff Joe maintains high levels of public approval for his controversial jail policies. Another correctional ideology related to retribution is deterrence. Initially, deterrence was a response to excessive punishment carried out during the 17th and 18th Centuries. With the Age of Enlightenment came the belief that punishment should be proportionate to the offense and that equality and justice should be incorporated when considering how to punish offenders.

Deterrence

As noted previously in the chapter, Bentham is the father of utilitarianism and was instrumental in developing theory about punishment, proportionality and deterrence. According to Bentham, punishment should serve a utilitarian purpose, in that is does the greatest amount of good for the largest number of individuals in society. Bentham (1789) believed punishment should serve four main functions:

1. Prevent all criminal offenses.
2. When it cannot prevent a crime, convince the offender to commit a less serious one.
3. Ensure that the offender uses no more force than is necessary.
4. Prevent a crime as cheaply as possible.

Bentham recognized that punishment was harmful and should only be used to deter individuals from committing crimes. Therefore, punishment must be comprised of three main elements: swiftness, certainty, and severity. Punishments that are swift occur relatively quickly after the commission of the crime. If too much time lapses between the offense and the actual time of punishment, the offender is less likely to be deterred from further criminal activity. Secondly, if the offender is certain that they will be apprehended and punished for a crime, they are more likely to be deterred from committing the crime. Conversely, the more an offender believes that he will not be punished or caught the more likely he will be to engage in criminal behavior. Lastly, punishment must be just severe enough to overcome the gain from a crime. Punishment that is too severe is unjust, and punishment that is not severe enough will not deter future criminal behavior (Bentham, 1789).

Deterrence is often broken down into two distinct categories or approaches. Specific deterrence is done to an individual offender to stop them from committing future offenses. If we punish the offender seriously enough, they will be discouraged from individual wrongdoing. General deterrence is done to an offender in the hopes that others will be deterred from committing a similar crime. If other citizens see an offender being punished for criminal acts, they will be discouraged from breaking the law because they do not want to face similar punishment. We use the offender as an example to others of what not to do. As noted earlier, if general deterrence is going to work, the punishment must be severe and certain enough to invoke fear in those who might consider engaging in criminal behavior. Although necessary to send a message that crime does not pay and will be punished, is it moral or ethical to severely punish an offender as an example to other "would-be" criminals? Are most individuals deterred by seeing another person punished or do they believe that they will not get caught?

How can society know how much punishment is enough to deter an individual from committing a criminal act? How do we know if a sanction is in the right proportion to the offense that was committed? One of the challenges we face is knowing how much to punish each individual offender—what might be a strong enough punishment for one particular offender, may do very little to deter another. Can we justify extreme punishments if it deters some offenders but is too harsh for others? Do current criminal justice policies and penalties deter individuals from committing crimes? Do offenders believe that they will be apprehended and punished? One study found that offenders believe there is very little chance they will be caught, and even if they are caught there is a good probability that they will receive a lenient punishment (Daniels, Baumhover, Formby & Clark-Daniels, 1999). Deterrence, regardless of its actual effectiveness, continues to be an accepted rationale for why we punish offenders in American society. Deterrence has received high levels of support in America due to its relationship with "get tough on crime" policies and is often touted by politicians as a rationale for crime legislation.

Thinking Questions

1. What are some common forms of retribution?
2. Describe the difference between general and specific deterrence.
3. What are your thoughts on Sheriff Joe's policies? Are they ethical?

Incapacitation

Incapacitation involves preventing offenders from committing future acts by removing them from society and not giving them the capacity to offend against citizens. Essentially, we are restraining offenders from committing further acts by isolating them from the place or persons upon which they are offending. In its simplest form we are reducing the temptation or seduction of crime by secluding the offender. This is traditionally done in America through incarceration, although this also could occur in the form of a suspended driver's license for offenses such as Driving While Intoxicated. We remove "dangerous" individuals from society and hold the offender until there is little or no risk that they will re-offend. One of the concerns with incapacitation is whether or not we are able to correctly or accurately predict who is likely to re-offend. We can release an offender who goes on to commit future crimes or continue to incarcerate an individual who may not re-offend. Should offenders be incarcerated based on what they might do or on what they have already done? Is it ethical to hold offenders because we fear they will engage in future criminality, even though they have not yet done so?

Often times, offenders deemed likely to repeat criminal offenses become those chosen most often for incarceration, as society would seem to benefit from their removal.

This type of selective incapacitation is apparent in states' habitual offender laws, also known as Three-Strikes laws, to combat career criminality. Habitual offender laws essentially allow a state to incarcerate an individual for natural life if the offender commits a specific number of felonies as outlined by state statutes (most states have this set at three) (Zimring, Hawkins and Samin, 2001). Should only serious felonies be considered as strikes, such as aggravated assault and rape, or should non-violent felonies be included when considering "strikes"? California's Three-Strikes law does allow for non-violent felonies to count as a strike. Not surprisingly, California, has incarcerated the most individuals under its Three-Strikes legislation. Recently, the Supreme Court upheld the constitutionality of habitual offender laws, so they are unlikely to go away in the near future. Unfortunately, there is no magic formula that can accurately predict who will and who will not engage in future crime. Incapacitation is not aimed at changing inmate behavior, but simply separating the offender from society. In contrast, rehabilitation is designed to create positive change within criminal offenders.

Rehabilitation

While retribution, deterrence, and incapacitation focus their attention on the criminal act committed by the offender and the appropriate level of response, rehabilitation focuses its attention on creating change within the offender. Rehabilitation is a term most closely related to the belief that the job of corrections is to change and restore an offender to a right status with society. The goal is to help the offender see the error of their previous ways and reenter society as legitimate and contributing citizens. Rehabilitation supports the idea that criminal sanctions should be an opportunity to promote positive change within the offender.

The roots of rehabilitation can be found in the positivist perspective. This focused its attention on applying scientific research to the study of human phenomena. In contrast with classical criminology, positivistic approaches focus more attention on studying the criminal rather than studying the crime. In positivistic criminology the factors that cause an individual to commit crimes are seen as biological, psychological or sociological. Rehabilitative efforts are clearly rooted in the idea that an offender needs help in responding and overcoming these forces. Rehabilitation is generally done in an offender-specific fashion such that each offender has a treatment plan that addresses their individual concerns and needs. A uniform approach to offenders will bring about the conditions necessary to invoke "change" within criminal offenders. As noted by one scholar,

> The rehabilitative ideal is the notion that a primary purpose of penal treatment is to effect changes in the characters, attitudes, and behavior of convicted offenders, so as to strengthen the social defense against unwanted behavior, but also to contribute to the welfare and satisfaction of others. (Allen, 1981, p. 2)

Rehabilitation is closely related to the medical model, in which criminal behavior was seen as an illness that needed to be treated or cured. Not surprisingly, rehabilitation seeks to "cure" offenders from the conditions that caused their crime whether they are psychological or environmental in nature. Thus, if criminal behavior is a result of things outside of the offender's immediate control, the offender should not be punished but should be treated. Rehabilitation programs were popular in American corrections until the mid-1970s, when research found that rehabilitative programs had little to no effect on reducing crime, because offenders deemed "rehabilitated" still committed crimes once released from incarceration (Martinson, 1974). Many opponents of rehabilitation utilized Martinson's study to declare that "nothing works" and that another strategy to deal with criminal behavior should be advocated. Does the American public support rehabilitative programs for offenders? Is there room for rehabilitation in an era when policies and politicians are drenched with "get tough" rhetoric? In a recent study of American voters, over 70 percent of those polled believed there should be rehabilitative services for offenders during and after incarceration (Krisberg & Marchionna, 2006). The study also found that those polled felt job training, drug treatment, mental health services, family support, mentoring, and housing were all very important services that should be offered to prisoners. While there might be perceived support for rehabilitative programs, there is a substantial monetary cost to taxpayers to run and implement offender programming. In the current fiscal economy it may be more and more of a challenge to implement offender programming when federal, state and local budgets are stretched to their limits. Can we rehabilitate offenders effectively and cheaply enough to keep offender programs in place?

Understanding your personal philosophy on punishment can be helpful in establishing how you will handle circumstances that involve the punishment of offenders, although it could be argued that every job in criminal justice involves placing an offender into a system of punishment.

Thinking Questions

1.   What are some of the ethical concerns with rehabilitation?
2.   Is rehabilitation for all offenders ethical?
3.   What is your punishment philosophy and how does it relate to your personal ethics?

Conclusion

Ethics can mean many different things to different people. In criminal justice, however, ethics should mean adherence to the mandates outlined in the Constitution and respect to professional codes of ethics. But, as you will see, remaining ethical is difficult for some to achieve, as they may be influenced by factors not consistent with fundamental rights guaranteed by our government. This book will take you through a journey of ethical dilemmas in criminal justice and provide you with ways to help make more ethically-sound decisions as a professional. You will learn about ethical hazards in the many areas of the criminal justice system and the different solutions implemented to help employees remember what their duties are as public servants.

References

Albanese, J. (2007). *Professional ethics in criminal justice: Being ethical when no one is looking.* New Jersey: Prentice Hall.

Allen, F. (1981). *The Decline of the Rehabilitation Ideal.* New Haven: Yale University Press.

Banks, C. (2008). *Criminal justice ethics: Theory and practice.* Thousand Oaks, CA: Sage.

Beccaria, C. (1764). *On Crimes and Punishment.*

Bentham, J. (1789). *Introduction to Principles of Morals and Legislation.*

Braswell, M.C., McCarthy, B.R., & McCarthy, B.J. (2008). *Justice, crime, and ethics.* Newark, NJ: Anderson Publishing.

Caldero, M.A., & Crank, J.P. (2004). *Police ethics: The corruption of noble cause.* Cincinnati, OH: Anderson Publishing.

Close, D., & Meier, N. (1995). *Morality in criminal justice: An introduction to ethics.* New York: Wadsworth Publishing Company.

Cole, D. (2003). *Enemy Aliens: Double standards and constitutional freedoms in the war on terrorism.* New York: The New Press.

Daniels, R.S., Baumhover, L.A., Formby, W.A., & Clark-Daniels, C.L. (1999). Police discretion and elder mistreatment. *Journal of Criminal Justice, 27,* 209–226.

del Carmen, R. *Criminal procedure: Law and practice.* Belmont, CA: Wadsworth.

Dreisbach, C. (2008). *Ethics in criminal justice.* New York: McGraw-Hill.

Flew, A. (1954). The justification of punishment. *Philosophy,* June.

Forst, B. (2009). *Terrorism, crime, and public policy.* New York: Cambridge University Press.

Krisberg, B., & Marchionna, S. (2006). Attitudes of US voters toward prisoner rehabilitation and reentry policies. *National Council on Crime and Delinquency page.* Retrieved October 27, 2010 from http://www.nccd-crc.org/nccd/pubs/2006april_focus_zogby.pdf.

Lipton, D., Martinson, R., & Wilks, J. (1975). The effectiveness of correctional treatment: A survey of treatment evaluation studies. Praeger Publishers.

Martinson, R. (Spring 1974). "What Works?—Questions and Answers About Prison Reform," *The Public Interest,* 22–54.

Roberg, R., Novak, K., & Cordner, G. (2005). *Police and society.* Los Angeles, California: Roxbury.

Seiter, R. (2004). *Corrections: An introduction.* New Jersey: Prentice Hall.

Souryal, S.S. (2010). *Ethics in criminal justice.* Cincinnati, OH: Anderson Publishing.

Wright, K.N. (1999). Leadership is the key to ethical practice in criminal justice agencies. *Criminal Justice Ethics, 18,* 68–69.

Zimring, F.E., Hawkins, G., & Kamin, S. (2001). *Punishment and Democracy: Three Strikes and You're Out in California.* New York: Oxford University Press.

Cases Cited

Atwater v. City of Lago Vista, 532 U.S. 318 (2001).

Kaupp v. Texas, 538 U.S. 626 (2003).

3

Ethics and the Evolution of Police

Chapter Objectives

- The student will understand the evolution of American police systems and practices
- The student will learn about the eras of policing
- The student will identify the ethical dilemmas associated with the various eras of policing
- The student will comprehend attempts to professionalize American police and the problems it created with the community
- The student will learn the ethical issues linked to the use of discretion
- The student will gain knowledge of community policing
- The student will be introduced to the ethics and community policing
- The student will understand the notion of the slippery slope with respect to police corruption

Introduction

Crime prevention is, and has always been, an invariable concern for societies around the world (Lab, 2004). Of course, each society differs in how they choose to maintain peace and tranquility. There are some societies, such as Japan and China, which opt to utilize more informal means of social control, although they do rely on the authoritative and coercive power of agencies that compose their justice systems when necessary (Chen, 2002; Braithwaite, 1998). In the United States, the primary means of maintaining order is to rely on the work of the police; the formal agents of social control. However, the strength of communities is also used to help achieve order (Lab, 2004; Roberg, Novak, & Cordner, 2005).

The evolution of policing in the United States began with a heavy reliance on citizens' ability to take matters into their own hands; a rudimentary form of *kinship* policing (Lab, 2004; Vago, 2003). Eventually, this informal system gave way to a more official manner where law enforcement, as well as order maintenance responsibilities, were vested in a few. From 1900 to 1970, attempts were made to professionalize the police, which meant encouraging them to make more ethical decisions (Peak & Glensor, 2002). In the end, such attempts at professionalization discouraged the community from partaking in crime prevention initiatives and further reinforced the so-called "us versus them" attitude between the police and the public (Greene & Pelfrey, 2001). During the late twentieth century until now, police organizations have tried to reverse the negative effects of past policing models and therefore have adopted a community policing philosophy that is inclusive of citizen input on everyday crime and disorder problems (Rosenbaum, 1988).

A look into the beginning stages of formal policing in this country may make some wonder why it has been difficult to divorce the field of policing from temptations to behave unethically. More recent stages in the evolution of policing, particularly with the adoption of community-oriented policing principles, can present problems for officers tying to make everyday ethical choices. This chapter will introduce you to the different eras of policing. Temptations to behave unethically existed in all three eras of policing.

Evolution of American Police Systems and Practices

Undoubtedly, our police system borrowed elements from the experiences and field tests of policing practices in England. Similar to England, we experimented with political appointees, such as the sheriff, the constable, and the justice of the peace, to coordinate initiatives to serve and protect communities very early in our history (Peak, 1997). During colonial times these political forces were in charge of enlisting all able-bodied men to join a loosely-organized police force and directing them to listen for the hue and cry of the citizenry in need of assistance. Those who refused this civic duty were reprimanded (Peak, 1997; Peak & Glensor, 2002).

The appointees were also in charge of other necessities of colonial life such as conducting elections, maintaining bridges, repairing roads as well as collecting taxes (Walker & Katz, 2005). Because policing was one of many tasks, it did not take long for the system to fail both in the colonies and in England. After all, some men were not too pleased with being forced to partake in policing matters and often neglected their civic duty (some even paid others to do their job) (Walker & Katz, 2005). More importantly, as populations gradually swelled due to urbanization and industrialization, crime rates increased (Peak, 1997). This made the basic model of policing highly inefficient. As a result, both in the colonies and in England, the watchman style of policing was soon adopted.

England naturally experimented with the watchman method of policing much earlier than in the colonies, In fact, the colonies' first test occurred in 1634 in Boston with unpaid night watchmen (Walker & Katz, 2005). By 1830, the city of Philadelphia experimented with paying men to serve during the day and night (Schmalleger, 2003). One year before, however, England was already conducting their first pilot test on a more professional police force after their watchman system of policing became inept at controlling and preventing crime. The London Metropolitan Police Act was enacted into law in 1829, under the direction of Sir Robert Peel, who is known as the father of modern policing (Peak, 1997). The Act underscored England's desire to move away from a fragmented and decentralized watchman policing scheme to a more formal and official role for those to be entrusted with the duty to protect society. Peel advocated a hiring practice for the new police force that was based on applicant's temperament (Peak & Glensor, 2002). This factor was a salient factor if Peel was to quell massive protests against a formalized police force.

Because inhabitants of London were wary of a centralized force, which they believed would serve the same function as an army and infringe on their freedoms, it was important for Peel to present a non-threatening group of officers, which later came to be known as the *bobbies*. Indeed, "Peel's attempts to appease the public were well-grounded; during the first three years of his reform effort, he encountered strong opposition. Peel was denounced as a potential dictator … and bobbies were referred to as general spies" (Peak & Glensor, 2002, p. 3). An amicable disposition was Peel's first attempt of appeasing the worried crowd. An additional way to gain public support and trust was through ethical conduct. Let's review the Peelian principles of policing for evidence of ethical decision-making.

1. The basic mission for which the police exist is to prevent crime and disorder.
2. The ability of the police to perform their duties is dependent upon the public approval of police actions.
3. Police must secure the willing cooperation of the public in voluntary observation of the law to be able to secure and maintain the respect of the public.
4. The degree of cooperation of the public that can be secured diminishes proportionately to the necessity of the use of physical force.
5. Police seek and preserve public favor not by catering to public opinion, but by constantly demonstrating absolute impartial service to the law.
6. Police use physical force to the extent necessary to secure observance of the law or to restore order only when the exercise of persuasion, advice, and warning is found to be insufficient.

7. Police, at all times, should maintain a relationship with the public that gives reality to the historic tradition that the police are the public and the public are the police; the police being only members of the public who are paid to give full-time attention to duties which are incumbent upon every citizen in the interests of community welfare and existence.
8. Police should always direct their action strictly towards their functions, and never appear to usurp the powers of the judiciary.
9. The test of police efficiency is the absence of crime and disorder, not the visible evidence of police action in dealing with it.

As you can see, the principles contain basic tenants of ethical decision-making such as demonstrating impartiality to the law, using reasonable force when necessary and, never abusing police authority. So, did these principles reach the shores of colonial America and influence our budding system of policing?

Thinking Questions

1. Compare and contrast policing in England and during colonial times.
2. What was the London Metropolitan Police Act?
3. What were citizens' reactions to the Metropolitan Police Act?
4. What did Sir Robert Peel think about ethics in policing?

Eras of Policing and Ethical Principles

Although it is debatable how many eras in policing have transpired over time, there seems to be agreement that there have been at least three major eras in American policing:

- The Political Era: 1830s–1900
- The Reform/Professional Era: 1900–1970s
- The Community Policing Era: 1970 to present

The Political Era

The Political Era was quite active in the extent of ethical violations committed by members of the police force in the various burgeoning cities across the United States. The era, as its name implies, was extensively influenced by local political bosses whose sole interest was retaining their stronghold on local affairs (Lyman, 2002). With a steady flow of immigrants moving to large cities in search of better employment prospects, constant riots, and an escalating crime and disorder rate, forced cities to resort to hiring and paying men to serve on a police force. As noted, Philadelphia was one of the first cities to pay for day and night watch services, followed by the city of New York (Schmalleger, 2003). But, police forces garnered their authority from political machines (as opposed to the constitution), primarily the alderman. The alderman was an elected official whose primary responsibility was to provide services to the constituents in his ward or neighborhood. One of these responsibilities included the formation of a police force (Walker & Katz, 2005).

Organizationally, police forces created under the "alderman system of policing" across the U.S. were highly decentralized, highly disorganized, and lacked any true supervision (Lyman, 2002). Police forces were simply composed of rank-and-file officers who were hired and fired at the discretion of the alderman. While surprising, the only manner in which a person could join the force during this time was to either bribe a politician to hire him or to receive the appointment of an office because of close personal ties with the politician (Purpura, 2001). Walker and Katz (2005) note that "police departments in the nineteenth century had no personnel standards ... officers were selected entirely on the basis of their political connections. Men who had no education, bad health, and criminal records were hired as officers" (p. 30).

Having a police force created by a politician and giving primary importance to his needs before attending to the community created significant ethical problems. However, the alderman system of policing was efficient in some respects. For instance, with the constant fear of losing the political seat, the alderman occupied his time finding solutions to crime and social disorder, as well as other problems such as unemployment, healthcare, runaway children, and the homeless. Needless to say, the function of the police was to help solve these problems. Law enforcement matters, while important to prevent riots which were an everyday occurrence, were of secondary importance. Their most important task was to help with a broad array of social services. They also helped enforce election laws and watched voter polling sites during elections (Peak & Glensor, 2002; Walker & Katz, 2005).

Peak and Glensor (2002) claim the politician-centered system of policing did have benefits. The first of which was attention to a number of social ills. Another advantage was the intimacy between the police and community. Because police officers resided in the same neighborhood they patrolled, they were able to give residents individualized attention. But, this also led to widespread police corruption. "The close identification of police with neighborhoods also resulted in discrimination against strangers, especially minority ethnic and racial groups ... which lead to officers practicing *curbside* justice"

(p. 8). Police corruption, which plagued every city during this era, also flour-ished because officers accepted bribes and payoffs for non-enforcement of laws related to drinking, gambling, and prostitution. The money was often divided among officers and helped defray their low wages (Peak & Glensor, 2002).

Thinking Questions

1. What was the Adlerman system of policing?
2. What were the advantages and disadvantages of policing during the Polit-ical Era?
3. What is curbside justice?

The Reform Era

With police corruption becoming rampant across cities, reform was crucial. The Reform Era, which spanned from the early 1900s to the 1970s, was influenced initially by a group of reform-minded individuals, knows as the Progressives (Pur-pura, 2001). The Progressives were middle-to-upper-class Americans who envi-sioned a government devoid of political influences and operating to truly serve the needs of the people (Lyman, 2002). In order to divorce politics from policing, it was necessary to accentuate the importance of deriving police authority from laws and the U.S. Constitution. It was not until this era that the Peelian principles were being incorporated into the mindset of our officers. In addition to being an "apo-litical public servant," the police were told that they must gain public trust and be held accountable for their actions. Citizens were encouraged to report incidences of police misconduct, corruption, or other misdeeds (Walker & Katz, 2005).

Gaining public support meant professionalizing the police. August Vollmer, chief of the city of Berkley, California from 1905 to 1932, is known as the fa-ther of police professionalism. He advocated for the training and education of officers. He was the first to hire college graduates and the first to organize college-level courses for officers (e.g., the police academy) (Walker & Katz, 2005). According to Walker and Katz (2005), professionalizing the police also required making the following changes:

- Defining policing as a legitimate profession and/or occupation. This meant that the police had to behave in such a way that gained the respect and trust of the community. This would be done by enforcing the law with impartiality.
- Appointing qualified personnel as chiefs of police. Rather than hiring politicians, efforts should be made to hire individuals with proven man-

agerial experience and/or who understand the law. It was during this time that lawyers were hired as chiefs in some departments.

- Raising personnel standards. This was the beginning attempt to implement screening mechanisms for applicants which included establishing minimum requirements for aptitude, health, and moral character.
- Introducing principles of scientific management. This involved centralizing command and control and making efficient use of personnel. This also meant implementing a quasi-military structure and organization for police departments that emphasized bureaucratic principles such as the implementation of policies and procedures and adherence to a chain of command.
- Using data, statistics and/or evidence-based crime reports to show the community that the police are being effective as well as to allocate resources. (pp. 35–36)

Change did not come easily or swiftly. For some police forces, change did not begin to take place until the late 1930s. Even with the changes, however, abuses of authority were still commonplace. In 1929, President Herbert Hoover appointed the Wickersham Commission to investigate ethical issues inherent in the criminal justice system, including the police (Peak & Glensor, 2002). In their findings, published under the *Report on Lawlessness in Law Enforcement*, the Commission found widespread examples of police misconduct including the physical abuse and torture of suspects. This added to other reports showing prejudice and bias in the enforcement of laws by police against racial minorities. Together, these examples fueled race riots in the first half of the twentieth century (Walker & Katz, 2005).

From 1930 to 1960, one of Vollmer's disciples, O.W. Wilson became instrumental in the eventual professionalization of the police during the 1960s and 1970s. Serving as chief of police in Wichita, Kansas from 1928 to 1935, then Dean of the University of California's School of Criminology from 1950–1960, and finally Superintendent of the Chicago Police Department from 1960–1967, Wilson advocated a new model of police administration (Walker & Katz, 2005). In his book *Police Administration* (1950), he called for the centralization of the command structure of police organizations and the establishment of a clear chain of command as well as the incorporation of specialized units. The special units were to be populated by officers based on skill and according to the frequency of crime. That is, the size and function of units were to be based on the amount of crime rates in a particular area and during particular times (Swanson, Territo, & Taylor, 2001). In a sense, this was an early attempt at determining crime hot spots and allocating resources (e.g., manpower) accordingly. This was also a first attempt to prove to the public that the police were effective and efficient crime fighters (Walker & Katz, 2005).

Efficiency also came in the form of technological advances. Although the patrol car made its appearance before World War I, its use was not prevalent until after the 1920s (Walker & Katz, 2005). The move from foot patrol to motorized patrol, however, did not fully occur until the 1960s. By then, the preferred method of responding to calls for service was to use the car. The patrol car was in line with Wilson's philosophy of police efficiency. After all, the car improved response time and citizens' perception of police. Other technological advancements helped improve efficiency; the two-way radio and the telephone. Making its debut in the late 1930s, the two-way radio allowed the police to remain on the streets while a dispatcher relayed information. Of course, the addition of the telephone, which was invented in 1877, and the gradual installation of the phone in residential homes during the early twentieth century allowed for citizens to stay in communication with the police (Walker & Katz, 2005).

While the police were making internal strides with respect to cleaning up their organizational structure, philosophy, and efficiency, crime and disorder did not dissipate (Purpura, 2001). Abuses of police authority, particularly against African Americans and Mexican Americans, were quite common. The Zoot Suit Riot sparked by racial tensions between police and Latinos occurred in 1943, in Los Angeles (Walker & Katz, 2005). The escalation of abuses continued and were documented by the Supreme Court in 1961. *Mapp v. Ohio* ruled that evidence gathered in violation of the Fourth Amendment was inadmissible in court. The Supreme Court had already ruled that it was wrong to use illegally-seized evidence in federal court. In the case of *Weeks v. United States* (1914), the Court held that evidence obtained illegally by any officer of the law, local or federal, could not be used in federal court because it violated the provisions of the Fourth Amendment. Because the Court did not specifically rule that illegally seized evidence could not be used in state courts, *Mapp v. Ohio* addressed this issue. The Court in *Mapp* said:

> Because it is enforceable in the same manner and to like effect as other basic rights secured by the Due Process Clause, we can no longer permit it to be revocable at the whim of any police officer who, in the name of law enforcement itself, chooses to suspend its enjoyment. Our decision, founded on reason and truth, gives to the individual no more than that which the Constitution guarantees him, to the police officer no less than that to which honest law enforcement is entitled, and, to the courts, that judicial integrity so necessary in the true administration of justice.

In 1966, the Supreme Court took on the issue of police misconduct with respect to interrogations. In *Miranda v. Arizona* (1966), it held that confessions were inadmissible in court if police did not first safeguard an individual's right against self-incrimination. Specifically, it said that suspects, under custodial interrogation, must be informed of their right to remain silent, their right to counsel, and their right to terminate an interrogation. Thus, the Court ruled:

> Unless other fully effective means are devised to inform accused persons of their right of silence and to assure a continuous opportunity to exercise it, the following measures are required. Prior to any questioning, the person must be warned that he has a right to remain silent, that any statement he does make may be used as evidence against him, and that he has a right to the presence of an attorney, either retained or appointed. The defendant may waive effectuation of these rights, provided the waiver is made voluntarily, knowingly and intelligently. If, however, he indicates in any manner and at any stage of the process that he wishes to consult with an attorney before speaking there can be no questioning. Likewise, if the individual is alone and indicates in any manner that he does not wish to be interrogated, the police may not question him. The mere fact that he may have answered some questions or volunteered some statements on his own does not deprive him of the right to refrain from answering any further inquiries until he has consulted with an attorney and thereafter consents to be questioned.

These cases exemplify the extent of police corruption and the giant steps taken by the Supreme Court to remedy this problem. But, tensions between the police and citizens continued and reached their height during the Civil Rights movement in the late 1960s. While the Civil Rights movement was fueled by discriminatory practices of the federal government against minorities in areas such as housing, education, and employment, they were also driven by instances of police brutality (Peak & Glensor, 2002). In 1965, President Lyndon B. Johnson appointed a commission, known as the *President's Crime Commission*, to study the problem. In 1967, they published a report entitled *The Challenge of Crime in a Free Society* and found that police brutality was an institutionalized norm within police organizations. The Commission called for the professionalization of police and recommended: (1) hiring qualified applicants, (2) training them, (3) managing and supervising them better, and (4) placing limits on police discretion. The National Advisory Commission on Civil Disorders, also known as the Kerner Commission, which found more than 200 incidents of race riots in 1967, recommended similar provisions

(Walker & Katz, 2005). The Commission further stated that violence and escalating crime rates would fail to decrease if the police did not seek true partnerships with the community.

Although the race riots contributed significantly to the notion of an "us versus them mentality" between the police and community, attempts at professionalization also had a similar outcome. The motorized patrol, as mentioned, had a pronounced effect on police practices but it also meant that officers only interacted with citizens when the latter beckoned (Uchida, 2001). Unlike during the Political Era, officers were distancing themselves from the public they were entrusted to serve. Also, in order to divorce the influence of politics from policing, especially opportunities for officers to practice curbside justice, officers were also told that their primary and only responsibility was crime fighting and/or enforcement of the law (Lyman, 2002). That is, their job was no longer to identify and find solutions to other social ills. This narrowing of job responsibilities limited their interactions with members of the community. When answering a call for service, they were also told to inform the public that the police were highly trained and capable of handling matters by themselves (Purpura, 2001). Officers were encouraged not to accept help from anyone not wearing a uniform. Finally, the "us versus them" approach was also achieved through the education of officers. As officers became better educated and trained, they too began to believe that it was their job to handle law enforcement matters without the help of the community. According to Uchida (2001), professional departments embodied a number of characteristics:

> First, the officers were experts; they applied knowledge to their tasks and were the only ones qualified to do the job. Second, the department was autonomous from external influences, such as political parties. This also meant that the department made its own rules and regulated its personnel. Finally, the department was administratively efficient, in that it carried out its mandate to enforce the law through modern technology and business-like practices. (p. 29)

Strained police-community relations were beginning to take a toll on crime and disorder problems. After all, isolating the community from helping to solve problems is counterproductive because citizens are the eyes and ears of the police (Rosenbaum, 1988). Some police departments established community relations teams to convince the public to become partners in the fight against crime (Greene & Pelfrey, 2001). But, as mentioned, the Civil Rights Movement, constant examples of police abuse of authority, and distrust in government fueled by many instances of discrimination, meant that attempts at community policing were futile (Walker & Katz, 2005). But, the police would soon realize that without community support, law enforcement and crime prevention duties were too difficult to achieve alone (Rosenbaum, 1988).

Thinking Questions

1. Who were the Progressives?
2. What did August Vollmer propose to professionalize the police?
3. What were some of the proposals to professionalize policing during the Reform Era?
4. What were the advantages and disadvantages to police professionalism?
5. What were the various findings from the different presidential commissions charged with investigating police issues?
6. What effect did the patrol car and education for officers have on community relations?
7. What was the role of the Supreme Court during the Reform Era?

The Community Policing Era

The Community Policing Era began in the late 1970s, but was especially well-defined during the 1980s and 1990s. The move toward a community policing philosophy was helped along the way by the following:

- In the mid-to-late 1970s, community crime prevention programs, such as Neighborhood Watch, received unprecedented support from the federal government. Funded largely by the Law Enforcement Assistance Administration and the National Institute of Justice, grants were given to police departments to improve or establish Neighborhood Watch organizations. By the 1980s, Neighborhood Watch gained momentum and was implemented across the United States (Rosenbaum, 1988; Lavrakas & Herz, 1982).
- Academic researchers found statistical evidence that the traditional model of policing, practiced during the Reform Era, was not effective in reducing and/or preventing crime. They also found that police would be ineffective in reducing and/or preventing crime without the help of the community. Furthermore, they found evidence to show that foot patrol was an effective means at preventing crime and disorder problems in neighborhoods (Walker & Katz, 2005).
- Congress passed the Violent Crime Control and Law Enforcement Act of 1994 that gave state and local police monies to implement community policing (Lyman, 2002).

Although community policing suffers from a "continuing search for a consistent definition" (Oliver and Bartgis, 1998, p. 491), the majority of definitions share a commonality:

> In community oriented policing, the police proactively act beyond simple crime fighting and law enforcement, rely on the citizenry, engage in tactics to target specific problems identified by the whole community, decentralize to the neighborhood level to be accessible, maintain constant contact and cooperation with the citizenry, work with other public and private sector organizations and continually evaluate strategies and community relations. (Pino, 2001, p. 200)

Community policing has been called a "revolution" (Oliver & Bartgis, 1998, p. 490) in the field that has brought about a philosophical change or reorientation in the crime-fighting roles of both the community and the police. However, community policing remains entrenched in an elusive search to find an accepted definition (Reisig & Giacomazzi, 1998). Numerous discussions and debates abound concerning the lack of consistent operational definitions for this style of policing (Eck & Rosenbaum, 1994). Difficulties in defining the conceptual elements that encompass community policing are only some of the semantic debates. For instance, discussions have also surfaced about implementation strategies, especially since there continues to be disagreement about whether community policing is a philosophy, an ideology, a tactic or a strategy (Trajanowicz et al., 1998; Kelling, 1994). The inability to discern the most appropriate label or definition does not preclude reaching a universal agreement on some of the basic tenets of community policing.

Rosenbaum and Lurigio (1994) contended that the basic tenets of community policing included (1) foot patrol, (2) neighborhood mini-stations and community centers, and (3) police organizing and outreach strategies. Foot patrol emphasized non-traditional police functions such as "attending community meetings, identifying community problems and needs; organizing citizen initiatives, resolving neighborhood disputes and making referrals to appropriate social service agencies" (p. 305). Neighborhood mini-stations and community centers affirmed a de-centralization of police services whereas police organizing and outreach strategies focused on soliciting residents to form and attend neighborhood crime prevention programs such as Neighborhood Watch (p. 306).

Lurigio and Skogan (1994), in their analysis of the Chicago Alternative Policing Strategy (CAPS), were more specific in their operationalization of community policing. For instance, they argued that community policing involved:

- Neighborhood orientation: Giving special attention to the residents and problems of specific neighborhoods, which demands that officers know their beats (i.e., crime trends, hot spots and community organizations resources) and develop partnerships with the community to solve problems.
- Increased geographic responsibility: Organizing police services so that officers are responsible for crime control in specific areas.
- Structured response to calls for service: A system of differential police response to citizen calls frees officers from the continuous demands of 911 calls.
- Proactive problem-oriented approach: Police focus on the causes of neighborhood problems rather than on discrete incidents of crime or disturbances. Attention is given to long-term prevention of these problems and to the signs of community disorder and decay that are associated with crime.
- Community and city resources for crime prevention and control: Part of the officer's role is to broker community resources and to draw on other city agencies to identify and respond to local problems.
- Emphasis on crime problem analysis: Requires efficient data collection and analysis to identify crime patterns and to target areas that demand police attention. (p. 318)

Adams, Rohe and Acury (2002), while consistent with previous operational definitions of community policing, posed a more simplistic definition. They argued that community policing was composed of three essential elements, the first being *shared responsibility* between the police and the community. The second element was *crime prevention* whereby officers and citizens would be vigilant to identify community problems and their solutions. The final element was *discretion* where officers are afforded the opportunity "to be creative in addressing community problems without resorting to arrest" (p. 402). Additionally, Adams et al. (2002) contended that changes must be made in relation to officer performance evaluations where performance was not solely based on response time, number of arrests and number of citations issued but rather on solving or reducing community problems.

Based on the discrepancies in operational definitions of community policing, it is logical to expect a natural variation among law enforcement agencies when implementing such a philosophy. Additionally, proponents of community policing such as Eck and Rosenbaum (1994) and Goldstein (1987) contend that the comprehensive organizational changes required by a community policing philosophy should be made in accordance with community needs and organizational readiness (i.e., acquiring resources, proper training of officers, minimal resistance by the organizational culture). Despite the natural-born inconsistencies in implementing community policing, Adams et al. (2002), Sims, Hooper, and Peterson (2002) and Webb and Katz (1997) argued that a significantly large number of law enforcement agencies in the United States profess to have adopted the tenets of community policing.

Thinking Questions

1. What are the basic elements of community policing?
2. Why is it so difficult to define community policing?
3. What responsibilities do officers and citizens have under a community policing model?

Does Community Policing Create Ethical Dilemmas in Policing?

One of the basic principles of community policing is empowering both the citizens and patrol officer so that, together, they may be able to more aptly resolve situations. As mentioned, this requires allowing officers more discretion to perform their duties. So, instead of only being able to arrest and/or issue citations, officers must "think outside of the box" and consult the community for the best possible solution. While garnering the input and help from the community is important, does it create problems? Does empowering the police and the community open a Pandora's Box to ethical violations?

Decentralization of authority usually grants patrol officers more discretionary powers and discretion has the potential to create many ethical dilemmas. Discretion, as you know, has been described as a needed element in policing but one that can lead down a spiraling road to corruption (Kleinig, 2008). In order for police to best identify and solve problems, within the mandates of community policing, they must "become one" with their community. Essentially, they must foster an intimate relationship with the community they serve in order to understand and solve problems. However, "becoming one" with the community, without crossing the so-called ethical-line in the sand, can be tricky. It is only natural for some officers and community members, in time, to become invested in each others' lives. Again, community policing encourages the development of friendship networks between the police and community. Eventually, an atmosphere of comfort and reciprocity develops. In other words, each becomes comfortable asking the other for favors. While favors may be innocuous in nature, such as citizens asking police to speak to teenagers

Gratuities

congregating on a street-corner, the door to asking/complying with favors has been opened. When that door is opened, gift exchanges for compliance to favors or requests may take place. Soon, each begins to justify the giving and/or receiving of gifts as appropriate.

For instance, it is not uncommon for citizens, particular store or business owners to show their gratitude to officers by offering free cups of coffee, free meals, or discounts in exchange for their attentiveness and presence at the store. While the giving of a free cup of coffee may be an innocent gesture and certainly is not the sole contributor to ethical violations or police corruption, the expectation, by the storeowner, of something in return is what establishes a "slippery slope." Ruiz and Bono (2004) argue that "what makes a gift a gratuity is the reason it is given; what makes it corruption is the reason it is taken" (p. 45). If the reason it is given and taken leads to favoritism, impartiality, and prejudice, then this begins the downward spiral of unethical behavior.

Box 3.1 Ethics in the News

The Republic (AZcentral.com)—November, 2013

Arizona Border Patrol Agent Gets Prison Term for Bribery

As a Border Patrol agent assigned to a special undercover unit in Yuma, Ivhan Herrera-Chiang's job was to stop criminals from smuggling drugs into the U.S.

Instead, the agent used his position to help drug traffickers bring methamphetamine, cocaine and marijuana across the border by providing them with secret information in exchange for bribes, according to court records and prosecutors.

On Tuesday, a federal judge sentenced Herrera-Chiang to 15 years in prison. He pleaded guilty in April to four felony counts of bribery.

"You have done about the worst thing a law-enforcement agent could do, especially a Border Patrol agent, and that is passed confidential information" to criminal organizations, U.S. District Judge Paul Rosenblatt said during a sentencing hearing in Phoenix.

Before he was caught and arrested in 2012, Herrera-Chiang provided maps of hidden underground sensors, lock combinations to gates along the U.S.-Mexican border and the location of Border Patrol traffic checkpoints to a former Arizona Department of Corrections officer, Michael Lopez-Garcia.

Lopez-Garcia, in turn, passed the information on to smugglers so they could evade detection and transport drugs into the country, according to court records and prosecutors.

Herrera-Chiang also improperly logged in to law-enforcement databases on his Border Patrol computer to run drug-seizure checks for Lopez-Garcia and even provided the physical description of a confidential informant in Mexico. That forced federal law-enforcement officers to rush in and rescue the informant to save him from hit men, according to court records.

About 10 Department of Homeland Security and Border Patrol agents, including several who assisted with Herrera-Chiang's investigation and prosecution, attended the sentencing.

They sat quietly in the back, across the courtroom from where about a dozen of Herrera-Chiang's family members and supporters sat. Some family members wept as Rosenblatt announced the 15-year sentence.

Herrera-Chiang's defense lawyer, Philip Seplow, pleaded with the judge to sentence Herrera-Chiang to only three years in prison, arguing that he was an "honorable" person who admitted he "did a horrible thing."

Herrera-Chiang did not know the information he provided to Lopez-Garcia, his boyhood friend, was being used to assist drug smugglers, although he admitted he should have known, Seplow said.

Herrera-Chiang also denied giving information to Lopez-Garcia about the confidential informant, and received only about $4,500 in bribes for providing other information, including the lock combinations and drug-seizure records, Seplow said.

Assistant U.S. Attorney Dominic Lanza said the case was "one of the most serious" Border Patrol corruption cases "in a long time."

"This is such serious misconduct, such tarnishing of the oath," Lanza said in asking Rosenblatt to sentence Herrera-Chiang to 15 years in prison.

Lanza said Herrera-Chiang's co-conspirator, Lopez-Garcia, told investigators that Herrera-Chiang received upward of $60,000 to $70,000 for the information he provided.

Regardless, Lanza said, "one dollar is too much" when selling confidential maps of underground sensors, lock combinations and "the identity of a confidential informant."

Lopez-Garcia pleaded guilty in May 2012 to several felony charges. He is currently serving a nine-year prison sentence.

Department of Homeland Security agents began investigating Herrera-Chiang and Lopez-Garcia in July 2011 after receiving a tip from a confidential informant.

Herrera-Chiang, a former Marine, joined the Border Patrol in August 2006. In March 2011, he was assigned to the Yuma Sector's Smuggling Interdiction Group, a plainclothes enforcement team responsible for conducting surveillance, detection and interdiction of drug traffickers and human smugglers, according to court records.

He actually began working with Lopez-Garcia before he joined the unit, starting around September 2010, helping smugglers in Mexico bring drugs into the U.S., according to court records.

Lopez-Garcia acted as the middleman, paying Herrera-Chiang to provide sensitive information, which Lopez-Garcia then passed along to drug smugglers in Mexico.

During that time, Lopez-Garcia was discovered five different times participating in drug-smuggling activities with the help of Herrera-Chiang.

Unknown to the two men, however, the drug-smuggling activities were actually being orchestrated by undercover DHS agents posing as drug smugglers, according to court records.

what about in communities hope gift

Kleinig (1996), in his "slippery slope" argument, said that "because even *giving is a duty rather than a gratuity* the appearance of a minor gratuity involves the same implicit rationale as a criminal offense and both were acts of illegitimate conduct, the former type of deviance should be included when defining police deviance" (cited in New- *Buddhist Cultures.* burn, 1999, p. 12). Basically, the acceptance of even the smallest "perks" such as free coffee is problematic because it changes the mindset of officers. Officers learn to rationalize that it is ethical to accept gratuities. Ruiz and Bono (2004), state that the acceptance of a free cup of coffee is "a gateway" to larger forms of police corruption because officers begin to believe they are entitled, by virtue of the uniform, to gratuities. They further state, "the acceptance of gratuities provides an opportunity for corrupt intent, whether the intent is initially that of the giver or the receiver. Once that opportunity has been grasped, officers will find themselves on a slippery slope of compromise and opportunism" (p. 45). Del Pozo (2005) notes that this is the moral hazard inherent in adopting a community policing philosophy.

Thinking Questions

1. What are the advantages and disadvantages of community policing?
2. What is the "slippery slope" argument?
3. When is the difference between a gift and a gratuity?

Conclusion

The history of policing in the United States is filled with instances of unethical conduct. In fact, some may argue that the police was born out of extreme corruption. But, as policing evolved, attempts were made to make the profession more ethical. Some attempts, however, were harmful to the relationship between the police and community. As such, a philosophy developed that was more inclusive of the input for citizens. While there is no doubt that our society favors the use of formal agents of social control, there is cognizance that without the community serving as the eyes and ears of the police, law and order would be difficult to achieve. Nonetheless, strategies that try to fuse the police with members of the public to become co-partners in the fight against crime and disorder, have led to abuses of power. Indeed, community policing presents opportunities to engage in unethical conduct.

Scenarios

1. As a recent graduate of the police academy, your next phase of training is to learn the ropes from a field training officer (FTO). You were lucky to be paired with a 25-year veteran of the department, knowledgeable of the formal and informal nature of the job. He is also a "legend" in the department, having been involved in the city's most infamous arrest. One day, while on patrol, your FTO invites you to lunch at his favorite restaurant. Being that you are eager to hear his war stories, you happily agree. After your meal, you take out your wallet to pay for him and yourself. Your FTO says, "No need … it's on the house. This is one of the reasons the restaurant is my favorite." What should you do?

2. Every day before going to work, you stop by the local convenience store for coffee and a newspaper. A few months ago, before reporting for your graveyard shift, you were in the habit of paying $1.50 for these items. Since you are no longer on graveyard shift, you introduce yourself to the morning clerk. She greets you and tells you that payment is not necessary for men and women in uniform. It's store policy, she says. Because you were running a little late, you feel that a full explanation of the "slippery slope" argument probably would take a few minutes to explain and perhaps not change her mind. So, you accept the free coffee and newspaper. After all, you tell yourself that it's only $1.50. One day the morning clerk tells you that she received a citation two days ago for a traffic violation. She also tells you that it's been difficult to pay bills lately and can't afford paying the citation plus the increase for her car insurance. She asks if there is anything you can do. What should you tell her?

3. Your department has recently implemented community-policing. As you know, this style of policing encourages more interaction between the police and residents. It has taken you months to earn the trust of residents in the neighborhood, especially the landlords of apartments that house the city's most notorious drug dealers. The landlords of several apartment buildings and you have been working on a solution to crime and disorder prob-

lems in and around these buildings. Since community-policing allows you to "think outside the box" you, together with the landlords, decide to evict known drug dealers. The landlords, however, also ask you to go along with a plan to evict tenants, who have not paid their rent, even though they are not crime suspects. They want you to accompany them when they inform the tenants they must vacate their apartment in two weeks or pay their back rent. What should you do?

4. At the last Neighborhood Watch meeting, residents were angry that the police department was not adequately addressing the issue of the city's homeless population. In fact, the residents were concerned that the police department was only interested in arresting homeless people. Your chief of police, however, has already expressed that she is not interested in solutions other than arrest. But, one of the residents is your biggest supporter of a police-youth afterschool league. He has contributed a large sum of money each year for youth activity projects. What should you do?

5. You are the Chief of a police department in a large metropolitan city. City Council has been critical of the many instances your officers have been on the news for misconduct, mainly for accepting bribes. Because you are tired of the criticism, you decide to do something. However, you also know that you must strike a balance between the wishes of City Council and the community who wants to show their appreciation to officers. What should you do?

References

Adams, R.E., Rohe, W.M., & Arcury, T.A. (2002). Implementing community-oriented policing: Organizational change and street officer attitudes. *Crime and Delinquency, 48*, 399–430.

Braithwaite, J. (1989). *Crime, shame, and reintegration*. New York: Cambridge University Press.

Chen, X. (2002). Social control in China: Applications of the labeling theory and the reintegrative shaming theory. *International Journal of Offender Therapy and Comparative Criminology, 46* (1), 45–63.

del Pozo, B. (2005). One dogma of police ethics: Gratuities and the democratic ethos of policing. *Criminal Justice Ethics*, Summer/Fall, 25–46.

Eck, J.E., & Rosenbaum, D.P. (1994). The new police order: Effectiveness, equity and efficiency in community policing. In D.P. Rosenbaum (Ed.), *The challenge of community policing* (3–27). Thousand Oaks, CA: Sage Publishing, Inc.

Goldstein, H. (1987). Toward community-oriented policing: Potential, basic requirements and threshold questions. *Crime and Delinquency, 33*, 6–30.

Greene, J.R., & Pelfrey, W.V. (2001). Shifting the balance of power between police and community: Responsibility for crime control. In J. Greene & S. Mastrofski (Eds.), *Community policing: Rhetoric or reality?* (435–465). New York: Praeger.

Kelling, G. (1994). Defining community policing. *Subject to Debate,* April, 3, 6.

Kleinig, J. (1996). *The Ethics of Policing.* Cambridge: Cambridge University Press.

Lab, S.P. (2004). *Crime prevention: Approaches, practices, and evaluations.* New York: Anderson Publishing.

Lavrakas, P.J., & Herz, E.J. (1982). Citizen participation in neighborhood crime prevention. *Criminology, 20*, 479–498.

Lurigio, A.J., & Skogan, W.S. (1994). Winning the hearts and minds of police officers: An assessment of staff perceptions of community policing in Chicago. *Crime and Delinquency, 40*(3), 315–330.

Lyman, M.D. (2002). *The police: An introduction.* Upper Saddle River, NJ: Prentice Hall.

Newburn, T. (1999). Understanding and preventing police corruption: Lessons from the literature. *Policing and Reducing Crime Unit: Police Research Series,* Paper 110. Retrieved October 10, 2010, from http://rds.homeoffice.gov.uk/rds/prgpdfs/fprs110.pdf.

Oliver, W.M., & Bartgis, E. (1998). Community policing: A conceptual framework. *Policing: An International Journal of Police Strategies and Management, 21*(3), 490–509.

Peak, K.J. (1997). *Policing America.* Upper Saddle River, NJ: Prentice-Hall.

Peak, K.J., & Glensor, R.W. (2002). *Community policing and problem solving: Strategies and practices.* Upper Saddle River, NJ: Prentice Hall.

Pino, N.W. (2001). Community policing and social capital. *Policing: An International Journal of Police Strategies and Management 25*, 457–471.

Purpura, P.P. (2001). *Police and community: Concepts and cases.* Boston: Allyn and Bacon.

Reisig, M.D., & Giacomazzi, A.L. (1998). Citizen perceptions of community policing: Are attitudes toward police important? *Policing: An International Journal of Police Strategies and Management, 21*(3), 547–561.

Roberg, R., Novak, K., & Cordner, G. (2005). *Police and society.* Los Angeles, California: Roxbury.

Rosenbaum, D.P. (1988). Community crime prevention: A review and synthesis of literature. *Justice Quarterly, 5*, 323–395.

Rosenbaum, D.P., & Lurigio, A.J. (1994). An inside look at community policing reform: Definitions, organizational changes, and evaluation findings. *Crime and Delinquency, 40*(3), 299–314.

Ruiz, J., & Bono, C. (2004). At what price a freebie? The real cost of police gratuities. *Criminal Justice Ethics*, Winter/Spring, 44–54.

Schmalleger, F. (2003). *Criminal justice today*. Upper Saddle River, NJ: Prentice Hall.

Sims, B., Hooper, M., & Peterson, S.A. (2002). Determinants of citizens' attitudes toward police. *Strategies and Management*, 24 (2), 200–215.

Swanson, C., Territo, L., & Taylor, R. (2001). Police administration. New Jersey: Prentice Hall.

Trajanowicz, R., Kappeler, V.E., Gaines, L.K., & Bucqueroux, B. (1998). *Community policing: A contemporary perspective*. Cincinnati, OH: Anderson Publishing Inc.

Uchida, C.D. (2001). The development of the American police: An historical overview. In R.G. Dunham, & G. P. Alpert (Eds.), *Critical issues in policing* (18–35). Prospect Heights, IL: Waveland Press, Inc.

Vago, S. (2003). *Law and society*. Upper Saddle River, NJ: Prentice Hall.

Walker, S., & Katz, C.M. (2005). *The police in America: An introduction*. Boston: McGraw-Hill.

Webb, V.J., & Katz, C.M. (1997). Citizens rating of the importance of community policing activities. *Policing: An International Journal of Police Strategies and Management*, 20, 7–23.

Cases Cited

Mapp v. Ohio, 367 U.S. 643 (1961).

Miranda v. Arizona, 384 U.S. 436 (1966).

Weeks v. United States, 232 U.S. 383 (1914).

4

Ethics and Police Work

Chapter Objectives:

- The student will understand the nature of police work
- The student will learn about the various ways officers learn ethics
- The student will examine the impact of the police subculture and the code of silence
- The student will explore how officers justify unethical behavior
- The student will comprehend studies on police deviance
- The student will learn about operant conditioning as an important element to police ethics
- The student will understand the *noble cause* and its relation to unethical behavior
- The student will explore avenues to instill ethical conduct in the field of policing

Introduction

Police can be aptly characterized as having government-endorsed, coercive muscle to help achieve harmony in society (Kleinig, 2008). Basically, they are given the privilege to enforce laws and the authority to physically and/or psychologically force individuals to comply with those laws. Roberg, Noval, and Cordner (2005) argue that the words *force* and *coercion* are one and the same because force "occurs any time the police attempt to have a citizen act in a particular way" (p. 315). Because of this power, ethics training should continuously be endorsed by police agencies across the country.

As mentioned in the last chapter, officers are also allowed to use discretion when fulfilling their duties as crime fighters (Walker & Katz, 2005). Because of their discretionary power, temptations to behave unethically usually surface. But, are temptations to behave unethically simply part of the nature of police work? Do officers learn immoral actions as part of their job or are they already unethical individuals prior to joining the force? Braswell, McCarthy, and

McCarthy (2008) explain that officers learn ethical, or unethical, conduct through occupational socialization and culturalization. That is, ethics is learned on the job. This chapter focuses on how and why officers may, at times, choose unethical conduct. It also discusses strategies to reinforce everyday ethics in the workplace.

Police Work

Today, it seems that more and more authority is given to police to intervene in the lives of the citizenry. This was certainly true after the events of September 11, 2001 and the passage of the Patriot Act (Cole, 2003; Forst, 2009). With well-justified concern over domestic and foreign terrorism, the federal government has exponentially increased police power in order to fight the War on Terror (Forst, 2009). Indeed, police are needed in society to maintain order and tranquility, especially with such apprehension over the security of our nation. Police are also our first line of defense against attacks, foreign or domestic. As such, ethics is important in law enforcement, as police must adhere to laws delineated in the U.S. Constitution. However, regardless of national security concerns, ordinary calls for service should be handled with ethical considerations and ethics should be practiced everyday in every situation.

The profession of law enforcement carries superior ethical dilemmas. Police work has been described as "morally dangerous" (Braswell et al., 2008, p. 49). Consider these examples:

- A citizen is driving in an area known by police to be a hot spot for selling drugs to minors. In the course of their routine patrol, two officers, in an unmarked car, notice the citizen and another individual sitting in a truck at an intersection stop-sign for more than one minute. All of a sudden, the citizen makes a right turn without signaling. Because failure to use the turn signal is a traffic violation, the officers stopped the truck. In plain sight, the officers observed plastic bags of crack cocaine. All occupants of the car were arrested on federal drug charges. Is it ethical for police to wait until a motorist commits a minor traffic violation in order to stop and search a car for motives unrelated to the traffic stop? Essentially, is it ethical for police to use a traffic stop to further an investigation into a possible drug dealer, knowing that they did not have probable cause to search the individual and/or the car prior to the traffic violation?
- A woman was convicted of second degree murder for the death of a 17-year-old boy, who died in a fire set in the mobile home where he lived

with the woman. Several days after the fire, the woman was interrogated by a police officer. The officer did not initially read the Miranda warnings because she was hoping to get a confession. In her distraught state, the woman finally confessed and afterward, the officer read the Miranda warnings. The officer, wanting to record the confession, cleverly asked the woman to summarize their past "un-Mirandized" conversation. The woman again confessed the crime and was eventually convicted of murder because of the confession. Is it ethical for the officer not to read the warnings because she knows the suspect is too distressed to realize she has the right to remain silent? What if there is no other evidence linking the suspect to the crime and without the confession, the murder remained unsolved? Is it ethical not to read the warnings in the last situation only?

- The state of Arizona recently enacted legislation that makes it a misdemeanor for immigrants in the state to be without required documents showing proof that they can live and/or work in the United States. It also allows police, during the course of a "lawful stop, detention or arrest" to ask about their immigration status. Furthermore, it allows officers, who have a reasonable suspicion that certain individuals are illegal immigrants, to question their status and conduct an arrest. Is it ethical for local and/or state police to check immigration status when they stop someone? Should they be allowed to conduct warrantless arrests of suspected illegal immigrants and criminalize them for failure to carry documentation?

- Living in a post-9/11 society, airport police sometimes rely on profiles to stop and question airline passengers. Should police use racial profiles to better secure our nation from foreign and/or domestic terror attacks? In order words, do the *ends justify the means*? In this case, does the possibility of preventing a terrorist attack justify the use of racial profiles?

There is no question that police work is loaded with pitfalls for unethical behavior. Temptations to behave unethically, even if the ends justify the means, as in the above examples, are ever present in law enforcement (Roberg et al., 2005). Many of the temptations are linked to the incredible amount of discretion afforded to police (Kleinig, 2008), however, they are also linked to the code of silence in the police force—a factor somewhat unique to this profession (Walker & Katz, 2005). It may also be linked to occupational socialization and culturalization, stress and, frustration (Braswell et al., 2008), therefore, ethics training is vital.

Temptations to act unethically are also faced by police supervisors and administrators and thus ethics training should not be required only for line-officers (Souryal, 2010). Command staff should also be included because there is considerable research that shows that low managerial supervision of line-officers and indifference toward the behavior of the rank-and-file perpetuates incidences of police deviance, including unethical conduct (Hughes, 2001; Walker & Katz, 2005; Purpura, 2001). Because unethical behavior can often lead to criminal and civil liability, all officers should receive instruction on ethical decision-making.

Learning Ethics *Learned Behavior*

Let's take a look at how officers learn ethics. Some of the hypotheses incorporate elements from theories in criminology that say ethical, or unethical, behavior is learned similarly to the manner in which an offender learns the techniques to commit a crime. But, there is another line of reasoning that assumes officers are unethical before even joining the police force.

The Values-Learned Perspective

The values-learned perspective is perhaps the most scholarly-established viewpoint as to how officers learn ethical and unethical behavior. This view holds that the most common manner is through social and/or cultural indoctrination to the police culture. Ethics are learned through the process of socialization and culturalization within a particular police agency (Braswell et al., 2008). The process of organizational socialization and culturalization seeks to "fuse the officer to the organization by providing him or her with a set of rules, perspectives, prescriptions, techniques, and tools necessary to participate in the organization" (Braswell et al., 2008, p. 58). Utilizing the perspective by sociologist Edwin Sutherland, unethical behavior can be learned through the process of socialization. Sutherland postulated that behavior was "learned, through the process of communication within intimate personal groups" (Akers, 2000, p. 72). Although his notion is usually applied to explain juvenile delinquency, his theory can be applied to ethics as well. Sutherland believed a person became deviant (delinquent) when he or she "had an excess of definitions favorable to law-violating behavior" (Akers, 2000, p. 72). Variations in deviance or criminality were explained by Sutherland to be caused by a differential association or the differences in an individual's exposure to deviant persons. Sutherland's premise that exposure to deviant persons increased the likelihood of engaging in deviance or criminality, did not imply that this behavior occurred in isolation. Rather, Sutherland contended that individuals were also exposed to those who held law-abiding standards. However, he argued that early exposure (priority) as well as the duration, frequency and intensity of inter-actions with deviant persons were variant factors that affected learning conforming or nonconforming behavior (Akers, 2000).

Sutherland's propositions of learning criminal behavior have surfaced in most of the studies on motivational causes for police deviance, including un-ethical behavior. Researchers have argued that the social context of learning to deviate occurs early in the career of the police officer, in particular during police-training academies (Hunt & Manning, 1991; Hodgson, 2001). This modality of association (priority) is accompanied by the "frequency," "duration," and "in-tensity" of interactions between cadets and police instructors. For instance, as part of basic training, cadets spend most of their time learning about the na-ture of police work from instructors, most of whom are current or former of-ficers. Some academies even prohibit cadets from leaving the premises and limit associations with families (Hodgson, 2001). Although varying in duration from several weeks to a few months, cadets receive intensive training ranging from civil and criminal law to officer safety. In addition, cadets receive thorough training on subcultural norms meant to develop an esprit de corps and meant to educate the trainees about the police worldview (Hodgson, 2001).

The bonding that occurs during the police training academy introduces cadets to a new perspective or lens to judge situations. As part of the indoc-trination process (some call it "the metamorphosis process"), cadets are grad-ually schooled to accept and believe that two separate worlds exist in policing—"us and them" (Kappeler et al., 1994). The "us versus them" attitude is "quickly generated to reflect the distinctiveness of the police officer status and the sus-picion thrown on others who are not in the club" (Hodgson, 2001, p. 535). Eventually, suspicion of anyone who does not wear the uniform leads to iso-lation from the community. Naturally, only those that wear the uniform can empathize with this isolation. It creates solidarity among the ranks and rein-forces the need to seek inclusion in the police subculture (Kappeler, et al., 1994; Hodgson, 2001).

The process of learning norms is inherent in any occupation, whether in the field of criminal justice or not. Members of particular associations or groups define normative behavior, which may be consistent with law-abiding behav-ior (Akers, 2000). In policing, members of the police subculture define ac-ceptable or unacceptable behavior. Depending on the ethos of the subculture, normative behavior may include definitions acceptable to law-violating or de-viant behavior (Hunt & Manning, 1991). For instance, one of the strongest cultural norms is maintaining the code of silence, which can invoke adminis-trative or legal sanctions if maintained and informal sanctions if broken. Es-sentially, even if the officer does not participate in the actual commission of the crime, reporting such behavior to superiors is considered norm-violating behavior within the subculture. On the other hand, not reporting such behavior is a violation of administrative policies and the law (Hunt & Manning, 1991; Sherman, 1978). The "blue curtain of secrecy," however, is likely to take precedence over administrative policies (Sherman, 1978, p. 47).

Differential associations with members of the police subculture, especially those who hold an excess of definitions favorable to law-violating behavior, may be sufficient motivational factors for deviant behavior. However, associating with fellow officers provides one of two viable explanations for police deviance. The other explanation is differential associations with street criminals. Police work requires that officers interact and communicate with those members of society who violate the law. Although most of these interactions do not occur within "intimate personal groups" they do occur with frequency and priority. Interactions with criminals and the intimacy between the officer and known felons are dependent on the type of assignment. Thus, officers assigned to vice squads may gradually consider criminals within their personal intimate groups. Evidence of this transformation has been provided by government inquiries into police drug-related corruption. Cited among the reasons why officers do not report or apprehend drug distributors was a need to protect members of the illegal narcotics operation (GAO, 1998). Again, this is a gradual transformation and the primary reason why police departments rotate officers in vice-squads after a certain period of time.

Box 4.1 On Border, Agents Struggle with Corruption

CBS News (AP) — August, 2009

Corruption along the U.S.-Mexican border takes many forms.

It can start as simply as a smuggler's $50 gift to the child of a reluctant federal agent, quickly escalating to out-and-out bribes. "Everyone does it," the agent, now in prison, recalls telling himself. Other times, county sheriffs greedily grab thousands from drug dealers. In a few instances, traffickers even place members in the applicant pool for sensitive border protection jobs.

An Associated Press investigation has found U.S. law officers who work the border are being charged with criminal corruption in numbers not seen before, as drug and immigrant smugglers use money and sometimes sex to buy protection, and internal investigators crack down.

Based on Freedom of Information Act requests, interviews with sentenced agents and a review of court records, the AP tallied corruption-related convictions against more than 80 enforcement officials at all levels—federal, state and local—since 2007, shortly after Mexican President Felipe Calderon declared war on the cartels that peddle up to $39 billion worth of drugs in the United States each year.

U.S. officials have long pointed to Mexico's rampantly corrupt cops and broken judicial system, but Calderon told the AP this isn't just a Mexican problem.

"To get drugs into the United States the one you need to corrupt is the American authority, the American customs, the American police—not the Mexican. And that's a subject, by the way, which hasn't been addressed with sincerity," the Mexican president said. "I'm waging my battle against corruption among Mexican authorities and we're risking everything to clean our house, but I think there also needs to be a good cleaning on the other side of the border."

In fact, U.S. prosecutors have been taking notice. Drug traffickers look "for weaknesses in the armor," said former prosecutor Yolanda de Leon in Cameron County, Texas.

One such weakness was her own county's Sheriff Conrado Cantu. With his thick mustache, ample belly and Western hat, Cantu was a backslapping natural in the political machine of Cameron County, population 335,000. The county includes Brownsville, Texas, directly across the Rio Grande from Matamoros, Mexico.

In no time, Cantu rose from constable to sheriff, a job he later acknowledged he was unqualified to hold. In 2005, he pleaded guilty to federal charges of running a criminal enterprise involved in extortion, drug trafficking and bribery. He's now serving a 24-year sentence for extorting money from drug traffickers and illegal gambling operations.

"If the opportunity came along he would take it," said de Leon.

Not all corruption charges that turned up in AP's checks were related to drug trafficking. The researched cases involve agents helping smuggle immigrants, drugs or other contraband, taking wads of money or sexual favors in exchange—or simply allowing entry to someone whose paperwork isn't up to snuff, all part of the daily border traffic that has politicians demanding that the U.S.-Mexico border be secured.

Court records show corrupt officials along the 2,100-mile U.S.-Mexico border have included local police and elected sheriffs, and officers with such U.S. Department of Homeland Security agencies as Immigration and Customs Enforcement and Customs and Border Protection, which includes Border Patrol. Some have even been National Guardsmen temporarily called in to help while the Border Patrol expanded its ranks.

As Calderon sent thousands of soldiers to northern Mexico to stop the gruesome cartel violence and clean out corrupt police departments, CBP, the largest U.S. law enforcement agency, boosted its border forces by 44 percent or 6,907 additional officers and agents on the southwest border.

At the same time, CBP saw the number of its officers charged with corruption-related crimes nearly triple, from eight cases in fiscal 2007 to 21 the following year—and began to crack down.

"Day in, day out, someone in our agency is approached and says no, but we operate in this high-threat environment," said James Tomsheck, assistant commissioner for internal affairs at CBP. "The reality of it is we are deeply concerned."

In the past 10 months, 20 agents from CBP alone have been charged with a corruption-related crime. At that pace, the organization will set a new record for in-house corruption; 90 employees have been charged with corrupt acts since October 2004. Agency officials expect those cases to continue to climb: There are 63 open criminal investigations—including corruption cases—against CBP employees.

At least as unsettling were the prospective agents who never got to commit their crimes: Four applicants for jobs in federal border law enforcement were not hired when polygraph tests and background checks confirmed they were infiltrators from drug trafficking operations, authorities said.

Such in-depth checks are conducted on only about 10 percent of applicants for border agent jobs, though such scrutiny will eventually be made standard for all applicants, according to Tomsheck. Meantime, officials are left to wonder: Are other gangsters working undercover for agencies charged with protecting the U.S. border?

CBP had more than 2,000 in-house discipline cases during the past three years, according to records obtained by the AP under the Freedom of Information Act. Most were minor, but about 100 reflected more serious, corruption-related incidents, many of which were later prosecuted.

The jump in corruption cases comes as CBP has increased its team of internal investigators from five three years ago to 220 today.

CBP's own investigation of corruption cases showed little correlation between minor disciplinary problems and the more serious instances of bribery and malfeasance.

"Virtually none of the employees arrested for corruption are employees that have serious misconduct issues," Tomsheck said. "Actively corrupt employees do everything they can to stay below the radar screen."

It can be heartbreaking to see agents switch sides for small amounts of money, said U.S. Attorney Tim Johnson, whose turf covers a long stretch of border from the Gulf of Mexico to Laredo, Texas. But, Johnson and other federal prosecutors say, "these cases will always have a priority" and must be prosecuted "to the fullest extent," to emphasize that corruption will not be tolerated.

"You can't allow people who work within the law enforcement community to compromise our mission. We would just lose control of everything down there," he said.

It's a lesson Mexico learned the hard way, ignoring for years corrupt police until Calderon began to replace them with military personnel.

In Texas, which has more than half the U.S. border with Mexico, the commission that oversees state and local law enforcement officers reported that criminal misconduct cases were opened against 515 officers in fiscal 2007 and 550 officers in fiscal 2008. Some form of disciplinary action was lodged against 324 and 331 peace officer licenses, respectively, in those years.

"The cartels increasingly recruit law enforcement officers on both sides of the border," Steve McCraw, then Texas's homeland security chief, told state lawmakers earlier this year. "It's not just a Mexico problem because of the amount of money involved. And as we've increased presence between the ports (of entry), there's an increased desire to recruit law enforcement personnel to move across the bridge or use them between the ports."

In-house CBP data shows corrupt agents fall into two categories—recent hires who are charged very quickly, indicating they took the jobs intending to break the law, and veteran agents who have worked for the agency for a decade or more before succumbing to the offers.

"From the Mexican cartels' point of view, it is cheaper to pay an official several thousand dollars to allow a load of narcotics to pass by than it is to risk having the shipment seized," Scott Stewart and Fred Burton, vice presidents of global intelligence firm Stratfor, wrote in a recent report. "Such bribes are simply part of the cost of doing business—and in the big picture, even a low-level agent can be an incredible bargain."

One such officer, a CBP agent convicted of taking money to smuggle illegal immigrants, was over his head with credit card debt, behind on child-support payments, about to lose his truck. His 10-year-old, whom he had taken to the mall for the day, wanted a football he couldn't afford.

That's when a friendly, familiar Mexican man pulled a $50 bill from a thick wallet and handed it to the agent's son, who snatched the money and dashed off to the Dallas Cowboys Pro Shop.

The father related the story in the visiting room of a federal prison in California where he is serving a four-year term.

"I was like, 'Wait son, hang on!' but he was gone, so happy with that money," said the former agent, whom prison officials allowed the AP to interview on condition of anonymity because convicted law enforcement officers are considered potential targets.

That was how it began, the ex-agent continued. A few weeks later, the Mexican man suggested that the officer let a man through his pedestrian checkpoint early one morning without asking questions. He'd get $5,000 for his trouble.

"I thought, 'Naaah, I can't do that.' Then I thought, 'Hell, my life's a mess. Everyone does it. If I'm caught I'll just say the guy got past me. I'll do it once. I could use the money,'" he recalled.

The cash came in handy. He bought clothes for his kids, jerseys for a youth team he coached; he made his truck payment, caught up on credit card bills.

The next time was easier, if less lucrative: $1,500 a person.

Nervously smoothing his prison-green scrubs, he said, "I really planned to stop." But then another offer came, even while colleagues warned him the FBI was snooping around. And then a woman he had illegally passed through named him when she was caught by an honest agent.

He was convicted for passing one person through. He paid $5,000 in fines in addition to the prison term.

"You want to know how many times I did this?" he asked. "Sixty-six. I kept a tally."

The men and women who were caught described their jobs as prestigious and well paid for the small border towns where they grew up. An entry-level CBP officer earns $37,000 a year in Laredo, and within a year is likely paid $41,000, well above the local average annual income of $25,000.

In border communities, the demarcation between countries is insignificant. People live on one side, work on the other; have a favorite barber on one side, but buy groceries on the other. The traffic is heavy, and constant.

Some of the border authorities were born in Mexico or are related to Mexican nationals. So do you let a colleague's Mexican aunt cross the border without a visa for a family birthday party? Or wave through a loaded truck that belongs to your bosses' brother-in-law without looking inside? Some agents said yes.

And so did some state and local officers. The deputy commander of a narcotics task force was caught in a sting operation protecting what he believed were loads of drugs moving through Zapata County; others have shaken down drug traffickers moving product through their turf.

In October, FBI agents arrested Starr County Sheriff Reymundo Guerra at his office as part of a sweep dubbed "Operation Carlito's Weigh." Guerra, the chief law enforcement officer for the border county of 62,000 people, had spent a decade as sheriff.

There was little public pressure for his ouster after his arrest and since he was running unopposed, Guerra was re-elected weeks later. County Judge Eloy Vera said the day of his arrest that Guerra, a mustachioed bear of man, was a "very good sheriff." He resigned only as a condition of his release pending trial.

In May, Guerra pleaded guilty to a drug trafficking charge for accepting thousands of dollars in exchange for passing information to a former Mexican law enforcement contact who he knew was working for Mexico's Gulf Cartel. Guerra once even gave false documents to one of his own deputies to close a drug trafficking investigation, prosecutors said.

Thinking Questions

1. Explain the values-learned perspective.
2. What effect does socialization and culturalization have on police ethics?
3. When and why does a police subculture develop?
4. Explain the "metamorphosis" process in policing.
5. Can interacting with criminals on a daily basis contribute to unethical behavior?

Learning to Justify Unethical Conduct

Maintaining the code of silence is one manner of normalizing deviant behavior as officers are socialized into thinking of the practicality or benefits of such behavior. However, the gradual normalization of behavior may be a function of learning techniques to neutralize or to justify the behavior. Sutherland did not disregard techniques of neutralization since he contended that in addition to learning skills needed for the commission of a criminal offense, individuals were schooled in the learning of rationalizations (Akers, 2000). In 1957, Sykes and Matza explored this notion in their study of juvenile delinquency. They hypothesized that juveniles who engaged in deviant behavior were not immune to feelings of guilt or shame. However, these feelings were ameliorated when, through the process of interaction with peer associations, they learned techniques to neutralize or justify their actions. These techniques also allowed them to engage in deviance and maintain a non-deviant identity. Included in the techniques to neutralize behavior were: (1) *denial of responsibility*, (2) *denial of injury*, (3) *denial of the victim*, (4) *condemnation of condemners*, and (5) *appeal to higher loyalty*.

Studies examining the characteristics of police work identified that actions that were defined as deviant or criminal by the dominant culture carried undertones of techniques of neutralization. For example, even before Sykes and Matza's (1957) formulation of their theory, others argued that "police accept and morally justify their illegal use of violence; such acceptance and justification arise through their occupational experience; and its use is functionally related to the collective occupation, as well as to the legal end of the police" (Cancino, 2001, p. 144).

According to Sykes and Matza (1957), individuals who claimed that their behavior should be excused due to an inability to control external or exogenous factors, used the technique of *denial of responsibility*. Kappeler et al. (1994) argued that this was a prevalent justification for police deviance. For instance, use of force was justified since officers had no control over a defiant citizen's behavior and were merely acting as a result of such confrontation. Also, citizen disrespect toward officers has been cited as the most common instance when this technique was used (Cancino, 2001). *Denial of injury*, an excuse used by individuals who believed that their actions were justified because there was an absence of harm or no apparent victim, provided police with a host of justifications for their deviant acts. Kappeler et al. (1994) noted that this technique was used when "police stole evidence from suspects for personal gain; when they violated the civil rights of citizens to make arrests or secure convictions; and when they abused authority to establish or maintain their personal sense of order" (p. 131).

Officers who claimed that their behavior should be excused because the individual was deserving of police action, relied on the technique of the *denial of the victim.* According to Sykes and Matza (1957), this technique altered the role of the victim and the transgressor, since the victim was believed to be causing harm to society. Officers who used this technique argued that they were justified in using force because the "victim" was causing harm to society. Chasing a fleeing felon, for instance, and causing serious risk of injury or death for the officer or citizens may help justify an excessive use of force (Kappeler et al., 1994).

Condemnation of the condemners "involves a reaction to the detection of deviance and a response to those who either allege or sanction deviance" (Kappeler et al., 1994, p. 135). In a police setting, this technique was used when officers perceived administrators to act in a hypocritical manner. Police resent administrators who reprimand or sanction behavior while they engage in similar behavior. *Appeal to higher loyalties,* was used to justify behavior when it was necessary to help or protect a colleague. This was the most common form of neutralization and it intimately related to association in the police subculture (Newburn, 1999; Hodgson, 2001; Hunt & Manning, 1991; Gaffigan & McDonald, 1997).

Thinking Questions

1.   According to Sykes and Matza, what are techniques of neutralization?
2.   How do officers neutralize their unethical decision?

Rewards and Punishments

As with the dominant culture, the police subculture retains the right to redefine normative behavior. Nonetheless, whether or not definitions remain constant over time (GOA, 1998), studies indicated that the rules of the subculture influence the behavior of cadets and police officers in general, even when the behavior was defined as deviant or criminal by the dominant culture (Kappeler et al., 1994; Hodgson, 2001; Hunt & Manning, 1991). However, decisions to follow the norms of the subculture were greatly influenced by operant conditioning.

Operant conditioning, as an element in criminological theory, was not discussed by Sutherland but was proposed by Burgess and Akers (1966). Burgess and Akers (1966) integrated elements of Sutherland's differential association with behavior theory to explain the learning mechanism associated with criminal behavior. They contended that criminal behavior was learned through a process of differential reinforcement whereby "operant behavior was conditioned or shaped by rewards and punishments" (Akers, 2000, p. 75). Rewards and punishments were dependent on past, present and anticipated future rewards and/or punishments and were affected by the position of the individual in the social structure (Akers, 2000). For instance, "the differential social organization of society and community, as well as the differential location of persons in the social class, race, gender, religion and other structures in society, provides the general learning contexts for individuals that increase or decrease the likelihood of their committing crime" (Akers, 2000, p. 82). Because Burgess and Akers (1966) also contended that learning could occur in non-social situations, later revisions of the theory included learning through imitation and modeling.

The social context for learning behavior for new cadets entering the police profession involves learning the rewards and punishments that are given when following or not following subcultural norms. As noted by Burgess and Akers (1966), rewards and punishments may be perceived or actual and dependent on past, present or future rewards and/or punishments. They may also be learned through imitation or the experiences (war stories) of others. During training at the police academy, cadets quickly learn the rewards that can be provided by abiding with subcultural norms. The most obvious reward is inclusion into the subculture. Inclusion provides the cadet with needed assistance for performing the job, such as protection and loyalty. Inclusion also shields the officer from negative or harassing comments made by citizens or other officers. Conversely, failure or refusal to abide with normative behavior brings isolation, ridicule, and harassment by fellow cadets (Hunt & Manning, 1991).

The perceived or actual punishments incurred by other members of the subculture are also important motivational factors that guide police deviant behavior. However, punishments do not necessarily need to be given only by members of the police subculture, but can be imposed by the police administrators, the larger dominant society, or the criminal justice system as a whole (Hughes, 2001). In the process of recognizing risks or punishments involved in engaging in criminally deviant behavior, the officer observes the actions taken against others and alters or adjusts behavior to avoid the imposition of penalties. The non-enforcement of policies by administrators and/or the lax punishments given to those officers convicted of criminal offenses by the criminal justice system may reinforce negative behavior. This is particularly salient for police officers that witness the rarity of administrative sanctions against those who engage in criminal behavior and the lax punishments imposed by the criminal justice system (Hughes, 2001).

Thinking Questions

1. What did Akers and Burgess say about rewards and punishments?
2. What effect do rewards and/or punishments have on police behavior?

Rational Choice Perspective of Learning Behavior

Rational choice theory has also been used to explain motivational for police deviance, including unethical behavior. Premised on eighteenth-century classical criminological assumptions, individual behavior was believed to have been guided by a natural hedonistic tendency to enhance self-interests and a rational calculation of weighing the risks and benefits involved in engaging in criminal behavior (Akers, 2000). Although much literature on police deviance dictates that it is a learned behavior, it does not negate the fact that officers may engage in a rational, or at least partial, calculation of the risks and benefits of engaging in deviant behavior. Thus, this rational choice argument does not discount that deviant behavior can be learned or amplified by structural processes within the organization and does not negate that those may be the primary motivational factors that cause police deviance. However, it is reasonable to argue that police officers may engage in a cognitive process whereby risks and benefits help form a decision to deviate. In addition, it is also reasonable to argue that officers may be guided by hedonistic tendencies to enhance self-interests and seek occupations where these interests may be enhanced.

The basic premise of eighteenth-century classical criminology was the individual's rational decision to engage in pleasure-enhancing actions and avoid those likely to impose pain. The cognitive process of decision-making (free-will) was characterized by a "rational calculation" to choose to obey or violate the law (Akers, 2000). Contemplation of engaging in law-violating behavior occurred after careful consideration of the consequences if the action was detected. It also involved a conscious realization of "their own experience with criminal punishment, their knowledge of what punishment is imposed by law and their awareness of what punishments has been given to apprehended offenders in the past" (Akers, 2000, p. 16). In essence, if the pain incurred was believed to outweigh the pleasure of the action, the individual was deterred from engaging in criminality. In addition, deterrence included the certainty, celerity, and severity of the punishment (Akers, 2000).

Classical criminology, entrenched in ideals of philosophers such as Beccaria and Bentham, characterized the individual's motivational cues to engage in criminality as originating from a human drive to "promote their own best interests" (Vold et al., 1998, p. 7); implying that individuals are "self-determining agents free to do as they wished and as their intelligence directs" (Vold et al., 1998, p. 7). It also implied a human tendency to avoid painful experiences. Recent applications of classical criminology have expanded the notion of deterrence theory through a formulation of rational choice theory. Although Bentham's moral calculus described the rational calculation of decision-making process of criminals (Akers, 2000), the 1980 version of choice theory borrowed extensively from the field of economics. Specifically, Becker (1968) argued that

> A person commits an offense if the expected utility to him exceeds the utility he could get by using his time and other resources at other activities. Some people become criminal therefore not because their basic motivation differs from that of other persons, but because their benefits and costs differ. This approach implies that there is a function relating the number of offenses by any person to his probability of conviction, to his punishment if convicted and to other variables, such as income available to him in legal and illegal activities, the frequency of nuisance arrests, and his willingness to commit the illegal act. (in Cullen & Agnew, 1999, p. 252)

Research on rational choice theory has revealed more contradictory findings than those proposed by Becker (1968). For instance, findings from several studies generally indicated that criminals do not possess the ability to engage in a full understanding of potential rewards and punishments (Akers, 2000). However, these finding do not negate that offenders participate in some form of decision-making process before the commission of the offense.

Classical criminology's deterrence theory and its extension through rational choice theory contain elements that are applicable to the study of police deviance, including unethical conduct. Literature on police deviance implies that officers engage in a rational, or at least partial calculation of weighing the rewards and punishments involved in engaging in any form of deviance. For instance, Hunt and Manning (1991) argued that the two greatest determinant factors that outweighed decisions to conform to law-abiding behavior were the benefits of maintaining membership in the police subculture and the benefits that resulted from engaging in the deviant act itself. Benefits of the act itself could be spending less time on paperwork or in court. For drug-related police deviance, the General Accounting Office (GAO) (1998) reported that benefits of engaging in such behavior were hedonistic, as officers stole money and drugs or conducted illegal searches with the aim of supplementing their income. The economic nature of their deviance was consistent with Becker's (1968) analysis.

Box 4.2 NYPD Cop Allegedly Took More than $1K in Cash from Brooklyn Construction Worker's Pocket during Stop-and-Frisk

The New York Daily News — October 8, 2014

The Brooklyn district attorney's office is investigating allegations that an NYPD cop swiped more than $1,000 from a man during a stop-and-frisk, then pepper-sprayed him and his sister when they complained, the Daily News has learned.

The encounter was captured on a cell phone video, which has been turned over to prosecutors and the NYPD Internal Affairs Bureau.

"One of the most disturbing things about the video is the other cops standing around watching and doing nothing to stop the wrongdoing," lawyer Robert Marinelli said Wednesday.

Marinelli represents the siblings who were pepper-sprayed — Lamard Joye, who claims the cop took $1,300 from his pocket, money that has still not been accounted for, and his sister Lateefah Joye, a professional basketball player in Europe, who tried to get the cop's badge number.

"I believe that this officer made an assumption that any money Mr. Joye possessed was obtained illegally and therefore he would not report the theft. This assumption was wrong. Mr. Joye is a hardworking taxpayer deserving respect," said Marinelli.

The brief clip begins with the unidentified cop pushing Lamard Joye against the fence of a basketball court at the Surfside Gardens housing project in Coney Island around 12:20 a.m. on Sept. 16.

Right before the recording began, according to Marinelli, Joye remarked to the cop, "Are you going to do to me what you did to the guy in Staten Island?" a reference to Eric Garner, who died in July after a cop put him in a chokehold.

What precipitated the Coney Island incident, and is not recorded on the video, according to Marinelli, were cops roughing up a young man named Terrell Haskins nearby, prompting Joye and his friends to shout, "Is that necessary?"

A group of cops confront Joye, whose arms are outstretched as he says to onlookers, "You see this?"

The cop appears to reach into Joye's pocket and pull out a thick wad of cash.

"Gimme my money!" Joye shouts, before the cop squirts him in the face with the spray.

Joye darts off and his sister begins arguing with the cop. An onlooker is heard yelling, "How ya gonna take his money?" "That's robbery" and "Get his badge number."

"I went to get his badge number and name," Lateefah Joye told The News. "I leaned over to see his badge. He pushed me away. I saw a two and a one and that's when he pepper-sprayed me in my mouth and my whole face."

Lateefah Joye, a graduate of Lincoln High School who played college ball at West Virginia University, said her brother was just trying to do the right thing by helping Haskins.

"I'm outraged," she said. "It's very outrageous. I've witnessed a lot of things cops have done. But what can you do? I'm not a violent person. I'm an athlete."

Her brother contacted Marinelli the next day, seeking legal help to get his money back.

The construction worker had withdrawn the cash from a bank a week earlier because the day of the incident was his 35th birthday and he was going to take his wife out on the town, Marinelli said.

The lawyer gave the video to the Brooklyn DA's chief civil rights prosecutor and also provided pay stubs, visual evidence of Joye cashing his paycheck at a check-cashing store and bank records documenting the withdrawal.

The Joyes, Haskins and the man who shot the video have all been interviewed by investigators.

"We are aware of the alleged incident and it is being actively and thoroughly investigated," Brooklyn District Attorney Kenneth Thompson said in a statement.

A police spokeswoman said, "The incident was precipitated by a call of a man with a gun. When officers arrived at the scene, they encountered numerous people at the location. As a result of the allegations, the matter is under investigation by the Internal Affairs Bureau and Civilian Complaint Review Board."

Last week, Police Commissioner Bill Bratton dropped a bombshell at a summit of top NYPD commanders when they viewed a video montage titled "What Would You Do?" showing clips of cops kicking and beating people who don't appear to be fighting back. He vowed to rid the force of any officer "who's so callous, so brutal, so corrupt, that they feel comfortable engaging in those acts of brutality, acts of corruption without fear."

There were 198 complaints against cops reported to the CCRB last year involving the use of pepper spray, down from 208 the previous year, said CCRB spokeswoman.

Patrolmen's Benevolent Association President Patrick Lynch said, "A 35-second-long video does not provide enough information about a police encounter to come to any conclusion about what transpired."

Although seemingly inconsistent with the basic premises of classical criminology and rational choice theory, it is within reason to assume that the officer may engage in a process of cognitive decision-making prior to the commission of the deviant act. As noted by Clarke and Cornish (1987), deviant behavior was a "function of choices and decisions made within the context of situational constraints and opportunities" (p. 8). In a police setting, these situational constraints and opportunities may have materialized as a result of differential associations with officers through social learning. Thus, rational choice exists within the realm of differential association since differential associations alter attitudes, values and views, which may affect officers' decisions to engage in deviance. In addition, rational choice exists within the realm of learned behavior.

Thinking Questions

1. What are the elements of classical criminology?
2. According to Hunt and Manning, what factors contribute to unethical decisions?

Predispositional Perspective

Are officers unethical before joining the force? This perspective holds that individuals' character, attitude, and especially value system is established early in life and occupational socialization has little, if any, impact on behavior. In terms of policing, this means that officers learn ethical or unethical behavior at a young age and are not influenced by the police subculture. The first to study this viewpoint was Rokeach, Miller, and Snyder in 1971. They found evidence to suggest that certain individuals are attracted to police work because of the authoritarian nature of the job. That is, they seek employment in the force because it gives them an outlet that matches their personality and allows them to be in an authority position. Caldero and Larose (2003) confirmed this finding. They determined that "individual value systems are more important than occupational socialization" (p. 162) in determining officers' workplace behavior. More specifically, they found:

1. Officer values are determined by particular characteristics of personality.
2. Officer values are unaffected by occupational socialization.
3. The values carried by officers are stable over time.
4. Education has little impact on values held by officers.
5. The police socialization process has little effect on the values of individual officers.

Indeed, there is evidence to suggest that an officer's value system, even if it is unethical in nature, is already established prior to joining the police agency and it does not change during occupational socialization. According to Crank and Caldero (2004), police work helps to accentuate existing personality traits.

The Noble Cause: What Really Happens

As part of legitimate police power, officers are granted the authority to engage in deceptive tactics, such as entrapment, telephone wiretapping, and undercover operations (Braswell et al., 2008). If utilizing a consequentialist perspective, we could argue that a positive outcome (e.g., preventing a crime from occurring) would justify the use of deceptive tactics. But, if we use a non-consequentialist approach, then we would have to look closely at the behavior of the officer. In this case, because the officer has a duty to uphold the law, together with constitutional mandates of due process and fairness, deceptive tactics would be considered unethical. Going back to the example of racial profiling, is it right to profile an individual based on race and/or ethnicity if it stops another terrorist attack?

According to Caldero and Crank (2004), sometimes ethics is forgotten because of the noble cause. Of course, this can lead to what they call *noble cause corruption.* Noble cause corruption is corruption committed in the name of good ends; corruption that occurs when police officers care too much. The noble cause is "a moral commitment to make the world a safer place to live" (p. 29), such as using profiles to prevent a terrorist attack. Carl Klockers (1983) referred to this as the "Dirty Harry" problem. In other words, it may be justified to commit a dirty act if it is for a good cause.

There are two factors that generally motivate officers to practice noble cause corruption. Caldero and Crank refer to these factors as "the smell of the victim's blood" and "the tower." As with the discussion on community policing, it is not uncommon for officers to begin to have empathy for community members especially if they interact with them on a daily basis. Soon, a relationship forms and police find themselves invested in the lives of the people they serve. This is, after all, one of the advantages of community policing. But, victims can affect police immensely. The desire to protect them, especially those victims who have suffered horrendous crimes such as sexual abuse or crimes against children, motivates some officers to circumvent the law. Thus, the "smell of the victim's blood" stimulates a need to protect those from harm. "The tower" is a metaphor used by Calderon and Crank to describe the civic duty of all officers. They explain that if there was a situation with an active shooter in a tower who has already killed several individuals, the first instinct for a police officer is to eliminate the shooter. Unlike any other profession, officers are taught to put their lives on the line to save others. Their life, in essence, is a commitment to the moral cause or to the noble cause. Thus, in order to preserve peace and tranquility, sometimes officers find it suitable to bend the law a little for a greater good.

Van Maanen's (1978) study, entitled *The Asshole*, adds that because officers are sometimes confronted with "assholes," who may or may not be lawbreakers, but are people who challenge their authority, police at times resort to street justice or street violence to protect society. Thus, they make moral judgments or decisions based on their authority to quell those who challenge their mandate. Nonetheless, commitment to the noble cause can lead to the belief that some ends are so important that any means to achieve them are acceptable. But, no matter how noble the end is, officers must accept that they must perform their civic duties within legal parameters.

As you can see, ethics is influenced by factors outside the boundaries of the Constitution. At times, the badge of public service is tainted by a belief that acting outside the parameters of the law is the only way to protect citizens. Other times, it is tainted by the interactions police have with recalcitrant law violators. In either case, it is unethical and against the law.

Thinking Questions

1. According to Caldero and Larose, are officers unethical before joining the force?
2. What is noble cause corruption?
3. What is the "Dirty Harry" problem in policing?
4. Explain Van Maanen's research.

Is It Too Late to Change?

If unethical behavior is inherent in police work, what can be done to deter officers from engaging in such conduct? If immoral behavior is part of the indoctrination process for police, is it too late to change their behavior? No it is not. Let's consider these options.

Assuming that behavior is learned on the job, officers can *unlearn* unethical behavior. This is usually achieved by rewarding officers for good deeds and reprimanding officers for misdeeds. Officers must be held accountable for their actions. Accountability means officers must take responsibility for their actions, good or bad. As was advocated by Sir Robert Peel, and later by multiple presidential commissions (e.g., the Wickersham Commission, the Kerner Commission) (Walker & Katz, 2005), officers should be held to a higher ethical standard and chastised for unethical conduct. It is important to note that accountability is only as successful as those within the organization want it to be.

You may remember the case of Frank Vincent Serpico. He was the New York City police officer who refused to accept bribes during the late 1960s, when corruption was rampant in the department. The Knapp Commission, who investigated his case and a multitude of incidences of corruption at NYPD, found that upper administrators were aware of corrupt actions and did nothing to stop and/or prevent it. Administrators were also indifferent to its occurrence (Walker & Katz, 2005). The Commission also noted that corruption became so widespread because of citizen apathy, meaning that citizens contributed to the problem because they were in the habit of offering bribes and/or knew it was occurring but did not take the time to report abuses of authority.

As was explained earlier, police management must be attuned to potential ethical dilemmas in order to first prevent problems from occurring, but they must also remedy problems once they occur. However, Souryal (2010) argues that managers are, at times, not attentive to such problems because the agency may suffer from what he calls "unenlightened management philosophies." Unenlightened management philosophies are those that place primary importance on protecting the manger (chief of police) and not the department. In essence, in order to cultivate ethical decision-making, managers must stimulate ethical correctness and the best way to do so is by example. Essentially, every individual in the department should strive to abide by the *Six Pillars of Character*—trustworthiness, respect, responsibility, fairness, caring, and citizenship (Josephson Institute, 2010). The Six Pillars of Character are ethical values to guide choices and the chief of police must be the first to set the example.

Box 4.3 Ramsey Beefs Up Philadelphia Police Ethics Strategies

The Philadelphia Inquirer—August 6, 2010

Faced with a growing number of officers in handcuffs, Philadelphia Police Commissioner Charles H. Ramsey announced plans Thursday to assign more officers to the department's Internal Affairs bureau, enhance officer training in ethics issues, and create new ways for officers to report misconduct among their colleagues.

Ramsey said he was not sure how many officers would be transferred to Internal Affairs, but said they would be assigned to a joint task force that works with the FBI in investigating police corruption. The department is also looking at ways to make Internal Affairs a more attractive assignment for officers, Ramsey said.

Much of the anticorruption plan focuses on preventing officers from making bad decisions. Whereas officers now receive most of their ethics training at the Police Academy, Ramsey said the department would create additional courses to help officers develop critical thinking and self-awareness throughout their careers.

Ramsey said the department would work to encourage officers to report colleagues when they see inappropriate behavior.

"The Police Department continues to ask the public to step up and report wrongdoing," Ramsey said. "We will ask no less of its own members."

The department is launching a hotline and e-mail address that go straight to Ramsey's office. Officers and the public can use them to anonymously report police misconduct. The phone number, which will be active Monday, is …

Ramsey has tasked Patricia Giorgio-Fox, deputy commissioner for organizational accountability, with implementing the new strategies.

He was spurred to announce the plan after Kenneth Crockett, a 26-year veteran of the 6,600-plus force, was charged last week with stealing $825 from a Northeast Philadelphia bar.

The announcement also followed the arrest of three police officers last month on federal charges of robbing a drug dealer.

Eleven officers have been arrested since March 2009, including two on murder charges stemming from off-duty shootings. Another officer was fired this year after admitting that he fabricated a story about being shot by a black man. In fact, the officer had shot himself.

Ramsey said Thursday that the department had opened investigations into several other officers, but declined to comment further.

"It's a cloud," he said of the spate of scandals. "And it's going to take time for that cloud to lift. But we're not going to run from it."

Ramsey has said attracting stronger recruits is a priority. Starting in 2012, new officers will have to be at least 21 and have three years of driving and two years of college classes under their belts. Standards now allow 19-year-olds with no college education and little driving experience to join the academy. The residency requirement has been modified in an effort to draw candidates from outside the city.

Police experts said implementing an anticorruption plan would not be easy. Some officers arrested recently were veterans and had nothing in their backgrounds that would indicate a predilection toward criminal acts.

A larger obstacle to fighting corruption is often a version of the "don't snitch" culture that officers battle when policing urban areas, said Rich Jarc, executive director of the Josephson Institute, a Los Angeles nonprofit that educates police departments on ethics. In many departments, Jarc said, it's all but demanded that officers stand together, and ratting each other out is discouraged.

"It doesn't mean that the department is totally corrupt," Jarc said. "But that cultural code of silence might be preventing some people from stopping this behavior."

Ramsey said Thursday that many officers had reported misconduct by colleagues, but that the department needed to reach those who remained hesitant to do so. After Crockett's arrest on theft charges last week, Ramsey said, more information came to light from officers who knew or suspected Crockett was not always going by the book.

"We've got to create an environment where people feel comfortable coming forward and reporting something," he said. "It's the right thing to do."

Of course, there are other ways for administrators to deal with unethical conduct. A clear zero-tolerance policy would be helpful (Ruiz & Bono, 2004). Officers must be cognizant that such behavior will not be tolerated. Standard operating procedures (SOP) for the department that explicitly describe unacceptable behaviors, including the acceptance of gifts, is important. The SOP must state which behaviors will not be tolerated and describe sanctions if violated. The use of written policy can be a useful tool because it will inform officers of ethical standards of behavior (Ruiz & Bono, 2004). Some departments also use an Internal Affairs Unit to conduct integrity tests. This strategy essentially checks the ethical conduct of officers, either those under suspicion for ethics violations or a random group, by creating real-life scenarios where officers' behavior can be observed and corrected, if necessary (Walker & Katz, 2005). Annual evaluations (or quarterly evaluations) of officers are also constructive. They can reward officers for ethical conduct or identify potential problems. Evaluations can be used in conjunction with early intervention systems. Early intervention (EI) systems, can store complaints against officers in an electronic database, and can systematically identify officers that have persistent complaints (Walker & Katz, 2005).

If none of the above influence ethical choices, liability will ensure compliance for individual officers and the department (Roberg et al., 2005). As disconcerting as this may seem, the courts may be one way to instill equity and justice into policing practices. After all, cases such as *Mapp v. Ohio* (1961) set forth rules on illegal searches and *Miranda v. Arizona* (1966) established the Miranda warnings to safeguard against coercive interrogation techniques by police. Of course, court intervention will have a detrimental impact on the department. This will stigmatize and tarnish the department's legitimacy for a long time. Legitimacy is needed to establish peace and tranquility in society. Without legitimacy in policing, mandates will be difficult to accomplish and the tarnished image of the department will be difficult to repair (Souryal, 2010). Of course, court intervention only goes so far. Courts cannot supervise day-to-day activities. They cannot ensure that the police comply with court decisions in every instance or ensure that police are aware of rulings that proscribe certain behaviors. As such, accountability from within the department is vital as is accountability to the public. But, accountability from other external forces may help too.

So, if the above internal strategies are not enough to extinguish unethical behavior, there are other strategies that can be used. Because some cases of unethical decision-making involve violations of the law, prosecution or the threat of prosecution, is one possible remedy. But before the problem reaches the courts, citizen oversight might be enough. Civilian review boards are composed of ordinary citizens from the community who review complaints against police and then provide a recommendation to the chief of police (Roberg et al., 2005). The media, a seemingly adversary of police organizations, can also be used to expose cases of unethical behavior (Walker & Katz, 2005). The media play an important role in police accountability. On a day-to-day basis, the media report on what the police are doing, whether such actions are heroic or unethical. In the latter case, reports of unethical conduct may help to awaken an unresponsive department to take action. Because the public is cognizant of the behavior, they can demand change. Once again, this will affect the legitimacy of the department and departments will need to take corrective actions to regain the public's trust.

Thinking Questions

1. What were the findings by the Knapp Commission?
2. What steps can a police chief take to end unethical behavior?
3. Describe the notion of zero-tolerance for unethical behavior.
4. What are the Six Pillars of Character?
5. What role can the Supreme Court, the media, and citizens play in police ethics?

Conclusion

No single strategy, whether internal or external, is the key to achieving ethical decision-making. Each of the different strategies has strengths and weaknesses, so a mixed approach to police ethics should be utilized. In a way, the use of internal and external strategies will be a form of checks and balances— a fundamental principle of democracy. But, it is important to understand how officers learn unethical behavior because solutions to problems may require starting with cadets and addressing the informal training that occurs at the police academy. If ethics is learned through the process of socialization early in the career of officers, a resolution must begin at this stage to help officers *unlearn* unethical behavior. It must then continue throughout their tenure if the solution is to be effective. If officers join the force with unethical values in place, it may be a little more difficult to change behavior. Unfortunately, sometimes it will require legal intervention that will ultimately tarnish the reputation of the department.

Scenarios

1. Every day between the hours of 7:30 a.m. to 8:30 a.m., you are assigned to monitor traffic flow at a school zone. Since the city and the department are trying to crack down on motorists speeding in school zones, you have been diligent in issuing citations for those driving above the speed limit. But, one day, you pull over a familiar face — the chief of police.

   a. Do you issue a citation or give her a warning?
   b. What are the repercussions in issuing a citation versus giving her a warning?
   c. What if the motorist was your mother? Would you issue a citation or a warning?

2. While on routine patrol, you are dispatched to a domestic violence situation. The dispatcher indicates that extreme caution should be taken because the alleged suspect is armed. You arrive at the house and can hear a man and a woman arguing as you exit your patrol car. You walk to the front door and are greeted by a fellow police officer, holding a gun and yelling at his spouse. His spouse has bruises on her arms and a black eye. From the verbal tirade, you piece together that his wife is having an affair. After diffusing the situation and convincing the officer to drop his weapon, what should you do?

   a. Do you arrest him or give him a warning that next time, he will be arrested?
   b. Would your decision be different if there were no bruises and/or injuries to the spouse?
   c. Would your decision be different if the officer was not holding a gun?
   d. Would your decision change if the officer was your brother?

3. You and your partner are dispatched to a call regarding a residential burglary. You arrive at the house but no one is home. So, you and your partner canvass the house and assess the situation. You notice, however, that your partner picked up an item from the bedroom dresser and placed it in

his pocket. You question his actions, but he denies taking anything from the house. What should you do?

a. Confront the officer one more time?
b. Ask the officer to empty his pockets?
c. Report the incident to your supervisor?
d. Forget you saw anything?

4. You're a rookie officer teamed with a veteran cop known for his aggressive tactics. One day, while patrolling a high-crime area, you pull up to a street corner and both of you notice teenagers slowly disperse as they see the patrol car. Because of his experience, the veteran officer tells you this corner is where most of the neighborhood drugs are sold. He tells you to follow his lead as he approaches one of the teens. He demands that the teen empty his pockets. The teen, however, ignores his request. Suddenly, you see the veteran officer slam the teen's head against the patrol car. He slowly empties his pockets but they produce no evidence of drugs. The officer releases his hold on the teen and tells him, this is his lucky day. What should you do?

a. Ignore what you saw?
b. Ask for a transfer to patrol with another officer but not report the real reason why you want the transfer?
c. Report the incident to your supervisor?

5. You and your partner are dispatched to the scene of a fight. When you arrive, two men are physically fighting but stop when you warn them they will be arrested. Your partner asks what's going on. One man begins to tell his side of the story but the officer stops him and wants to hear the story from the other man involved in the fight. Your partner determines that the fight began when the man telling his side of the story made a racial slur against the other, a Mexican-American. When the man repeats the slur, the officer laughs and tells both parties to go home. No incident report is filed. What should you do?

a. Complete an incident report?
b. Confront the officer about his behavior?
c. Notify your supervisor that you think your partner is racist?

6. Your supervisor tells everybody on his beat that the chief will be making a report to City Council about crime in the city. With the fear of crime increasing due to drug-related violence, it is important for the chief to convey that the city is safe by showing decreasing crime rates. Therefore, the supervisor tells you and the other officers to downgrade certain crimes. For

instance, attempted car thefts will be downgraded to vandalism and aggravated assaults will be downgraded to simple assaults. What should you do?

7. Patrol cars are equipped with cameras and they automatically begin recording when the siren is activated. Your partner is keenly aware of this and has from time to time turned off the camera especially when pulling over female drivers. When questioned by administration, he simply says that the camera must not have been working properly. What should you do?

   a. Tell your supervisor the truth?
   b. Go along with your partner's lies?
   c. Simply ignore the situation?

References

Akers, R.L. (2000). *Criminological theories.* Los Angeles: Roxbury Publishing Company.

Becker, G.S. (1968). Crime and punishment: An economic approach. In Cullen, F.T., & Agnew, R. (Eds.), *Criminological theory: Past to present* (251–253). Los Angeles, CA: Roxbury Publishing Company.

Braswell, M.C., McCarthy, B.R., & McCarthy, B.J. (2008). *Justice, crime, and ethics.* Newark, NJ: Anderson Publishing.

Burgess, R.L., & Akers, R.L. (1966). A differential association-reinforcement theory of criminal behavior. *Social Problems,* 14, 128–147.

Caldero, M.A., & Crank, J.P. (2004). *Police ethics: The corruption of noble cause.* Cincinnati, OH: Anderson Publishing.

Caldero, M., & Larose, A. (2003). Value consistency within the police: The lack of a gap. *Policing: An International Journal of Police Strategies and Management,* 24(2), 162–180.

Cancino, J.M. (2001). Walking among giants 50 years later: An exploratory analysis of patrol officer use of violence. *Policing: An International Journal of Police Strategies and Management,* 24(2), 144–161.

Clarke, R.V., & Cornish, D.B. (1987). Understanding crime displacement: An application of rational choice theory. *Criminology,* 25(4), 933.

Cole, D. (2003). *Enemy Aliens: Double standards and constitutional freedoms in the war on terrorism.* New York: The New Press.

Cullen, F.T., & Agnew, R. (1999). *Criminological theory: Past to Present.* Los Angeles, CA: Roxbury.

Fishbein, D. (1997). Biological perspectives in criminology. In S. Henry & W. Einstadter (Eds.), *The criminology reader* (92–110). New York: New York University Press.

Forst, B. (2009). *Terrorism, crime, and public policy.* New York: Cambridge University Press.

Gaffigan, S.J., & McDonald. (1997). *Police integrity: Public service with honor.* Washington, D.C.: U.S. Department of Justice.

General Accounting Office (1998). *Report to the Honorable Charles B. Rangel, House of Representatives: Information on drug-related police corruption.* General Accounting Division: Washington, D.C.

Hodgson, J.F. (2001). Police violence in Canada and the USA: Analysis and management. *Policing: An International Journal of Strategies and Management,* 24(4), 520–549.

Hughes, T. (2001). Police officers and civil liability: The ties that bind? *Policing: An International Journal of Police Strategies and Management,* 24(2), 240–262.

Hunt, J., & Manning, P.K. (1991). The social context of police lying. *Symbolic Interaction,* 14(1), 153–169.

Josephson Institute (2010). Making ethical decisions. Retrieved October 10, 2010, from http://josephsoninstitute.org/MED/index.html.

Kappeler, V.E., Sluder, R.D., & Alpert, G.P. (1994). *Forces of deviance: Understanding the dark side of policing.* Prospect Heights, Illinois: Waveland Press, Inc.

Kleinig, J. (2008). *Ethics in criminal justice.* New York: Cambridge University Press.

Matsueda, R.L. (1998). The current state of differential association theory. In Truab, S.H., & Little, C.B. (Eds.) *Theories of Deviance* (pp. 261–291). Itasca, Illinois: F.E. Peacock Publishers, Inc.

Newburn, T. (1999). Understanding and preventing police corruption: Lessons from the literature. *Policing and Reducing Crime Unit: Police Research Series,* Paper 110. Retrieved October 10, 2010, from http://rds.home office.gov.uk/rds/prgpdfs/fprs110.pdf.

Purpura, P.P. (2001). *Police and community: Concepts and cases.* Boston: Allyn and Bacon.

Roberg, R., Novak, K., & Cordner, G. (2005). *Police and society.* Los Angeles, California: Roxbury.

Rokeach, M., Miller, M., & Snyder, J. (1971). The value gap between police and policed. *Journal of Criminal Justice,* 27(2), 353–382.

Ruiz, J., & Bono, C. (2004). At what price a freebie? The real cost of police gratuities. *Criminal Justice Ethics,* Winter/Spring, 44–54.

Sherman, L.W. (1978). *Controlling police corruption: The effects of reform policies. Summary Report.* Washington, D.C.: U.S. Department of Justice.

Souryal, S.S. (2010). *Ethics in criminal justice.* Cincinnati, OH: Anderson Publishing.

Sutherland, E. (1947). *Principles of criminology.* Philadelphia: Lippincott.

Sykes, G.M., & Matza, D. (1957). Techniques of neutralization: A theory of delinquency. *American Sociological Review,* 22, 664–670.

Van Maanen, J. (1978). The asshole. Retrieved October 10, 2010, from http://petermoskos.com/readings/Van_Maanen_1978.pdf.

Vold, G.B., Bernard, T.J., & Snipes, J.B. (1998). *Theoretical criminology.* New York: Oxford University Press.

Walker, S., & Katz, C.M. (2005). *The police in America: An introduction.* Boston: McGraw-Hill.

Williams, F.P., & McShane, M.D. (2010). *Criminological theory.* New Jersey: Prentice Hall.

Cases Cited

Mapp v. Ohio, 367 U.S. 643 (1961).
Miranda v. Arizona, 384 U.S. 436 (1966).

5

Officers of the Court
Ethical Responsibilities of a Lawyer

Chapter Objectives

- The student will understand the ethical responsibilities of lawyers
- The student will understand the underlying reasons for the ethical responsibilities of lawyers
- The student will understand the different sources of ethical obligations
- The student will understand the ethical duty of competency
- The student will understand the ethical duties of loyalty and communication
- The student will understand the requirement that legal fees be reasonable
- The student will understand the different types of legal fees
- The student will understand the unique challenges when lawyers represent individual charged with crimes
- The student will understand limitations on trial publicity
- The student will understand the need to protect client funds and property

Introduction

The legal profession is governed by standards of professional responsibility which are often referred to as ethics rules. National and state codes provide guidance regarding appropriate conduct for lawyers. National standards are developed by the American Bar Association. ABA membership is voluntary and, unlike many state bar associations, is not required for lawyers. The current ABA standards, The Model Rules of Professional Conduct, were adopted by the ABA House of Delegates in 1983 and were developed to serve as a model for states to follow when developing their own rules of professional conduct (www.abanet.org). The Model Rules also contain Comments to each rule. Comments provide additional information which supplements the policy contained in the rule. Comments may also offer illustrations or examples to aid in the interpretation of the rule. Often, comments have as much authority as the Model Rule.

The ABA has been proactive in working to ensure the ethics rules reflect the realities of modern law practice. In 2009, the ABA created the Commission on Ethics 20/20, which serves to review the rules in light of technology advances and global practices. This commission makes recommendations for modifications to the rules that will make them consistent with emerging technology and international practices.

While the ABA Model Rules provide guidance from the national organization, each state is free to develop its own Rules of Professional Conduct. With the exception of California, all states have adopted the ABA Model Rules of Professional Conduct (www.abanet.org). After the adoption of the Model Rules, states modify or add provisions to meet local needs. Adoption of the ABA Model Rules does not necessarily mean that the Model Rule and the state rule are identical. In addition to the ABA Model Rules and state rules, state law and court rules should be consulted when questions of professional responsibility occur.

The following chapter will discuss the primary professional responsibilities of lawyers and provides the text of the ABA Model Rules to illustrate those responsibilities. Unfortunately, one chapter is not sufficient to address all of the professional responsibilities of lawyers. In law school courses, professional responsibility and ethics require a full semester. The following chapter is devoted to those responsibilities which are essential.

Responsibilities of a Zealous Advocate

Above all, professional responsibility requires lawyers to serve as a "zealous advocate." A zealous advocate is a lawyer who advocates for their client to the extent permitted by law and the rules of ethics. Therefore, the best interest of the client should be the prevailing consideration for a lawyer. However, as an officer of the court, the lawyer must be conscious of ethical responsibilities as well as the interests of justice when advocating for his or her client. Initially, one may conclude that zealous advocacy refers only to activities which occur in the courtroom. We picture a lawyer emotionally and forcefully arguing their client's case before a jury in a packed courtroom. This certainly is a picturesque notion of zealous advocacy. However, for most lawyers, courtroom advocacy is only one dimension of the many roles they fulfill.

Ethical rules address the varied dimensions of functioning as a lawyer. There are many independent duties or dimensions which culminate in the responsibility to zealously protect the interests of a client. How does an attorney ensure that they function as a zealous advocate for their client? One way to conceptualize the duty to serve as a zealous advocate is to examine the most basic ethical responsibilities for lawyers. These "building blocks" normally include the following duties: competence, diligence and communication. We begin with an examination of these basic responsibilities.

Duty of Competence

Lawyers are expected to understand the law and possess the requisite knowledge, training and experience necessary to represent their client. The duty of competence requires lawyers to be knowledgeable and informed when giving advice and in their actual representation of the client. ABA Model Rule 1.1 states as follows: "A lawyer shall provide competent representation to a client" (http://www.abanet.org/cpr/mrpc/rule_1_1.html). Competent representation requires the legal knowledge, skill, thoroughness and preparation reasonably necessary for the representation. Consider for a moment, however, that most lawyers are "general practitioners." General practitioners are engaged in the general practice of law and therefore accept a variety of cases including criminal defense, family law, wills and estates and real estate matters. Can lawyers reasonably remain competent in that many areas of the law? Generally speaking, the answer is "yes." However, in this modern age of instant access to changes in the law via legal databases such as Westlaw and Lexis, it has become increasingly demanding.

As a result, some lawyers elect to specialize in a certain area or certain areas of the law. Specialization allows lawyers to restrict their practice to a few areas or a single area of the law. For example, lawyers may elect to specialize in family law, criminal law, insurance defense, probate law or bankruptcy, among many other fields. Specialization may be determined by the lawyer or the nature of the firm that the lawyer works for. In other words, a lawyer may decide that they enjoy a particular area of the law and are likely to be successful in that area, or a lawyer may work with a firm that is limited to a certain area of practice. This is very common with firms who practice in the area of insurance defense. These firms primarily represent insurance companies and work to defend individuals with insurance coverage who are sued.

Another important role for a lawyer is that of "counselor." To provide legal counsel to prospective or current clients requires lawyers to be able to advise clients about the law and the impact of the law upon their personal situation. Clients seek legal counsel in an effort to obtain information about their legal rights and to assist them when making important decisions. As such, professional and ethical guidelines require lawyers to remain knowledgeable so that they may give appropriate and current advice to his or her client.

ABA Model Rule 2.1 Advisor

In representing a client, a lawyer shall exercise independent professional judgment and render candid advice. In rendering advice, a lawyer may refer not only to law but to other considerations such as moral, economic, social and political factors that may be relevant to the client's situation.

(http://www.abanet.org/cpr/mrpc/rule_2_1.html)

For example, consider the critical nature of the decision that a criminal defendant must make regarding whether or not to testify. While criminal defendants may not be forced to testify in criminal trials due to the 5th Amendment privilege against self-incrimination, there are reasons that testifying may be necessary or helpful to the defendant. This decision is an extremely complex one and can be affected by a variety of factors. The assistance of competent legal counsel is essential. What if the lawyer representing a criminal defendant in a murder trial was unaware of a recent Supreme Court decision which impacted the decision to waive the privilege against self-incrimination? Failure to advise the client about the impact of this court decision could potentially have a devastating impact on the defense. Given the grave and often permanent impact of bad legal advice, lawyers are duty-bound to remain knowledgeable. It is not an excuse to later explain to a client who has been convicted and imprisoned that "I did not know about that case." While the preceding example is a bit extreme, it is offered to illustrate the importance of competency.

The duty of competency also requires lawyers to provide competent representation to their client. In other words, the lawyer must be competent to handle the case, to prepare the necessary paperwork and to understand the procedures which apply. Whether a lawyer is competent to handle a particular matter can depend on a variety of factors, including: the lawyer's training and experience, the complexity of the case, the nature of the case and whether the lawyer is able to devote the necessary time to competently represent the client in this particular legal matter. Lawyers are expected to be objective and honest in their assessment of their own competency. A lawyer must be sure they are competent enough to take the case.

If a lawyer is not competent to take the case, ethical guidelines require that the lawyer either: (1) work with another lawyer who is competent in that area of the law; (2) decline the case and refer the client to another lawyer; or (3) take the case only if the lawyer is able to become competent in that particular area of the law. This final option is somewhat surprising, however, with some legal matters, a lawyer may be able to acquire the level of knowledge necessary to competently handle the case despite not having prior experience with this type of case.

For example, a young trial attorney could be approached by one of his existing clients about a family law matter. The lawyer normally restricts his practice to criminal defense, but after meeting with the client learns that this legal matter is fairly simple and, more importantly, not contested. The lawyer, after consulting with a colleague who specializes in family law, estimates that the case will take approximately 10 to 20 hours of work to complete. The lawyer has recently concluded a murder trial and, aside from a few small cases, has time to "get himself up to speed" on the family law matter. Moreover, his colleague is willing to assist him at no cost to the client. Is the lawyer competent to accept the family law matter? Given the facts, this seems reasonable. Recall that the lack of prior experience with a particular type of case does not necessarily itself render a lawyer incompetent with regard to a certain type of case.

In order to "encourage" lawyers to remain competent, ethical guidelines and state licensing requirements mandate lawyers to engage in continuing education. These requirements are designed to ensure that lawyers remain informed regarding changes in the law, procedure and ethical responsibilities. The specific number of Continuing Legal Education hours, also known as CLE, varies from state to state. However, if lawyers fail to satisfy the minimum number of hours, penalties such as fines or suspension from practice may be imposed. If concerned or curious, potential clients may contact the state bar association to determine whether the lawyer is in good standing. Unfortunately, in some cases, mere completion of continuing legal education hours does not guarantee that a lawyer is competent.

Competent legal advice and representation requires only pursuing or bringing those claims into court which have merit. Claims that do not have merit are considered to be frivolous, or without a "basis in law or fact." The United States Supreme Court, in *Smith v. Robbins* (2000) characterized frivolous claims as those which are "lacking in arguable issues."

Simply because a client is not likely to prevail does not mean the case is frivolous. Rather, lawyers have a duty to assess whether there is an objective and reasonable basis in law or fact which justifies bringing the claim into court. The following are examples of frivolous claims or cases:

- No basis in law or fact exists to support the claim.
- Underlying motive for initiating the case is to harass or injure another.
- The attorney is unable to make a good faith argument in support of the case.

- The attorney is unable to make a good faith argument for reversal of existing law.

In the majority of states, it is both unethical and a violation of local court rules to file a frivolous claim. ABA Model Rule 3.1 contains the prohibition on frivolous claims.

> **ABA Model Rule 3.1 Meritorious Claims and Contentions**
> A lawyer shall not bring or defend a proceeding, or assert or controvert an issue therein, unless there is a basis in law and fact for doing so that is not frivolous, which includes a good faith argument for an extension, modification or reversal of existing law. A lawyer for the defendant in a criminal proceeding, or the respondent in a proceeding that could result in incarceration, may nevertheless so defend the proceeding as to require that every element of the case be established.
> (http://www.abanet.org/cpr/mrpc/rule_3_1.html)

Duty of Diligence

In addition to being competent, ethical guidelines require that lawyers be diligent in their representation of clients as well as in the operation of their law practice. The duty of diligence requires lawyers to take the appropriate and timely steps to advance the legal interests of their client. Lawyers must be zealous when representing a client and ensure that they are actively engaging in pursuit of their client's claim. The duty of diligence requires a lawyer to avoid procrastination, unnecessary delay and lapses in attention to the case. In other words, a lawyer is obligated to promptly attend to the case. Inadequate staff, heavy caseloads or personal issues have not been accepted by disciplinary committees or courts as sufficient excuses for the failure to diligently pursue a client's case.

> **ABA Model Rule 1.3 Diligence**
> A lawyer shall act with reasonable diligence and promptness in representing a client.
> (http://www.abanet.org/cpr/mrpc/rule_1_3.html)

> **ABA Model Rule 3.2 Expediting Litigation**
> A lawyer shall make reasonable efforts to expedite litigation consistent with the interests of the client.
> (http://www.abanet.org/cpr/mrpc/rule_3_2.html)

Consider the case where a trial attorney is going through a divorce and has developed a drinking problem. The stress of her personal situation is causing her professional responsibilities to suffer. She has failed to file two personal injury cases within the statute of limitations and is later sued by her clients for malpractice. Her clients also file a complaint with the state bar association for her failure to remain diligent. Does the lawyer's personal situation excuse her negligence? No. While the lawyer's personal situation certainly explains her conduct, it does not excuse her negligence for legal purposes.

The duty of diligence also includes the responsibility to follow the case through to its conclusion. An exception to this responsibility may occur if the client terminates the representation. Otherwise, the lawyer is required to finish the case. What if the relationship between lawyer and client has deteriorated to the point that the lawyer is unable to continue to effectively represent the client? The lawyer may terminate the representation. However, special care must be taken by the lawyer to notify the client and to advise them about any deadlines, statutes of limitations and the need to secure substitute legal representation. In situations where the case is pending in court, the lawyer must file a "Motion to Withdraw" requesting permission from the court to withdraw from the case. The lawyer must be prepared to establish why he or she is unable to continue to represent the client after which, the court may decide whether the lawyer will be allowed to withdraw from the case. Ultimately, the judge will determine whether withdrawal will be allowed.

Thinking Questions

1. What are the ABA model rules of conduct?
2. Name and describe some of the duties and responsibilities of a lawyer. Which ones seem more challenging than others?
3. What does it mean for a lawyer to be competent? Diligent?

Duty to Communicate

One of the most common complaints brought against lawyers is the failure to communicate with clients. While modern lawyers are extremely busy individuals who spend many hours in court, depositions and in meetings, the duty to keep their clients informed about their cases is considered to be a fundamental professional obligation. Simply put, lawyers are ethically required to communicate with their clients to ensure that the client has information regarding the status of his or her case.

The duty to keep a client informed is central to ensuring effective and productive legal representation. The duty to communicate applies to issues such as the status of a case, the presence or absence of settlement offers, discussion about strategy and any other matters which may affect the representation. The duty to communicate and provide information to clients also requires lawyers to provide accurate information to their clients. In order to make informed decisions about their case, clients must be presented with truthful information.

The duty to communicate with clients requires lawyers to communicate in a reasonable manner. What is reasonable will vary depending on the case. For example, it is rarely necessary for a client and lawyer to speak every week. This may change, however, if the client's case is involved in a trial. In the latter situation, the client and lawyer may need to speak daily to determine the most appropriate strategy, review witness testimony and other issues.

The ethical duty to communicate does not specify the means of communication. However, lawyers are most comfortable with written communications and may use correspondence such as letters or emails to communicate important information to their clients. Written forms of communication allow the lawyer to communicate with his or her client and to have a record of that communication. Written forms of communication are often preferred to establish attempts to contact when the lawyer has difficulty reaching the client. This evidence may prove critical later if the client files a complaint against the lawyer.

ABA Model Rule 1.4 Communication

(a) A lawyer shall:

(1) promptly inform the client of any decision or circumstance with respect to which the client's informed consent, as defined in Rule 1.0(e), is required by these Rules;

(2) reasonably consult with the client about the means by which the client's objectives are to be accomplished;

(3) keep the client reasonably informed about the status of the matter;

(4) promptly comply with reasonable requests for information; and

(5) consult with the client about any relevant limitation on the lawyer's conduct when the lawyer knows that the client expects assistance not permitted by the Rules of Professional Conduct or other law.

(b) A lawyer shall explain a matter to the extent reasonably necessary to permit the client to make informed decisions regarding the representation.
(http://www.abanet.org/cpr/mrpc/rule_1_4.html)

Confidentiality

A hallmark of the duty to provide legal representation is the duty to maintain the confidences of the client. The duty to maintain confidentiality applies to any and all information which "relates to the representation." Therefore, the obligation to maintain confidentiality applies to a significant amount of information. Also, the duty to maintain confidentiality applies to any information which relates to the representation even if the source of that information is not the client. Information which relates to the representation and received by the attorney from third parties must also be protected. The primary underlying justification for the duty of confidentiality is the need to encourage open and honest discussions between lawyers and their clients (or prospective clients). Knowing that all information relating to the representation will remain confidential allows clients to openly discuss their legal situation with a lawyer. Fully presenting the facts to the lawyer ensures that the client will receive appropriate and correct advice. Moreover, the duty provides assurance to the lawyer that they are more likely to receive all necessary information so that they may provide correct advice. Therefore, the benefits of the duty of confidentiality enure to the lawyer and the client.

The need to maintain confidentiality is triggered even before the lawyer is hired. During an initial consultation between a prospective client and a lawyer, all information relating to the representation is confidential. This assurance allows prospective clients to meet with lawyers and freely discuss their cases in an effort to select a lawyer.

The duty of confidentiality is not limited by the duration of the representation. In other words, once the case is over or the lawyer no longer represents the client, any information obtained must be kept confidential. Legal scholars refer to this ethical obligation as the "continuing duty of confidentiality." Former clients can rest assured that information regarding their case will remain confidential. In certain circumstances, the client may consent to the disclosure of confidential information. However, disclosure should only occur after the client has been advised of the advantages and disadvantages of disclosure. Situations which may necessitate disclosure include the following:

• The need for the lawyer to communicate or consult with other lawyers

- The need for the lawyer to communicate or consult with expert witnesses
- During certain settlement negotiations

Provided the client consents to disclosure, the lawyer may share information which "relates to the representation" in order to more effectively pursue or resolve the case.

The situations described above are those which are fairly common and may often arise during the course of legal representation. In contrast, there are numerous exceptions to the duty of confidentiality. Situations which constitute exceptions to the duty of confidentiality do not require consent from the client before disclosure can be made. The lawyer is not obligated to maintain confidentiality under these circumstances. The most common exceptions to the duty to maintain confidentiality include the following circumstances:

- Prevention of a crime or fraud
- Prevention of death or serious bodily injury
- Prevention of perjury
- To assist the lawyer with a defense to a dispute between the lawyer and client
- To assist the lawyer with a defense to a claim of misconduct or a crime
- To allow the lawyer to otherwise comply with the law or a court order

The ethical duty to maintain confidentiality extends to members of the lawyer's staff. While staff are not personally bound by professional ethics rules that apply to lawyers, these individuals are bound by the terms of their employment. State ethics rules and guidelines require lawyers to take reasonable measures to ensure that non-lawyer staff members such as paralegals, legal assistants, investigators, administrative assistants and interns do not disclose client information. Lawyers, therefore, should explain the duty of confidentiality to all staff members, provide training and if appropriate, require staff to sign a confidentiality agreement. While these measures do not always prevent the disclosure of information, the existence of these will assist the lawyer to establish that he or she implemented measures designed to protect clients.

Technological advances have significantly increased the efficiency of lawyers however, those advances come with risks. The use of a growing variety of technological methods also increases the likelihood that client information may be compromised. As such, lawyers must ensure that safeguards are in place to secure the use of email, facsimile and other methods.

Without consent by the client or existence of an exception, accidental or intentional disclosure of client information by the lawyer or a staff member may result in disciplinary action for the lawyer. Depending on the circumstances, sanctions may range from reprimand to disbarment. Before we leave our discussion of confidentiality, we should briefly examine the distinction between the attorney-client evidentiary privilege and the ethical duty of confidentiality. The attorney-client evidentiary privilege is a testimonial privilege which, like the ethical duty of confidentiality, protects communications between lawyers and clients. There are many similarities between the two, but there are also differences. The similarities include the following:

- The underlying justification (to encourage open and honest discussion)
- Applies to communications which occur during the lawyer/client relationship
- Applies to initial consultation (prospective clients)
- Does not end with the termination of the relationship or conclusion of the case
- Applies in civil and criminal matters
- Consent to disclose information may be given by the client only
- May not be used to conceal crime, fraud or perjury

The most significant difference between the testimonial privilege and the ethical duty of confidentiality is form. The testimonial privilege is an evidentiary principle which may be invoked by the client or the lawyer to avoid providing testimony about privileged communications between the two. Second, the ethical duty of confidentiality is broader in scope. The ethical duty renders all information relating to the representation private. This duty applies in all settings, not only when the lawyer is asked to testify. Obviously, there is considerable overlap between the two. To simplify matters, consider the relationship between the ethical duty and the privilege as follows: all information relating to the representation is confidential and if the lawyer is asked to testify about that information, the lawyer or client may assert the testimonial privilege. The client may also assert the privilege if he or she is called to testify. However, once the client waives the privilege, the lawyer may not reassert the privilege.

The client is the "holder" of the privilege and therefore only the client possesses the authority to waive the privilege. Waiver of the privilege may occur verbally or through the conduct of the client. Waiver of the evidentiary privilege may occur if the client discusses his conversations with the lawyer with others, allows third parties to attend meetings with the lawyer where privileged conversations occurred or consents to testify about privileged conversations.

ABA Model Rule 1.6 Confidentiality of Information

(a) A lawyer shall not reveal information relating to the representation of a client unless the client gives informed consent, the disclosure is impliedly authorized in order to carry out the representation or the disclosure is permitted by paragraph (b).

(b) A lawyer may reveal information relating to the representation of a client to the extent the lawyer reasonably believes necessary:

(1) to prevent reasonably certain death or substantial bodily harm;

(2) to prevent the client from committing a crime or fraud that is reasonably certain to result in substantial injury to the financial interests or property of another and in furtherance of which the client has used or is using the lawyer's services;

(3) to prevent, mitigate or rectify substantial injury to the financial interests or property of another that is reasonably certain to result or has resulted from the client's commission of a crime or fraud in furtherance of which the client has used the lawyer's services;

(4) to secure legal advice about the lawyer's compliance with these Rules;

(5) to establish a claim or defense on behalf of the lawyer in a controversy between the lawyer and the client, to establish a defense to a criminal charge or civil claim against the lawyer based upon conduct in which the client was involved, or to respond to allegations in any proceeding concerning the lawyer's representation of the client; or

(6) to comply with other law or a court order.

(http://www.abanet.org/cpr/mrpc/rule_1_6.html)

Conflicts of Interest

Before accepting representation, lawyers must evaluate whether a conflict of interest exists or could develop. A conflict of interest occurs when the lawyer may be placed in a situation where conflicting loyalties may impair the representation a lawyer is able to provide. Because a lawyer has a duty to remain loyal to his or her client, the lawyer must avoid situations where the commitment to the client's case may be jeopardized or adversely affected by other interests. "Other interests" may include the interests of another existing client, a former client, a third party, or the lawyer's own self interests. ABA Model Rules 1.7 and 1.9 set forth the lawyer's responsibility to maintain loyalty to current and former clients.

The essence of a conflict of interest is that there is another relationship that will potentially cause the lawyer to compromise his or her loyalty to a client. There are many types of conflicts which could impair a lawyer's loyalty or create divided loyalties. However, given our limitations in this chapter, we will cover the most basic principles.

The law is extremely clear on the issues of conflict and loyalty. Lawyers owe their clients undivided loyalty. This expectation is derived from the principle that "trust" is the essence of the lawyer-client relationship. As with many other professions (physician, accountant, therapist), the layman should be able to trust the professional from whom they seek advice and assistance. The existence of trust allows the professional and the client to work together in a mutually beneficial fashion to advance the interests of the client. As such, the lack of loyalty would significantly undermine the professional relationship. The ability of the lawyer to provide independent advice to the client may be compromised by the interests of others. Prior to accepting representation of a client, a lawyer should evaluate and assess whether the lawyer's duty or obligation to another (client, family member, self) would impair the lawyer's ability to advise and represent the client.

The clearest type of conflict exists where undertaking representation of the prospective client would have a direct and negative impact on a current client. In other words, if accepting the new client would require the lawyer to advance a position or interest which is directly adverse to the existing client, then a conflict of interest exists and the lawyer should not agree to represent the new client. Legal scholars often refer to this type of conflict as "direct adversity." For example, a lawyer could not represent two clients who are suing each other. Those clients clearly have adverse interests and therefore a lawyer would not be able to represent each individual effectively.

Consider a case where the lawyer has represented a husband and wife for many years in matters involving their business. Unfortunately, the couple has now decided to divorce. Each spouse approaches the lawyer about representation in the divorce. Can the lawyer represent either the husband or the wife? No. The husband and wife are both current clients. Representing one against the other would clearly be a conflict of interest. The lawyer should refer each spouse to another lawyer for the divorce.

A second type of conflict occurs when the lawyer's loyalty or ability would be impaired due to the lawyer's duty to protect the interests of another client, a third party or the lawyer's personal interests. Here, acceptance of representation of the second client would limit the ability of the lawyer to protect the interests of another. While it would not be directly adverse (client vs. client) as in the first type of conflict, it would have a negative impact. For example, consider a case where an individual meets with a lawyer about suing a corporation for negligence. The lawyer's parents (not the lawyer) own 50% of the stock in the corporation. Should the lawyer accept the negligence case? Probably not.

While the lawyer does not have an ownership interest in the corporation, he or she has a family relationship with owners of a significant amount of corporate stock. As such, the lawyer's relationship with the third parties may inhibit or limit his or her ability to provide independent advice to the client.

ABA Model Rule 1.7 Conflict of Interest: Current Clients

(a) Except as provided in paragraph (b), a lawyer shall not represent a client if the representation involves a concurrent conflict of interest. A concurrent conflict of interest exists if:

(1) the representation of one client will be directly adverse to another client; or

(2) there is a significant risk that the representation of one or more clients will be materially limited by the lawyer's responsibilities to another client, a former client or a third person or by a personal interest of the lawyer.

(b) Notwithstanding the existence of a concurrent conflict of interest under paragraph (a), a lawyer may represent a client if:

(1) the lawyer reasonably believes that the lawyer will be able to provide competent and diligent representation to each affected client;

(2) the representation is not prohibited by law;

(3) the representation does not involve the assertion of a claim by one client against another client represented by the lawyer in the same litigation or other proceeding before a tribunal; and

(4) each affected client gives informed consent, confirmed in writing.

(http://www.abanet.org/cpr/mrpc/rule_1_7.html)

ABA Model Rule 1.9 Duties to Former Clients

(a) A lawyer who has formerly represented a client in a matter shall not thereafter represent another person in the same or a substantially related matter in which that person's interests are materially adverse to the interests of the former client unless the former client gives informed consent, confirmed in writing.

(b) A lawyer shall not knowingly represent a person in the same or a substantially related matter in which a firm with which the lawyer formerly was associated had previously represented a client

(1) whose interests are materially adverse to that person; and

(2) about whom the lawyer had acquired information protected by Rules 1.6 and 1.9(c) that is material to the matter; unless the former client gives informed consent, confirmed in writing.

(c) A lawyer who has formerly represented a client in a matter or whose present or former firm has formerly represented a client in a matter shall not thereafter:

(1) use information relating to the representation to the disadvantage of the former client except as these Rules would permit or require with respect to a client, or when the information has become generally known; or

(2) reveal information relating to the representation except as these Rules would permit or require with respect to a client.

(http://www.abanet.org/cpr/mrpc/rule_1_9.html)

Lawyers must also be cautious when provided with a chance to engage in business opportunities with clients. While business or financial transactions with clients are not always a conflict of interest, we discuss them in this section due to the potential of these situations to create a conflict of interest between the lawyer and client. As such, lawyers must be especially careful when engaging in business or financial ventures with their clients. While states vary with regard to accepted and prohibited business transactions between lawyers and clients, the overriding consideration for lawyers is that the transaction be:

- Fair to the client
- Reasonable to the client
- In writing
- Provides client with opportunity to seek independent counsel regarding the transaction

Ethics rules and guidelines clearly seek to protect the client in such situations and presume that the lawyer is the professional and therefore possesses certain skills and knowledge which the client does not. More importantly, the lawyer-client relationship is built on trust and therefore a client may be more susceptible to overreaching by the lawyer due to the trust that exists. In order to prevent overreaching or deception, ethics rules proscribe limitations.

ABA Model Rule 1.8 Conflict of Interest: Current Clients: Specific Rules

(a) A lawyer shall not enter into a business transaction with a client or knowingly acquire an ownership, possessory, security or other pecuniary interest adverse to a client unless:

(1) the transaction and terms on which the lawyer acquires the interest are fair and reasonable to the client and are fully disclosed and transmitted in writing in a manner that can be reasonably understood by the client;

(2) the client is advised in writing of the desirability of seeking and is given a reasonable opportunity to seek the advice of independent legal counsel on the transaction; and

(3) the client gives informed consent, in a writing signed by the client, to the essential terms of the transaction and the lawyer's role in the transaction, including whether the lawyer is representing the client in the transaction.

(b) A lawyer shall not use information relating to representation of a client to the disadvantage of the client unless the client gives informed consent, except as permitted or required by these Rules.

(c) A lawyer shall not solicit any substantial gift from a client, including a testamentary gift, or prepare on behalf of a client an instrument giving the lawyer or a person related to the lawyer any substantial gift unless the lawyer or other recipient of the gift is related to the client. For purposes of this paragraph, related persons include a spouse, child, grandchild, parent, grandparent or other relative or individual with whom the lawyer or the client maintains a close, familial relationship. (http://www.abanet.org/cpr/mrpc/rule_1_8.html)

Lawyers as Witnesses

Lawyers are also prohibited from serving in dual roles during trials. Dual roles as advocate and witness may result in conflict and confusion. As such, ethics rules prohibit lawyers from serving as a lawyer in a trial where it is likely that the lawyer will be called as a witness. This prohibition ensures that the role of lawyers during trials is abundantly clear. Lawyers are advocates and therefore should not involve themselves in representation where it is likely that they will become a witness during a trial. Witnesses are called upon to offer testimony and provide evidence in cases. As an advocate, a lawyer's role is restricted to presenting evidence to the court and advocating for his or her client. It is important to note that the prohibition applies only to cases where it is likely that the lawyer will be called as a witness in a *trial*. However, as with most rules, there are exceptions.

ABA Model Rule 3.7 Lawyer as Witness

(a) A lawyer shall not act as advocate at a trial in which the lawyer is likely to be a necessary witness unless:

(1) the testimony relates to an uncontested issue;

(2) the testimony relates to the nature and value of legal services rendered in the case; or

(3) disqualification of the lawyer would work substantial hardship on the client.

(b) A lawyer may act as advocate in a trial in which another lawyer in the lawyer's firm is likely to be called as a witness unless precluded from doing so by Rule 1.7 or Rule 1.9.

(http://www.abanet.org/cpr/mrpc/rule_3_7.html)

Thinking Questions

1. What is the duty to communicate?
2. Describe the ethical considerations in client confidentiality.
3. What are some potential conflicts of interests with lawyers? How does this involve ethical conduct?
4. What are some of the special concerns when lawyers serve as witnesses?

Representing Individuals Accused of Crimes

Lawyers are often asked, "How can you represent criminals?" If a lawyer engages in criminal defense work, they will be asked this question. However, this question provides us with an opportunity for understanding the true role of a lawyer in the American legal system. Recall our earlier discussion about the key components of a lawyer. Lawyers have a legal and ethical obligation to serve as an advocate for their clients, even if those clients have unpopular causes. This duty does not require lawyers to be friends with clients or endorse their views or behavior. Rather, the lawyer has a job to do.

Effective lawyers are able to remain objective and disconnect from the allegations against their clients and let's face it, some lawyers do a better job of this than others. Those who do are able to advance the interests of their client, and protect their rights whether the client is accused of shoplifting or homicide. While the penalties are much different, the lawyer's obligation remains the same. Moreover, all defendants are presumed innocent until *proven* guilty. The lawyer's responsibility is to ensure that the government meets the burden of proof. When defending individuals accused of crimes temptations abound. Lawyers who do not remain objective may view their role as requiring them to use any means necessary to win the acquittal of their client. However, defense lawyers are officers of the court and therefore are duty bound to ensure that their actions and conduct are at all times consistent with the law and professional ethics.

Candor with the Court

As an officer of the court, lawyers have a duty to be candid with the court. This duty applies in all cases, civil or criminal. However, we discuss this issue in this section due to the complexity of representing individuals at risk of losing their liberty or lives. The obligation to be candid with the court and to avoid the presentation of false evidence includes criminal defense attorneys. Lawyers may not make false statements to the court and are required to disclose certain facts when the failure to disclose those facts would allow fraud or perjury to occur. Lawyers are also prohibited from offering false evidence to the court. If a lawyer becomes aware that a client has lied on the stand (perjury), the lawyer has a duty to make the court aware of the false testimony. ABA Model Rules 3.3 and 3.4 provide guidance on the duties associated with candor and fair play.

The duty to be candid with the court can be uniquely complex in criminal cases. Defendants have the right to testify in their own defense if they so choose. However, if a lawyer knows that the defendant's testimony will be untruthful ethics rules require the lawyer to take certain actions. Those actions may include questioning the defendant on only those matters about which they will offer truthful testimony or notifying the court that the defendant will testify in "narrative form."

Narrative form involves the defendant taking the stand and telling his or her story without questioning by defense counsel. In situations where defense counsel elects to proceed in this manner, the lawyer will notify the court and prosecutor before the defendant takes the stand. This method of testifying allows the lawyer to avoid participation in the presentation of false testimony to the court. The reality of such situations is that once the court and prosecution have been advised by the lawyer that the defendant will testify in narrative form, they are essentially on notice that the defendant may commit perjury. In other cases, the lawyer is not aware of the false testimony until after the defendant has testified. In those situations, the lawyer may not remain silent, but has an ethical duty to notify the court of the perjury.

Due to these difficulties, many criminal defense lawyers do not ask their clients whether they are, in fact, guilty. More importantly, a criminal defense lawyer does not need to know whether the defendant committed the crime in order to prepare and present a defense at trial. Defense attorneys are trained to evaluate the government's case, to assess any weaknesses, to challenge evidence and present a cogent defense theory. As a result, actual knowledge of a client's guilt is not necessary to the work that needs to be done by the defense lawyer. As you have now seen, actual knowledge of a client's guilt often significantly impairs the lawyer's ability to present the case. Therefore, during the initial consultation, many lawyers will proactively advise the prospective client not to disclose his or her actual guilt to the lawyer.

ABA Model Rule 3.3 Candor Toward the Tribunal

(a) A lawyer shall not knowingly:

(1) make a false statement of fact or law to a tribunal or fail to correct a false statement of material fact or law previously made to the tribunal by the lawyer;

(2) fail to disclose to the tribunal legal authority in the controlling jurisdiction known to the lawyer to be directly adverse to the position of the client and not disclosed by opposing counsel; or

(3) offer evidence that the lawyer knows to be false. If a lawyer, the lawyer's client, or a witness called by the lawyer, has offered material evidence and the lawyer comes to know of its falsity, the lawyer shall take reasonable remedial measures, including, if necessary, disclosure to the tribunal. A lawyer may refuse to offer evidence, other than the testimony of a defendant in a criminal matter, that the lawyer reasonably believes is false.

(b) A lawyer who represents a client in an adjudicative proceeding and who knows that a person intends to engage, is engaging or has engaged in criminal or fraudulent conduct related to the proceeding shall take reasonable remedial measures, including, if necessary, disclosure to the tribunal.

(c) The duties stated in paragraphs (a) and (b) continue to the conclusion of the proceeding, and apply even if compliance requires disclosure of information otherwise protected by Rule 1.6.

(d) In an ex parte proceeding, a lawyer shall inform the tribunal of all material facts known to the lawyer that will enable the tribunal to make an informed decision, whether or not the facts are adverse.

(http://www.abanet.org/cpr/mrpc/rule_3_3.html)

ABA Model Rule 3.4 Fairness to Opposing Party and Counsel

A lawyer shall not:

(a) unlawfully obstruct another party's access to evidence or unlawfully alter, destroy or conceal a document or other material having potential evidentiary value. A lawyer shall not counsel or assist another person to do any such act;

(b) falsify evidence, counsel or assist a witness to testify falsely, or offer an inducement to a witness that is prohibited by law;

(c) knowingly disobey an obligation under the rules of a tribunal except for an open refusal based on an assertion that no valid obligation exists;

(d) in pretrial procedure, make a frivolous discovery request or fail to make reasonably diligent effort to comply with a legally proper discovery request by an opposing party;

(e) in trial, allude to any matter that the lawyer does not reasonably believe is relevant or that will not be supported by admissible evidence, assert personal knowledge of facts in issue except when testifying as a witness, or state a personal opinion as to the justness of a cause, the credibility of a witness, the culpability of a civil litigant or the guilt or innocence of an accused; or

(f) request a person other than a client to refrain from voluntarily giving relevant information to another party unless:

(1) the person is a relative or an employee or other agent of a client; and

(2) the lawyer reasonably believes that the person's interests will not be adversely affected by refraining from giving such information.

(http://www.abanet.org/cpr/mrpc/rule_3_4.html)

Duty to Provide Effective Representation

In criminal matters, defense lawyers have both an ethical and constitutional obligation to provide effective representation. The Sixth Amendment requires that criminal defendants receive effective assistance of counsel. The leading case on the effective assistance of counsel is *Strickland v. Washington* (1984). In *Strickland*, the United States Supreme Court endorsed its previous holdings in cases such as *Powell v. Alabama* (1932), *Johnson v. Zerbst* (1938) and *Gideon v. Wainwright* (1963) wherein the Court held that the constitutional right to counsel is necessary to ensure that a criminal defendant receives a fair trial. As such, the mere fact that legal counsel is present during legal proceedings is not in and of itself sufficient to conclude that the defendant has received effective counsel. Counsel must participate and provide a defendant with adequate advice regarding his or her legal rights and trial strategy.

According to *Strickland*, in order to demonstrate that legal counsel was not effective, criminal defendants must establish the following: 1) deficient performance by counsel and 2) counsel's performance actually prejudiced the defense. To obtain a reversal of a criminal conviction or sentence, the defendant has a significant burden to establish that counsel committed error and that those errors resulted in a trial that was not fair. The second requirement of "actual prejudice" to the case has proven to be the most difficult prong of this standard to establish. In many cases, despite errors by defense counsel, sufficient evidence exists to establish guilt. Therefore, the defendant is unable to establish that but for the performance of counsel (or lack thereof), the result at trial would have been different. In other words, the defendant is unable to show that the conduct of the lawyer caused the guilty verdict or sentence.

Conflict of Interests in Criminal Cases

Lawyers must also evaluate existing or potential conflict of interests in criminal matters. The ethical rules are the same and require lawyers to determine whether their ability to serve either client will be impaired. If so, the lawyer must not undertake the representation. In certain criminal matters, a lawyer may be asked to represent co-defendants who are each charged with crimes arising out of the same set of circumstances. Such cases are extremely rare and for good reason. In such cases, the lawyer must ensure that protecting the interests of or presenting an effective defense for one client will not limit his or her ability to do the same for the co-defendant. Given the frequent need to shift blame to co-defendants in criminal cases, the ability of a lawyer to effectively represent co-defendants is likely to be constrained. As such, many lawyers will not consider this type of representation but rather, advise defendants to secure independent and separate representation. Not only does separate representation reduce the likelihood of an ethical violation due to a conflict of interest, it will also remove a potential future appellate challenge to the effectiveness of the representation for purposes of the Sixth Amendment.

Trial Publicity

While everyone enjoys a First Amendment right to free speech, commentary about pending legal matters may be restricted due to the potential impact on the fairness of legal proceedings. While most of us immediately think of prosecutors and law enforcement when limitations on trial publicity are mentioned, these limitations apply equally to defense lawyers in criminal cases. Ethics rules commonly restrict the amount and nature of commentary which may be made by lawyers involved in legal matters. The underlying intent of these restrictions is to safeguard and promote fair legal proceedings and ensure, to the extent possible, that cases are tried in the courtroom and not the media.

Public Communication

Ethics rules in the majority of states and ABA Model Rules have a general prohibition on "extrajudicial" statements (statements outside the courtroom). Extrajudicial statements are those "that a reasonable person would expect to be disseminated by means of public communication which the lawyer knows or reasonably should know may have a significant likelihood of material prejudice upon an adjudicative proceeding." This standard was upheld by the United States Supreme Court in *Gentile v. State Bar of Nevada* (1991) finding that the speech of lawyers may be restricted in order to preserve fairness of legal proceedings. Thus, restrictions commonly found in state ethics rules were held in *Gentile* not to violate the First Amendment.

In cases involving ethical violations, much of the attention is devoted to (1) the lawyer's knowledge and (2) whether the statement carried with it a substantial likelihood of material prejudice. Material prejudice occurs when the statement would likely influence a juror or witness. In order to provide some guidance on the latter issue, ABA Model Rules and state ethics rules often include "safe harbor" provisions which set forth certain statements which will not violate the prohibition. These statements commonly include the following:

- the claim, offense or defense involved and, except when prohibited by law, the identity of the persons involved;
- information contained in a public record;
- that an investigation of a matter is in progress;
- the scheduling or result of any step in litigation;
- a request for assistance in obtaining evidence and information necessary thereto;
- a warning of danger concerning the behavior of a person involved, when there is reason to believe that there exists the likelihood of substantial harm to an individual or to the public interest; and
- in a criminal case, in addition to the information above:
  (i) the identity, residence, occupation and family status of the accused;
  (ii) if the accused has not been apprehended, information necessary to aid in apprehension of that person;
  (iii) the fact, time and place of arrest; and
  (iv) the identity of investigating and arresting officers or agencies and the length of the investigation.

(http://www.abanet.org/cpr/mrpc/rule3.6.html)

In addition, the ABA Model Rules allow lawyers to make statements " … that a reasonable lawyer would believe is required to protect a client from the substantial undue prejudicial effect of recent publicity not initiated by the lawyer or the lawyer's client." Such statements may only contain " … such information as is necessary to mitigate the recent adverse publicity" (http://www.abanet.org/ cpr/mrpc/rule3.6.html).

Now that we've identified statements or subjects about which lawyers may make extrajudicial statements, what areas should be avoided? The following types of statements are generally prohibited by state ethics codes, court rules or state law. Again, lawyers must be familiar with those topics prohibited in the state where the lawyer practices. Interestingly, the ABA Model Rules do not set forth a list of prohibited topics, but rather only identify permissible topics as discussed in the preceding paragraphs.

- Character, credibility, reputation or criminal record of a party, suspect or witness.
- Identity of witnesses or information regarding the anticipated testimony from a party or witness.
- Information regarding a plea, confession or admission.
- Test results or the failure to submit to a test.
- Information regarding evidence which may be presented at trial.
- Personal opinions regarding the guilt or innocence of a defendant.
- That an individual has been charged with a crime absent an acknowledgement that a charge is merely an accusation.

While ethics rules and guidelines apply to lawyers, the rules also contemplate the risk of using agents to accomplish what the lawyer may not. As such, most ethics codes further prohibit the use of agents (investigators, staff, etc.) to make statements that the lawyer may not make. If a lawyer enlists the assistance of another to do so, the lawyer will have committed an ethical violation.

Lawyers as Authors

Many successful lawyers have become successful authors as well. Lawyers such as F. Lee Bailey, John Grisham, Nancy Grace and Marcia Clark and others have authored best sellers. While Grisham and Grace are known for their legal thrillers, Bailey and Clark wrote about actual cases in which they were involved. Do ethical issues exist for lawyers who want to describe their experiences in a book or movie?

ABA Model Rule of Professional Conduct 1.8(d) provides some guidance on this issue. Rule 1.8 provides "[p]rior to the conclusion of representation of a client, a lawyer shall not make or negotiate an agreement giving the lawyer literary or media rights to a portrayal or account based in substantial part on information relating to the representation" (http://www.abanet.org/cpr/mrpc/rule1.8.html).

Similar rules can also be found in state ethics codes. These rules are designed to protect the client from overreaching by lawyers who stand to profit from books or movies which portray the client's case. Agreements between the client and lawyer may, however, be negotiated following the conclusion of the representation. Thus, once the case is over, the restriction no longer applies. However, clients should always secure independent legal representation with regard to the negotiation of the agreement.

Thinking Questions

1. Discuss the ethics of representing people accused of crimes.
2. What is candor with the court?
3. What is effective representation?
4. What are some of the ethical responsibilities that lawyers have in dealing with trial publicity?

The Cost of Legal Representation

The cost of legal representation can be very expensive. As professionals, lawyers charge fees for their services and clients should expect to pay for legal services. Fee arrangements, however, should be discussed during the initial consultation so that the prospective client has a clear understanding of the type of fee charged, the amount of the fee and the method of payment.

Types of Fees

Three types of fees are generally charged by lawyers. These include the hourly fee, contingency fee or flat fee. An hourly fee is a set amount per hour. For example, the lawyer may charge $150.00 per hour for "office time" and $200.00 per hour for "court time." Such fees are not unusual and differences in the hourly rate for office and court time are increasingly common. If an hourly rate will be used for the legal matter, the prospective client should inquire about the amount of the hourly rate, billing practices, and an estimate of how many hours similar legal matters typically require. It is common for lawyers to use hourly rates in many types of cases such as estate matters, domestic relations cases, and real estate.

A contingency fee is a percentage of the amount of damages which are ultimately awarded in the client's legal matter. Personal injury cases are typically handled in this manner. We so often hear lawyers in television commercials make statements such as "there is no fee, unless I recover for you." This type of statement refers to the contingency fee. Contingency fees are prohibited in certain cases. The ABA Model Rules and the majority of state ethics codes prohibit the use of a contingency fee in domestic relations and criminal defense cases. In domestic relations cases, a contingency fee may not be charged for obtaining a divorce or property settlement. However, in some states, contingency fees may be used when a lawyer is hired to collect past due alimony or child support.

Contingency fees typically range from 30% to 50% of the recovery. For example, consider the case where a plaintiff successfully sues a drug manufacturer for damages caused by side effects of a drug. Let's assume the Plaintiff recovers $100,000 in damages. The lawyer and client agreed to a 30% contingency fee if the case settled and a 40% contingency fee if the case required a trial. The case settled prior to trial so the lawyer is entitled to a fee of $30,000. The lawyer may also be entitled to reimbursement for any expenses paid for by the lawyer such as expert witness fees, deposition fees, investigators, mileage, etc. Expenses are generally paid outside of the contingency fee, but only if this is specifically set forth in the contingency fee agreement. In other words, the lawyer would be entitled to $30,000 plus reimbursement for expenses. Assuming the lawyer could prove that she incurred $7,000 in expenses, the total compensation for the lawyer would be $37,000 in this case. However, if the agreement indicates that the lawyer's fee will be calculated on the "net recovery" a different calculation would be utilized. Using net recovery, the lawyer's 30% contingency would be calculated on $93,000 ($100,000 less $7,000 expenses). As such, the 30% contingency fee would be $27,900. In our hypothetical, the difference in calculation did not make a significant difference in the lawyer's fee. However, in other cases where expenses are higher, there can be a considerable difference.

A flat fee is a certain sum which the lawyer establishes as his or her fee for a certain type of case. It is not uncommon to see advertisements such as "Uncontested divorce, $99." This is an example of a flat fee. Potential clients, however, should beware of unusually low prices for legal matters. This is not to say that clients should be wary of all flat fees. Rather, a flat fee may be a useful tool when working with a lawyer to negotiate payment for a certain service. The fee is established at the outset and the client knows exactly what the final bill for services will contain. This type of certainty can be extremely advantageous. For example, an estate lawyer who is asked to prepare a will and a trust may establish a flat fee for that service. Flat fees are generally used in cases where the amount of time required to complete the matter can be reasonably predicted.

Written Fee Agreements

With each type of fee, the fee agreement should be in writing and easily understood. Lawyers should explain the agreement and its contents to the client before the client signs the document. Written agreements are strongly encouraged by the ABA Model Code as well as state ethics codes and serve to protect both the lawyer and the client. However, it is important to note that most ethics codes, including the ABA Model Rules, do not *require* fee agreements to be in writing, except when a contingency fee is involved. The best practice for lawyers, however, is to have every fee agreement in writing.

If a contingency fee will be charged the fee agreement must be in writing. States differ with regard to whether the contingency agreement must be signed by the client. However, it difficult to conceive of a valid "agreement" without some objective indication that the client agreed to the terms. In certain cases, the failure of having the contingency fee in writing has resulted in a determination that the fee was unreasonable.

The ABA Model Rules clearly set forth the requirements of a written contingency fee agreement. ABA Model Rule 1.5(c) requires that the agreement set forth the (1) percentage to be charged; (2) the method of calculation of the fee and expenses; (3) whether expenses are deducted before or after calculation of the contingency fee; and (4) expenses that the client is liable for in cases where there is no recovery. Lastly, lawyers should provide an itemized statement of charges, fees and expenses to the client. Again, clarity and transparency are the goals with any fee agreement. The agreement should be fair and reasonable in light of the factors set forth above.

Ethics codes, laws or court rules do not establish minimum or maximum fees which may be charged. However, ethics codes do require that fees should not be "unreasonable." As such, lawyers have an ethical responsibility to ensure that the fee charged in a particular case is a reasonable one. The reasonableness of a fee can vary dramatically given the type of the case. As a result, the ABA Model Rules and state ethics codes provide factors which should be considered when evaluating whether a particular fee is "reasonable." These factors include, but are not limited to, the following:

- The time and labor involved, the novelty and difficulty of the questions involved and the skill required to perform the legal service properly;
- The likelihood, if apparent to the client, that the acceptance of the particular employment will preclude other employment by the lawyer;
- The fee customarily charged in the locality for similar services;
- The amount involved and the results obtained;
- The time limitations imposed by the client or by the circumstances;
- The nature and length of the professional relationship with the client;
- The experience, reputation and ability of the lawyer or lawyers performing the services; and
- Whether the fee is fixed or contingent.

(http://www.abanet.org/cpr/mrpc/rule1.5.html)

Indigent Clients

The American system of justice places a high value on competent and effective legal representation and most would agree that those who come to court with competent representation often receive very different results. Our commitment to the provision of competent legal representation is illustrated throughout the legal system. In criminal cases, the Sixth Amendment of the Constitution requires competent legal representation, regardless of the ability to pay. In other cases, the Constitution may not require appointment of counsel, but our society and the legal profession certainly understand the need.

Indigency is a term used to describe individuals who are needy or poor and without the ability to pay for legal services. Because the essence of the legal profession is service, when lawyers take the oath and obtain a license to practice law, the commitment to serve the public is inherent. Advocacy for access to justice, regardless of one's ability to pay, continues to be a high priority for national and state bar associations.

The ABA Model Rules and the majority of states strongly encourage lawyers to engage in *pro bono publico* legal service. *Pro bono publico* is literally translated as "for the good of the public." In many states, lawyers must report the number of *pro bono* hours they provide on an annual basis or make a financial contribution to the state bar to fund legal services for the poor. Often these funds are utilized to establish volunteer lawyer programs or legal assistance programs.

ABA Model Rule 6.1 states that "every lawyer has a professional responsibility to provide *pro bono* legal services to those unable to pay." The ABA recommends that lawyers provide at least 50 hours of *pro bono* legal service each year with the majority of those hours provided directly to poor individuals or to charitable, religious, civic, community organizations that are designed to address the needs of the poor. The remaining hours may include legal services for the protection of civil liberties or services to charitable, religious, civic, community or educational organizations for no fee or a reduced fee where payment of a standard fee would deplete the resources of the organization; services for a reduced fee to persons of limited means; or participation in activities for the improvement of the law, legal system or legal profession. The ABA also encourages lawyers to contribute financial support to organizations that assist the poor with legal services.

The ABA standard of 50 hours per year is considerably higher than those found in most states. However, most codes refer to the number of hours as "aspirational" in nature and therefore not binding. Thus, professional codes should be viewed as establishing a goal for lawyers. In addition, most state codes allow for exemptions or exceptions to the obligation to provide *pro bono* services.

For example, lawyers who are prohibited from the practice of law due to their employment, lawyers who are no longer active members of the bar or lawyers who have been suspended from the practice of law are not required to provide *pro bono* service.

Lawyers are often called upon to accept court appointments. These are most common in criminal cases where the defendant is indigent and cannot afford to retain private counsel. Public defenders are typically utilized in these matters. However, situations may arise where the public defender is unable to take the case due to a conflict of interest, high caseload or other issue. Moreover, in many rural areas, public defenders are the members of the bar who are appointed to a case because no public defender position or office exists.

As with *pro bono* service, lawyers are strongly encouraged to accept appointments when called upon to do so by the court. In fact, ABA Model Rule 6.2 and most state codes state that lawyers should accept appointments by the court, unless good cause exists not to do so. Good cause to decline a court appointment may include the following:

- Accepting the case may cause the lawyer to violate an ethical rule or law
- Accepting the case may cause the lawyer to suffer undue financial burden
- The client or the cause is so repugnant to the lawyer that effective representation may be jeopardized
- Lack of expertise in the area of the law required to properly defend the case

A lawyer must establish to the court that good cause exists to avoid accepting the appointment. Absent good cause, lawyers may be subject to disciplinary actions if they refuse to accept an appointment. Of those listed above, the lack of expertise is often cited as the most common reason for seeking to be excused from an appointment. Moreover, the lack of expertise alone is not sufficient to avoid the appointment. Rather, if the lawyer argues that he or she lacks expertise in the area of the law, the lawyer must also demonstrate to the court that it would pose an undue or unreasonable burden for the lawyer to educate themselves in order to become competent. Only if the lawyer is able to establish that he or she lacks the necessary expertise *and* would be unduly burdened by a requirement to educate themselves to the point of competency will lawyer be excused from the appointment.

Unlike the obligation to provide *pro bono* service, lawyers are compensated for their work on court-appointed cases. While the fees may be less than those customarily charged, reasonable fees and expenses will be approved by the court. In court-appointed cases where the state, county or municipality is paying for the legal services, lawyers are required to submit a motion for payment with an itemized accounting of all charges. Following review by the court, the request for payment of fees and expenses may be approved, reduced or denied.

For lawyers, the ability to pay creates no differences in the professional and ethical obligations owed to the client. Whether the lawyer is involved in the case in an effort to provide services to the poor or due to court appointment, the lack of a fee paid by the client has no bearing on the quality of service the client should receive and more importantly, provides no excuses for the failure to provide competent legal service. Simply put, the lawyer should conduct themselves as they would for a client who is paying for services.

The Unauthorized Practice of Law

The ABA Model Rules and State Rules of Professional Conduct work to provide standards to govern and guide the legal profession. The rules work to ensure that lawyers conduct themselves in a lawful, ethical and professional manner when interacting with clients, the judicial system, fellow lawyers and the public. In other words, the license to practice law carries with it both privileges and responsibilities. Those without a license to practice who engage in the provision of legal services are not subject to those professional responsibilities and as such pose a unique danger to the public. Protection of the public is the primary goal.

To deter individuals from engaging in the practice of law without a license, state laws criminalize this behavior with penalties that range from fines to prison sentences. Additionally, the ABA Model Rules and state ethics codes address this issue as well. Generally speaking, the unauthorized practice of law occurs in a few common situations. The first situation arises where a licensed lawyer provides legal services in a state where they are not licensed. Lawyers must be licensed in the state where they intend to practice. As such, lawyers must be licensed in each state where they intend to provide legal services. Some exceptions to the requirement to be licensed in multiple states exist where a lawyer will offer legal services in another state on a temporary basis. In these situations, a lawyer may seek to be admitted to practice in another state on a temporary basis and for a limited purpose. This refers to admission *pro hac vice*.

A second situation which may involve the unauthorized practice of law occurs when non-lawyers provide legal services. Paralegals, legal assistants, legal secretaries and court clerks often possess sufficient legal expertise to assist with certain legal matters. However, these individuals are prohibited from doing so. Non-lawyer personnel working in law firms are often allowed to assist clients to the extent required by their professional duties. However, they are not compensated to perform legal services, but rather to serve as support staff to the lawyers in the firm. As such, despite having a certain level of legal knowledge, non-lawyer legal professionals are not allowed to charge for their services or utilize discretion to advise other individuals about their legal rights or remedies.

The restrictions on the unauthorized practice of law do not apply to individuals who elect to represent themselves in legal matters. The United States Supreme Court has held that individuals have the right to represent themselves in legal cases as long as they are able to competently do so. As such, the trial court must make a determination that the individual can do a reasonably competent job. The Sixth Amendment includes the right to proceed *pro se* (represent oneself) in a criminal trial. However, once the individual elects to proceed *pro se*, they do so at their own peril and may not excuse their conduct or lack of legal knowledge.

Lastly, the restrictions on the unauthorized practice of law have not been found to prohibit the use of "writ-writers" in prisons. Writ-writers are inmates who assist other inmates with the preparation of legal documents. The inmate who files the challenge is typically functioning *pro se*.

Abuse of Power and Privilege: When Lawyers Cross the Line

As discussed earlier, national and state rules of professional conduct, state laws and court rules are designed to ensure that lawyers conduct themselves in a lawful, ethical and professional manner when interacting with clients, the judicial system, fellow lawyers and the public. Unfortunately, as with any profession, there are those individuals who elect to operate outside the boundaries of professional, ethical and moral standards. Transgressions may occur in many forms and may involve violations of professional standards as well as federal or state criminal laws or both. When these cases arise, it is harmful to the legal profession and those honest, hardworking lawyers who we rarely see in the news. Some of the most troubling and infamous cases involve bribery and misuse of client funds.

Bribery

Bribery cases typically involve unscrupulous lawyers, judges or jurors. In these cases, there is some offer of benefit to the judge or juror in exchange for a certain result in a case. Lawyers who engage in this behavior have violated not only their professional code of ethics, but state and/or federal criminal laws. These cases undermine not only the legal profession, but the legal system as well. The notion of a fair system that works to provide a just result is damaged when individuals engage in bribery. ABA Model Rule 3.5(a) provides the general prohibition against unlawful influence. Criminal charges that may be brought in such cases include bribery, obstruction of justice, wire fraud, conspiracy and others.

> **ABA Model Rule 3.5 Impartiality and Decorum of the Tribunal**
> A lawyer shall not:
> (a) seek to influence a judge, juror, prospective juror or other official by means prohibited by law;
> (b) communicate *ex parte* with such a person during the proceeding unless authorized to do so by law or court order;
> (c) communicate with a juror or prospective juror after discharge of the jury if:
>> (1) the communication is prohibited by law or court order;
>> (2) the juror has made known to the lawyer a desire not to communicate; or
>> (3) the communication involves misrepresentation, coercion, duress or harassment; or
>
> (d) engage in conduct intended to disrupt a tribunal.
> (http://www.abanet.org/cpr/mrpc/rule_3_5.html)

Misuse of Client Property

By virtue of their profession, lawyers are often entrusted with client funds and property. Ethics rules provide guidance on the manner in which lawyers should treat client funds and property. The overriding restriction regarding client funds and property is that they remain separate. Client funds should not be deposited into the lawyer's personal or business accounts and should only be deposited and held in a separate trust account. Failure to keep funds or property separate is referred to as commingling. Commingling client funds or property with a lawyer's personal funds or property may result in disciplinary action. Converting client funds or property to the lawyer's own use is theft and may be prosecuted as such.

Lawyers must maintain records which document the receipt and disbursement of client funds and property. Most state ethics rules provide a specific time-frame during which such records must be maintained following termination of the lawyer-client relationship. These time frames typically require records to be kept for periods ranging between five to ten years.

A tragic case involving trial lawyers who are accused of defrauding their clients of millions of dollars in fees occurred in Kentucky. Three lawyers, Shirley Cunningham, William Gallion, and Melbourne Mills, represented clients in personal injury cases against the manufacturer of the diet drug, Fen-Phen. The lawyers were accused of stealing $65 million dollars in fees from their clients. As a result of the allegations, the lawyers faced federal prosecution for criminal offenses, were permanently disbarred for ethical violations and face civil suits filed by more than 400 of their former clients.

ABA Model Rule 1.15 Safekeeping Property
(a) A lawyer shall hold property of clients or third persons that is in a lawyer's possession in connection with a representation separate from the lawyer's own property. Funds shall be kept in a separate account maintained in the state where the lawyer's office is situated, or elsewhere with the consent of the client or third person. Other property shall be identified as such and appropriately safeguarded. Complete records of such account funds and other property shall be kept by the lawyer and shall be preserved for a period of [five years] after termination of the representation.
(b) A lawyer may deposit the lawyer's own funds in a client trust account for the sole purpose of paying bank service charges on that account, but only in an amount necessary for that purpose.
(c) A lawyer shall deposit into a client trust account legal fees and expenses that have been paid in advance, to be withdrawn by the lawyer only as fees are earned or expenses incurred.
(d) Upon receiving funds or other property in which a client or third person has an interest, a lawyer shall promptly notify the client or third person. Except as stated in this rule or otherwise permitted by law or by agreement with the client, a lawyer shall promptly deliver to the client or third person any funds or other property that the client or third person is entitled to receive and, upon request by the client or third person, shall promptly render a full accounting regarding such property.
(e) When in the course of representation a lawyer is in possession of property in which two or more persons (one of whom may be the lawyer) claim interests, the property shall be kept separate by the lawyer until the dispute is resolved. The lawyer shall promptly distribute all portions of the property as to which the interests are not in dispute. (http://www.abanet.org/cpr/mrpc/rule_1_15.html)

Thinking Questions

1. Discuss ethics and legal fees and the different types of fees that are charged.
2. What are some of the ABA recommendations for reasonable fees?
3. What are some ethical considerations with indigent clients?

4. What are some of the abuses of power and privilege a lawyer can engage in? What would stop them from doing so?

Conclusion

The practice of law has become increasingly complex. Lawyers must be educated and informed about the law, business practices and the rules of ethics. This chapter attempts to present an overview of the most basic ethical consideration for modern lawyers. However, even a cursory review of those considerations leaves one with an appreciation of the complexity of the legal profession.

The ABA Model Rules in conjunction with state rules, state law and local court rules attempt to create guidelines and mandates which work to create a legal system which fulfills its purpose. These rules also work to instill public confidence and trust in the legal system and the lawyers which function within that system. Ultimately, these rules work to protect citizens from unethical behavior by lawyers.

Failure to abide by these ethical responsibilities may result in a variety of disciplinary measures. These include reprimand, suspension, fines, and removal from office or disbarment. Therefore, once an individual becomes a lawyer, he or she must understand and appreciate the unique position they now occupy and be willing to earn the public trust and confidence that has been bestowed upon them.

Scenarios

1. A lawyer's neighbor has been having trouble with local teens vandalizing his property. The neighbor has discussed these problems several times with the lawyer while outside working in their yards. While arriving home from the office one evening, the lawyer observes three teens damaging the neighbor's mailbox. He recognizes the teens because he has a son in the same grade. The lawyer provides the names and addresses of the teens to the neighbor so that the neighbor may file a criminal complaint. Due to the extent of the damage, the neighbor decides to also bring a civil claim against the teens and requests that the lawyer serve as his lawyer in that case. Can the lawyer serve as an advocate in this case? Why or why not?

2. A lawyer has been retained to handle a divorce case for Suzy Smith. Mrs. Smith contacts the lawyer every day by telephone and/or email to obtain information related to her case. At this time, the case is in the discovery phase and lawyers are working with their clients to exchange documents and potential witness lists before trial. The trial will begin in approximately 90

days. The lawyer has a caseload of approximately 400 active files and is extremely busy. However, if Suzy Smith does not hear from the lawyer each day, she threatens to file a complaint with the state bar. Does the lawyer have a duty to communicate with Suzy each day? Why or why not?

3. A lawyer has represented Stevie Snake for many years. Mr. Snake has had many run-ins with the law and requires representation in criminal cases from time to time. To date, the lawyer has represented Mr. Snake in a robbery case, theft case and shoplifting case. Mr. Snake schedules an appointment to meet with the lawyer to discuss "an important legal matter." During the meeting, Mr. Snake indicates that he is in "big trouble" and needs cash. He informs the lawyer that he has a Rolex watch he needs to sell quickly. He asks if any lawyers in the firm may be interested in a "great deal." The lawyer suspects the watch was stolen in the robbery case where the lawyer represented Mr. Snake. The lawyer communicates his suspicions to Mr. Snake and Mr. Snake leaves the office in a hurry. Is the lawyer required to maintain confidentiality in this scenario? Can he notify the police? Why or why not?

4. A paralegal is hired by law firm to assist lawyers with preparation of trial documents. The paralegal's primary duties are to assist trial lawyers organize evidence and exhibits for upcoming trials. While assembling a trial notebook for an upcoming personal injury case, the paralegal sees a personal and romantic letter written to the client by a Dr. Jones. Dr. Jones is married to the best friend of the paralegal. The paralegal is enraged and believes she has a moral duty to advise her best friend about the letter. Has an ethical violation occurred if the paralegal discloses the information to her best friend? May the paralegal's supervising lawyer be held responsible for the disclosure?

5. Robbie the Robber is on trial for armed robbery. He and his attorney meet the week before trial to discuss strategy. During the meeting, Robbie indicates that he did rob the convenience store, but only because he needed money for his mother's upcoming surgery. Robbie advises his attorney that he would like to testify in his own defense at trial. He believes the jury will be sympathetic and will understand why he was so desperate. His attorney advises Robbie not to testify due to his extensive criminal records (this could be introduced to impeach his credibility). Rather, his attorney advises that he should allow his mother to testify about her medical condition. Robbie insists on testifying. During the trial, Robbie takes the stand and much to his lawyer's surprise, testifies that he was in another state at the time of the robbery. He denies any participation in the events. What should the lawyer do?

6. A lawyer represents a 17-year-old juvenile who has been charged with homicide and rape. The case has resulted in a significant amount of publicity and public outcry about out of control teen violence. The victim in the case was a young mother of two toddlers whose husband was serving in the military in Afghanistan at the time of the murder. The lawyer has evidence to show that his client, however, did not commit the crime. Rather, the evidence will reveal that the juvenile's 22-year-old brother committed the crimes. Can the lawyer defend his client in the press? What statements can he make? Why or why not?

7. A lawyer has been hired to represent an individual in a personal injury matter. The lawyer has been practicing for many years and believes in doing business "with a handshake and a smile." He agrees to take the case on a contingency basis and the client agrees that the lawyer will receive 30% if the case settles before trial, 40% if trial is required and 50% if the case is tried and an appeal is necessary. The lawyer's secretary hears the lawyer and client discuss these percentages. They shake hands and the client leaves. The case goes to trial and the Plaintiff (client) wins. The lawyer prepares an itemized account of his fees (40%) and expenses. The expenses total $20,000. The client is surprised by the amount of the expenses and states that he will not pay those. Can the lawyer collect the expenses? Why or why not?

8. A lawyer receives a call from the judge's administrator indicating that the judge intends to appoint the lawyer to represent a defendant in a capital murder case. The case is likely to go to trial and the state is seeking the death penalty. The lawyer practiced criminal law for many years, but for the last five years he has devoted his practice to wills and estates due the toll the stress of litigation took on his health. He is not excited about the prospects of being involved in a death penalty case. Specifically, he is concerned about his health and the effect the representation may have on his existing clients. He would like to refuse the appointment. May he do so?

9. A local court clerk routinely assists individuals with the completion of legal forms. A young lady comes into the court clerk's office one afternoon and requests assistance with filing a divorce. The lady explains that she is being abused by her husband and needs to file for a quick divorce. The lady has met with three lawyers, but she is unable to pay their fees. The court clerk pulls examples of forms from another case file and explains to the lady what language the "judges like to see in the forms." The lady goes home and prepares her forms. These forms are later filed with the court and the case is placed on the docket for a hearing two months later. The lady explains to

the court that she is representing herself and that her husband has agreed to the divorce. The judge inquires about her ability to complete the forms and the lady explains that the court clerk helped her with the forms and the information that should be contained in the forms. Has the court clerk engaged in misconduct?

10. A prospective client has an appointment to meet with a local lawyer about a suit against his employer for wrongful termination. On the day of his meeting, the prospective client brings his best friend with him to hear what advice the lawyer gives. If the friend attends the meeting between the lawyer and his client, will the information that is discussed be confidential? What if the lawyer is called to testify about the conversation? Does the information satisfy the lawyer-client privilege?

References

American Bar Association Model Rule of Professional Conduct 1.3
American Bar Association Model Rule of Professional Conduct 1.4
American Bar Association Model Rule of Professional Conduct 1.5
American Bar Association Model Rule of Professional Conduct 1.7
American Bar Association Model Rule of Professional Conduct 1.8
American Bar Association Model Rule of Professional Conduct 1.9
American Bar Association Model Rule of Professional Conduct 1.15
American Bar Association Model Rule of Professional Conduct 2.1
American Bar Association Model Rule of Professional Conduct 3.1
American Bar Association Model Rule of Professional Conduct 3.2
American Bar Association Model Rule of Professional Conduct 3.3
American Bar Association Model Rule of Professional Conduct 3.4
American Bar Association Model Rule of Professional Conduct 3.6
American Bar Association Model Rule of Professional Conduct 3.5
American Bar Association Model Rule of Professional Conduct 3.7
American Bar Association Model Rule of Professional Conduct 6.2

Cases Cited

Gentile v. State Bar of Nevada, 501 U.S. 1030 (1991).
Gideon v. Wainwright, 372 U.S. 335 (1963).
Johnson v. Zerbst, 304 U.S. 458 (1938).
Powell v. Alabama, 287 U.S. 45 (1932).
Smith v. Robbins, 528 U.S. 259 (2000).
Strickland v. Washington, 466 U.S. 668 (1984).

6

Prosecutors and Judges
Ethical Responsibilities of Public Servants

Chapter Objectives

- The student will understand the ethical responsibilities of judges
- The student will understand the ethical responsibilities of prosecutors
- The student will understand the underlying reasons for heightened ethical responsibilities for judges and prosecutors
- The student will understand the different sources of ethical obligations
- The student will understand the need for an independent and impartial judiciary
- The student will understand the concept of judicial discretion
- The student will understand the duty to establish and protect courtroom decorum
- The student will understand the concept of *ex parte* communications
- The student will understand the need for recusal or disqualification
- The student will appreciate the difference between an advocate and a minister of justice
- The student will understand restrictions on the dissemination of information
- The student will understand the duty to disclose exculpatory evidence
- The student will understand the duty to convict only guilty persons
- The student will understand limitations on interactions with represented and unrepresented individuals

Introduction

Judges and prosecutors each have unique roles to play in the American legal system. They are lawyers and therefore, with the exception of a few judges, they are subject to the ethical responsibilities discussed in the previous chapter. Due to their unique roles, additional ethical considerations and responsi-

e individuals. This chapter will examine those special eth-
judges and prosecutors.

...ost important distinction between judges, prosecutors and
,ᴐ is the requirement that judges and prosecutors always remain objective. While defense attorneys have a duty to be a zealous advocate for their
client and work towards the primary goal of defending their client, judges and
prosecutors must, above all, be committed to the following: (1) preservation
of justice; and (2) protection of a defendant's constitutional rights. Thus, judges
and prosecutors must work to ensure that defendants in criminal cases have fair
trials. They must place the interests of justice above all else.

Ethical responsibilities for judges and prosecutors are governed by professional ethical rules, state statutes and case law. They must be aware of and familiar with the restrictions and duties imposed on them by a variety of sources.
Ethical rules are typically developed by national and state bar associations.
These rules set forth ethical guidelines for judges, prosecutors and attorneys.
Ethical issues are also addressed by state statutes and court opinions. While
most of these sources are consistent with each other, differences do arise from
time to time.

Ethical Issues and Judges

In the American legal system, the judge is a neutral actor who should function as an impartial and objective guardian of justice. To ensure that judges
are impartial and objective, ethical guidelines, state statutes and case law impose strict requirements on those individuals who serve as judges. Judges should
behave in a manner that is above reproach, so ethical guidelines are strict.
These guidelines are designed to ensure that the public can have faith and confidence in the judiciary and, in turn, the legal system.

Integrity and Independence of the Judiciary

Judges are expected to be completely independent and objective. The requirement of an independent judiciary is critical to American notions of blind
justice. Most of us have seen a statue of Lady Justice wearing a blindfold. This
represents the ideal that all should have an equal opportunity before the law.
The sense of having a fair hearing is critical to the American legal system.

A judge can best be viewed as a referee. He or she is responsible for (1) ensuring that the court proceedings are conducted in a fair and impartial manner; (2) enforcing court rules; (3) instructing the jury on the law; and (4)

ruling on matters which arise. As such, of paramount importance is that the judge be impartial and objective. He or she should not be inclined to rule in favor of one side or the other due to external factors, but rather should make decisions based solely on the evidence which is presented in court.

Because judges are held in such high esteem, the manner in which they are selected is important. However, the method used to select judges is often debated. Today, there are three possible methods of selecting judges. These include: appointment, election, and the merit system. The method of selection varies among the states with some states using more than one method. Others, however, use only one method. The federal system is a system which uses only one method to select judges. In the federal system, judges are nominated for appointment by the President of the United States.

In jurisdictions which utilize appointment to select judges, such appointments are made by the chief executive. The chief executive of a state is the governor, while the chief executive (for purposes of the federal system) is the President of the United States. In jurisdictions which use appointment to select judges, judicial nominees must be confirmed by the state legislature or Congress.

Appointment is the oldest method of selecting judges. The use of appointment as a method of selecting judges is criticized by those who believe that judges should be elected by the citizens. They believe that appointment results in the selection of judges whose ideology is most consistent with that of the appointing executive and therefore infringes on the notion of a neutral and detached judge. However, others strongly advocate for appointment as the preferred method of judicial selection. Advocates for this method suggest that appointment by the chief executive and confirmation by the legislature or Congress is a preferred method to ensure that capable and qualified candidates are appointed.

Other jurisdictions select judges by popular elections. Election of judges by the voting public began during the 1800s. Advocates for this method of judicial selection argue that elections are the most democratic form of judicial selection. As with other elections, the voting public chooses the winning candidate. Critics, however, question whether elections produce the most qualified judges or just the most popular.

Elections may be partisan or non-partisan. Partisan elections occur when judicial candidates declare their political affiliation (Republican, Democrat, Independent, etc.) and are identified as such on the election ballot. Non-partisan elections occur when judicial candidates do not declare a political affiliation and therefore no political affiliation is listed by their name on the ballot.

The third method of selecting judges is referred to as the merit system. This system is often referred to as the "Missouri Plan" because Missouri was the first state to formally adopt this method of judicial selection. The Missouri Plan, or merit system, has grown in popularity since the 1940s with more than 20 states now using some version of this method. The merit system is designed to ensure that potential judicial candidates are well-qualified for such positions. The merit system blends characteristics of the other two methods. A non-partisan nominating commission begins the process by selecting several potential qualified candidates. The governor then selects his or her choice from that list. The final step in the process occurs when the individual selected by the governor stands for election. This is referred to as retention. The chief executive participates initially by selecting qualified candidates and the voting public has the final voice in the matter when the candidates stand for election. For many, this method satisfies the need to ensure that qualified candidates are selected, but also allows the democratic process to work.

The Duty to Judge

Ultimately, our society expects judges to function as adjudicators. All states' ethical guidelines impose upon judges the duty to hear those cases which are assigned to the court. Thus, without a legitimate reason for recusal (stepping aside), judges are expected to hear those matters which come into their courtroom. The duty to hear cases which are brought into court carries with it the duty to remain knowledgeable about developments in the law. This is often referred to as the duty of competence. As such, judges must remain competent to hear legal matters. We often hear the phrase "ignorance of the law is no excuse." This holds true for judges as well. Judges are duty-bound to ensure that they are familiar with the law and, if not, to engage in independent research so that they understand the possible legal issues that could arise in their courtroom.

Judges, like attorneys, are obligated by ethical guidelines and state statutes to attend continuing legal education sessions on an annual basis. While the exact number of hours varies from state to state, members of the legal profession have a professional and ethical duty to make sure they remain educated and are able to competently assist clients and litigants. Failure to remain competent in the law may be a disciplinary issue. As such, a judge may be deemed incompetent or unqualified for the position if he or she fails to educate themselves.

When adjudicating matters, judges are also required to ensure that their decisions are based on the law and not based on personal or partisan interests.

In other words, the judge should, at all times, remain independent. Judges should not be motivated by personal bias, prejudice or favoritism towards one party. Additionally, judges should not be influenced by fear when deciding cases. The fear of political loss or the fear of retribution are examples of real factors which could potentially influence the outcome of decisions. As such, judges have to work extremely hard to ensure that their motivations are based solely on the law.

Judicial Discretion

Judges possess a vast amount of discretion over matters which come before them. Discretion refers to the ability to exercise one's judgment. For example, while certain issues are controlled by statute or case law, many areas of the law are within the discretion of the judge. Certain matters over which judges possess broad discretion are:

- rulings on the admissibility of evidence
- sentencing
- use of expert witnesses
- scheduling and docket management

For example, when imposing a sentence upon an individual who has been convicted of a crime, the judge may have discretion to determine the type, length or nature of the sentence. Assume an individual is convicted of armed robbery in a state where the statute indicates that individuals convicted of armed robbery may be sentenced to a term of imprisonment not less than five (5) years but not more than twenty (20) years. In such situations, the sentencing judge would have the discretion to determine the exact length of the sentence as long as it was within the parameters established by the statute. Thus, the judge could be acting both legally and ethically if a sentence of 6 years or 18 years was imposed. The judge has the ability to impose a relatively light sentence or a relatively harsh sentence. While judges have vast discretion regarding many matters, they must always ultimately act within the confines of the law.

Thinking Questions

1. What are some responsibilities of the judiciary?
2. What are the methods used to select judges? Discuss the ethical concerns of the different methods.

3.   What are some areas in which judges have discretion?

Judicial Decorum and Conduct

At all times, judges are expected to conduct themselves in a professional manner and maintain the integrity of the judiciary. Ethical guidelines require judges to act in a dignified and unbiased manner both in their professional and personal capacity. This duty requires judges to avoid association with certain groups, avoid engaging in certain behaviors and any appearance of impropriety. The duty to avoid even the appearance of impropriety is based on the need for the public to have confidence in the integrity of the judiciary. Simply stated, judges are held to a higher standard. When one accepts a position as judge, their behavior must not only conform to the dictates of the law, but they must be cognizant that other behaviors which are not illegal or immoral may cast a negative light upon the judiciary and therefore undermine public confidence. Judges must take care to avoid behaviors, speech or other conduct which may give the appearance of impropriety. Examples of behavior which may give the appearance of impropriety and are found in judicial ethics provisions throughout the states include the following:

- Association with groups or individuals who have known biases, prejudice or engage in criminal behavior
- Association with groups or individuals who engage in discrimination or discriminatory behavior
- Attending events where inappropriate behavior occurs
- Making inappropriate comments
- Conveying the impression to the public that the judge can influence cases

Judges are also expected to maintain courtroom order and decorum. Courtrooms should be professional environments where the business of the court can be conducted. The judge, with the assistance of bailiffs, is charged with the responsibility to maintain a civil atmosphere. Judges are authorized to expel individuals who are disruptive, loud or boisterous from the courtroom. While certain cases are emotional, lawyers, parties and observers are expected to conduct themselves in a respectful manner when in court. The duty to maintain courtroom order and decorum applies equally to the judge. Judges are prohibited from engaging in unprofessional behavior while in the courtroom. Examples of such behavior may include: intimidating witnesses, speaking in a hateful manner to parties or attorneys, making disparaging comments or attempts to harass or humiliate individuals appearing in court.

Ex Parte Communications

Rules of ethics, statutes and case law strictly prohibit *ex parte* communications between judges and attorneys or parties involved in a case. *Black's Law Dictionary* defines *ex parte* as "on one side only." As such, *ex parte* communications are those which occur between the judge and only one side of a case. Historically, this practice was referred to as "earwigging." In order to ensure that each side of the case has an opportunity to interact in a fair manner with the court, rules prohibit judges from communicating with attorneys or litigants when the other side is not present. Thus, in a matter which is pending before the judge or may be brought before the court in the future, judges have a general duty to avoid *ex parte* communications.

Ex parte communications are prohibited for a variety of reasons. First, such communications may give the impression or appearance that one side of the case has the judge's "ear," so to speak. This may be interpreted as an unfair advantage. Second, *ex parte* communications are prohibited to ensure that judges behave in a manner which ensures fairness in legal cases. To communicate with one side without the other present can undermine the ability of the court to remain impartial or give the appearance that one side has an unfair advantage with the court. Finally, *ex parte* communications may subtly influence the judge, despite the best of intentions. The possible penalties for engaging in *ex parte* communications range from disqualification or the case to more extreme disciplinary actions.

In the majority of jurisdictions, there are exceptions to the prohibition on *ex parte* communication. Common exceptions include emergency situations, scheduling issues or situations where the communication is unlikely to give one side of the case an unfair advantage. For example, emergency situations may include cases where a victim of domestic violence seeks a temporary restraining order. Many state statutes have procedures which allow the victim to obtain a temporary restraining order on an *ex parte* basis without the presence of the alleged perpetrator.

Recusal and Disqualification

In matters where judges are unable to remain independent and impartial, ethical responsibilities impose a duty upon the judge to recuse him/herself from the case. The duty to recuse or disqualify oneself is grounded in the need to maintain the impartiality and integrity of the judiciary.

In general, judges are presumed to be impartial. In order to overcome this presumption, a motion to recuse must be filed. A motion is a request of certain actions from the court. For example, there are motions to suppress evidence, motions for change of venue and motions for new trial. The motion to recuse must be filed in a timely manner and set forth the basis for the recusal request. In other words, the party seeking to disqualify the judge, must prove that a sufficient reason exists which would impair the judge's ability to fairly decide the case. Suspicion alone is not a sufficient basis to have a judge recuse themselves.

In general, state ethics provisions require recusal of a judge in two situations: (1) a specific basis for disqualification or (2) circumstances which would lead a reasonable person to question the judge's impartiality. In either situation, if proven, the judge must recuse themselves from the case. Specific bases for recusal include the following situations:

- Prior or existing relationship (familial, business, social or romantic) between the judge and a party, attorney or witness in the case
- Judge has a financial or personal interest in the outcome of the case
- Judge has previously served as an attorney in the case
- Judge has personal knowledge about the case
- Judge has bias or prejudice towards a party in the case
- Judge previously worked with attorneys who serve in the case
- In cases where the judge may be called as a witness
- Judge or a member of the judge's family is related to a party or attorney or has an interest in the outcome of the case

In these cases, judges are required to recuse themselves on their own. If the judge fails to recuse him or herself, a motion to recuse may be filed by one or both of the parties in the case. In certain states, the parties in a case may consent to the continued service of a judge where a specific basis for recusal exists. Consenting to service of a judge who should be recused is risky and is usually not advisable.

However, other situations exist where a reasonable person may question the judge's impartiality. In these situations, the judge should also recuse him or herself from the case. These situations may include a variety of circumstances but the essence of the inquiry is whether those circumstances would lead a reasonable and objective person to question the judge's impartiality. Generally speaking, a judge's previous rulings on cases or rulings in the present case are not sufficient to establish a basis for recusal unless these rulings indicate a certain bias or prejudice. Also, the mere fact that litigants or attorneys have made campaign contributions to the judge's political efforts is not necessarily a basis for recusal. Rather, in the latter two situations, the party seeking recusal must establish that the impartiality of the court is compromised.

While the primary expectation of judges is to serve as an adjudicator, a working courtroom requires judges to also serve in an administrative capacity. Most state ethical guidelines also address the administrative dimension of being a judge. As such, ethical responsibilities also apply to the judge when serving in an administrative capacity. As with other administrators, judges are required to engage in the following duties:

- Supervision of court personnel
- Training of court personnel
- Hiring and firing of court personnel
- Ensure that cases are heard and disposed of in a timely manner
- Ensure that litigants have access to the court system

Thinking Questions

1. What are some examples of judicial impropriety?
2. What are reasons why a judge should recuse himself from a case?
3. What is *ex parte* communication? What is it used for?
4. What are some administrative duties of judges?

Judges as Witnesses

In rare situations, judges may find themselves involved in cases where they may be a potential witness. Most state ethics rules and state statutes require recusal of the judge in situations where he or she has involvement or knowledge of a case which may cause the judge to be a potential witness. But, what occurs when the involvement or knowledge occurs after the case has begun or in another unusual situation? In those cases, a judge would not be aware that he or she should recuse themselves at the outset of the case. While such situations are extremely rare, the Federal Rules of Evidence offer some guidance. The subject of a judge serving as a witness in a case is treated as a matter of competency by the Federal Rules of Evidence. Federal Rule of Evidence 605 states that "[t]he judge presiding at the trial may not testify in that trial as a witness." Moreover, Rule 605 does not require an objection to be made to the judge testifying as a witness in order to preserve the error on appeal. In other words, the error is deemed to be so clear, that an attorney need not object (http://www.law. cornell.edu/rules/fre/ACRRule605.htm). State competency laws and rules of evidence contain similar prohibitions on judges testifying as witnesses in trials over which they are presiding. While modern practice deems judges incompetent to testify in these situations, at common law, a judge was competent to testify during a trial over which he was presiding.

But, what about trials where the judge is not presiding? May a judge testify in other cases? The prohibitions that we have just discussed would not apply and therefore the judge would be competent to serve as a witness.

Extra-Judicial and Political Activities of Judges

When accepting the position of judge, individuals also accept that considerable personal sacrifice is required. During the selection process, whether by appointment or election, and later, upon selection, the personal and professional conduct and activities of judges are significantly restricted. The following discussion will examine the most common restrictions on the conduct and activities of members of the judiciary.

Practice of Law

Once an individual is selected to be a judge, they may no longer engage in the practice of law. For many judges, this transition means giving up a rewarding career as an advocate. Individuals who spent their professional lives advocating on behalf of others must now ensure that they conduct themselves in an impartial and objective manner. As such, judges may no longer practice law. The "practice of law" can include a variety of activities. These include giving legal advice, preparing legal documents, or other activities which involve the dissemination of information about one's legal rights or obligations. Due to this restriction, judges take special care to avoid giving litigants or attorneys advice or suggestions regarding practice in his or her courtroom. This can be especially frustrating for *pro se* litigants who are not represented by an attorney who may inquire about their case and the best manner in which to proceed. Members of the judge's staff are also prohibited from the practice of law and must take care to ensure that their conduct or behavior cannot be construed as such.

In most states, once selected to serve as a judge, the individual has a certain amount of time during which they may continue to practice law with the goal of concluding cases which they have begun. States vary with regard to the amount of time a judge may continue to practice, but generally, the timeframe ranges from six months to one year. This enables the judge/former attorney to ethically and professionally conclude those legal matters which have been filed without jeopardizing their client. Such an exception allows clients to have continuity of representation. In most jurisdictions, cases which have not been filed by the judge/former attorney must be referred to other attorneys. In most states, judges are allowed to receive fee payments for legal work they performed prior to becoming a judge. However, judges may not receive referral fees where they performed no work on the case.

Speech

Judges must ensure that their conduct, including their speech, does not undermine the impartiality or integrity of the judiciary. Judges may not comment on cases which are pending in their courts. Such comments must not be made in public or in private. Judges are also generally prohibited from criticizing or praising jurors for a particular verdict in a case. Such comments may imply that the judge appreciates the verdict. In contrast, it is generally permissible for judges to thank jurors for their service. The latter reflects gratitude for civil service whereas the former may imply that the judge is favorably disposed to a particular verdict or party.

For many judges, teaching in higher education becomes a professional opportunity. In most jurisdictions, there is no ethical prohibition on teaching. In such cases, judges are often relied upon to serve as adjunct or part-time professors in law schools, universities and junior colleges. This is not only a valuable professional experience for the judge, but a meaningful opportunity for students. Students, in such situations, have the opportunity to receive instruction and mentoring from a member of the bench who possesses valuable practical knowledge about our legal system.

Social speech is also subject to restrictions. Judges are prohibited from engaging in speech which includes jokes or derogatory comments about a particular group. For example, statements, comments or behavior which may give the impression that the judge is biased or bears prejudice toward particular groups are not permissible. Such statements may also impugn the integrity of the judiciary.

Political Activities

Upon selection, judges must essentially become apolitical beings. While judges retain their right to vote, other political activities are significantly restricted. Judges are generally prohibited from engaging in political speech, fundraising or otherwise aligning themselves with political organizations. Again, the underlying concern is that alignment or affiliation with political causes or interests may interfere with the independence of the judiciary. For example, during the campaign and while on the bench, judges must be careful about statements which tend to indicate favor for a particular cause or ideology.

In states which allow judges to be elected in partisan elections, political affiliation is a reality of the campaign and election. However, post-election and in states that utilize non-partisan elections or appointment to select judges, political activities must cease. This prohibition, however, does not extend to members of the judge's family.

In many jurisdictions, judges or judicial candidates are prohibited from directly accepting campaign contributions. Rather, judges must rely on election committees and other third parties to handle such matters. This practice is designed to ensure that knowledge of campaign donor identity or the amount of a contribution would not impair the judge's objectivity. Moreover, many states impose limits on the amount of campaign contributions by individuals or organizations. In states which use election as the method of judicial selection, efforts to ensure that judicial elections are free from undue influence of political organizations and advocacy groups is becoming increasingly complex.

Items of Value

Items of value, including gifts, are subject to certain restrictions. In general, judges and their immediate family members are prohibited from receiving items of value which are tendered for the purpose of receiving special favor or are given by an individual who is likely to be involved in a legal matter which would come before the judge. In contrast, items of value which are considered "ordinary social hospitality" are not generally prohibited by ethical guidelines. However, courts, disciplinary committees and legal scholars have struggled to fully define what constitutes "ordinary social hospitality."

The majority of jurisdictions utilize an objective test when determining whether an item of value constitutes "ordinary social hospitality." An objective test asks what a reasonable person, knowing all of the facts and circumstances, would conclude. In contrast, a subjective test would focus on what the individuals involved in the transaction believed. Cases involving the receipt of an item of value are typically decided on a case by case basis due to the sheer number of situations that may possibly arise. As such, rather that identifying a laundry list of items which are prohibited to be exchanged, courts and ethics rules may set forth certain factors which should be considered when attempting to determine whether an item of value constitutes ordinary social hospitality. Examples of such factors may include the following:

- Value of the item
- Nature of the item (gift, loan, favor, bequest)
- Occasion for the gift (engagement, wedding, birthday, etc.)
- Intent of the donor
- Intent of the donee (recipient)
- Relationship between the donor and the donee

- Whether such items are generally exchanged between individuals with such relationships
- Likelihood that the donor may appear before the judge

Consideration of these factors may assist a court or an ethics panel to determine whether the judge violated ethical guidelines when he or she or a family member accepted the item of value. For many members of the judiciary, refusal of all items of value from individuals other than family members may be the easier practice.

Thinking Questions

1. What are some responsibilities of the judiciary?
2. What are the methods used to select judges? Discuss the ethical concerns of the different methods.
3. What are some areas in which judges have discretion?
4. Describe and discuss "ordinary social hospitality."

Ethical Issues and Prosecutors

Like judges, prosecutors are charged with the duty to ensure that justice prevails in the American legal system. As such, the primary goal of prosecutors is not to convict individuals of crimes, but to ensure that individuals charged with crimes receive a fair trial. As with judges, ethical guidelines, statutes and case law are designed to ensure that prosecutors function in a manner consistent with traditional notions of justice. The following sections examine the most critical ethical considerations for prosecutors.

Prosecutorial Discretion: Minister of Justice vs. Advocate

Unlike defense attorneys, prosecutors have a broader scope of concern in criminal matters. Defense counsel is charged with providing his or her client with a competent and aggressive defense, ensuring that the defendant receives a fair trial and safeguarding the constitutional rights of the defendant. The chief obligation of a defense attorney is to protect their client. Prosecutors, however, while employed by the government (county, state, or federal) are likewise ethically commanded to ensure that criminal defendants receive a fair trial and are not deprived of their constitutional rights. As a result, prosecutors are often referred to as a "minister of justice" as opposed to an "advocate."

This ethical obligation is contrary to common perceptions of prosecutors. In general, our society views prosecutors as individuals who represent the government and are charged with the responsibility to convict guilty persons. Most do not understand that, while prosecutors are expected to be effective advocates for the government, they are officers of the court and are ultimately charged with the pursuit of justice. Within that endeavor, prosecutors must ensure that the rights of criminal defendants are protected. Thus, an enduring ethical challenge for prosecutors is the need to strike an appropriate moral, legal and ethical balance between the commitment to pursue justice; the public and political demand for convictions; and ensuring that the constitutional rights of criminal defendants are protected.

In the American legal system, the liberty of citizens is protected to such an extent that society is willing to tolerate the possibility that if the full spectrum of legal and constitutional rights is enforced during a criminal trial the result may be that a guilty person could occasionally go free. That the guilty would go free is more tolerable to American notions of justice than the possibility that an innocent person would be convicted or denied his or her legal protections. As discussed earlier, prosecutors are ethically bound to utilize the resources of the government in a manner to ensure that the legal process and the rights of criminal defendants are protected. Thus, prosecutors have a duty to seek prosecution and conviction of only those individuals who are guilty of crimes.

The duty to convict only guilty persons includes the ethical responsibility to initiate criminal charges only in cases where there is merit. In other words, before seeking an indictment or filing an information, the case should have a legal and factual basis and not be frivolous in nature. The United States Supreme Court, in *Smith v. Robbins* (2000), characterized frivolous claims as those which are "lacking in arguable issues."

However, a frivolous case does not refer to an action where success is unlikely. Thus, the mere fact that the person filing the case may lose in court does not render the matter "frivolous." Rather, frivolous cases would include the following:

- No basis in law or fact exists to support the claim
- Underlying motive for initiating the case is to harass or injure another
- The attorney is unable to make a good faith argument in support of the case
- The attorney is unable to make a good faith argument for reversal of existing law

Prosecutors are also ethically bound to ensure that each criminal charge is supported by probable cause. Probable cause requires that there is objective proof that the defendant did in fact commit the crime. Thus, before filing charges or pursuing charges filed by law enforcement, a prosecutor has an independent duty to ensure that probable cause exists.

As discussed earlier, prosecutors have an ethical obligation to ensure that the rights of criminal defendants are protected. A component of that responsibility is to ensure that criminal defendants are aware of their legal and constitutional rights. A fundamental constitutional right for criminal defendants is the Sixth Amendment right to counsel. In order to ensure that criminal defendants are aware of this right, most jurisdictions impose upon prosecutors an ethical duty to advise unrepresented criminal defendants of their right to legal counsel and to provide information regarding how to obtain an attorney. If necessary, prosecutors should allow additional time and opportunity for criminal defendants to obtain counsel. In certain instances, this may necessitate a continuance or delay of legal proceedings.

Interaction with Unrepresented and Represented Individuals

In general, ethical guidelines are extremely protective of unrepresented individuals. Ethics rules in the majority of American jurisdictions address the interaction of lawyers with individuals who are not represented by counsel. This includes the interaction of prosecutors with individuals, such as witnesses, suspects or defendants who are not represented by an attorney.

When individuals are not represented by legal counsel, ethics rules specifically forbid prosecutors from obtaining waivers of important legal rights. These rights may include the right to counsel, the right to a preliminary hearing, the right to a jury trial and many others. These prohibitions reflect an attempt to shield unrepresented individuals from the consequences of decisions made without the benefit of competent legal advice.

A more general prohibition which applies to all attorneys is what has come to be known as the "anti-contact rule." The anti-contact rule does not specifically apply to prosecutors, but most versions of this rule do not specifically exclude prosecutors either. As such, prosecutors must be mindful of the rule and be familiar with the approach taken in the state in which they practice. In the past, the United States Department of Justice suggested not only that this rule should apply to prosecutors in criminal matters, but should apply with more force than in civil cases. In *Minnick v. Mississippi* (1988), a dissenting justice persuasively advocated for the application of anti-contact rule to apply to prosecutors in criminal cases by stating, "[if] the rule obtains in civil cases where money is at stake, why not where the executioner approaches."

The origins of the anti-contact rule can be traced to the early 1800s in Hoffman's treatise. The rule is a general prohibition against contact or communication by attorneys with individuals who are represented by counsel. In other words, if an individual has retained an attorney to represent them in a divorce, an attorney for the other side of the case cannot ethically contact the individual regarding the divorce. The objective of this prohibition is to create a barrier between the client of another and the opposing attorney. Such practice ensures that opposing attorneys cannot exact concessions from individuals who are represented by their own legal counsel.

In order to violate this rule, the attorney must be aware or have knowledge that the individual is represented by counsel and disregard that knowledge. Therefore, contact by an opposing attorney who has no knowledge of the representation would not be an ethical violation. Moreover, in most states, it is not an excuse or defense that the represented individual initiated the contact with the opposing attorney. It is the opposing attorney that has the ethical obligation to discontinue the communication and advise the individual that they are ethically prohibited from speaking. If the opposing attorney has received consent from the other attorney or if the opposing attorney is otherwise authorized by law to contact the individual, no ethical violation will have occurred.

Lastly, in order to constitute an ethical violation, the contact must relate to the subject for which the individual has retained a lawyer. For example, suppose John Smith retains an lawyer to represent him in a divorce from his wife. The wife's lawyer also regularly represents an insurance company. During the divorce action, Mr. Smith is involved in a car accident. Mr. Smith elects not to retain a lawyer to represent him in the personal injury matter. The lawyer for the insurance company (his wife's divorce lawyer) now needs to contact him regarding settlement of his accident claim. May the attorney ethically do so? Yes, provided the interaction with Mr. Smith will only involve the car accident and not the divorce. But, what if the proceeds from the settlement of the car wreck could be considered marital property in Mr. Smith's state of residence? The division of marital property is an issue directly related to the divorce. Given the ethical implications, the safest course of action may be for another lawyer in the law firm which represents the insurance company to contact Mr. Smith.

Several common exceptions to the anti-contact rule do exist. These include situations where the contact does not relate to the subject of the representation. However, navigating the complex relationship among or between "subjects of representation" can be difficult as illustrated by the situation with Mr. Smith in the preceding paragraph. Next, the anti-contact rule applies to lawyers only. Therefore, parties to the action could speak directly to each other.

Another exception includes cases where there is consent from the represented person's lawyer or contact is authorized by law. This is a frequent area which raises concerns when prosecutors, rather than regular lawyer, are involved. While it is clear that prosecutors could not contact defendants who are represented by counsel regarding the crime for which the defendant has obtained legal counsel, what if the prosecutor would like to contact the defendant about another crime? Many jurisdictions, as well as the American Bar Association, would conclude that the prosecutor is allowed to contact that individual as long as the contact relates to a separate case. However, we learned a valuable lesson earlier. Whether an issue is entirely distinct or separate may not always be clear at the outset.

In the world of criminal justice, the use of undercover agents and informants in criminal investigations is often a necessity. However, from an ethical perspective, prosecutors may not use undercover agents, informants or law enforcement to contact individuals that the prosecutor or lawyer would be prohibited from personally contacting. If such cases, the agent, informant or officer is acting as the "alter ego" of the prosecutor or lawyer. If this occurs, the contact can result in an ethical violation despite the fact that a third party was involved.

Duty to Disclose Exculpatory Evidence

Exculpatory evidence is evidence which tends to negate guilt or mitigate the offense in criminal matters. In other words, it is evidence which may be helpful to a defendant. In all jurisdictions, prosecutors have both an ethical and constitutional obligation to disclose exculpatory evidence which may impact guilt or sentencing in criminal cases. In many states, this duty to disclose exculpatory evidence is also addressed by local court rules. As such, the duty of prosecutors to disclose exculpatory evidence is controlled by case law, court rules and ethical guidelines.

The leading case on the constitutional issue of disclosure of exculpatory evidence is *Brady v. Maryland* (1963). In *Brady*, the United States Supreme Court held that the "suppression of evidence favorable to an accused upon request violates due process where the evidence is material either to guilt or punishment, irrespective of the good faith or bad faith of the prosecution." Thus, the *Brady* Court set forth a strict liability approach which does not rely on the good or bad faith of the prosecutor, but rather is primarily concerned with the need to ensure that criminal defendants are afforded a fair trial.

In future cases, the Supreme Court has clarified the *Brady* rule. For example, in *United States v. Bagley* (1985), the Court held that the constitutional obligation to disclose exculpatory evidence only applies to evidence which is "material" to guilt or punishment. In order to be considered "material" evidence must have the potential to impact the outcome of the case. In conclusion, the *Bagley* Court further held that the prosecutor is not required " ... to deliver his entire file to defense counsel, but is only required to produce evidence, favorable to the accused, that, if suppressed, would deprive the defendant of a fair trial."

An important requirement of the *Brady* rule is that the defendant must first request the disclosure of exculpatory evidence. The defendant's request, therefore, triggers the constitutional duty to disclose. As a result, a constitutional violation would only occur when the prosecutor fails to disclose exculpatory evidence following a request by the defendant. In many states, however, ethics rules impose a more general duty to disclose on prosecutors. These rules do not condition the duty of a prosecutor to disclose exculpatory evidence on the request by a defendant. Rather, prosecutors have a duty to disclose exculpatory evidence whether or not the defendant makes a formal request.

Duty of Full Disclosure to Grand Jury

In many states, the ethical duty of prosecutors to make full disclosure of exculpatory evidence also applies in grand jury proceedings. In grand jury proceedings, prosecutors present their side of the case. If the grand jury finds sufficient evidence to indict, a true bill of indictment is granted. If there is not sufficient evidence to indict, the grand jury would return a "no bill." Certainly, there is a need to ensure that a grand jury has all material evidence prior to making a decision regarding indictment. However, there is inconsistency among the state ethics rules, case law and the ABA Model Rules. As such, it is incumbent upon prosecutors to be familiar with their state's approach to this issue.

As such, it is incumbent upon prosecutors to be familiar with their state's approach to this issue.

In *United States v. Williams*, the Supreme Court addressed this issue and held that federal prosecutors are not required to disclose exculpatory evidence to a federal grand jury. The Court held that the imposition of the duty to disclose upon the grand jury would transform the nature of the grand jury from accusatory to adjudicatory. The Court further held that " ... the Fifth Amendment presupposes an investigatory body acting independently of either the prosecuting attorney or the judge" and thus, "imposing upon the prosecutor a legal obligation to present exculpatory evidence in his possession would be incompatible with the system."

Dissemination of Information to the Public

Criminal cases can often generate significant interest. As such, prosecutors are often faced with requests from the media and public regarding the status of a case. The need or desire for information must be balanced against the duty to ensure that criminal defendants are able to receive a fair trial. As such, ethics rules provide limitations on the nature of information which may be released prior to and during trial.

In general, lawyers are prohibited from making extrajudicial statements to the media or the public which a lawyer reasonably should know would pose a substantial risk of prejudice to a future trial or other legal proceedings. Generally, information which should not be disclosed may include the following:

- Character, credibility, reputation or criminal record of a party, suspect or witness;
- Identity of witnesses or information regarding the anticipated testimony from a party or witness;
- Information regarding a plea, confession or admission;
- Test results or the failure to submit to a test;
- Information regarding evidence;
- Personal opinions regarding the guilt or innocence of a defendant; and
- That an individual has been charged with a crime absent an acknowledgement that a charge is merely an accusation.

Given the long list of information which may have a prejudicial impact, the question remains, what information is generally acceptable for dissemination? In general, lawyers are not prohibited from making statements which include information regarding the identity, residence, occupation and family status of the accused; information necessary to aid in the apprehension of a suspect, the fact, time and place of an arrest or the identity of participating investigating agencies.

Moreover, in many jurisdictions, prosecutors' offices are charged to ensure that law enforcement agencies should respect these restrictions as well. Given the complexity of the restrictions on dissemination of information in criminal cases, modern law enforcement agencies often employ public information officers who are specifically trained to deal with requests for information from the media and the public. Public information officers may be sworn or civilian and are able to ensure that appropriate information is disseminated.

Use of Agents to Avoid Ethical Obligations and Limitations

Clearly, there are many limitations on the conduct of prosecutors. These limitations and restrictions are designed to strike a meaningful balance between the necessary work of prosecutors to pursue criminal charges against individuals suspected of criminal activity and the right of criminal defendants to have a fair trial. Many jurisdictions impose further responsibility on prosecutors to ensure that law enforcement or other agents have not engaged in behavior that would be prohibited for the prosecutor. In our earlier discussion regarding interactions with represented and unrepresented parties, the use of police or undercover agents to carry out what a prosecutor would be prohibited from doing directly was discussed. In cases where third parties are functioning as the "alter ego" of the prosecutor as a mechanism to avoid ethical restrictions, an ethical violation may be imputed to the prosecutor. Establishing that a third party acted as the "alter ego" of the prosecutor would be determined on a case by case basis given the variety of situations which may arise. Obviously, the clearest scenario would include those cases where prosecutors direct law enforcement to engage in certain forms of conduct that the prosecutor is unable to.

These rules are designed primarily to prevent prosecutors from using others to engage in conduct which the prosecutor is prohibited from. However, one must consider that the ability to charge prosecutors with control over or hold prosecutors accountable for the conduct of law enforcement officers can be extremely complex. First, a variety of law enforcement agencies (state, local, or federal) may be involved in a criminal investigation. Because prosecutors may be state, local or federal, they may not possess the authority to control the conduct of certain agencies. Second, establishing that third parties were acting as the "alter ego" of a prosecutor can be complicated. The perceptions and intent of both the prosecutor and agent are relevant and may vary considerably during the course of an investigation.

Thinking Questions

1. What are some of the duties of a prosecutor?
2. Discuss exculpatory evidence and how prosecutors should handle this evidence.
3. What are some of the ethical issues in dealing with dissemination of information to the public?
4. What are examples of frivolous cases?

Box 6.1 ABA Model Rule 3.8 Special Responsibilities of a Prosecutor

The prosecutor in a criminal case shall:

(a) refrain from prosecuting a charge that the prosecutor knows is not supported by probable cause;

(b) make reasonable efforts to assure that the accused has been advised of the right to, and the procedure for obtaining, counsel and has been given reasonable opportunity to obtain counsel;

(c) not seek to obtain from an unrepresented accused a waiver of important pretrial rights, such as the right to a preliminary hearing;

(d) make timely disclosure to the defense of all evidence or information known to the prosecutor that tends to negate the guilt of the accused or mitigates the offense, and, in connection with sentencing, disclose to the defense and to the tribunal all unprivileged mitigating information known to the prosecutor, except when the prosecutor is relieved of this responsibility by a protective order of the tribunal;

(e) not subpoena a lawyer in a grand jury or other criminal proceeding to present evidence about a past or present client unless the prosecutor reasonably believes:

(1) the information sought is not protected from disclosure by any applicable privilege;

(2) the evidence sought is essential to the successful completion of an ongoing investigation or prosecution; and

(3) there is no other feasible alternative to obtain the information;

(f) except for statements that are necessary to inform the public of the nature and extent of the prosecutor's action and that serve a legitimate law enforcement purpose, refrain from making extrajudicial comments that have a substantial likelihood of heightening public condemnation of the accused and exercise reasonable care to prevent investigators, law enforcement personnel, employees or other persons assisting or associated with the prosecutor in a criminal case from making an extrajudicial statement that the prosecutor would be prohibited from making under Rule 3.6 or this Rule.

(g) When a prosecutor knows of new, credible and material evidence creating a reasonable likelihood that a convicted defendant did not commit an offense of which the defendant was convicted, the prosecutor shall:

(1) promptly disclose that evidence to an appropriate court or authority, and

(2) if the conviction was obtained in the prosecutor's jurisdiction,

(i) promptly disclose that evidence to the defendant unless a court authorizes delay, and

(ii) undertake further investigation, or make reasonable efforts to cause an investigation, to determine whether the defendant was convicted of an offense that the defendant did not commit.

(h) When a prosecutor knows of clear and convincing evidence establishing that a defendant in the prosecutor's jurisdiction was convicted of an offense that the defendant did not commit, the prosecutor shall seek to remedy the conviction.

(http://www.abanet.org/cpr/mrpc/rule_3_8.html)

Conclusion

In the American legal system, judges and prosecutors are vested with a significant amount of public trust and confidence to carry out their duties. In order to ensure that these legal actors conduct themselves in an ethical manner, heightened professional obligations and responsibilities are required. Underlying these heightened obligations is the need to protect the integrity of the legal system and to ensure that criminal defendants have the right to fair proceedings. Failure to abide by these ethical responsibilities may result in a variety of disciplinary measures. These include reprimand, suspension, fines, and removal from office or disbarment. Therefore, once an individual accepts a position as a judge or prosecutor, he or she must understand and appreciate the unique position they now occupy and be willing to earn the public trust and confidence that has been bestowed upon them.

Scenarios

1. A judge is presiding over a death penalty trial. During the trial, the prosecutor seeks to qualify an expert witness to testify about the DNA evidence in the case. After satisfying all legal rules regarding an expert witness, the prosecutor calls the witness to the stand to be qualified. The expert testifies about his education and experience. The defense objects to the qualification of the individual as an expert witness because his graduate degrees are from online degree programs. The judge agrees and denies the prosecution's request to qualify the individual as an expert witness in the area of DNA. May the judge rule in this manner? Why or why not?

2. During a murder trial, the mother of the victim is very emotional (understandably). The judge has instructed the audience that they are to avoid making comments or having emotional outbursts during the legal pro-

ceedings. When the defendant takes the stand, the mother of the victim repeatedly yells at the defendant. The judge requests that the bailiff escort the mother out of the courtroom. May the judge have the mother removed? Why or why not?

3. The local prosecutor was recently elected as a trial judge. A few weeks later, she is attending a cocktail party held in her honor and to celebrate her election as judge. All are having an enjoyable time and as the evening goes on and the judge is visiting with a group of former colleagues who begin discussing cases. One of the lawyers has had a bit too much to drink and begins making derogatory comments about "people who sue drug companies." What should the judge do? Why?

4. A family court judge is doing her weekly shopping at the supermarket on Saturday. While there she sees a local lawyer that she has known for many years. In fact, the two attended law school together. They meet on an aisle and begin catching up. During their discussion, the lawyer brings up a divorce case that is pending on the judge's docket. The lawyer represents the wife and informs the judge that the wife was taken to the emergency room after a domestic violence incident the previous evening. The case is set for a hearing to obtain a temporary restraining order on Monday morning before the judge. May the judge discuss the case? Why or why not?

5. A lawyer has recently been elected to serve as a judge. In the state in which the lawyer practiced law and has now been elected, the time to conclude all existing cases is six months. The lawyer is able to conclude all cases which had been filed within that time period. However, while the lawyer/judge is packing up his law office, a prospective client comes to visit. The client has a million-dollar personal injury claim and would like to hire the lawyer/judge to represent her. The lawyer/judge explains that he is unable to do so, but will refer her to a competent personal injury lawyer. The lawyer/judge makes the referral and contacts the other lawyer. The second lawyer offers to pay the lawyer/judge a "finder's fee" for sending such a wonderful case to him. May the lawyer/judge accept the fee? Why or why not?

6. In a state which selects judges in non-partisan elections a local trial judge is asked to be the keynote speaker at the local Democratic Party Annual Celebration. The judge is a lifelong Democrat and is honored by the request. The judge agrees to be the speaker. May the judge speak at this function? Why or why not?

7. Two lawyers married after law school. They each went on to have successful careers as trial lawyers and the husband was eventually elected as a judge. The wife continued to practice law and was deeply involved in local politics. For her longstanding service to the Republican Party the lawyer was named "Republican Lawyer of the Year" and given an award. The award included a ten-day cruise in the Mediterranean. May she accept the award? Why or why not? May the judge accompany her on the cruise? Why or why not?

8. A prosecutor receives a file concerning the armed robbery of a convenience store. The police have arrested Randy Robber, a career criminal with a length criminal history. The prosecutor reviews the file and has doubts about whether Randy Robber could have committed the crime. The prosecutor believes Randy Robber was actually in another state in jail at the time of the robbery, but cannot verify this. The police chief begins contacting the prosecutor's office to see when the matter will be presented to the grand jury. The prosecutor shares his concerns with his boss, the District Attorney. The DA instructs the prosecutor to present the case to the grand jury at its next session. May the prosecutor proceed with the case? Why or why not?

9. During a pre-trial hearing in a murder case, the prosecutor receives a written request from a defense attorney to provide the defense with all information contained in the file of the prosecutor. The prosecutor objects and argues that he is not required to turn over the entire file. Based on the authority of *Brady v. Maryland* (1963) the defense disagrees and demands a copy of the file. Does the Constitution require the prosecutor to provide a copy of the entire file to the defense?

10. A prosecutor is having his weekly meeting with staff investigators. The investigator reports that he is having difficulty contacting a witness for an upcoming trial. The witness is also a defendant in another case which the prosecutor's office is investigating and is out on bond in that case. The witness/defendant is not represented by a lawyer in her case, but says she is looking for representation. The investigator finally locates the witness and is able to question her about the original case. During the interview, the investigator also questions the witness/defendant about the case where the witness is charged with a crime. The investigator reports the information to the prosecutor following the interview. May all of the information be used by the prosecutor? Why or why not? Has the prosecutor committed an ethical violation? Why or why not?

References

American Bar Association Model Rule of Professional Conduct 3.8

Federal Rules of Evidence Rule 605

Fox, L.J., S. Martyn and A. Pollis, Editors. (2009). *A Century of Legal Ethics: Trial Lawyers and the ABA Canons of Professional Ethics*. Chicago, IL: American Bar Association.

Garner, B. (2009). *Black's Law Dictionary*. 9th Edition. West Publishing Co.

Hoffman, D. (1836). *Fifty Resolutions in Regard to Professional Development*.

Hoffman, D. (1846). *A Course of Legal Study*.

Morgan, T. and R. Rotunda. (2006). *Professional Responsibility: Problems and Materials*. 9th Edition. New York, New York: Foundation Press.

Cases Cited

Brady v. Maryland, 373 U.S. 83 (1963).

Minnick v. Mississippi, 498 U.S. 146 (1988).

Smith v. Robbins, 528 U.S. 259 (2000).

United States v. Bagley, 473 U.S. 667 (1985).

United States v. Williams, 504 U.S. 36 (1992).

Additional Websites

http://www.abanet.org

http://www.law.cornell.edu/rules/fre

7

Correctional Institutions
Ethics in Prisons and Jails

Chapter Objectives

- The student will understand how important staff are to the safe and ethical running of a correctional institution
- The student should be aware of how the institutional environment effects ethical behavior of staff members
- Identify the different types of correctional staff members and the unique ethical challenges they face
- Understand the importance of training
- The student will understand how offender management effects ethics
- The student will gain knowledge about the correctional officer subculture and its effect on ethics
- The student will learn the types of inmate personalities and how these influence the ethics of staff members
- The student will become aware of the types of offender manipulation that occur in prison
- The student will learn practical strategies to use in avoiding offender manipulation
- The student will be given tools to become a professional and ethical correctional employee

Introduction

The term "corrections" is used to describe the part of the criminal justice system that carries out the sentence imposed by the courts. The sentence is carried out by a system that is comprised of many parts including, but not limited to: correctional institutions, probation and parole, day reporting centers, electronic monitoring programs, boot camps and halfway houses. This chapter will focus mainly on institutional corrections and the ethical operations of jails and prisons in the United States. Jails are short term places of confinement that house pre-trial detainees and individuals with sentences of less than one year, or in some cases two years. Prisons, by contrast, are facilities that house offenders with sentences longer than one to two years and only house individuals who have been sentenced. While there are inherent differences between these two types of correctional institutions, how to engage in ethical practices within them is very much the same. This chapter is meant to serve as a practical examination of ethical issues that are encountered within correctional facilities. Major ethical challenges that employees face will be discussed as well as strategies and skills that can be practiced by correctional staff to avoid common mistakes.

In America, incarceration is one of the main ways that we punish offenders who have broken the law. According to the Bureau of Justice Statistics, 2,305,908 million persons were incarcerated in a jail, state or federal prison facility by the end of 2013 (BJS, 2014). Correctional facilities impact millions of lives. How they are run and the manner in which the employees carry out their duties has a profound effect on those incarcerated, the employees themselves, and the public. Correctional institutions are not like any other place. They are their own unique world with smells and sounds and a language that is unlike any other. Activities and existence outside of these facilities are termed by those incarcerated and those who work with them as the "free world," further separating institutional life from outside life. For both the inmates and the staff, this distinction creates a sense that what happens "inside" is separate from activities on the "outside." For those that work within the walls and fences, remaining ethical and professional is a challenge, particularly when faced with "clients" who may see them as the enemy. Consequently, inmates may also see correctional institution staff as targets to be exploited for contraband or special favors. Ethics and accountability are key components in the successful operations of correctional facilities. The first portion of this chapter will focus on the institutional environment and its effect on ethics.

The Institutional Environment

Picture your ideal work environment: the type of place that you have always dreamed of working. Imagine the smell, the surroundings, the sound level, your co-workers, and your clients. Where do you go for lunch and who goes with you? What is the tone of voice you use and the manner in which you speak to those around you? Conversely, picture yourself standing in the middle of a cellblock. Visualize the dayroom, or common living area. What are the sounds that you hear? Picture what you are wearing and the sights and smells around you. Clearly, not everyone gets to go to work in their perfect work environment, but most individuals can agree that correctional facilities are unlike most other work environments. Considered by most in the public to be a "necessary evil," jails and prisons house individuals that are deemed unfit to participate in society. Unlike other jobs where clients come to you willingly, "clients" of correctional institutions are there against their will. The prison environment is far removed from the norms and values that operate in the "free world." As noted by Crouch and Marquart (1990, p. 273):

> The ghetto like atmosphere of a maximum-security prison is quite overpowering to the uninitiated. Perhaps as many as 2000 men live, eat, work, urinate, sleep, and recreate in a very limited concrete steel building. This concentration of life presents the new guard with an unfamiliar and at the very least distracting sensory experience as simultaneously he hears doors clanging, inmates talking or shouting, radios and televisions playing, and food trays banging; he smells an institutional blend of food, urine, paint, disinfectant and sweat. What he sees is a vast array of inmate personalities portrayed by evident behavior styles.

Understanding the unique physical environment of the prison is one of many factors that play a role in understanding ethics in the correctional environment. Each institution has a formula or a "recipe." There are many ingredients that make up each unique correctional facility, but all have three main correctional components: (1) a building/facility, (2) correctional staff, and (3) inmates. The next portion of this chapter discusses these three main features and their impact on ethics.

The Building/Facility

Prison Design

Each building is designed in a particular fashion. Older facilities are often made up of one long hall-way with cellblocks and other buildings extending from it (telephone pole design). This design was popular between the 1920s and 1970s and designed to easily isolate riots or disturbances (Roberts, 1997). Newer facilities, such as the campus style, look more like college campuses with buildings spread out over the prison complex. Construction impacts correctional ethics because each prison design brings with it special considerations. Older facilities may be in disrepair or have places that are "blind-spots" or "nooks," which inmates and officers might use to conduct unethical conduct. Modern facilities often rely on technology to help with prison operations, such as automated locks or camera systems. Features such as these can help to encourage officers and inmates to behave ethically as potential wrongdoing might be videotaped. On the other hand, officers may become complacent and rely too heavily upon technology to do their job for them. Technology will continue to be an important consideration in ethics and institutional corrections (http://www.wired.com/science/discoveries/news/1997/12/8583).

Facility Location

It is also important to understand the impact of facility location; where the facility is actually located. Many prisons are located in rural areas. Conflicts may arise between inmates and officers because some inmates may come from more urban settings and the officers from a rural environment. Rural settings also provide additional isolation, where accountability and oversight of personnel are potentially reduced. In some instances, officers or other prison staff are sent to work in facilities in a location unknown to them. Urban correctional facilities have location concerns as well. In many situations, officers come from the same neighborhoods as the offenders, and may feel pressured to help out someone from their neighborhood. Consideration of community support and their perception of corrections and staff who work there can also have an impact on how officers feel about and perform their jobs. How is prison staff perceived by the community? Does the community embrace or reject having a prison in "their town"? Researchers have concluded that there is very little support from the community towards correctional officers and that this can cause stress on correctional staff (Cullen, Link, Wolfe, & Frank, 1985; Glenn, 2001; Lambert et al., 2002). These factors may make a prison staff member's job easier or more difficult depending upon the level of community support (http://northstatescience.blogspot.com/2007/07/prison-town-usa.html; http://www.prison policy.org/scans/building.html).

Custody Level

Another important consideration in the institutional environment is the custody level of the institution. Each custody level brings with it unique ethical challenges. Prisons are generally broken down into four distinct custody designations:

1. **Super-Max (also known as High-Security)**: These facilities house the "worst of the worst" and generally have inmates on "lock-down" for 23 out of 24 hours a day. Inmates have limited contact with officers and virtually no contact with other offenders. Examples of these facilities include the ADX Florence in Colorado, Red Onion in Virginia, and Pelican Bay in California. Famous inmates who are in Supermax include: the "Unabomber" Theodore Kaczynski and Salvatore "Sammy the Bull" Gravano, of the Gambino crime family.

2. **Maximum Security:** These facilities are exemplified by fortress style prisons with high walls and towers. Inmates generally live in cells and prison schedules are regimented to follow a strict routine. Maximum security facilities were designed with security in mind (diminishing the possibility of escapes and reducing inmate violence) and focus on custody first and programming second. Examples of these facilities are Attica in New York, Rahway (now East Jersey State Prison) in New Jersey, and USP Lewisburg.

3. **Medium Security:** Many medium security facilities physically resemble maximum security, but the organization and prison atmosphere is less severe and less structured. Medium security prisons differ greatly depending upon each agency's mission and model. Some medium facilities may be more rehabilitative, while others may be transitioning maximum security inmates into medium custody and still closely resemble a maximum security facility.

4. **Minimum Security:** Inmates housed in minimum security facilities are usually felons with clean records, the least violent, or inmates in special programming such as Substance Abuse treatment or Mental Health treatment. Offenders may live in dormitory style housing, have more frequent and open movement throughout the correctional facility, and have more access to programs and rehabilitation than in other facilities (Clear, Cole, & Reisig, 2010).

Each custody level provides distinctive challenges for correctional employees. Super-max inmates may seek to get special privileges from officers such as extra time outside of their cells or ask officers to pass things from inmate to inmate. Because inmates in Super-max and Maximum security spend less time out of their cells, they may seek to obtain information or privileges that are readily available to minimum security inmates. Other ethical challenges may come in the form of officers misusing authority or using excessive force, or feeling pressure to do so from other officers (Glenn, 2001).

Inmates in medium and minimum security may want officers to overlook "trafficking and trading" (passing commissary or other goods to another inmate which is generally against prison policy) or gambling. Inmates might also try to cross boundaries by initiating physical contact with prison staff or attempting to obtain contraband, as they generally have more access to prison staff. Games that inmates play will be discussed further in the section on avoiding offender manipulation.

Box 7.1 Hot Ethical Issues in Correctional Facilities

Cell Phones are one of the hottest items on an inmate's "to get" list. In many states phone calls are a rare commodity, therefore, inmates will go to great lengths to gain access to the outside world. The issue with cell phones is that they are small, transportable, common, and easy to obtain, especially with the "pay as you go" phones that can be discarded when the minutes are used. Cell phones pose a major security risk as these calls are not monitored for content and criminal activity like calls made by the offenders on prison phones. Not only does the content of these calls pose a risk, but the source of the phones is cause for concern as well. If officers and other prison staff are willing to bring in cell phones, it is not inconceivable for them to bring in other contraband such as drugs or weapons. As cell phones get smaller and cheaper, it is not a problem likely to go away. For further info on cell phones in prison see the following web links.

http://www.msnbc.msn.com/id/25625860/wid/11915829
http://www.npr.org/templates/story/story.php?storyId=6248833

The institution environment should not be overlooked when examining ethics and correctional institutions. The next portion of the chapter will focus on the staff members employed to manage and maintain our correctional facilities.

Thinking Questions

1. Describe some of the physical conditions of institutional confinement.
2. How does facility location impact correctional ethics?
3. Name and describe the four custody designations.
4. Compare and contrast how maximum and minimum custody inmates might differ in the ethical challenges they present to correctional staff.

Correctional Staff

Correctional institutional staff is organized in a hierarchy—the warden or superintendent sits at the top, assistant wardens down through sergeants are the middle rungs, with correctional officers on the lowest tier. While each prison differs slightly, prison staff most often include the following employees:

- Administration—wardens, superintendents, assistant wardens and other employees who run the prison
- Programming—medical doctors, nurses, counselors, psychologists, caseworkers and ministers. This category could also include contract employees who work in food service or maintain machinery.

- Maintenance/Facilities—physical plant supervisors, work crew supervisors, Food Service Managers, Industry Supervisors
- Custodial Supervisory Staff—captains, lieutenants, sergeants
- Line Staff—correctional officers
- Volunteers—prison ministry, Alcoholic Anonymous/Narcotics Anonymous Sponsors

Generally, correctional workers are divided into two distinct categories: (1) Non-custodial staff/personnel and volunteers and, (2) Custody/Security staff which make up correctional officers and their supervisors.

Non-Custodial Staff/Personnel and Volunteers

Non-custodial staff varies depending upon each correctional department but generally involves treatment staff (nurses, counselors, etc.) and other support staff (administrative assistants, teachers). Included in this group are volunteers. Volunteers may function as clergy or in some instances as treatment staff. Volunteers provide valuable services to correctional institutions. Volunteers must be prepared to encounter offenders who are willing and ready to manipulate and use religion or treatment as a way in which to obtain special favors or contraband. According to Christian Ministries to Offenders (2006), good traits in a prison volunteer include:

- Reliable and emotionally stable; able to accept responsibility and take independent action when necessary;
- Self-confident without the slightest hint of brusqueness or conceit;
- Firm but fair—adherence to the rules with a patient, constructive and creative manner;
- Not anxious to impress or cherish inflated ideas of their own importance;
- Always searching for the truth and not gossiping or spreading rumors;
- Neat in appearance and a friendly personality without becoming overly familiar;
- Humble, sympathetic, understanding without divulging their own personal problems;
- Adapting to change, maintaining enthusiasm, dispelling prejudice and growing allegiance to our entire ministry as a whole; and
- Alert, able to make decisions accurately and fairly, and concerned with the welfare of both the inmate and the credibility of the overall ministry in the facility.

Additionally, this volunteer group includes an entire page in their manual on avoiding offender manipulation, which includes the following suggestions applicable to all staff employed in the correctional setting:

- Be careful of the you/me situation. A secret or privileged communication between two persons may very readily not be valid in a court of law. You, as volunteers, should never do or say anything you would be embarrassed to share with your peers. A "secret" confided by you gives the other person the advantage of taking liberties if you want the secret to be kept.
- KEEP IT IN THE OPEN! This is probably the most important advice of all. It is most often the key to preventing or stopping the game playing process. Manipulators don't want to be too open because a knowledgeable onlooker may expose the manipulation process.
- Be knowledgeable of proper institution procedures relating to avenues confined persons can pursue to acquire needs. People asking "favors" generally already know whether or not you can grant them. You will most likely be judged negatively if you agree to something you should not, or do not agree to something you should.

This was my mistake

(http://www.tdcj.state.tx.us/pgm&svcs/AUGUST%202007%20Volunteer_
Orientation%20Handbook.pdf)

Treatment staff and other non-custody staff are often faced with challenges specific to their positions or role within the institution. Nurses may face inmates asking for special privileges or extra medication because they are "sick." Inmates may also play up their need for compassion with treatment staff and pit the "uniform" staff against the treatment staff. Most non-uniform or non-custodial staff are placed in job positions with more of a "helping" role, while custody staff stress security and enforcing rules. While institutions need individuals with this orientation to assist in rehabilitating offenders, the staff must make every effort to guard against offender manipulation. The Illinois Corrections Nurse II Outline of Job Knowledge, Skills and Abilities outlines two key features related to staff and inmates of Corrections: (1) Requires ability to maintain security of the work and comply with all facility rules, regulations, policies and directives and (2) Requires ability to adhere to detailed rules of conduct with regard to appropriate interaction with inmates or students. Although often forgotten, the non-custody employees are essential to the safe and effective running of a correctional facility. It is vital that all employees understand how essential it is that they remain ethical and professional at all times.

A starting point for any correctional professional, regardless of job, is the American Correctional Association's Code of Ethics.

American Correctional Association Code of Ethics

1. Members shall respect and protect the civil and legal rights of all individuals.
2. Members shall treat every professional situation with concern for the welfare of the individuals involved, and with no intent for personal gain.
3. Members shall maintain relationships with colleagues to promote mutual respect within the profession and improve the quality of service.
4. Members shall make public criticism of their colleagues or their agencies only when warranted, verifiable, and constructive.
5. Members shall respect the importance of all disciplines within the criminal justice system and work to improve cooperation with each segment.
6. Members shall honor the public's right to information and share information with the public to the extent permitted by law subject to individuals' right to privacy.
7. Members shall respect and protect the right of the public to be safeguarded from criminal activity.
8. Members shall refrain from using their positions to secure personal privileges or advantages.
9. Members shall refrain from allowing personal interest to impair objectivity in the performance of duty while acting in an official capacity.
10. Members shall refrain from entering into any formal or informal activity or agreement which presents a conflict of interest or is inconsistent with the conscientious performance of duties.
11. Members shall refrain from accepting any gifts, services, or favors that is or appears to be improper or implies an obligation inconsistent with the free and objective exercise of professional duties.
12. Members shall clearly differentiate between personal views/statements and views/statements/and positions made on behalf of the agency or Association.
13. Members shall report to appropriate authorities any corrupt or unethical behaviors in which there is sufficient evidence to justify review.
14. Members shall refrain from discriminating against any individual because of race, gender, creed, national origin, religious affiliation, age, disability, or any other type of prohibited discrimination.

15. Members shall preserve the integrity of private information; they shall refrain from seeking information on individuals beyond that which is necessary to implement responsibilities and perform their duties; and members shall refrain from revealing nonpublic information unless expressly authorized to do so.

16. Members shall make all appointments, promotions, and dismissals in accordance with established civil service rules, applicable contract agreements, and individual merit, rather than furtherance of personal interests.

17. Members shall respect, promote, and contribute to a work place that is safe, healthy, and free of harassment in any form.

Using this basic guideline as a starting point will help to steer any potential employee in the right direction. While each staff member plays a vital role in operating the facility, it is correctional officers and uniform personnel that are considered to be the backbone of the institution because of their continuous contact with inmates.

Correctional Officers

Correctional officers are a unique and distinctive human resource in the criminal justice system. The correctional officer, more so than any other employee in the correctional environment, is in constant contact with offenders. The correctional officer's primary function is custody and control of inmates. More simply, they serve to protect the public by keeping offenders secure and controlled from the outside world. Many nicknames have been used to describe custody staff, including, "hacks," "screws," "turnkeys," "keepers," "guards," and "Bossman" or "Bosslady." The American Correctional Association (ACA) approved a resolution to discontinue the use of the term "prison guard" utilizing the "correctional officer" title instead (ACA, 1993). This coincides with the shift in correctional ideologies and the dramatic increase in the inmate population. The "old philosophy" of dealing with inmates became obsolete as inmates began to win lawsuits and were granted rights through judicial intervention.

Under the old philosophy, any regulation issued by the prison system was deemed valid. Prisoners had little if any rights, and were virtually "slaves of the state" (del Carmen, Ritter, & Witt, 2002). Correctional officers had broad discretion and handled inmates as they saw fit, with little fear of reprisal or discipline. As noted by Marquart (1986), to not participate in the discipline of offenders was seen as a "weakness" by other guards. In a recent book about the condition of corrections in the State of Texas the author concluded that, "Correctional officers are human beings, contrary to what the media may project ...

They come in both sexes, all races, and all sizes. Correctional officers can always count on four things: being understaffed, unprotected, underpaid, and underappreciated" (Glenn, 2001, p. xiii). Those four factors create a setting where correctional officers are under external and internal pressure and must remain steadfast against potential ethical pitfalls. *← which happen all the time*

Thinking Questions

1. Name and describe the different types of correctional staff.
2. What are some of the unique challenges to treatment/non-custodial staff?
3. What are some of the key components of the ACA Code of Ethics?
4. Hypothesize some of the ways the custody and non-custody staff differ and how this relates to correctional ethics.

Offender Management

Training

The first step in learning how to manage offenders is training. Training should serve three main purposes. First, officers who have received proper training are often better prepared to act decisively when encountering a broad range of situations (riots, fights, verbal conflicts, etc.). Second, training in any organization leads to increased effectiveness and productivity. Third, a good training program will foster unity and cooperation (Josi & Sechrist, 1998). Essentially, training is the foundation for managing offenders. Quality of and effort put into training are the springboard of the correctional career. This is also the time when many officers and employees develop their ethics persona — in essence the type of officer that they will be. Institutional ethics begin with training. Many correctional departments mandate that their correctional officers attend an academy. For example, the Federal Bureau of Prisons requires that all staff attend the 3-week training course, as all staff are "correctional workers first." After successful completion of the academy, they then report to their institution and receive further training, known as On-the-Job Training (OJT). While few would argue that the formal training is unnecessary, or is not a key component in becoming a correctional officer, the real test involves the trainee becoming submerged in the prison society.

Many states are now assigning Field Training Officers or Mentors to help new correctional officers with the transition. The Field Training Officer (FTO) is used to guide the new officer, helping them to integrate the classroom instruction they received in the academy into more practical and usable techniques of managing offenders. Unfortunately, this relationship can also cause problems if the mentors are not ethical or see little value in teaching the new officer anything (Dial, 2007). It is not uncommon for new officers to be told that they are to forget everything they learned at the academy as they will be taught everything they need to know at the institution. Supervisors in charge of the FTO/Mentoring program must pay careful attention to how and with whom new officers are placed to ensure that they are given ethical and appropriate information. Web link: http://www.doc.state.vt.us/about/policies/rpd/106-06-academy-field-training-officer-fto.

Thinking Questions

1.   Why is training so important to correctional officers?
2.   What are the two types of training and how are they different?
3.   How does effective training encourage ethical behavior?
4.   What types of training should be included for correctional officers?

Managing Offenders

Once the correctional officer has received training, he/she is placed out on their own managing offenders. How does one correctional officer handle large numbers of inmates on a cellblock or in the chow hall? How can an officer realistically supervise hundreds of inmates and ensure that they comply with the rules? Do correctional officers really have "power" over inmates? Sykes (1958) believed that the "power" of the correctional officer could be corrupted, and noted the "defects of total power." Sykes contended that it was impossible to control large numbers of inmates and meet the demands of their supervisors without being co-opted by the inmates. Essentially, the officer might overlook small or minor rule infractions to gain compliance in other more serious areas, such as control of dangerous contraband or fighting. Simply stated, an officer might be more likely to let inmates break minor rules (i.e., hanging a clothes line in a cell, or letting an inmate be in the dayroom in a t-shirt versus a uniform shirt) so that the inmates will obey major rules (making and using a tattoo gun, stabbing an inmate in the recreation yard). This philosophy can potentially lead officers to troublesome situations. If inmates feel that an officer is willing to break small rules, they may believe that the officer will be willing to overlook "major" rules. Sykes (1958) argued that the officer had little or no power other than that which the convicts granted to him. Hepburn (1985) identified five ways in which an officer might exert their power:

1. Legitimate Power—(the formal authority to take charge over inmates) Hepburn noted, "the prison guard has the right to exercise control over prisoners by virtue of the structural relationship between the position of the guard and the position of the prisoner" (Hepburn, 1985, p. 146).
2. Coercive Power—(the ability to punish) Coercion is at the heart of prison environment and is sometimes used as a method of control by correctional officers.
3. Reward Power—(rewards to gain compliance) Correctional officers have a direct effect on work assignments, housing locations, and access to recreation and commissary. While those mentioned before are considered to be formal rewards, correctional officers may also reward inmates by overlooking minor rule infractions or granting an inmate a "favor."
4. Expert Power—(special abilities, skills, or expertise that inmates perceive as a form of expert power) An example of this could be an industry foreman who is skilled in carpentry or plumbing. When the foreman tells an inmate to complete a task he may do so because he believes that the foreman is more knowledgeable than he is and respects his expertise.
5. Referent Power—(respect) This was noted by Hepburn as "persuasive diplomacy," a leadership style that gains compliance because the inmates respect and admire the CO.

Hepburn (1985) believed that, of the five bases of power, officers relied most heavily upon legitimate and expert power to gain compliance from inmates. Coercive and reward power was found to be the least effective means of control. Rewards are often given out unfairly, dependent upon particular officers' biases and dislikes. An inmate might face harsh punishments for their actions from one officer, while the action carried out with another correctional officer might gain a reward. Coercive power may backfire if the offender feels like they are being punished unfairly. This might also be the cause of small or large scale cellblock disturbances, if a small or large group of offenders believes they are the target of unfair or unusually harsh punishment.

Most correctional departments encourage correctional staff to be firm, fair and consistent. Once inmates know how an officer operates their cellblock or work area they adapt to and live their life according to an officer's "shift personality." If inmates know that the correctional officer follows and enforces the rules, they will, more often than not, follow them. The use of rewards is often misconstrued by offenders as favoritism and can create larger problems if offenders perceive it as a weakness, believing that the officer can be manipulated. If an officer does their job and the inmate does his, rewards are not necessary.

The "reward" for the inmate is not having to face disciplinary action or increased scrutiny. It is vital to the new correctional officer that they quickly determine how they are going to supervise the inmates placed in their control.

Officers need to learn their institutional environment due to the fact that each prison has its own flavor and character. Maximum security institutions may have different procedures than minimum security institutions. Does the institution house a particular type of offender, and if so, do the policies dictate a different course of action? What is the tone or pace set by the shift supervisors? What are their expectations? If a shift supervisor expects an officer to search a certain number of cells and bring out quantities of contraband, it is important to understand how this fits into the shift and institutional mission.

Many new officers are afraid to ask questions of senior officers and supervisors. While the "new boot" may face some teasing initially, supervisors and senior officers will generally respect a new staff member for seeking out their advice, rather than making mistakes or getting into a situation that could have been avoided. It cannot be stressed enough that officers must know and rely on agency policy. *Correctional employees must know policy!* An officer cannot maintain an ethical demeanor if they do not know what the agency expects of them. Undoubtedly, it will make the officer's job easier if they know upfront what the offenders can and cannot do. The offenders know what they are supposed to do, but rely on correctional staff to enforce the policies.

Officers and staff who do not enforce or know the rules will generally have inmates who do not follow them. Following agency policy is the surest and safest course of action. The mountains of paperwork that one receives in the training academy are for the officers' consumption. Not only do they want officers to read it, but they expect that correctional staff are and will continue to be aware of the policies that guide conduct on and off duty. Knowing the agency's expectation of employees and the offenders is a way that correctional employees can be and remain ethical if they follow the policies. Knowing policy is only the first step, as the second step is actually putting the policy into practice.

Thinking Questions

1. What are the five bases of correctional power?
2. Which type of power is the most effective?
3. What are some examples of rules that officers follow?
4. Speculate about what rules or policies would have the most profound impact on staff members and ethics.

The Correctional Officer Subculture: Influences on Ethical Behavior

A large portion of social science research focuses on the subculture of the police officers and its effect on supervisors, police officers, and the public. Research has also been conducted to indicate if there is a similar subculture amongst correctional officers. These attitudes and beliefs impact how individuals within the group setting chose to act. The correctional subculture has a profound impact on ethical or unethical behavior by correctional employees. Kaufman (1988) further concluded that correctional officers held a similar set of beliefs that made them distinct and unique from treatment staff and prison administrators. Kaufman (1988, p. 86) identified nine norms that constitute the correctional officer code:

1. Always go to the aid of an officer in distress.
2. Don't "lug" drugs (bring them into the institution for an inmate to use).
3. Don't rat on another officer.
4. Never make a fellow officer look bad in front of the inmates.
5. Always support an officer in a dispute with an inmate.
6. Always support officer sanctions against inmates.
7. Don't be a "white hat" or a "goody-two-shoes."
8. Maintain office solidarity versus all outside groups.
9. Show positive concern for fellow officers.

Correctional officer subcultures impact the socialization of correctional trainees and their ethical framework. The recruits observe and imitate senior officers. The inherent rules within the subculture can create unethical behavior such as: Don't rat on another officer. Officers might be encouraged to overlook unethical behavior by co-workers to remain true to the "brotherhood." Pointing out wrong-doing by an officer can potentially be seen as choosing inmates over staff, which can cause alienation and exclusion from the group. However, officers must remember that their job is not to cover up the wrongdoing of their co-workers, but to protect the public and carry themselves with integrity. Officers are also put under pressure to side with another officer, even if the officers are wrong or acting outside of agency policy. Generally, it is considered to be good practice to take the officer aside after the inmate has left, and talk to the officer about their conduct. Continued misconduct or policy violations by officers no matter how small or large can lead to big problems in the institution. Initially, an individual might find reporting the situation uncomfortable, but prevention of loss of life or serious contraband (drugs, guns) is more important than protecting group solidarity. Inmates, by and large, respect officers who model integrity and ethical behavior. If they know an officer will "do the right thing," they are less likely to try to manipulate them or violate rules in their presence. Crouch and Marquart (1980) assert that the subculture influences a new officer:

- How to perceive inmates—Traditionally, inmates are viewed as the "enemy" or as "non-human." The correctional officer's main job is to ensure security and enforce rules and regulations. While officers have different styles of dealing with offenders, most officers strongly dislike inmates as a whole, and may often look for opportunities to "screw over" an inmate (this could be by making an offender late for a visit with family). Most new officers learn these attitudes from other correctional officers. Some correctional staff have inmates that are on an officer's trouble maker "list," while staff are also aware and remember those inmates that are less likely to cause trouble. New officers often generate their own lists in a similar fashion to those that mentored them. Inmates, regardless of their actions, are not to be trusted.
- How to anticipate trouble—Trouble can come from any inmate at any time, but more often than not, there are signs that problems are developing. This could be a change in noise in the cellblock area, whether it be extremely quiet when normally loud or very loud when usually quiet. Refusal or apprehension of an offender when asked to be searched could also be a sign of "trouble." The senior officer is important in conveying this type of information to new officers as they understand the workings of the institution, and know what is usual or unusual for that specific prison.
- How to manage inmates—As noted above, officers handle inmates differently. Women may often use more psychological pressure or techniques to gain compliance, where men might use physical force. The FTO may offer strategies for dealing with offenders. Offenders are not carbon copies, and senior officers often help new officers understand how to deal with mental health inmates, as well as inmates of other races. The subculture as a whole would encourage as little interaction as possible. The author, a former FTO at a correctional institution, encourages females to abide by the "30-second rule." If offenders cannot convey their request in thirty seconds or less, then their discussion could possibly be an attempt to engage in staff manipulation. The most frequent heard advice given by correctional officers to trainees is to tell an inmate "NO." If an officer is not certain of the answer, always answer no, and then find out the answer later.

The correctional officer subculture has both positive and negative effects. The subculture can help other correctional officers find support in a job and environment that is full of stress and pressure. Few people understand the world of the corrections like other correctional officers, which has led some correctional agencies to develop correctional officer led trauma support teams to assist officers in need.

Unfortunately, the subculture also promotes negative behavior. The subculture may encourage officers to act in ways that violate their personal and ethical beliefs, which may cause inner conflict and strife. Officers may engage in deviance or excessive use of force and expect or assume that another correctional officer will look the other way or even be willing to lie to protect a fellow officer. Officers who do not follow the unwritten code may be ostracized and left to fend for themselves. Socializing outside of the institution is not uncommon, and the author of this chapter was often invited to after work functions sometimes known as "choir practice." Failure to attend these functions, regardless of reason, was seen as alienating yourself from the "group." Perceptions of weakness in prison are not looked upon positively by other officers, and being "friendly" with offenders is an immediate cause for other correctional staff to separate themselves from the weaker officer. Unfortunately, this might only lead the officer to cling more tightly to the offenders who offer protection and sympathize with the ostracized officer (Worley & Cheeseman, 2006). This solidifies the need to pay careful attention to the younger, less experienced officers through training and mentoring. The subculture might also encourage negative coping mechanisms, such as excessive drinking (Dial, 2007). It could also be argued that the correctional officer subculture has changed as corrections itself has changed.

Thinking Questions

1. What are some of the elements of the correctional officer subculture?
2. How could the subculture influence the ethics of other officers?
3. What is the 30 second rule? Why is it important?
4. Does the integration of women and minorities into the correctional officer workforce change the subculture? Why or why not?

Gender and Ethics in Corrections: Cross-Gender Supervision and Beyond

Gender makes up a large portion of who we are and how human beings interact with one another. Clearly, gender also plays a role in corrections and how an employee interacts with offenders. This section will pay particular attention to cross-gender supervision, when women supervise men and men supervise women. Understanding the unique challenges and dilemmas raised by cross-gender supervision is essential in becoming an ethical corrections professional. It would seem that even though there are a large number of female correctional officers who work at male institutions some still feel like outsiders in a male dominated world. Research by Britton (1997) asserts that women still face challenges such as inmate sexual harassment, and male officers feeling like prison is not a place for females to work in.

Women Supervising Male Offenders

Female officers are an important resource for correctional agencies, particularly when many correctional departments are short staffed. One southern state reported that as of June 30, 2008, their agency had 9,535 (40.8%) female correctional officers and 13,809 (59.2%) male correctional officers (TDCJ-CID, 2008). With many agencies having large numbers of female correctional staff that primarily work at male institutions, training is crucial.

Graham (1981) noted essential ingredients for females working in all male institutions:

1. Using one's head—having a normal amount of intellect and common sense. It means understanding that the female brain is capable and not limited by the female body or by others' perceptions of one's capability. It should also reflect the notion of relying on the brain as the most important tool in dealing with conflict and offender issues. Physical strength may not be nearly as effective as mental toughness and learning through time and experience what battles to fight and when.
2. Developing correctional skills—learning the equipment, the law, the programs, the security, and the secrets of how to find out what is going on in the inmate community. This is obtained though observation and experience as well as listening to senior officer suggestion about how to find contraband, hiding spots, how to sense trouble, how to talk to offenders, etc. For many officers this process takes time. As with many things, officers learn from mistakes or from the mistakes of others.
3. "Having corrections in your blood"—if corrections is in your blood you don't mind going back to work at night, you don't mind going to work early and coming home late; you spend a lot of time in the cellblocks and on the yard, talking to the inmates, and you find yourself thinking and talking corrections just about anytime anyone will listen.

This process often occurs as the individual becomes more involved with other correctional officers. When you socialize with correctional staff and in some cases, live with them, prison or jail is the topic everyone can relate to. As noted by Dial (2007), some officers from the beginnings of their careers have corrections "in their blood." Characteristics of these individuals are as follows: high aptitude for finding contraband, willing to study policies and procedures, belief that they could and would make rank very quickly, and a general enthusiasm for the work.

4. Ability to tolerate stress and constant pressure—this is often the most difficult problem for both men and women managing a correctional institution (Graham, 1981, p. 134). As noted in a previous chapter, stress has profound effects on individuals and influences their behavior in many ways. The ability to generate and maintain positive coping mechanisms is paramount in maintaining ethically solid correctional practices. Women working in all male correctional facilities may have to develop support networks to deal with the specific challenges that they face. Additionally, it is important to know the limits of oneself, to notice changes in behavior or feelings so that the stress and pressure do not become overwhelming and unmanageable.

Jurik (1988) discussed five strategies that women utilize to avoid traps and stereotypes. Table 7.1 has an overview of these strategies.

The problem for many females working in corrections is that many of them have chosen the job by default and not as a sought after career decision (Marquart, Barnhill, & Balshaw-Biddle, 2001). This attitude often causes females working in male institutions to become susceptible to offender manipulation. Additionally, women working in male institutions may face scrutiny from male officers. What is crucial for a female officer to be ethical and successful is to understand the potential types of problems that she may face and be prepared in advance as to how to handle them. Male offenders will use different approaches in deciding to see if you are willing to engage in behavior outside of policy, including bringing in contraband that is minor (food, gum, envelopes, etc.) or major (drugs, guns, cell phones) or engaging in a romantic or sexual relationship. During the period of 2009–2013, thirty-five defendants pleaded guilty to charges ranging from corruption to racketeering for smuggling drugs and contraband into the Baltimore City Detention Center (Anderson, 2015). At the center of the scandal was Tavon White, a leader of the Black Guerrilla Family Gang (BCF). While incarcerated in the facility he fathered five children with four correctional officers. The BCF gang members were able to facilitate their criminal activity by convincing jail staff to put them in "workingman" posts,

Table 7.1

STRATEGIES	OVERVIEW OF COMPONENTS
Projecting a "Professional Image"	• Applies rules in courteous, consistent, and assertive manner • Deals with other prison personnel in a courteous and assertive manner
Demonstrating Unique Skills	• Female presence limits aggressive behavior from inmates • Using communication and crisis management skills to diffuse conflict • Individual competence in unique areas such as writing or special investigation
Emphasizing Teamwork	• Assist other officers in handling altercations • Emphasize the effort of the team in handling crisis situations and providing "back-up"
Using Humor as a Distancing Device	• Develops camaraderie with co-workers • Handles sexist remarks • Eases inmates' tension
Using Sponsorship to Enhance Positive Viability	• Balance between isolation and being too closely identified with a sponsor (seductress label) • Provides recognition of abilities for advancement

which include jobs such as cleaning and maintenance—tasks that give inmates more freedom to move around within the jail. This case underscores the benefits of rotating officers to different units, particularly in cases where management and close supervision is more difficult.

More information on games inmates play will be provided in the inmate section of this chapter.

Men Supervising Women

Seventy percent of correctional officers who guard female inmates are men, which can create a highly sexualized environment (Calhoun & Coleman, 2002). A simple solution is to end cross-supervision for both sexes, and only allow male correctional officers to work with male inmates and vice versa. This, however, infringes upon the rights of both sexes to have the equal opportunity to work as correctional officers. The research suggests that if correctional employees remain professional and "do their jobs," the incidence and prevalence of illegal conduct can and will go down. In recent years, <u>female prisoners have been able to restrict supervision by male correctional officers by showing a history of abuse or psychological harm.</u>

Box 7.2 Ethics in The News

The Colorado Independent — May 23, 2008

Former corrections officer accused of sexual misconduct, rape

An arrest warrant has been issued for a former prison guard with the Colorado Department of Corrections who is facing both civil and criminal charges of sexual misconduct with inmates, including rape.

The corrections officer failed to appear in court on Tuesday for criminal charges of unlawful sexual conduct with a female inmate he used to supervise, according to Denver district court records. A civil suit filed earlier this month accuses the same guard of raping a female inmate while she was in state custody.

District court records show that 37-year-old Lashawn Terrell, a former sergeant at the Denver Women's Correctional Facility, was first charged by state authorities with engaging in sexual relations with an inmate in 2006. The sexual acts were reported to have taken place from June to October that year, according to legal statements in the case.

Court records show that Terrell was arrested for the first offense and incarcerated briefly before being released on a $10,000 bond in November 2006.

The case is still pending, and clerks with the district court confirmed that a warrant had been issued for Terrell for failure to appear for a hearing on Tuesday.

On May 13, Mari Newman with Killmer, Lane & Newman, a legal firm that focuses on civil rights issues, filed a lawsuit against Terrell and the state corrections department claiming that the former guard raped and sodomized an inmate at the women's correctional facility in 2006 and that the department had failed to act to stop the abuse.

It is unclear whether there is more than one accuser since the names of possible sexual assault victims are redacted before records are made public.

Newman did not respond to a request for comment, but according to the legal brief, Terrell is alleged to have coerced the female inmate into engaging in sexual acts in the kitchen cooler area in the facility during her work assignment program.

Terrell then "proceeded to treat [the inmate] as a virtual sex slave," even though the inmate "told him she did not want to have sex with him," according to the brief. In exchange for the sexual acts, Terrell is alleged to have given the inmate small amounts of "money, stamps, and coffee."

According to the lawsuit, the rapes escalated to a point where the inmate was forcibly sodomized by Terrell and physically injured in the rectal area, causing long-term bowel difficulties. The legal brief states that a cellmate notified department authorities when she noticed the inmate was bleeding upon returning to her cell.

The suit also claims that other inmates at the women's facility had seen Terrell raping or engaging in sexual behavior with other inmates, and that the corrections department was negligent in letting such things happen in a state facility.

In response to inquires about Terrell and the two legal cases, department spokeswoman Katherine Sanguinetti said she could not comment on pending litigation. The department has yet to respond to the suit in court.

Attempts to contact Terrell were unsuccessful.

(http://www.coloradoindependent.com/4263/former-corrections-officer-accused-of-sexual-misconduct-rape)

The National Institute of Corrections (NIC) offers a thirty-six hour course specifically related to supervision of female offenders, including cross-gender supervision. Interestingly, no state or federal appeals court has forbidden male officers from supervising female inmates in the showers. Many states, such as Oregon, consider it to be sound practice not to allow male officers to view female inmates in the shower areas. The Arizona Department of Corrections has a four-hour training block specifically relating to the issue of cross-gender supervision. States are not mandated to provide cross-gender supervision training, although it is an essential element in creating a safe and effective prison environment. With the passage of the Prison Rape Elimination Act of 2003, one of the recommendations to the standards committee could be the inclusion of cross-gender supervision training in all Correctional Officer Academy courses. The Prison Rape Elimination Act was enacted by Congress to address rape and sexual assault in prison and to hold correctional agencies accountable. A warden at a state prison facility also offered strategies for staff working with female offenders:

1. Staff has to be aware and understand that there are gender related differences for women, both emotionally and physically. They treat and react to situations differently, mostly being emotional issues, as many are battered or abused in their life.
2. Most of our policies are geared towards the male offender and are sometimes difficult to manifest into female corrections. A great example is gang related issues. They do not place female gang members in administrative segregation based solely upon their memberships. Making it difficult to control and restrict participation, recruiting and extortion activities.
3. Women form relationships and bonds on a much broader scheme than do the males. Women form families while incarcerated and a much larger percentage participate in homosexual activities.

4. Women need to maintain a much closer contact with family and children than do men. They want to form closer relationships with staff and other offenders than the males do.
5. There is the perception that women are much more difficult to work with than men, therefore, they tend to have much more fluctuations in their attitudes each day.
6. Women offenders tend to assume a male staff member who is professional and courteous "likes" her. In some cases it is the first time she has been treated fairly or with compassion by a male. Consequently, they tend to try to establish relationships (many men unfortunately fall for this).

Paramount to all staff acting in an ethical and professional manner is that they remember that they are there for a job, not for social interaction and not to provide goods and services to offenders. Inmates will attempt to engage officers regardless of gender or sexual orientation into a relationship whether it is platonic or sexual.

Thinking Questions

1. What is cross-gender supervision?
2. What are the unique ethical challenges it brings?
3. What are strategies for ethical success for female officers? Male officers?

Inmates

Offenders are the final component of the correctional institution that plays a major role in the ethical conduct of those working within them. Without offenders, there would be no need for correctional institutions. Society has deemed it necessary to remove these individuals from wider society and place them into a correctional facility. The key to being an ethical corrections employee is to understand the nature and personality of the inmate, and also to know the types and forms of manipulative activity that they will attempt to engage in. The first portion of this section addresses typical inmate personalities.

Personality of Inmates

Retzlaff, Stoner, and Kleinsasser (2002) identified the three types of personalities that are most common among inmates:

The first is narcissistic personality. According to the Diagnostic and Statistical Manual of Mental Disorders (DSM-IV-R), an individual with Narcissistic Personality Disorder has at least five of the following qualities:

1. Grandiose feelings of self importance, and believes they should be recognized as superior, regardless of whether or not they have adequate achievements to back up their claims.
2. Pre-occupied with self-fulfilling fantasies.
3. Believes he or she is "special" and has unique problems understandable by high status or other "special" people.
4. Requires constant attention and admiration.
5. Feels over-entitled.
6. Exploitive.
7. Lacks empathy.
8. Preoccupied with feelings of envy.
9. Shows arrogant, haughty attitudes or behaviors.

Individuals with this type of personality are always looking out for themselves and generally view relationships as a way in which to obtain something. The offenders will try to exploit other offenders and staff in an attempt to make their prison time as comfortable as possible.

Antisocial personality is the second most common type of inmate personality, according to Retzlaff et al. (2002). Antisocial Personality Disorder is described by the following characteristics:

1. Failure to conform to social norms with respect to law abiding behavior. Actions that are grounds for arrest are performed repeatedly.
2. Deceitfulness in the form of lying repeatedly, conning others for personal gain or pleasure.
3. Impulsiveness: a failure to plan for the future.
4. Irritability/aggressiveness.
5. Risk taking behavior: disregard for the safety of themselves or others
6. Irresponsibility: Failure to sustain good work behavior, honor financial obligations.
7. Lack of remorse.

This type of offender blames their mistakes on others and never takes responsibility for their actions. This inmate is also looking for ways to "get one over" on the staff and may view staff as individuals to be "conned" for sex or other favors.

The final personality type is that of the Histrionic personality, of which offenders have the following characteristics:

1. Are uncomfortable unless he or she is the center of attention.
2. Shift emotions rapidly.
3. Act very dramatically as though performing before an audience with exaggerated emotions and expressions, yet appears to lack sincerity.
4. Constantly seek reassurance or approval.
5. Are gullible and easily influenced by others.
6. Are excessively sensitive to criticism or disapproval.
7. Have a low tolerance for frustration and are easily bored by routine, often beginning projects without finishing them or skipping from one event to another.
8. Do not think before acting.
9. Make rash decisions.
10. Are self-centered and rarely show concern for others.
11. Have difficulty maintaining relationships, often seeming fake or shallow in their dealings with others.
12. Threaten or attempt suicide to get attention (Cleveland Clinic, 2008).

Not every offender has the narcissistic, antisocial, or histrionic personality although they may exhibit traits from each one. It is also possible that the offender does not exhibit any of the above personality characteristics. Knowing the offender's personality is an important step in knowing the types of games they might play with staff. Inmates also live by an underground set of rules known as the inmate code.

Inmate Subculture/Code

Inmates go through a process called prisonization, learning how to manage within the institution and learning how to "get along" with staff members. According to Sykes (1958), there are five elements of the inmate code:

1. Don't interfere with inmate interests.
2. Don't fight with other inmates.
3. Don't exploit inmates.
4. Maintain yourself/be tough.
5. Don't trust guards or the things they stand for.

It has been argued that the inmate code is weakening, as offenders see benefits in ratting out other offenders, or running interference on another inmate's scam to gain favor with staff or administration. Each prison has its own inmate social atmosphere and elements of the inmate code are often in varying degrees at different levels. What can be gained from understanding the code and its relationship to ethical management of offenders is that staff and offenders live by different sets of norms. Offenders are often more than willing to cross the line and mingle with officers or other staff members, if it provides them with certain benefits. Knowing the offender mindset and how it fits into the subculture of the inmates will help staff members to avoid offender manipulation, which is discussed in the next portion of the chapter.

Thinking Questions

1. What are the three most common types of offender personalities according to Retzlaff et al. (2002)?
2. Which offender personality do you think poses the most ethical challenges to the staff?
3. What is the inmate code?
4. Hypothesize some of the other personality traits of offenders and how they might affect the ethics of staff members.

Avoiding Offender Manipulation

One of the ways in which employees begin to slide down the ethical slippery slope in corrections is through inappropriate relationships with inmates, by being manipulated by offenders, or both. While correctional officers are often susceptible to offender manipulation because of their continuous contact with offenders, it is important to emphasize that all persons who work in the institutional environment are potential targets. Offender manipulation occurs at many levels and with all types of staff members. If an individual believes they are not a potential target, they are mistaken. Inmates want to do time as easily and comfortably as possible and want to face as little interference from staff in their quest to do time their way. Not surprisingly, the inmates' desired way of doing time does not often coincide with institutional rules and regulations.

Officers and other prison staff control a variety of inmates' activities such as work assignments, access to the recreation yard, access in and out of the cellblock, telephone and TV use, mail, food, and control of possessions in their cell just to name a few. Manipulating or gaining additional access to some of these prison commodities can provide great benefit to the inmate. Gaining contraband can be done through the prison underground. Morgan Freeman's character Red, in *The Shawshank Redemption*, ran the underground prison store. Paying for some privileges or paying off gambling debts can come by paying for them through commissary items such as cigarettes, soups, soaps, sodas, or even sardines. Each desired privilege or contraband item has a price, dic-

tated by whoever is in control of the underground store. If the offender does *like me*
not wish to participate in this underground commodity or finds the prices too
high, they can try to obtain goods and services by getting them from officers
and other prison staff through manipulation and deception. Coinciding with
their desire to "take back" the control, offenders have time to watch and observe their "prey." Inmates who are continually sizing up officers are trying to
figure out if they are susceptible or have weaknesses that can be exploited. Worley and Cheeseman (2006) found that inmates watched for and sought out officers with certain perceived or observed characteristics. Table 7.2 provides an
overview of these characteristics.

Table 7.2

TYPE OF PROBLEM	CHARACTERISTICS
Social Isolation *This one sounds like me*	• Likely to be below average in appearance • Low self-esteem, shy • Limited opportunities for relationships in the outside world
Relationship Failures	• Abusive relationship • Sexually promiscuous • Recently separated or divorced
"Wild" Social Lives	• Comes to work tired and/or "hung over" • Sleeps on the job • Generally gregarious and outgoing
Financial Problems	• Likely to be perceived as "greedy" • Appearing to only want to make a "one-time, quick buck"
Job-Related Problems	• Does not get along well with supervisors • May identify more with inmates than other staff members • Is likely to have been disciplined before

Offenders see officers with problems as officers with potential to be "turned."
Through spending time getting to know how each officer thinks and feels, inmates may "groom" officers for sexual favors or to bring in contraband. Some
of these grooming techniques as observed by the author of this chapter are:

Friendly Fella: This inmate will generally talk about anything that they
observe as an interest of the officer. This may include sports, family,
cars, religion, or hobbies. This tactic is used to generate feelings that

he/she is not so different from me. This tactic may take many months to come to fruition and usually starts by asking for small things that appear benign at the outset but are used as a way of getting the officer to bring in bigger items (i.e., a piece of gum, a soda, etc.).

Prince Charming: This particular inmate is always there to lend a helping hand. They will offer to carry things for correctional staff or hold "jiggers" (prison slang for watching out for the staff member or when supervisors are headed in the staff member's direction). They are excruciatingly polite and always put themselves on the staff's side when staff are there (they may mock staff or make fun of staff after the shift to "save face" with the offender population). When dealing with officers of the opposite sex, these inmates will extend additional courtesies such as opening doors or attending to the correctional employee. This is often used in conjunction with the third type of offender technique.

Flattering and Complimenting Companion: Much like Prince Charming they attend to officers, but may not be so inclined to act out the "model inmate" role. These inmates engage in telling officers how attractive and how smart they are. These inmates pay meticulous attention to changes in hairstyle, perfume/cologne, weight, etc., complimenting each change, and spinning perceived negative changes into a way to pay positive attention to the employee (i.e., an officer's weight gain may turn into a comment about how the offender finds "thick" women attractive, or that the new look is healthy). It should also be noted that flattery is not singled out for staff members of the opposite sex, but can also be used on same-sex officers (i.e., "I saw your car in the parking lot the other day. Is that new? It's a sweet ride," or "I love your make-up, that color is great with your hair."). Comments like those above may seem benign or small, but to the offender, they are part of a large test. Gauging the reaction to the above comments allows them to take steps forward or alter the plan so that they can determine an area of weakness.

The Teammate: This offender watches to see which officers are in conflict and chooses to side with one, particularly if the offender has observed other weaknesses in the officer. The inmate will then "take up" for the one officer, while encouraging further discord and conflict behind the scenes. This offender will spread rumor and innuendo, while maintaining allegiance to the chosen officer.

These tactics are often used in conjunction with one another or in differentiating patterns dependent upon the needs/desires of the offender at the time, and the opportunities that present themselves. Offenders who are adept at manipulation know how much and with whom they will use their deception upon.

Cornelius (2001) discusses the CHUMPS approach as a way in which correctional officers and staff can avoid offender manipulation:

C = Controlling yourself and not being complacent
H = Helping offenders to help themselves
U = Understanding the offender subculture and understanding yourself
M = Maintain a safe distance
P = Practice professionalism in adhering to policies and procedures
S = Stopping yourself from being stressed out so you are not vulnerable (Cornelius, 2001, p. 72).

Controlling oneself and not being complacent are at the center of ethical correctional practices. Complacency breeds corruption, and if an employee fails to uphold or ignores rule violations offenders will take advantage of the situation and the officer. The following news article stresses how complacency can lead to serious consequences.

Box 7.3 Corrections in the News

New York State Department of Correctional Services — March 19, 2004

Commissioner: Staff complacency contributed to escape from Elmira prison

Commissioner Glenn S. Goord today released his report into the July 7, 2003, escape by two inmates from the maximum-security Elmira Correctional Facility in Chemung County.

The report concludes that complacency on the part of employees — from administrators to line staff, combined with the egregious behavior of three workers — contributed to the first escape in 19 years from the prison that today houses 1,840 inmates.

The report is available as an Adobe PDF under the Press Release section on the Department's website: www.docs.state.ny.us.

In the report, Commissioner Goord said, "The escape of inmates Timothy Vail and Timothy Morgan was avoidable. It resulted from complacency manifested in a widespread breakdown in Departmental practices, long-time policies and security procedures. The inmates recognized and took advantage of these lapses. Staff complacency allowed the inmates to identify, smuggle and utilize contraband and other material to enable their escape."

While most of the necessary corrective actions cited in the report were completed within the first few months following the escape, the report was withheld until Vail's sentencing this afternoon in Chemung County Court on the escape incident. Morgan had been sentenced last Oct. 31.

Commissioner Goord said, "There is little doubt that had there been strict adherence to established policy, procedure and practices, the escape would have been thwarted. The dedicated staff at Elmira last saw an escape in 1984. Its excellent record led to a mood of complacency, exhibited by staff over-familiarity with Vail, lax tool control, spotty inmate frisks and incomplete cell searches. Count procedures and perimeter security requirements were not followed. Failures in basic correctional practices, regarding supervision of inmates, alertness and observation, contributed to the inmates' success in escaping the proverbial 'security envelope' — the cell."

Three employees are being served with notices of discipline seeking their dismissal from state service. Served this morning at the prison were civilian instructor Gary Silvers and Correction Officer James Davenport. Correction Officer Richard Mustico will be served when he reports for his next duty assignment. They will continue to work as they undergo the disciplinary process.

In a letter to the public included in the report, Commissioner Goord said, "I want to assure the public and our employees that the Elmira Correctional Facility remains a secure work site, safe for the Chemung County community that surrounds it."

Investigators found that virtually all materials used in the escape were obtained from Carpentry Shop #4, including a sledgehammer head clearly stamped "Shop 6." The shop closed in the 1980s. It was later relocated and reopened as the current Shop #4. The sledgehammer head had since been used in Shop #4 as a door stop, until Vail smuggled it out to the double cell he and Morgan shared. The sledgehammer was not, as was alleged at the time of the escape, "stolen from a prison construction site" with "insufficient security staff coverage."

Vail had also been given a chair from the carpentry shop to take back to his cell. But, before doing so, he filled its hollow metal legs with approximately 100 screws that would be used to chip away at the concrete ceiling in the cell.

Vail also took a guide from a jointer planer in the carpentry shop and smuggled it to their double-cell, as well as a stabilizer bar from a table saw. Both were used to hammer screws into the concrete. Neither of these items, the sledgehammer head or the screws hidden within the chair legs were detected as the inmates smuggled them through prison security checkpoints back to their cell.

No contraband was discovered during three searches of their cell during the period the investigation found the inmates were implementing their escape plan.

The investigation also debunked allegations that noise from "blaring televisions" prevented officers from hearing the inmates hammering into the concrete ceiling of their cell. The cell from which the inmates escaped is 120 feet down the cell block, and three stories above, the single communal TV on the ground floor of the cell block. The officers' station is also on the first floor: 10 feet beyond the inmates' cell and then more than 20 feet down a side corridor. Those distances preclude noise from that TV from being a factor. There were only a handful of incidents in which staff issued inmates disciplinary tickets in recent months for refusing orders to follow regulations and use personal headphones to listen to their 12-inch, black-and-white in-cell televisions. Thus, sound from in-cell televisions did not present a diversion.

"Policies and procedures exist for a reason," Commissioner Goord said. "In any job site, work standards and expectations fall when complacency sets in. The staff at Elmira has recommitted itself since last summer to ensuring that all security procedures are now followed, and that accountability is being maintained in shops throughout the prison.

"I intend that this report will now become a self-auditing tool for every prison in the state," Commissioner Goord said. The state's 70 prisons today house 64,928 inmates.

(http://www.doccs.ny.gov/PressRel/2004/ElmiraEscape1.html)

Complacency can cause danger to those inside and outside of the facility. It is also important for a correctional employee to exert control over their actions and keep themselves "in check." As the one in charge of keeping offenders in line, the importance of being firm and remembering that their role is to enforce rules and maintain institutional order cannot be overlooked. Being mentally tough and staying strong are important components in maintaining control and avoiding offender manipulation. Offenders are often persistent and may ask for the same favor many different ways. As noted previously, "NO" said firmly and with conviction in a consistent manner will eventually allow offenders to see that the correctional staff member "sticks to their guns." As noted by Cornelius (2001), the job of the staff member is to be "nosy" and to ask questions as a way of controlling offenders. A key to control is awareness: awareness of offenders, what they can and cannot do, and what is going on around them. The most successful correctional staff are those that are thorough, yet efficient. Offenders will do their best to evoke sympathy, empathy, fear, or anything else that will cause the staff member to acquiesce to their request.

This leads us to the H, or helping offenders to help themselves. Cornelius (2001) notes that helping occurs when officers begin to help offenders understand accountability and responsibility for their actions. The officer must help the offenders to understand that there are boundaries and that they must follow them, much like members of society follow norms and laws. In essence, correctional staff can help offenders learn how to take care of themselves by forcing them to do so. They will ask for favors, ask correctional staff to fill out their paperwork, offer excuses and justifications. The best way for the staff to handle this is to ensure that offenders learn that actions have consequences. Offenders should be given the proper paperwork and information they need to become successful outside of prison, but they should follow the proper policies and procedures to get it. Another way in which staff members can help offenders to help themselves is by modeling good behavior. If a staff member fails to follow the rules, it is unreasonable to expect that an inmate will do so. Inmates observe officers to see who is ethical and who is not, so they can pick out potential marks for their "con games." Correctional officers who speak professionally and handle themselves with integrity and fairness can help offenders to model good behavior.

U signifies understanding the offender subculture and understanding yourself. While this chapter has already briefly discussed the offender subculture, one should remember the mindset of the inmate. This is not meant to imply that all offenders are bad people. Correctional institutions are places where offenders are deprived of certain goods and privileges, and generally, human nature dictates that we all, including inmates, want to live as comfortably as possible. Personal self awareness of strengths and weaknesses prevents becoming ensnared in ethical pitfalls, such as offender manipulation.

Correctional staff members need to be aware of, or notice a change in personal attitude. Also, correctional officers should be cautious about sharing too much personal information with an offender. This ties in with the idea of complacency, in that staff begin to see offenders as "friends," and share things that they should not. Taking an inventory of oneself is not any easy task, but honest self assessment is important in maintaining an ethical demeanor and relationship with offenders. The M, in the CHUMPS approach by Cornelius (2001), is maintaining a safe distance. This is one of the most important ways that staff members can avoid offender manipulation and stay ethical and professional. Correctional employees are taught to maintain a boundary between staff and offenders, and yet many offenders will spend hours trying to weaken this boundary line. As noted above in inmate grooming styles, offenders will use many techniques to get closer to staff members including:

- Flattery/you are the only one — "You look so nice today," "You are the best teacher I have ever had," etc.
- Common ground — we both like football, we are the same religion, we are not so different ("we would be friends on the outside").
- Favors or extra work — offenders getting your coffee, waiting on you, willing to do extra work for you.
- Companionship/socialization — talking to a staff member about "mundane" things, noticing changes in a staff member and providing a shoulder to lean on, or someone to talk to if the staff member just needs to talk.

Many of these tactics are used to create the ultimate boundary violation—romantic and/or sexual involvement with the correctional worker. It is also very important to note that offenders are open to sexual relationships in many cases with same sex employees as well as opposite sex employees. This being said, no one is off limits when it comes to engaging in staff and offender relationships. With the increase of female correctional officers working in male institutions, it is not uncommon for female staff to become entangled in inappropriate relationships with male offenders.

Box 7.4 Floyd County Corrections Officer
Admitted Having Sex with Inmate

News & Tribune—August 9, 2008

A former Floyd County Corrections Officer admitted to having sex with an inmate and even going to his mother's house to get pills for him, according to a probable cause affidavit filed in the Superior Court Wednesday.

Michelle A. Hurst, 39, of Borden, told detectives that she had sexual intercourse with an inmate, 31-year-old Craig Proctor, on at least two occasions in July. She also gave Proctor oral sex two other times, she told police.

From June 12 to June 23, Proctor made 40 calls to Hurst's cell phone. In the phone calls which were taped, Hurst discussed how she was going to bring tobacco products and a cell phone delivered to him in his jail cell.

Hurst also said she went to Proctor's mother's house three times and had his mother give her pills to take to give Proctor, according to the affidavit. She brought him two loratabs and three other pills, she said.

On another occasion, she brought him Makers Mark and Wild Turkey whiskey and an MP3 player.

Hurst was employed by the Floyd County Sheriff's Department from April 5 until July 21, 2008. Sheriff Darrell Mills said she was still on probationary status, and he was able to fire her immediately after hearing of allegations.

Detectives officially began investigating Aug. 4, according to the affidavit.

Mills said that he monitors his employees closely and does not tolerate anything unprofessional.

"This shows that the system is working," Mills said.

Hurst was charged with sexual misconduct by a service provider and trafficking with an inmate, both class C felonies. She was also charged with trafficking with an inmate, as a class A misdemeanor.

A class C felony is punishable by two to eight years in prison and up to a $10,000 fine.

Hurst's next court appearance is scheduled for Monday. Bond was set at $50,000.

While many new officers and employees are susceptible to relationships with offenders, staff members with many years of experience can also be manipulated. It is very important to keep a safe distance from offenders physically and emotionally. There should always be a safe distance zone from which offenders must stay away from staff members (an arm's length minimum is a good starting point). Offenders will continually try to test these boundaries and see if the officer will stand their ground. P in the CHUMPS approach stands for practicing professionalism in adhering to policies and procedures (Cornelius, 2001). As noted earlier in the chapter, to be a corrections professional who is ethical is to know the policies and procedures and to follow them consistently and regularly with all offenders. Included with professionalism is how an officer comes to work. Offenders are less likely to try to manipulate officers who follow grooming standards and come to the prison dressed in a neat uniform. Offenders often perceive officers who come to work dressed in wrinkled attire as not caring about the institution or the policies and procedures. Professionalism is a large part in detracting offenders from attempting to manipulate staff and in presenting an image that offenders can respect and emulate. The final part of the CHUMPS approach is stopping oneself from being stressed out (to avoid becoming vulnerable). Regardless of career choice, stress and job burnout can cause individuals to do things they would never have considered under other circumstances. Knowing and recognizing signs of stress and turning to positive coping mechanisms to alleviate the stress will help correctional employees from facing dismissal or disciplinary actions, due to the stress that caused them to become vulnerable to offender manipulation.

Thinking Questions

1. Why do offenders try to manipulate staff members?
2. What are the types of offender grooming techniques?
3. What does CHUMPS stand for?
4. What are some ways that staff can guard against offender manipulation?

Conclusion

Ethics in the correctional environment is the key to running a safe and effective correctional institution. Violations in ethics can lead to drugs in the institution, an increase in gang activity, an increase in weapons, riots, and in some cases, death. Ethical violations also undermine public confidence in correctional institutions and the criminal justice system. Correctional staff members at all levels within the institution impact how offenders do their time. Understanding the institution's environment, types of staff members, and the inmates that are housed there can give anyone considering a career in corrections insight into the types of situations that one might face. Correctional institutions are tough environments where staff members are asked to make large numbers of offenders follow the rules, while the offenders are attempting to find ways of getting around the rules. Correctional facilities are looking for quick thinking, mentally tough individuals who can and want to do a good job. Becoming an effective employee begins and ends with ethics. Without ethics, or a solid foundation in knowing what you can and cannot do both inside and outside of the institution, correctional employees run the risk of placing themselves in harm's way, literally or metaphorically.

Scenarios

1. You are a correctional officer assigned to a medium security facility. Part of your assigned duty is to screen offender mail for content and suspicious activity. Upon scanning a letter from Offender Smith you notice that he alludes to the fact that he is trying to get an unnamed staff member to bring in contraband for him and is expecting their first delivery this week. What do you do?

   a. What if the officer mentioned is your best friend? What if the officer mentioned is your worst enemy? What if it is your supervisor? What if the person mentioned is the warden?

2. You have a "trustee" work crew who is cleaning the administrative office area of the facility after administration has gone home. You see an officer you want to talk to but that would leave the inmate alone in the human resource area. What do you do?

   a. What if a supervisor calls you over to speak to you?

3. You are working with a female officer and you notice that a male inmate is spending large amounts of time talking with the female officer, including after rack time and lights out. The female officer is a senior officer with 10 years of experience. How do you handle the situation?

   a. What if the female officer is new with 2 months of experience? What if the officer is male and the inmate is female? What if the officer and the inmate are of the same gender?

4. You are off duty and go out to dinner in a nearby town 30 miles away. At the restaurant you notice a fellow correctional officer eating dinner with family members you have seen visiting an inmate at your facility. How do you handle the situation?

   a. What if the person having dinner with the correctional officer is a former inmate? What if the correctional officer is having dinner with a supervisor (you can clearly see that the dinner is romantic and not platonic)?

5. While at home watching the local news you see footage from a bank robbery. One of the robbers looks identical to a correctional counselor at your facility. The police have set up a hotline for information. How do you proceed?

6. While doing a cellblock search during a unit lockdown you notice that Supervisor Green is taking snack cakes and food items from offenders. You see the supervisor and he offers you a snack cake as he passes by commenting, "grocery shopping at its finest." How do you handle the situation?

   a. What if the supervisor was taking jewelry? Does it change if the offender is not present when the "taking" occurs? What if the offender does not speak up when the item(s) is taken? What if the offender calls you in to testify on his behalf?

7. A male offender comes up to you and tells you that he has been raped by another male offender. You have seen the two offenders together constantly and most staff and inmates assume they are a "couple." How do you proceed with the allegation?

   a. What if a female inmate claimed she had been raped by a female inmate? What if the inmate alleges sexual misconduct from a staff member? What if the inmate is a known complainer who is always looking to sue the institution?

8. You are a laundry officer. While doing tool and product inventory before taking over the shift you notice that 5 gallons of a chemical is missing (this chemical is sometimes used by inmates to huff or get high). The officer on the shift before you is known for allowing inmates to use as little or as much of the chemicals as they want and being very lax with offender shakedowns. When you ask him where the chemicals have gone he just shrugs his shoulders and comments that no one really cares about the inventory. What do you do?

   a. What if the warden has just issued a crackdown on contraband?

9. You are doing a cell search with an officer and you notice him putting pictures in his pocket. When you ask him what he is doing he tells you that he is going to add them to his "prison picture collection." He tells you that he has hundreds of pictures from inmates that he has collected over the years. What do you do?

   a. What if the officer is taking soft-core pornography magazines?

10. You are about to take over shift at the perimeter tower (picket). When doing your inventory, you notice that a round of ammunition is missing. The officer offers to go to the store and get matching ammo to replace the missing round. What do you do?

11. You are invited to a shift party after work and by the time you arrive many of your co-workers are intoxicated. You notice two officers "making out" who you know are both married to other people. A friend and fellow officer comes up to you and offers you a hit off his "pipe." How do you handle the situation?

12. You are working the post near the front entry at 2 in the morning. You are in charge of deciding who can initially come into the institution. The assistant warden come to the front door and appears to be intoxicated and smells like alcohol. The assistant warden demands entry on to the facility even though it is against policy to let anyone into the facility under the influence of drugs and alcohol. What do you do?

13. You are the video camera operator for a cell extraction. The use of force has turned ugly and the lieutenant tells you to cut the tape, even though you see that the situation with the inmate is not resolved and it is against agency policy to turn off the camera. The inmate is screaming, officers are screaming and you notice a pool of blood forming by the inmate's head. How do you handle the situation?

   a. What if there is no pool of blood and the inmate appears to not be suffering or in any duress? What do you write in your report? What if you are called into to court to testify about what you saw and what would you say on the stand?

14. An inmate has been asking you for various items all day which are nuisance items and against regulations (i.e., extra toilet paper, going to the recreation yard after last call for recreation, bringing chow hall food into the cellblock). You have told the inmate "no" and the offender is growing in agitation. The offender tells you to kiss his ass and that you are a @&%#* piece of ^%#@$. What do you do?

References

American Correctional Association (1993). *National Standards*. Lanham, MD: American Correctional Association.

Anderson, J. (February, 2015). Former gang leader at center of jail scandal sentenced. *The Baltimore Sun*. Retrieved from: http://www.baltimoresun.com/news/maryland/crime/blog/bs-md-ci-tavon-white-sentencing-20150209-story.html.

Britton, D.M. (1997). Perceptions of the work environment among correctional officers: Do race and sex matter? *Criminology*, 35(1), 85–105.

Bureau of Justice Statistics (2013). Prisoners in 2013. Retrieved May 15, 2015 from http://www.bjs.gov/index.cfm?ty=pbdetail&iid=5109.

Calhoun, A.J., & Coleman, H.D. (2002). Female inmates' perspectives on sexual abuse by correctional personnel: an exploratory study. *Women & Criminal Justice*. 13(2/3), 101–124.

Christian Ministries to Offenders (2006). Ministry Training Materials.

Clear, T., Cole, G., & Resig, M. (2010). *American Corrections*. Florence, KY: Wadsworth Publishing.

Cornelius, G. (2001). *The art of the con*. Lanham, MD: American Correctional Association.

Crouch, B.M., & Marquart, J.W. (1990). Resolving the paradox of reform: Litigation, prisoner violence, and perceptions of risk. *Justice Quarterly*, 7, 103–123.

Crouch, B., & Marquart, J. (1980). On becoming a prison guard. pp. 63–106 in *The Keepers: Prison guards and contemporary corrections*, edited by B. Crouch. Springfield, IL: Charles Thomas Publishers.

Cullen, F.T., Link, B.G., Wolfe, N.T., & Frank, J. (1985). The social dimensions of correctional officer stress. *Justice Quarterly*, 2, 505–533.

del Carmen, R., Ritter, S., & Witt, B. (2002). *Briefs of Leading Cases in Corrections*. Cincinnati, OH: Anderson Publishing.

Dial, K.C. (2007). Training Day: A Typology of Correctional Academy Trainees and the Academy Experience. *American Criminal Justice Association LAE Journal*. December 2007.

Glenn, L.B. (2001). *The largest hotel chain in Texas*. Austin, TX: Eakin.

Graham, C. (1981). Women are succeeding in male institutions. In B.H. Olsson (ed.)*Women in Corrections*, 27–36. American Correctional Association.

Hepburn, J.R. (1985). The exercise of power in coercive organizations: A study of prison guards. *Criminology, 23*, 145–164.

Josi, D.A., & Sechrist, D.K. (1998). *The changing career of the correctional officer: Policy implications for the 21st century*. Boston: Butterworth-Heniemann.

Jurik, N.C. (1988). Striking a balance: Female correctional officers, gender role stereotypes, and male prisons. *Sociological Inquiry, 58*, 291–305.

Kauffman, K. (1988) *Prison officers and their world.* Cambridge, MA: Harvard University Press.

Lambert, E.G., Hogan, N.L., & Barton, S.M. (2002). Satisfied correctional staff: A review of the literature on the correlates of correctional staff job satisfaction. *Criminal Justice and Behavior, 29,* 115–143.

Marquart, J.W. (1986). Prison guards and the use of physical coercion as a mechanism of prisoner control. *Criminology, 24,* 347–366.

Marquart, J.W., Maldine, B.B., & Balshaw-Biddle, K. (2001). Fatal attraction: An analysis of employee boundary violations in a southern prison system, 1995–1998. *Justice Quarterly, 18,* 878–891.

Roberts, J. (1997). *Reform and retribution: An illustrated history of American prisons.* Lanham, MD: American Correctional Association.

Sykes, G. (1958). *The society of captives.* Princeton, NJ: Princeton University Press.

Texas Department of Criminal Justice Human Resources (2008). *Correctional Officer profile Data.* Huntsville, TX: Texas Department of Criminal Justice.

Worley, R., & Cheeseman, K. (2006). Guards as embezzlers: The consequences of "nonshareable problems" in prison settings. *Deviant Behavior, 22,* 203–222.

Additional Websites

http://www.baltimoresun.com/services/newspaper/printedition/wednesday/maryland/bal-md.mcguinn05mar05,0,6697262.story

http://www.insideprison.com

http://www.innocentinmates.org/vanstory/prisonlike.html

http://www.corrections.govt.nz/public/pdf/safety/pps-wwmp.pdf

http://www.apsu.edu/oconnort/3300/3300lect06.htm

http://www.prisoncommission.org/public_hearing_1.asp

http://www.aca.org

http://www.nicic.org

8

Ethics in Probation, Parole, and Community Corrections

Chapter Objectives

- The student will understand how community corrections differs from institutional corrections
- The student should be aware of the many roles that community corrections staff play
- The student will identify the unique challenges that officers face in the community
- The student will understand how offender management effects ethics
- The student will gain knowledge about the different personality types of probation/parole officers
- The student will become aware of the types of offender manipulation that occur in probation, parole and community corrections
- The student will learn practical strategies to use in avoiding offender manipulation
- The student will be given tools to become a professional and ethical community correctional employee

Introduction

As noted in Chapter 7, corrections is the part of the criminal justice system that carries out the sentence imposed by the courts. Specifically, community corrections is a term that is used to describe punishments that are generally completed outside of prison walls or fences. This could include a variety of punishments or sentences including, but not limited to:

- *Probation*—The release into the community of a defendant who has been found guilty of a crime, typically under certain conditions, such as paying a fine, doing community service or attending a drug treatment program. Violation of the conditions can result in incarceration.

- *Parole*—Any form of release of an offender from imprisonment to the community by a releasing authority prior to the expiration of his sentence, subject to conditions imposed by the releasing authority and to its supervision, including a term of supervised release.
- *Work camps*—Work camps are minimum security facilities where offenders often live while they are not working. Offenders generally work during the day (for the agency that is imposing their sentence) and then stay in the facility during non-working hours. Many work camps have more freedom than traditional correctional facilities and are often used as an alternative to traditional incarceration or as a pre-release program for offenders who are getting out of jail or prison soon.
- *Boot camps* (shock incarceration programs)—Short-term prison programs run like military basic training for young offenders, adult and youthful felons.
- *Intensive supervision probation*—Intensive Probation places tightened restriction on defendants who cannot comply with or who are not appropriate for standard probation supervision. It is often seen as the "last chance" prior to a prison sentence. Enhanced supervision may include curfew restrictions, increased office and home visits, increased alcohol and drug testing and stricter fee collections.
- *House arrest/Home detention*—Under a house arrest program, the offender serves a jail sentence in their own residence rather than in a jail or prison cell. The person, in some cases, wears an electronic monitoring device. Individuals serving this type of sentence are generally allowed to leave home for work or as determined by the probation/parole officer.
- *Work release*—Work release programs generally allow greater freedom in which offenders who follow a Monday–Friday work week attend work and live at their homes on those days, and serve their sentences two days at a time on weekends. Depending on the terms of the program, the prisoner may serve his or her sentence in a halfway house or home confinement while not working. Other work release programs can be offered to prisoners who are nearing the end of their terms and looking for a reintegration into civilian life, with a possible offer of full-time employment once the offender is released.
- *Non-residential drug and alcohol programs*—Programs designed to treat an offender's drug and/or alcohol addiction through outpatient treatment and counseling.
- *Electronic monitoring*—Electronic monitoring allows the release of a person into the community, during what could of otherwise been time in jail,

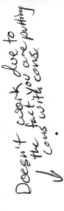

requiring the individual to record his or her whereabouts at all times or on regular intervals using electronic or telecommunication devices.

- *Halfway house*—A halfway house is a residence designed to assist persons, especially those leaving institutions, to reenter society and learn to adapt to independent living. Halfway houses aim to assist in community transition, and may provide vocational training, counseling, and other services.

The task of community corrections is generally placed on the shoulders of probation and parole personnel. The American Probation and Parole Association (APPA) is an international association composed of members from the United States, Canada and other countries actively involved with probation, parole and community-based corrections, in both adult and juvenile sectors. All levels of government including local, state/provincial, legislative, executive, judicial, and federal agencies are counted among its members (APPA, 2010). Probation and parole are terms that *should not* be used interchangeably.

People charged with a crime and placed on probation serve their sentence in the community under the supervision of a probation officer and must adhere to specific conditions which are set by the judge. A sentence of probation is, in most cases, accompanied by a "suspended sentence" to imprisonment (Alarid & del Carmen, 2010). As long as probationers adhere to the designated conditions of their probation, they remain free in the community. If a probationer violates the conditions, however, his or her probation can be revoked (terminated) and the offender may be sent to prison to finish the term of the original sentence. A violation of a condition of probation is not necessarily an automatic revocation. The revocation is always up to the Judge. They are the only persons allowed to revoke a probation sentence. The officer and/or State can request revocation but it is ultimately up to the Judge. For example, someone who is given a sentence of three years probation also receives a suspended three year sentence to prison. If, on the last day of the second year of probation the probationer's probation status is revoked (terminated), he or she will be sent to prison for the remaining one year in order to complete the original sentence.

Parole, on the other hand, is a conditional early release from prison which, like probation, is served in the community, under supervision, and is subject to specific conditions. How early prisoners are released in their prison sentence depends, in part, on how well they behave while in prison. The amount of time taken off the end of their original prison sentence is called "good time." For every day an inmate behaves properly in prison, good time may be awarded (Alarid & del Carmen, 2010). The grounds upon which an inmate accumulates good time varies from state to state, as well as how and when a prisoner is eligible for parole, if at all. Parole, like probation, can also be revoked if the conditions are violated. Parolees who violate the conditions of their parole may be sent back to prison to complete their sentence. Revocation of parole is also often at the discretion of the parole officer (Hanser, 2009).

The environment of community corrections is quite different than that of institutional corrections. In a prison or jail, many variables are accounted for and offenders have limited access to items such as drugs and/or alcohol. In the community, offenders have access to many types of illegal substances, as well as opportunities to break the law or break the conditions of their proba-tion/parole. Because offenders on probation and other community sanctions have more contact with the "free world," those tasked with ensuring that they follow the conditions of their sentences have more discretion than correctional officers. This chapter will discuss the role that probation and parole officers play in the criminal justice system and the unique challenges that they face. Particular emphasis will be placed on how these particular criminal justice professionals deal with ethical dilemmas and decision making.

Thinking Questions

1. What are some of the types of community corrections?
2. How are probation and parole similar? How are they different?
3. What is the APPA?
4. What role do probation and parole officers play in community corrections? Why is ethics so important to them?

The Personnel of Community Corrections

Traditionally, the most prominent of community corrections jobs is that of the probation officer. Probation officers are different than other correctional officers in many aspects. As a general rule most probation officers are required to have a Bachelor's degree (typically a degree in the behavioral or social sci-ences) whereas correctional officers are generally only required to have a GED or high school diploma. Probation officers also have a great deal of discretion, particularly in comparison to correctional officers, and are less restricted by policy manuals and rule books. One other major area of difference is that pro-bation officers are often certified peace officers and have powers afforded to law enforcement officers (i.e., powers of arrest) such as being allowed to carry a gun. Discretion, as noted in previous chapters has a profound effect on the way in which a criminal justice professional does their job. Discretion is also an area in which individuals can get into ethical "hot water," by taking the boundaries of discretion too far.

Probation officers serve many functions and generally are housed under a local or state judicial system. One of those most distinctive aspects of the probation officer's job is the dual function that is an inherent part of the work. Probation officers perform both investigative and supervision functions. As noted in a Massachusetts job posting, probation officers are required to fill many roles.

The probation officer, under the direct supervision of the chief probation officer, first assistant chief probation officer, or assistant chief probation officer, investigates thoroughly offender personal history, background and environment; reports findings to the court and is prepared to make appropriate recommendations on dispositions; periodically interviews probationers to determine the effectiveness of probation supervision and areas in which casework counseling are needed; refers probationers to social resources in the community for assistance in rehabilitation; enforces court orders; recommends revoking of probation and/or modification of court orders when necessary (http://www.mass.gov/courts/probation/po.html).

Probation officers are asked to do many things, which all have an impact on offenders and members of the community that they serve. In order for officers to known what is expected of them the APPA has established a code of ethics. Box 8.1 outlines the APPA's Code of Ethics.

Box 8.1 APPA Code of Ethics

1. I will render professional service to the justice system and the community at large in effecting the social adjustment of the offender.

2. I will uphold the law with dignity, displaying an awareness of my responsibility to offenders while recognizing the right of the public to be safeguarded from criminal activity.

3. I will strive to be objective in the performance of my duties, recognizing the inalienable right of all persons, appreciating the inherent worth of the individual, and respecting those confidences which can be reposed in me.

4. I will conduct my personal life with decorum, neither accepting nor granting favors in connection with my office.

5. I will cooperate with my co-workers and related agencies and will continually strive to improve my professional competence through the seeking and sharing of knowledge and understanding.

6. I will distinguish clearly, in public, between my statements and actions as an individual and as a representative of my profession.

7. I will encourage policy, procedures and personnel practices, which will enable others to conduct themselves in accordance with the values, goals and objectives of the American Probation and Parole Association.

8. I recognize my office as a symbol of public faith and I accept it as a public trust to be held as long as I am true to the ethics of the American Probation and Parole Association. (APPA, 2010)

Probation and parole officers serve the entire community and are asked to consider both the needs of the offender and the needs of the citizens within the community (including the victims). This can be an almost impossible task as these officers often have large caseloads and may have more than one role they are asked to play (Alarid & del Carmen, 2010).

The Probation and Parole Officer Subculture

As noted in previous chapters, both police officers and correctional officers are part of a subculture. The subculture of probation and parole officers is not perceived to be as prevalent as that of correctional officers or police officers and research on this subculture is not nearly as prominent. Because of their higher levels of education, more autonomous work environment, integration into the community, the need for a subculture or for group cohesiveness may be seen as unnecessary. As noted by Pollock (2010), there are three general characteristics that could be found among a group of community corrections employees:

1. *Individualism*—Because each officer oversees their own caseload it is expected that they will manage this and make decisions about what is best for their clients and the community with little input from others in their office. Consultation on small levels will often occur. To offer unsolicited opinions or to openly criticize another officer's decisions would be seen as a violation of the autonomy and flexibility given to community corrections personnel. In particular, seasoned officers would find help or opinions unwanted or, in some cases, even offensive.

2. *Lethargy (Apathy)*—This term refers to the idea that personnel should have a low level of overall work output. In general, community corrections personnel are perceived as overworked and underpaid and to go above and beyond for the agency would be seen as having little benefit for the employee. Also, as caseloads increase and the number of officers decrease, officers may feel as though they will never be able

to manage the workload and may feel compelled to "give up" or see little value in doing "extra" work.

3. *Cynicism*—Working with criminals is not an easy task. Officers, from
the very beginning (through training and working with other officers), may view offenders as untrustworthy, devious, and not worth
attempting to rehabilitate. If officers do believe in the goodness and
capacity for change in their clients they may face ridicule or be ostracized by the other officers.

These attitudes and beliefs can have a profound effect on how the officers work
their caseloads and how they perceive other officers and the profession in general. Secondly, cynicism and apathy can lead probation officers to take short-
cuts which can cause them to act unethically. Officers who do little or no work
may not be properly supervising offenders and may be overlooking obvious
criminal activity which could be harming the public they are tasked with protecting. It could also be argued that by not doing a job they are getting paid
to do, they are being unethical.

Much in the same way that correctional officers develop strategies to deal with
working in a prison, so too do probation and parole officers adapt to their
unique work environment by taking on different roles to handle the job. The
type of officers that they are also heavily influences their personal and professional ethics. Klockars (1972) came up with a typology of four main types of
community corrections officers:

1. *Law Enforcers*—Officers who see themselves as law enforcers view
obeying the law as essential and focus on the authority and enforcement aspects of their jobs. Officers who fall into this category
emphasize their court-ordered authority to carry out their duties
and tend to write up most, if not all, violations of the conditions of
probation.

2. *Time Servers*—Time servers are similar in philosophy to law enforcers,
but are unwilling to change their ways and are not concerned with
using new technologies or new policies. These officers choose not to
go over any expectation and do the minimum work requirements as
outlined in their department policy. It could be said that they just follow the rules and make no attempt to understand or change them.

3. *Therapeutic Agents*—These officers see their roles as rehabilitators and
agents of social change. They are willing to help motivate positive
changes in offenders and encourage them to see the value in living as
productive members of society. They may see themselves more as a
counselor and life coach and show offenders on their caseload respect

and concern, desiring for them to succeed in integrating themselves back into society.

4. *Synthetic Officer*—This officer sees the value and necessity in balancing both the law enforcement and therapeutic aspects of their work. They attempt to balance the authoritarian and helping aspects of the profession, although this can cause role conflict for the officer.

As noted by Alarid and del Carmen (2010) officers may or may not hold on to one type of work style for their career, although the combination of personality and work style tends to determine how an officer will interact with offenders. The type of community corrections officer a person chooses to be will have a great impact on the ethical orientation of the officer as well. Law enforcers might be more prone to ethical violations that involve exaggerating on a violation report to get the offender sent to jail/prison. The time server might overlook violations because they do not want the hassle of the paperwork or having to add additional face-to-face meetings to their caseload. Conversely, the therapeutic agent might overlook a violation because they believe the offender deserves a second chance, although this could be viewed as unethical, depending upon the type of crime the offender committed. Everyone is susceptible to ethical violations regardless of personality or job orientation.

Thinking Questions

1. What are the three general characteristics of community corrections personnel? Which do you see as the most important in relationship to ethics?
2. What are the four types of probation officers?
3. What ethical violations could occur based on probation officer orientation?
4. How is the community corrections subculture different than the correctional officer or police subculture?

Fulfilling the Dual Roles: An Ethical Challenge for Probation Officers

One of the main areas in which probation officers have discretion is in the area of making sentencing recommendations to the court. In the area of investigation the probation officer is tasked with conducting Pre-Sentence Investigation Reports (PSI). The court generally orders a PSI after an offender's conviction or submission of a guilty plea. The judge then uses it to guide their decision in sentencing an offender and may also serve as a guide in determining classification decisions once an offender is placed in the correctional system. A PSI normally begins with the officer collecting basic background information from the offender and then clarifying and verifying for accuracy. PSIs also contain information on prior criminal history, IQ, work history, drug and alcohol use, social history and a sentencing recommendation. According to Clear, Cole, and Resig (2011) judges follow the PSI sentencing recommendation 70–90% of the time.

Clearly, the PSI is a document that potentially holds within it a great deal of power. If probation officers fail to verify information or fail to consider information with objectivity, serious ethical violations could occur. Because of high caseloads, officers may casually look over or not re-check every detail in the PSI. Additionally, an offender could potentially face prejudice based on a probation officers thoughts and feelings about their background and criminal history. Because judges, more often than not, follow the sentencing recommendations, there is enormous potential for officers to abuse or misuse the power, discretion and authority given to them. Even if it is just a human mistake or clerical error, a blunder on a PSI has the possibility to mean the difference between time in jail or probation. Acting ethically in community corrections begins with how personnel conduct the PSI, since it is a foundational part of sentencing and impacts not only the offender, but the victim and society in general.

Probation officers also deal with family members in a much closer proximity than many other criminal justice professionals. In many cases, officers meet with offenders in their homes and encounter family members who may be hostile or who resent the fact that their family member is on probation. Additionally, family members might be involved in criminal enterprise and may be a negative influence on the offender. Family members can, however, be a great help in keeping an offender from re-offending. Having supportive family members who encourage the offender and help them from falling back into crime can be a valuable resource to both the offender and the probation officer.

Probation officers must be mindful of maintaining a professional demeanor when dealing with family members (and all members of the community). Additionally, officers must also maintain a safe physical and emotional distance from offenders and family members so as to not become targets of manipulation or become entangled in inappropriate relationships.

Box 8.2 Ethics in the News

Los Angeles Times—February 21, 2010

At least 11 Los Angeles County juvenile probation officers have been convicted of crimes or disciplined in recent years for inappropriate conduct involving current or former probationers, including several cases of molesting or beating youths in their care, a *Times* investigation has found.

Additionally, two other officers are the focus of internal affairs investigations for allegedly having sex with probationers.

The Times identified the cases through court documents, law enforcement records and department sources. Probation officials said they were prohibited by law from discussing the details of officers' misconduct.

Among the incidents:

- A probation officer had sex with three youths in the detention hall where she worked—in laundry, supply and interview rooms. She was sentenced last year to four years in prison after pleading guilty to five counts of felony sexual abuse.

- A probation officer caught on tape beating a youth in a juvenile hall recreation room was convicted last year of battery and sentenced to 24 months' probation.

- A probation officer was sentenced to a year in jail last year for directing five teenagers under her care to beat another youngster who she mistakenly believed had stolen her cellphone.

Los Angeles County probation officers are responsible for protecting 3,000 youths in 21 halls and camps, one of the nation's largest juvenile justice systems.

The department, with an annual budget of about $700 million, has been the subject of federal investigations in recent years for failing to prevent, report and document child abuse.

The Times examined records from the last four years—a period during which county officials hired Robert Taylor to head the agency with the mandate of reforming the department, including providing better oversight of officers. At the time he took over, the department was struggling with violence in its halls and camps and persistent criticism that it was doing little to help the juvenile offenders in its care.

Probation officials have sustained 102 allegations of officer misconduct involving youths at the county's halls and camps over the last three years, according to a department source who asked not to be identified because he was not authorized to release the information publicly. The source said many of the sustained cases involved complaints of excessive force. Department officials did not disclose how many officers were involved in misconduct or the extent of any discipline.

Taylor retired Feb. 5. Former Ventura County probation chief Cal Remington was appointed as acting chief to assess the department before the new chief, Alameda County probation chief Donald H. Blevins, takes over April 19.

During his tenure, Taylor said he tried to be more proactive than his predecessors, coordinating undercover internal investigations with the Los Angeles County Sheriff's Department.

For example, he said a probation sting with sheriff's deputies at Central Juvenile Hall in 2008 led to the arrest of a probation officer suspected of dealing marijuana to youths. The officer was fired, but has not been criminally charged, according to county officials.

"Unfortunately, we have people who fail to meet expectations and when they do, we deal with them with a disciplinary system that is swift and sure and produces the desired outcome," Taylor said. He said he did not consider the current personnel problems any worse than what other large law enforcement agencies face.

Taylor acknowledged at least one effort to monitor staff and probationers has fallen short: Many of the more than 600 security cameras at county detention halls and camps are broken. Last month, county supervisors approved spending $1.2 million to determine how best to replace some cameras and other security equipment at a juvenile camp and three halls.

Many critics say poor oversight has hampered the department's efforts to identify abusive staff.

Two years ago, federal investigators found that the department failed to investigate and document officer abuses, including excessive use of force on probationers.

The department has eight internal affairs investigators to review hundreds of complaints leveled against 6,200 probation officers each year, including about 2,900 sworn officers working with juveniles. By contrast, the Los Angeles Police Department has 271 internal affairs investigators for 9,900 sworn officers; the Los Angeles County Sheriff's Department has about 30 internal affairs investigators for about 10,000 sworn officers.

A 15-member probation commission appointed by county supervisors is supposed to monitor the department and advise the probation chief. Commissioners can ask the probation chief to investigate alleged misconduct, and if probation officials fail to take action, they can bring complaints to county supervisors. But they rarely do and have never forced the department to disclose probation personnel records, said commission President Don Meredith, a retired Glendale police lieutenant.

"When we bring it up, they say they can't discuss it with us because it's internal matters, confidential," Commissioner Jo Kaplan said of the alleged misconduct. "We have no oversight."

Teachers who work at probation camps and halls are required by law to report suspected abuse but often don't because they are afraid of the consequences, said Mark Lewis, president of the teachers union, the Los Angeles County Education Assn.

"There is this belief that if I report something or file a child abuse report against a probation officer, that probation is not going to come when I need them ... or they're going to set me up," Lewis said. "So there is a tendency not to report."

Even if someone wanted to report misconduct, they may have found it difficult: The phone number on websites and signs posted in the halls and camps for the Probation Department's ombudsman was inoperable until three weeks ago, when a spokeswoman responding to calls from The Times said an "urgent work order" had been submitted to repair it.

* * *

Former Probation Officer Kimberly Hald, 37, describes herself as a "soccer mom" who made some bad decisions during a difficult time in her life. Prosecutors say she's a predator who had sex with three teenage boys—ages 16 to 18—at a detention hall for more than a year.

Starting in August 2006, Hald had sexual encounters with the teenagers at Central Juvenile Hall where she worked as a probation officer, according to court records. She bought her victims' silence with treats, including hall passes, food from home and cellphone access, the records show.

Hald became infatuated with the probationers, prosecutors said, sending them letters with provocative photos of herself. She even got a tattoo with the initials of one of the youths.

Hald was caught when one of the youths resisted her advances in a hallway, a scuffle ensued, and he reported her, according to prosecutors. Even after she was arrested and suspended from her probation job, Hald continued to visit the youth at the jail and gave him money. She was later convicted of sexual abuse and sentenced to four years in prison.

Taylor said it would have been difficult to catch Hald because she was well-educated and showed no signs of misconduct. "She was a married mother of three children with advanced college degrees," he said.

Hald declined to be interviewed. But in a letter sent from prison in response to an inquiry from The Times, she blamed her problems on a troubled marriage and expressed remorse. "I did not take the probation job seriously," she wrote.

"I was vulnerable due to a very bad domestic violence situation, and I let myself be carried away by the endless compliments and flattery of the young men," Hald wrote. "Bottom line, I had a consensual relationship with a young man who was 17 and I stupidly thought I was in love with. Everything else I did was completely inappropriate, unethical and extremely unprofessional."

* * *

Ademole Turner's career as a probation officer ended when a surveillance camera captured him hitting a boy in the face.

Video footage from the July 20, 2007, encounter in the recreation room at Los Padrinos Juvenile Hall shows the former college football star hitting a 16-year-old boy in the face, throwing him to the floor and kicking him at least once, prosecutors said.

The confrontation began when the boy approached another youth and asked about his gang affiliation, authorities said. Turner, 32, immediately interceded and struck the teenager. The youth had a bloody nose and bruised face, prosecutors said.

Downey police called to investigate Turner screened the tape and gave it to prosecutors, who charged Turner with assault by an officer, assault likely to cause great bodily injury, child abuse, corporal injury to a child and attempting to dissuade a witness from reporting.

Turner pleaded no contest to misdemeanor battery last year as part of a plea deal. He was sentenced to 24 months' probation and 50 hours' community service. A father of three, he quit his probation job and was teaching math and coaching football at a high school in Gardena.

Turner's attorney, Charles J. McLurkin, said there were "extenuating circumstances" that led to the beating, noting that his client was not properly trained to supervise violent youths.

"This is an issue of the training the county did not provide," McLurkin said.

Probation Department spokeswoman Kerri Webb disputed that allegation, saying that all probation officials are trained consistent with state standards.

* * *

When Probation Officer Diane Buchanan couldn't find her cellphone, she was convinced one of the boys she supervised at Barry J. Nidorf Juvenile Hall in Sylmar had stolen it, prosecutors said.

Court records tell how Buchanan, 39, first strip-searched the youths. Failing to find the phone, she questioned them.

Racial tensions had been simmering for weeks between black and Latino youths at the facility, the youths testified. One of the black youths alleged that a Latino detainee, Miguel Jimenez, had stolen the phone and flushed it down a toilet.

Buchanan believed him and started planning her revenge, prosecutors said.

On her way to Jimenez's cell, she approached a group of youths and told them she would unlock Jimenez's cell, then let them run past her to beat him up, according to court testimony.

"She told us to go in there and get him for the phone," one of the youths told investigators. "If I didn't do it, I was going to be with him."

Five youths attacked Jimenez, beating and kicking him as he lay on the floor. Jimenez, then 17, was in detention for vandalism. He cowered as the youths laughed and beat him, according to court records. He said Buchanan, who he called "Miss B," refused to intervene.

Buchanan left after a few minutes, locking the door and leaving Jimenez with numerous bumps and scrapes. He was not allowed to see a doctor until the next day, when another probation officer noticed his injuries and persuaded him to report the attack.

Buchanan later found her cellphone — in the parking lot. A grand jury charged Buchanan with child abuse. In May, she was convicted and sentenced to a year in jail.

Jimenez was being held at North County jail last week on assault charges and could not be reached for comment. But his brother Jorge Jimenez, 26, of Los Angeles said Jimenez was still upset about the beating.

"He feels betrayed," Jorge Jimenez said. "He was at a place where he was supposed to be rehabilitated, and instead this happened."

(http://www.streetgangs.com/cops/022110_la_juvenile_probation)

Although the above story outlines juvenile probation officer misconduct, probation officers who supervise adults are equally as likely to fall victim to these situations or temptations, or they could be actively engaging in wrongdoing by taking advantage of their position. The additional role of functioning as a supervisor of offenders will be discussed in the next section of the chapter.

Thinking Questions

1. Describe and discuss the dual role of probation officers. How can this create ethical dilemmas?
2. What is a PSI? What is it used for?
3. How can family members help or hinder the job of a probation officer?
4. Based on the news story in the above section, how can officers become better equipped to avoid misconduct?

Supervision in the Community

Both probation and parole officers work with offenders while they are living within the community. This is in stark contrast to officers who work in a prison environment and, as such, the ethical challenges that both groups encounter can have distinct differences. One of the challenges in supervising offenders who are within the community is making decisions about whether or not a revocation recommendation should be made. A revocation recommendation occurs when an offender fails to meet a condition of their supervised release. If revocation occurs they will either complete the remainder of their sentence in jail or prison or, as in the case of parole, be returned to prison to serve out the remainder of their original prison sentence.

Probation and parole officers do not have the actual power of revocation. They make a recommendation to the authority (judges or parole boards) and a decision is made to determine whether or not the offender should face revocation (Hanser, 2009). Reasons why a person could face revocation are listed below:

- *A new crime was committed*—If an offender while on probation or parole commits a new crime or crimes they will face revocation. Generally, it is a standard condition of probation and parole to not commit any crime (felony or misdemeanor), be in the proximity of areas of known criminal activity, or to be seen in the company of people who have committed or are suspected of committing criminal activity.
- *Leaving the jurisdiction without prior approval*—Most offenders on any form of community supervision must let their officer know if they plan to leave the area of jurisdiction, which varies based on conditions of probation/parole (could be a city, county, or state). Dependent upon what their particular conditions outline, the offender must notify the officer, obtain approval, and can then leave the jurisdiction. In most cases, approval for leaving a jurisdiction is given for funerals, weddings and case-by-case bases, as each offender is unique.
- *Non-payment of fees/fines*—Probation and parolees may face a series of fines or fees associated with being under community supervision. Failure to pay these fees or fines can result in revocation.
- *Positive drug test/failure to abstain from alcohol*—Because taking illegal drugs is against the law, offenders on probation and parole are not allowed to take certain substances (i.e., marijuana, heroin, cocaine, methamphetamine). Additionally, offenders may also be tested or required to refrain from certain prescription medication. Offenders are generally also not allowed to drink alcohol or visit places that sell alcohol (in some places this includes restaurants that serve alcohol). Typically, as a standard condition of probation/parole, offenders are required to take drug tests and may also be required to pay for them. In some places, they may also be required to take antabuse, which is a drug that makes a person sick if they drink alcohol.
- *Failure to meet conditions*—If an offender has not committed a crime or failed a drug test they can still face revocation if they fail to meet any of the additional conditions outlined in their probation or parole contract.

As outlined in Appendix A this could be failure to report to an appointment, being in a place they are not supposed to be, or a failure to maintain employment.

Box 8.3 Sample Probation Fees

All adult offenders are charged a one-time probation fee based upon the period of probation ordered at the time of sentencing.

Probation Term:	Fee Amount:
6 months	$60
1 year	$120
2 years	$240
3 years	$360
4 years	$480
5 years	$600
6 years	$720

Payment is due within 60 days of sentencing however, payment plans can be arranged with the supervising agent.

UA Fees:

Adult offenders are charged **$25** for positive UAs only. Payment is due at the time of testing.

Cognitive Thinking Skills Fees:

The cost of the adult Cognitive Thinking Skills program is **$200**. Payment is due prior to the start of class. Payment plans are available upon request.

(http://www.co.pine.mn.us/index.asp?Type=B_BASIC&SEC={38244D80-A5F6-4CCD-8575-86EBC70BFB3B})

As an ethical probation or parole officer it is essential to not abuse the power and discretion given to you when considering an offender for revocation. A violation report (or the lack of one) can have serious consequences for both the offender and the community. If the officer looks the other way when an offender has failed a drug test or is found in possession of a weapon, there are risks to the community, regardless of the reason why a violation report is not filed. If the officer is fearful or is bribed, it is clearly a breach of ethical conduct. If the officer fails to file a report because the offender is likeable, has a legitimate excuse or this is the first offense, it could still be argued that the officer has a duty to protect the citizens of the community and should file a violation report. On the other hand, is it realistic or feasible for an officer to file a violation report every time that any offender violates any condition of probation, no matter how large or small? Due to large caseloads the idea that an officer would be able to file a report for every violation (even if they wanted to) seems unlikely. This issue is of great concern to individuals working within community corrections. Officers who report every violation may view officers who do not as corrupt or weak. On the other hand, officers who do not file reports may see the value in giving offenders a chance to succeed, especially if the violation is a small one. There is no easy answer to the question of what, if any, violations should or could be overlooked.

An ethical professional should not fall temptation to favoritism, accepting money or services in exchange for ignoring violations, and should avoid manipulation tactics from offenders. Another area of concern is to resist the urge to "pencil-whip" or falsify paperwork. All of these will be discussed at great length in the next section of the chapter. Another area of probation and parole officers' work life is the task of making the numerous essential daily supervisory decisions regarding the probationers/parolees on their caseload.

Thinking Questions

1. What are some of the fees associated with probation?
2. What are some of the unique challenges in dealing with family members?
3. What are some of the unique challenges of supervision in the community?

Community Corrections and Caseload Supervision

Probation and parole officers are granted discretion in many areas including whether or not to file violation reports and what sentence they initially recommend to the judge in the PSI (Alarid & del Carmen, 2010). Additionally, officers are assigned a caseload of offenders whom they manage and supervise with high levels of discretionary authority. When discussing caseloads and ethics, it is important to discuss the issue of how many offenders are assigned to any one officer and what type of offenders they are supervising. Hanser (2009) noted that the APPA in 1991, attempted to outline an ideal caseload size but found that exact numbers were less effective as each probation and parole agency could best determine its ideal caseload and officer needs. Additionally, Burell (2006) noted three main reasons that making ideal caseload recommendations is difficult:

- *Not all offenders are alike*—Offenders are different (offense, gender, race, prior criminal history, etc.) and have different needs.
- *Court system/judicial assignment of conditions*—Judges assign probationers and parolees to different sets of conditions and caseload supervision varies depending upon what conditions offenders receive.
- *Differences in jurisdictions*—Each community is different and each community has different job opportunities, criminal enterprises, as well as legal and community corrections policies.

Clearly, there are limits to the number of offenders that personnel in community supervision can handle. A caseload of 500 offenders would be unrealistic to effectively manage, although in some cases even a caseload of 50 offenders might be too much if they are special needs offenders.

Box 8.4 Ethical Considerations When Dealing with Special Needs Offenders

There are a variety of special needs offenders that could be assigned to a probation or parole officer. Some examples of special needs offenders are: sex offenders (adult and juvenile), mentally ill offenders or offenders with mental health issues, gang members, female offenders and geriatric offenders. These offenders are at greater risk of re-offending, have much more individualized treatment plans, or are feared more by the public (sex offenders) and therefore are seen as needing more intensive supervision. In the case of sex offenders officers who have sex offender caseloads are often given additional training to learn how to best handle not only the particular needs of the offender but also of the community. It could be argued that officers who handle special needs offender caseloads are given additional responsibility with limited additional resources. In regards to ethical considerations, not all officers are capable of or are willing to manage special needs offenders. Officers who manage offenders with mental health concerns must take special care when considering treatment options and how to best help them to reintegrate into the community. Lack of proper attention with a sex offender caseload, for example, could potentially lead to citizens becoming victims. Additionally, because of the nature of their offenses, sex offenders are at greater risk for ridicule from citizens and community corrections personnel. Professionalism and careful consideration is necessary when dealing with special needs offenders, not only for their welfare and success but also for the welfare of the community they serve.

Additional resource: See the Arizona guidelines for the safe and effective management of sex offenders http://antipolygraph.org/documents/az-sex-offenders.pdf.

While there is a huge debate as to what constitutes an ideal caseload, for the probation officer working the caseload, the issues are primarily how to manage the numbers they are given and how to do so in a way that both follows policies and procedures and is ethical. Officers also must balance the fact that they are asked to do a great deal with limited resources (Alarid & del Carmen, 2010). Large numbers of offenders can cause officers to take short-cuts, by doing such things as not visiting the offender while filling out paperwork or filing violation reports. A community supervision officer might use informal sanctions rather than formal reports to gain offender compliance. Theoretically, informal handling of offender violations is against probation policy. Realistically, given the resource and time constraints, officers may feel the need to handle small scale violations informally to reduce paperwork and additional follow-up appointments. Large community corrections caseloads have been linked with higher rates of crime (Worrall, Schram, Hayes, & Newman, 2004), so there will be continued debate as to what a reasonable and effective caseload should be.

Probation and parole officers have many other issues that are part of caseload management. In some instances officers may face ethical dilemmas in dealing with offender employment. In some instances, the offender may have not disclosed to their employer that they are on probation or parole. The presence of the probation officer checking on the offender could jeopardize the offender's employment. Even if the offender has disclosed their criminal status to their employer, employers may find the presence of an officer intrusive to their operations.

Officers could also be faced with the issue of offenders' personal lives spilling over into the area of caseload management. For example, an offender may be beginning a relationship with an individual who is unaware that their significant other is under community supervision. Does the probation officer have a duty to inform the other person about the criminal history? This could also emerge as an issue if an offender has HIV/AIDS (of which we will talk more about in Chapter 12) or any other communicable disease and whether they should inform intimate. In general, health histories are protected by HIPAA (Health Insurance Portability and Accountability Act) although this does not always extend to probationers or parolees. Most states have laws that govern the confidentiality of HIV/AIDS so officers have a legal duty not to inform others of this condition. There is less clarity on disclosing health information in cases such as hepatitis or herpes.

Caseload management is also different depending on location and size of the jurisdiction. In large counties, such as Dallas County, Texas, officers who have a conflict of interest with a client can pass the offender to another officer more easily than in a smaller county where only one officer has the entire caseload. Different jurisdictions also have different types of resources. A larger department such as Cook County, Illinois has a staff of 520 probation officers, 90 sworn managers and 210 administrative and support staff members with a yearly budget of close to $41 million (Cook County Illinois, 2010). By contrast, Clay County, Illinois has three probation officers and one full time secretary (Clay County Illinois, 2010). Caseload management will clearly be different in both counties and the ethical dilemmas faced by the officers and staff could be quite different.

Thinking Questions

1. What are some of the reasons that numbers are not often given for ideal caseloads?
2. What are some of the unique challenges in managing a community corrections caseload?
3. What are some of the differences in managing a caseload in a small vs. large jurisdiction?
4. Hypothesize some of the challenges in managing a caseload of probationers. Parolees?

Corruption

In the same way that police officers are tempted to engage in various forms of corruption, probation and parole officers also have opportunities to engage in corrupt behavior. Offenders may attempt to bribe officers to overlook violations by giving them money or by offering to perform a service for them (i.e., an offender with construction skills may offer to build a deck or complete a home improvement project for the officer). It is also possible that the officer will engage in a "quid pro quo" form of corruption where they will tell the offender that unless they give them money or provide a service they will face a revocation of probation or parole.

In 1972 the Knapp Commission on police corruption found that there were two types of corrupt police officers: grass eaters and meat eaters. Grass eaters are police officers who accept gratuities and receive small payments from contractors, tow-truck operators, gamblers and store owners but do not pursue payments or seek out opportunities to engage in corrupt behavior. As the opportunities arise, they engage in them. By contrast, meat eaters are officers who spend a large amount of time aggressively seeking out situations they can exploit for financial gain. An example of this is shaking down pimps and drug dealers for money. This type of police corruption is exemplified by fictional LAPD narcotics detective Alonzo Harris (portrayed by Denzel Washington) in the movie Training Day. These same typologies apply to probation and parole officers as they apply to police officers.

A probation or parole officer could engage in grass eating through taking advantage of opportunities such as payments for fixing a drug test, or by getting free meals or merchandise from grateful merchants or offender family members. In the same way a community corrections officer could participate in meat eating by stealing drugs or money from their offenders or demanding sexual favors to stay out of jail or prison.

There are no easy answers in how to stop corruption although some simple steps taken by any criminal justice agency could be a starting point.

1. Strengthen leadership—Lead by example by having your top level administrators and supervisors act in the same manner in which you want line community corrections personnel to act.
2. Creating and developing clear policies and procedures that "draw the line" and make it clear to the officers and the community what behaviors are and are not ethical. Violations of written policies must be followed up with formal disciplinary action. Policies should be in written format to decrease confusion as opposed to just "talking about ethical behavior."
3. Emphasize corruption control at the selection and training phase of community corrections. This would include greater focus on each applicant's integrity recruitment phase (background checks, integrity and psychological testing) as well as providing more anti-corruption and ethics training at the initial academy and follow up training during on the job.

Box 8.5 Probation Officer Accused of Fixing Drug Tests

A district court probation officer is accused of taking bribes in exchange for clean drug test reports. William Garcia, 39, works with people involved in domestic violence and family court cases. He was arrested at work Tuesday after investigators said he took two $20 bills that were given to an informant as bait. Garcia is jailed on a $100,000 cash bond. He faces bribery, extortion and perjury charges.

Thinking Questions

1. Why does corruption in community corrections occur?
2. Compare and contrast grass eaters and meat eaters.
3. Brainstorm some ways to stop corruption amongst probation and parole officers.
4. What are some ways that staff can guard against offender manipulation?

Conclusion

Ethics in the community correctional environment is an essential part of the job. Violations in ethics can lead to serious consequences for both the offender and the community. If community corrections officers engage in grass eating or meat eating, harm will be done to their agency, the offender, and the citizens in the community where they work. Being able to effectively manage the caseload and the unique challenges of working with offenders while they are living in the community is of great importance. The use of discretion by probation officers in the PSI and in making daily supervision decisions has profound ethical implications. Both probation and parole officers have to decide how to manage their offenders and decide what type of officer role they take on as they make daily supervision decisions. Because of the close interaction that they have with the public community corrections personnel need to be aware of the ethical challenges they face and also become knowledgeable of the resources available to them to avoid corruption, coercion and burnout.

Scenarios

1. You are supervising a first time felon who was sentenced to probation. The offender has done well for 6 months and then fails a urinalysis drug test for marijuana. The offender does not disclose this to you when you meet. How do you handle the situation? Would your decision be different if the offender tested positive for heroin?

2. You notice that a fellow parole officer is spending large amounts of time with one particular offender (beyond that of how often parolees and the officer meet). When you ask the officer they tell you that the offender is just "needy" and has more problems than some of the other offenders. You overhear the offender and officer talking about highly personal information

about how the officer is in a failing marriage and has financial problems. The offender used to be a high ranking drug dealer. What do you do?

3. You are a probation officer with a intensive supervision caseload of sex offenders. One of the offenders on your caseload has informed you that he overheard another offender in group talk about how he found a great place to find "fresh meat." What do you do? What if the offender confesses that he has gone to this place but has not picked up any of the young boys yet?

4. You are invited over to another officer's house for a cookout. The officer proudly shows you their home and their new addition and deck. The officer winks and says that he got a great deal on labor. You know that the officer has offenders on their caseload that are experienced contractors. When you ask the officer who did the work, they smile and say they have connections. What do you do?

5. You have a caseload of 125 offenders and are having a hard time keeping up. An officer who has been with the agency for 15 years tells you that they devised a new system that helps to manage the paperwork. The officer explains how they "pencil-whip" the paperwork. What do you do?

References

Alarid, L., & del Carmen, R. (2010). *Community Based Corrections.* Florence, KY: Wadsworth Publishing.

American Probation and Parole Association (2010). Code of Ethics. Retrieved October 2, 2010. http://www.appa-net.org/eweb/DynamicPage.aspx?Site=APPA_2&WebCode=IA_CodeEthics.

American Probation and Parole Association (2010). Mission Statement. Retrieved October 27, 2010 http://www.appanet.org/eweb/DynamicPage.aspx?WebCode=IA_Introduction.

Burrell, B. (2006). *Caseload Standards for Probation and Parole.* Retrieved October 10, 2010. http://cdpsweb.state.co.us/cccjj/PDF/Research%20Documents/APPA%20Caseload_Standards_PP_0906.pdf.

Clay County (2010). *Probation.* Retrieved October 1, 2010. http://www.claycountyillinois.org/index.aspx?page=19.

Clear, T., Cole, G., & Resig, M. (2010). *American Corrections.* Florence, KY: Wadsworth Publishing.

Cook County (2010). *Division of Adult Probation.* Retrieved October 1, 2010. http://www.cookcountycourt.org/services/programs/adult-probation/profile.html.

Hanser, R. (2009). *Community Corrections.* Thousand Oaks, CA: Sage Publications.

Klockars, C.B. (1972). A theory of probation supervision. *Journal of Criminal Law, Criminology and Police Science,* 63, 550–557.

Pollock, J. (2010). *Ethical Dilemmas and Decisions in Criminal Justice.* Florence, KY: Wadsworth Publishing.

Worrall, J., Schram, P., Hayes, E., & Newman, M. (2004). An Analysis of the Relationship Between Probation Caseloads and Property Crime Rates in California Counties. *Journal of Criminal Justice* 32:231–241.

Additional Websites

http://www.appa-net.org
http://www.aca.org
http://www.nicic.org
http://www.appa-net.org/eweb/docs/appa/pubs/SMDM.pdf
http://www.dallasnews.com/sharedcontent/dws/news/texassouthwest/stories/
DN-ujday3main_13pro.ART.State.Edition2.4237295.html
http://www.vcn.bc.ca/bcpoa/survivm5.htm

Appendix A: Conditions of Probation and Parole (Clackamas County, Oregon)

Conditions of Probation

1. Pay supervision fees, fines, restitution or other fees ordered by the Court.
2. Not use or possess controlled substances except pursuant to a medical prescription.
3. Submit to testing of breath or urine for controlled substance or alcohol use if the probationer has a history of substance abuse or if there is a reasonable suspicion that the probationer has illegally used controlled substances.
4. Participate in a substance abuse evaluation as directed by the supervising officer and follow the recommendations of the evaluator if there are reasonable grounds to believe there is a history of substance abuse.
5. Remain in the state of Oregon until written permission to leave is granted by the supervising officer.

6. If physically able, find and maintain gainful full-time employment, approved schooling, or a full-time combination of both. Any waiver of this requirement must be based on a finding by the Court stating the reasons for the waiver.

7. Change neither employment nor residence without prior permission from the Department of Corrections or a county community corrections agency.

8. Permit the supervising officer to visit the probationer or the probationer's work site or residence and to conduct a walk-through of the common areas and of the rooms in the residence occupied by or under the control of the probationer.

9. Consent to the search of person, vehicle, or premises upon the request of a representative of the supervising officer if the supervising officer has reasonable grounds to believe that evidence of a violation will be found, and submit to fingerprinting or photographing, or both, when requested by the Department of Corrections or a county community corrections agency for supervision purposes.

10. Obey all laws, municipal, county, state, and federal.

11. Promptly and truthfully answer all reasonable inquiries by the Department of Corrections or a county community corrections agency.

12. Not possess weapons, firearms, or dangerous animals.

13. Report as required and abide by the direction of the supervising officer.

14. If under supervision for, or previously convicted of, a sex offense under ORS 163.305 to 163.465, and if recommended by the supervising officer, successfully complete a sex offender treatment program approved by the supervising officer and submit to polygraph examinations at the direction of the supervising officer.

15. Participate in a mental health evaluation as directed by the supervising officer and follow the recommendation of the evaluator.

16. If required to report as a sex offender under ORS 181.596, report with the Department of State Police, a chief of police, a county sheriff, or the supervisory agency: (a) when supervision begins; (b) within 10 days of a change of residence; and (c) once each year within 10 days of the probationer's date of birth.

Addendum to Judgment

Addendum to Judgment — Substance Abuse Package

1. Obtain a substance abuse evaluation as directed by the probation officer, follow through with any treatment recommendations, including inpatient treatment, and comply with all follow-up treatment.
2. Not use or possess alcoholic beverages (including "near beer"), illegal drugs or narcotics, and shall notify the probation officer of any medical prescriptions given by a doctor.
3. Do not enter or frequent any establishment whose primary income is derived from the sale of alcoholic beverages.
4. Shall not frequent places where narcotics are used, sold or kept.
5. Shall not possess any narcotics paraphernalia, including smoking devices, and shall not associate with any person known to use, sell or possess any illegal drugs or narcotics.
6. Submit to monitored testing at the direction of the probation officer and at the defendant's own expense.
7. Take Antabuse if medically able and at the direction of the probation officer.
8. Not drive without a valid license and insurance and shall be subject to the requirements of the Guardian Interlock System according to DMV policies for a hardship license.
9. If the crime of conviction is a DUII, you must attend a DUII Victim's Panel within 60 days of this judgment.
10. Attend Alcoholics/Narcotics Anonymous meetings at the direction of the probation officer.
11. Submit defendant's person, residence, vehicle or property to search by the probation officer at any time without benefit of a search warrant when the probation officer has reasonable grounds to believe that such a search will reveal evidence of a violation of this probation.

Addendum to Judgment — Sex Offender Package

1. Have no contact with any female or male under the age of 18, unless authorized by your probation officer.
2. Consent to and cooperate with polygraph examinations and penile plethysmograph assessments when deemed necessary by the therapist and/or the probation officer.
3. Be financially responsible for all counseling costs incurred by the victim(s).

4. Consent to the sharing of assessment and treatment information between public and private agencies, agents and persons who are deemed essential in assessing, monitoring, and mediating treatment for sexual deviancy problems.

5. Not possess or use at any time any type of pornography including, but not limited to written, telephonic, computer-based pictures, video tapes or audio tapes, and cannot frequent establishments associated with the sex industry.

6. Enter and complete a sex offender treatment program as directed by the probation officer.

7. Consent to, and cooperate with, any plan deemed necessary by the probation officer and/or therapist to maintain and monitor offense-free behavior for the duration of this probation.

8. Not be involved in any organizations which would place defendant in direct contact with children, i.e., Boy Scouts, Girl Scouts, 4-H, Big Brother or Big Sister programs, Sunday school teaching, etc.

9. Not frequent or visit places that exist primarily for the enjoyment of children, i.e., circuses, amusement parks, zoos, etc.

10. Must register as a sex offender pursuant to Oregon Revised Statutes.

11. Submit to blood testing for DNA purposes and HIV testing with release of information to the victims(s).

12. Submit defendant's person, residence, vehicle or property to search by the probation officer at any time without the benefit of a search warrant when the probation officer has reasonable grounds to believe that such a search will reveal evidence of a violation of this probation.

Addendum to Judgment — Financial Crimes Package

1. Advise current and any future employer, including temporary agencies, of this probation and the nature of the crime. Probation officer may discuss the details of the crime of conviction with the employer.

2. Provide probation officer with employment information and allow communication between employer and probation officer for purposes of monitoring compliance with probation conditions.

3. Do not accept any employment which includes the handling of money, i.e., cash, checks, credit cards, or bank cards, accounts payable, without obtaining permission from your probation officer and making a full disclosure to the employer.

4. Do not change employment or job duties without prior permission of the probation officer and report any changes in supervisor to the probation officer immediately.

5. Permit the probation officer to visit your place of employment.

6. Provide complete personal financial records, i.e., tax records, household income and expenses, bank statements, etc., to the probation officer upon request.

7. Prior to engaging in any financial transaction over $200.00, you must obtain permission from the probation officer.

8. Must submit to polygraph examination at your own expense upon request of parole/probation officer pertaining to employment and financial matters only.

9. Submit defendant's person, residence, vehicle or property to search by the probation officer at any time without benefit of a search warrant when the probation officer has reasonable grounds to believe that such a search will reveal evidence of a violation of this probation.

Board of Parole and Post Prison Supervision
General Conditions of Supervision

1. Pay supervision fees, fines, restitution or other fees ordered by the Board.

2. Not use or possess controlled substances except pursuant to a medical prescription.

3. Submit to testing of breath or urine for controlled substance or alcohol use if the offender has history of substance abuse or if there is a reasonable suspicion that the offender has illegally used controlled substances.

4. Participate in a substance abuse evaluation as directed by the supervising officer and follow the recommendations of the evaluator if there are reasonable grounds to believe there is a history of substance abuse.

5. Remain in the State of Oregon until written permission to leave is granted by the Department of Corrections or a county community corrections agency. Offender automatically waives extradition if offender absconds supervision out of State.

6. If physically able, find and maintain gainful full-time employment, approved schooling, or a full-time combination of both.

7. Change neither employment nor residence without prior permission from the Department of Corrections or a county community corrections agency.

8. Permit the supervision officer to visit the offender or the offender's residence or work site and to conduct a walk-through of the common areas and of the rooms in the residence occupied by or under the control of the probationer.

9. Consent to the search of person, vehicle or premises upon the request of a representative of the supervising officer if the supervising officer has reasonable grounds to believe that evidence of a violation will be found, and submit to fingerprinting or photographing, or both, when requested by the Department of Corrections or a county community corrections agency for supervision purposes.

10. Obey all laws, municipal, county, state, and federal.

11. Promptly and truthfully answer all reasonable inquiries by the Department of Corrections or a county community corrections agency.

12. Not possess weapons, firearms, or dangerous animals.

13. Report as required and abide by the direction of the supervising officer.

State of Oregon Board of Parole and Post Prison Supervision Special Conditions

1. Offender shall be evaluated by a mental health evaluator and follow all treatment recommendations.

2. Offender shall continue to take any psychiatric or psychotropic medication that was prescribed prior to or at the time of release from custody until otherwise directed by a physician. At the direction of the parole officer, the offender shall undergo a psychiatric evaluation and take any medications recommended. The offender shall comply with a medication monitoring program at the request of the parole officer.

3. Offender shall have no contact with minor females and shall not frequent any places where minors are likely to congregate (e.g., playgrounds, school grounds, arcades) without prior written approval from their supervising officer.

4. Offender shall have no contact with minor males and shall not frequent any places where minors are likely to congregate (e.g.,

playgrounds, school grounds, arcades) without prior written approval from their supervising officer.

5. Offender shall submit to random polygraph tests as part of a sex offender surveillance program. Failure to submit to the tests may result in return to the Department of Corrections custody. Specific responses to the tests shall not be the basis for return to the Department of Corrections.

6. Offender shall enter and complete or be successfully discharged from a recognized and approved sex offender treatment program which may include polygraph and/or plethysmograph testing. Offender shall abide by a prohibition of sexually deviant materials, activities or behavior that the offender may use for the purpose of deviant sexual arousal, unless otherwise allowed by the Parole Officer in writing.

7. Offender shall pay court ordered restitution to the clerk of the court of the county of sentencing (ORS 137.106, OAR 255-065-0005).

8. If required to report as a sex offender under ORS 181.595, report with the Department of State Police, a Chief of Police, a County Sheriff or the Supervising Agency: when supervision begins, within 10 days of a change in residence and once a year within 10 days of the person's date of birth.

9. Offender shall not possess or use intoxicating beverages.

10. Other: Special Conditions may be imposed that are not listed above when the Board of Parole and Post Prison Supervision determines that such conditions are necessary.

11. Offender shall have no contact direct or indirect with those listed.

12. Consent to search of computer or other electronic equipment upon the request of the supervising officer, or their representative, if the supervising officer has reasonable grounds to believe that evidence of a violation will be found.

13. Sex Offender Package:

    a. Agreement to comply with any curfew set by the board, the supervisory authority or the supervising officer.

    b. A prohibition against contacting a person under 18 years of age without the prior written approval of the board, supervisory authority or supervising officer.

    c. A prohibition against frequenting, without the prior written approval of the board, supervisory authority or supervising officer, a place where persons under 18 years of age regularly congregate.

d.   A prohibition against working or volunteering at a school, day care center, park, playground or other place where persons under 18 years of age regularly congregate.

e.   Entry into and completion of or successful discharge from a sex offender treatment program approved by the board, supervisory authority or supervising officer. The program may include polygraph and plethysmograph testing. The person is responsible for paying for the treatment program.

f.   A prohibition against any contact with the victim, directly or indirectly, unless approved by the victim, the person's treatment provider and the board, supervisory authority or supervising officer.

g.   Unless otherwise indicated for the treatment required under subparagraph (e) of this paragraph, a prohibition against viewing, listening to, owning or possessing any sexually stimulating visual or auditory materials that are relevant to the person's deviant behavior.

h.   Agreement to consent to a search of the person or the vehicle or residence of the person upon the request of a representative of the board or supervisory authority if the representative has reasonable grounds to believe that evidence of a violation of a condition of post-prison supervision will be found.

i.   Participation in random polygraph examinations to obtain information for risk management and treatment. The person is responsible for paying the expenses of the examinations. The results of a polygraph examination under this subparagraph may not be used in evidence in a hearing to prove a violation of post-prison supervision.

j.   Maintenance of a driving log and a prohibition against driving a motor vehicle alone unless approved by the board, supervisory authority or supervising officer.

k.   A prohibition against using a post-office box unless approved by the board, supervisory authority or supervising officer.

9

Ethics in Security and Loss Prevention

Chapter Objectives

- The student will understand the importance of ethics in private security
- The student should become aware of the unique elements of loss prevention
- The student will gain knowledge of interrogation and investigation in private security
- The student will learn the importance of *Miranda* warnings in private security
- The student will understand the shopkeeper's privilege
- The student will become aware of the Retail Shoplifting Task Force

Introduction

While perusing the compact disc section of a Sam's Club in Santa Fe, New Mexico, a woman was accused of shoplifting CDs and subsequently strip-searched by a store loss prevention agent and a Santa Fe police officer. No stolen property was recovered as a result of the apprehension or search, according to the plaintiff's attorney. The plaintiff maintained that the police officer and the store loss prevention officer should have been able to determine whether the suspect had shoplifted compact discs without forcing her to disrobe (*Albuquerque Journal*, 2005). Although all criminal charges were dropped against the plaintiff, she alleged that the city of Santa Fe, the police officer involved, and Sam's Club were guilty of false imprisonment and causing her "lasting emotional damage from the trauma of being stripped" (Pawloski, 2005, p. 1).

Shoplifting is probably the most common crime that occurs in retail businesses. However, as the example above shows, the importance of exercising sound discretion when carrying out routine investigative duties cannot be over-emphasized. When shoplifters are detained and searched illegally there is an identifiable victim. However, many investigative activities that take place in the field of private security involve actions that occur out of public view. As society has evolved, the private security industry has become increasingly dependent on technology with tools such as exception reporting and closed-circuit television. The expansion of private security investigations and duties pose many ethical dilemmas for professionals that will ultimately impact the longevity and success of one's career in the field.

This chapter focuses on ethical issues that confront private security personnel, and specifically, retail investigations. Two points must be noted regarding this topic and the scope of this chapter. First, the field of private security is too broad and thus the ethical issues related to all private security duties are too diverse to cover adequately in one chapter. Second, there are few empirical studies on this topic—most research on ethics in the criminal justice field focuses on police, probation, parole, and corrections. Although the chapter addresses ethics in the retail security industry, many of the same principles and practices are transferrable to other private security professionals such as private investigators and corporate (non-retail) security professionals.

Privatization and Public Service

Without debate, the private security field has grown immensely in the past few decades. Privatization is "the trend of making services and functions, that are traditionally performed by public entities the province of private, for-profit entities, usually companies" (Nemeth, 2010, p. 2). As of 2000, the number of private security employees was approximately 2 million, more than four times the number of personnel in public law enforcement. Cunningham, Strauchs, and Van Meter (1990) identified 4 primary reasons for the growth in the private security industry:

- A surge in workplace-related crime;
- A rise in fear of crime;
- Fiscal constraints on state and public expenditures; and
- An increase in security resources designed for the protection of private businesses.

As is the case in the public sector, private security professionals face a diverse range of ethical issues when performing their work. First, the "for-profit" aspect of privatization means that private security businesses exist primarily for the reason of generating revenue, as opposed to public agencies. In addition, because much of what occurs in the private security industry is out of public view there is less media attention toward misconduct on the part of private security personnel. How often do you see stories concerning misconduct on the part of private security personnel on your local television news programs? The amount of coverage devoted toward any area of the private security industry pales in comparison to police-related deviance. Second, state tort law is the primary source of legal action against private security individuals, whereas public law largely regulates the conduct of government actors (Baum, 2008). Chapter 10 discusses the application of state and federal laws to the conduct of public officials. Many of these laws have no relevance to private security personnel. For example, the federal and constitutional laws that apply to police, probation, and parole officers are not the same for private security personnel. In some ways, the law gives private security more flexibility to investigate crime but gives public officials more protection against liability. For instance, private security investigators are not subject to the normal warrant requirement that applies to searches and seizures conducted by government officials. This, however, does not mean that a person working in private security cannot be sued for false arrest or violating another's expectation of privacy. We will address the legal issues that apply to private security work later in the chapter, but first it is necessary to provide some background information on the privatization movement and explain the roles and functions of individuals working in these areas.

Establishing a Culture of Ethical Behavior

Creating a culture of strong ethical behavior in the loss prevention and security field is no different than with most other professions. Loss prevention and security professionals are bestowed some unique authority to investigate matters relating to company profitability and fraud, and as a result, they have access to certain types of sensitive information, such as employee records, financial data, as well as surveillance equipment that can be abused. Albrecht et al. (2016) notes that organizations use five main strategies to cultivate a strong ethical foundation:

(1) Ensuring senior management officials model appropriate behavior;
(2) Proper hiring and screening of employees;
(3) Communicating expectations to employees regularly and conducting training as necessary to reinforce expectations;
(4) Cultivating a positive work environment; and
(5) Establishing an effective process for addressing fraud when it occurs (p. 72).

Unethical behavior on the part of an organization's leader has a ripple effect across the organization, resulting in lower morale and cynicism among employees. Further, because security and loss prevention personnel are given special authority, any unethical behavior on their part is viewed as more condemning than misconduct committed by other employees. The analogy here is similar to misconduct on the part of police and correctional officials. In other words, we expect prisoners to violate prison rules just like we expect employees to occasionally commit criminal acts. But when security professionals engage in misconduct it becomes exponentially more difficult for the organization to accomplish its objectives due to the lack of confidence among employees and the public. This is why it is important for security managers to model ethical and appropriate behavior for their subordinates (Trautman, 2008).

Another best practice in establishing a climate of integrity and ethics is proper screening of employees prior to hiring them. Routine background checks should also consist of reference checks and a review of the employee's previous work history. A lack of employment stability is a sign that the employee may not be good risk to the company. In addition, the type of access the employee has should be taken into consideration when hiring employees. The risk of fraud is heightened in cases where companies are opening new store locations reorganizing their company structure. As an investigator for a major U.S. retail organization, this author investigated a chain of cash thefts in the bookkeeping department of a new store location. Malfunctioning video equipment in the area was a compounding issue, but eventually the ex-employee admitted to the frauds totaling ten-thousand dollars in loss to the company. The case highlights the importance of monitoring new employees in sensitive areas or areas that do not have established protocols.

Communicating expectations to employees about the importance of good service and respect to the community is another hallmark of creating a solid ethical framework within an organization. The job of loss prevention and security professionals is similar to that of senior leadership—they must communicate about ways to prevent and deter fraud and be able to respond effectively when there is a crisis. Hertig (2008) recommends the following ways to improve ethics among security officers through effective communication:

(a) post an ethics code in the workplace,
(b) model ethical behavior,
(c) mandate that security officers sign an ethics code each year,
(d) cultivate an atmosphere that promotes communication between security managers and subordinates,
(e) conduct ethics training for employees on a periodic basis, and

(f) include specialized ethics training for security personnel (Hertig, 2008).

A fourth method of fostering a strong work ethic among security professionals is to ensure policies are clearly written for employees so that there is no perception of favoritism or special treatment for certain employees. Loss prevention and security professionals are not always supervised as closely as other employees, thus they have more opportunities to work on specialized assignments. This can sometimes result in perceptions of special treatment by other staff that security professionals can do whatever they choose. A way to remove this perception is for security professionals to identify tasks that can be accomplished in a team setting. Creating a culture of teamwork is an important strategy to ensuring that lines of communication remain open and that employees feel comfortable coming forward with information if needed. This is critical, as research shows that it is employees and management, rather than investigative staff, who discover most frauds (Albrecht, et al., 2016).

A final method to ensuring that ethical conduct is maintained in the workplace deals with actual methods used to investigate different types of theft or fraud. It is important that security managers maintain the integrity of investigations by not discussing the details of pending cases with other employees. This may seem commonsense to many, but the business environment is much different than conducting street crime investigations. It is inevitable that some employees will monitor the activity of loss prevention and security personnel out of sheer interest, excitement, or fear of detection. Thus the methods used to investigate employees must be surreptitious in nature. Use of closed-circuit television, accounting procedures, selected witness interviews with management are more appropriate strategies than overt strategies that are likely to result in security breaches, which threaten the stability of the organization (Fay, 2006; McCrie, 2001).

Loss Prevention and Retail Security: General Duties

The growth in the retail security and loss prevention industry is directly tied to economic growth in the private sector. During the 1990s, the industry experienced unprecedented growth fueled primarily by two factors: (1) significant economic growth in retail industry, and (2) increased risk to profit loss due to technologically-based crime and operational loss. Retail executives observed the need to expand their loss prevention and security departments to address these new demands. In the last several years, however, the retail industry has suffered major cutbacks and the impact of downsizing and industry reorganization has caused many modifications to the traditional duties of a retail investigator. Information on the impact of the downsizing and corporate security reorganization comes from The National Retail Security Survey conducted by the National Retail Federation (NRF) and the University of Florida. The survey reports that retail losses due to theft and operational loss decreased in 2009 to 1.44 percent to retail sales, down slightly from 1.51 percent in 2008 (Grannis, 2010). Although the amount of loss as a percent to sales has only slightly declined, overall retail sales have also dropped 7.3% during the period 2008–2009.

The "traditional" loss prevention investigator typically performs duties exclusive to theft and fraud investigation, but may also perform many operational tasks. The organizational chart and respective divisions of loss prevention departments vary significantly depending on the company's size, but a general format is depicted in Figure 9.1.

Figure 9.1 Organizational Structure of a Typical Loss Prevention Department

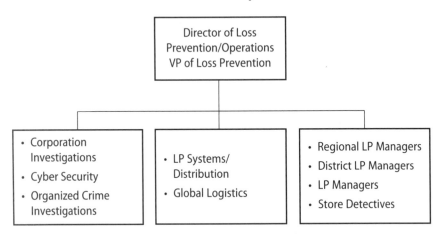

The work of an hourly loss prevention investigator can be monotonous and droning. In order to be promoted, however, most individuals will inevitably work their way up the corporate ladder from an hourly position. Entry level investigators are typically confined to one store and perform a simple daily routine. On the occasion that an investigation occurs or a shoplifter is apprehended, the investigator's role in the process is relatively limited. Once an investigator proves that he or she has the necessary leadership skills to be successful, he or she may be promoted. The next level supervisor in a loss prevention department is commonly the loss prevention manager. The loss prevention manager typically supervises 2–10 investigators depending on the size of the store or company.

The traditional role of the loss prevention investigator encompasses duties such as:

- Apprehending shoplifters
- Investigating and apprehending employees involved with internal theft
- Investigation of check and credit card fraud
- Conducting operational audits and inspections

Shoplifter Apprehensions

The business of apprehending shoplifters poses many ethical dilemmas. To begin, corporate loss prevention apprehension policies require that investigators observe a shoplifter (1) approach a merchandise selection area, (2) select the merchandise, (3) conceal the merchandise or maintain the item in open view throughout the entire incident, (4) fail to make an attempt to pay for the item, and (5) maintain constant surveillance of the suspect and property throughout all of these steps. It is quite common for investigators to miss one of the above mentioned steps, but still apprehend the suspect. When this occurs there is a clear violation of loss prevention policy, but the reality is that store loss prevention agents frequently make apprehensions on shoplifters despite breaks in surveillance. Failure to maintain surveillance after a suspect conceals merchandise is probably the most common step that is missed in the process. This occurs not because investigators are lax in their duties, but because it is often difficult to avoid being detected by the suspect while maintaining visual observation. There are two main reasons why store investigators overlook company detention policies. First, a normal reaction for the investigator is for their judgment to be overcome by the excitement of having witnessed a theft, which increases the potential for what is referred to as a "bad stop." A bad stop occurs when an investigator stops an alleged shoplifter and does not recover the suspected stolen property. A second reason is related to individual egotism. Some store investigators often enjoy the notoriety from their coworkers and their supervisor when they have made a successful apprehension. They also know that their value as an investigator is directly measured by the number of apprehensions they conduct. Hence, hourly investigators may feel an overwhelming compulsion to "get stats," which leads to occasional violations of the 5-step protocol.

In an effort to crack down on problems associated with shoplifting, retail businesses have formed Retail Shoplifting Task Forces, which are essentially comprised of investigators from different retail businesses sharing intelligence on shoplifting schemes. This is a good example of the professionalization movement in private retail security to improve the quality of investigations.

Use of Force Against Shoplifters

Most states have recognized the shopkeeper's privilege, which is the authority of the business representative to use reasonable force to detain shoplifters until the police arrive to take them into official custody. The act of detaining shoplifters amounts to a citizen's arrest as opposed to an arrest by a police officer. What is reasonable varies according to facts and circumstances. Below is an example of Oregon's citizen's arrest statute.

133.225 Arrest by private person.

(1) A private person may arrest another person for any crime committed in the presence of the private person if the private person has probable cause to believe the arrested person committed the crime. A private person making such an arrest shall, without unnecessary delay, take the arrested person before a magistrate or deliver the arrested person to a peace officer.

(2) In order to make the arrest a private person may use physical force as is justifiable under ORS 161.255.

In response to increased litigation in the area of shoplifter apprehensions, many companies have adopted "no-chase" polices that forbid store security agents from engaging in pursuits beyond a set distance from the store's entrance or exit. Unlike police officers, store security agents are not permitted to carry weapons or have any means of self-defense against a suspect who becomes aggressive during an apprehension attempt. The desire to make a successful apprehension can result in poor decision-making in the use of force by store loss prevention agents. An example of this problem occurred in *Gaines v. Nordstrom* (2007). In this case, Nordstrom loss prevention agents became involved in an altercation with a suspected shoplifter (Gaines) near a cashier check-out area because he was wearing merchandise that had not been paid for. The agents eventually subdued and handcuffed Gaines then escorted her to a detention room where she was held for approximately an hour until the Portland Police arrived. The court found in favor of the plaintiff, opining that "there must be objectively reasonable indicia that Gaines actually engaged in the actus reus of theft, i.e., that she took, appropriated, obtained or withheld the clothes from Nordstrom" (p. 6). Since Gaines never actually left the store with the property, the agents did not have probable cause to make the apprehension and thus they were not entitled to immunity.

Box 9.1 Dillard's Cited in Racial Profiling Suit

The Commercial Appeal (Memphis, TN) — October 22, 2005

LITTLE ROCK — A new lawsuit accuses department store chain Dillard's Inc. of engaging in racial profiling in efforts to thwart shoplifters . Eight plaintiffs sued the company in U.S. District Court in Little Rock, saying it wrongfully accused black customers of shoplifting at stores in Arkansas, Tennessee and Florida. The suit alleges Dillard's employees or security workers questioned the plaintiffs when they were in the stores and accused them of stealing merchandise. The office of Dillard's general counsel refused to comment Friday on the suit, which was filed Monday. Dating back to the 1990s, Dillard's has been the target of lawsuits that alleged the company discriminated against blacks. The suits alleged black customers were unreasonably searched, questioned or denied service at stores across the South. Dillard's has denied those allegations.

In one complaint, a Texas jury in 2001 awarded about $800,000 to the family of a black man who died after being hogtied during a confrontation with security and police at a Dillard's store. Jurors held Dillard's liable, while clearing the City of Houston and its police.

In another case, Dillard's was ordered to pay a $1.2 million verdict to a black woman who was detained for shoplifting in a store in Overland Park, Kan. Paula Hampton had just bought an Easter outfit for her niece's 1-year-old son and was redeeming a coupon for men's cologne samples when the guard interrupted the transaction.

This year, Dillard's was the target of a federal class-action suit that accused its hair salons of using a dual pricing system, one for black customers and another for white and similar groups.

Source: Associated Press, "Dillards cited in racial profiling suit," *The Commercial Appeal,* Memphis, TN. October 22, 2005. Reprinted with permission.

Thinking Questions

1. What are common pitfalls associated with human deception judgments?
2. What sorts of pressures/obstacles do loss prevention personnel face when conducting interviews/interrogations?
3. How is productivity assessed and how does job performance affect the manner in which interviews/interrogations are conducted?

The Ethics of Interviewing and Interrogation

Retail businesses commonly outsource interview and interrogation training to private security firms such as John E. Reid and Associates, Wicklander & Zulawski, and Stan Walters' Kinesic Interviewing Technique. Each of these firms has different approaches and recommended strategies to conducting interviews and interrogations. However, a similarity among the three methods is how they define interviewing and interrogation. Interviewing or the non-accusatory interview focuses on fact-gathering to the extent that sufficient information is obtained to make a determination about the suspect's involvement in a crime. For example, if ten people had access to a safe where money was stolen, each person may be interviewed regarding the incident. The investigator's job in this regard is to determine what inconsistencies exist and to make an initial judgment about each suspect's truthfulness without accusing or implying that he or she may be guilty. If 2 of the 10 individuals indicate fact inconsistencies suggesting deception, then it is ethically permissible to interrogate each person. Moreover, interrogation consists of one or more accusation strategies that are designed to obtain accurate and truthful information from a person suspected of committing the act.

In the last decade, there has been a steady stream of false confession cases casting scrutiny toward police interviewing and interrogation tactics (Porter & Ten Brinke, 2008). Research shows that police lie detection accuracy rates range from 50–60% in experimental settings (Bond & DePaulo, 2006; Aamodt & Mitchell, 2006). However, there is very little published research on the lie detection ability of private investigators, including retail security personnel. Despite this empirical gap in the research literature, there is little reason not to believe that many of the same issues affecting police officials also affect private security investigators. Having an awareness of the limitations and potential biases affecting interviews and interrogations will result in a stronger ethical foundation for professionals in the field.

Common Pitfalls in Lie Detection

The two fundamental ethical issues underlying interviews and interrogations deal with the methods that are used to elicit information and the consequences they have for individuals. Error in human deception judgments is related to various cognitive and behavioral tendencies inherent to the criminal investigation process. Confirmation bias, for example, is the tendency for investigators to seek out behaviors or statements that confirm initial judgments of guilt or innocence and to disregard information that negates these initial judgments (Kassin, Goldstein, & Savitzky, 2003). In fraud investigations, for instance, it is common practice to begin the investigation by compiling documentary evidence (paper trail) suggesting a suspect's culpability. The process of seeking out information to corroborate the documentary evidence may, in turn, influence an investigator's perspective on the way questions are asked or the degree to which the investigator remains open-minded about the suspect's responses. However, a paper trail that suggests a person is guilty may be easily justified during an interview, negating any need to pursue the interrogatory process. For instance, managers and supervisors sometimes instruct employees to perform "customer satisfaction" transactions such as price adjustments that may look suspicious on paper but in reality no criminal activity has occurred.

In addition to the potential for confirmation bias, there are likely circumstances in which an interviewee falsely confesses (intentionally or unintentionally) to private security interviewers. Kassin and Wrightsman (1985) developed a taxonomy for differentiating between types of false confessions: (1) voluntary, (2) compliant, and (3) internalized. For instance, employees may provide voluntarily confessions strictly for attention, guilty conscience, or a perceived material benefit such as drawing unemployment from their employer. These interviews usually concern policy violations where no criminal charges are likely to occur.

Under the second type, compliant false confessions, the person interviewed may feel compelled to confess or admit culpability based on promises of leniency or avoiding prosecution altogether. It is common for an interviewer to stress the potential for criminal prosecution against an employee, even if he or she is aware that insufficient evidence exists, for the sole reason of obtaining resolution of the case. Internalized confessions involve those situations where employees are led to believe they are guilty when they are in fact not. This type of confession may occur in the context of a policy violation that is connected to some form of real or perceived criminal activity. For instance, an employee may mistakenly fail to scan merchandise at the cash register but an investigator's perception may be that the act was intentional. During an interview with the employee the investigator may convince the person that the mistake was due to negligence and thus the same as theft.

The most valid data on interrogation technique efficacy (real and perceived) comes from surveys from law enforcement officers, observational studies, and experiments. The assumption is that an innocent person would never confess to a crime they did not commit; and therefore, lying to the suspect (legal, although perhaps unethical) would not trigger a confession from an innocent person. As in police investigations, private investigators may feel inclined to lie to suspects to obtain a desired response. So the question becomes: Is lying to obtain a truthful statement (albeit a confession or admission) unethical? To answer this question, it is useful to differentiate between two types of lies — extrinsic and intrinsic. Intrinsic lies involve the presentation of false information or evidence about the case to obtain the desired response from the suspect. This is also called the false evidence ploy. Conversely, extrinsic lies have to do with legal issues involving the courts or police. For instance, an investigator may indicate to the suspect that he or she will urge the court to be lenient if there is "cooperation" (in the form of a confession) in the investigation.

One may argue that investigators need to be able to embellish the facts in order to persuade a suspect to tell the truth. An informal survey of retail security professionals published in a loss prevention magazine indicates that lying to elicit a confession is a norm in the private security field (Virgillo, 2010). In the study, one respondent noted:

> If I have all the evidence I need before I walk in the door, depending on the scenario, I will say whatever is required to get to the truth out of a person. As long as I do not make false promises, lying is certainly allowable, acceptable, and part of the process to bend the truth to whatever the subject will relate to. Bottom line, I tell them whatever I need to tell them to get to the truth. (Virgillo, 2010, p. 4)

In addition to the practice of lying during interrogations, there is the issue of selecting the appropriate rationale and articulating that rationale to the suspect to obtain the desired response. The interview rationale is the strategy that the interviewer will use to establish rapport with the suspect, minimize the seriousness of the act, or convince the person that cooperation (in light of the evidence) is their best interest. Investigators can inflict serious emotional damage on a suspect by emphasizing the moral reprehensibility of their actions in order to obtain the goal of a confession. One respondent in the same study reported:

> I've certainly witnessed interrogations using rough-house tactics like saying the subject would never see their kids again or saying they won't be prosecuted if they admit.

The legal parameters governing private security interrogations are different from those governing government officials. For instance, the *Miranda* requirement that requires police to advise suspects that they are entitled to counsel prior to any custodial interrogation does not apply when private security individuals conduct investigative interviews. In other words, private (nongovernmental) individuals who conduct investigative interviews do not have to tell suspects that "anything you do or say may be held against you in a court of law." Frequently, employees will ask the person at the start of the interview a question like "Are the police going to be called?" It is customary for private security agents to respond with the answer "that depends on how cooperative you are." In many cases, the result is that the person conducting the interview already knows whether the police are going to be called but withholds that information from the suspect for two reasons. First, obtaining a written confession is critical to case resolution and many investigators assume that the suspect will be more willing to provide a written statement as long as they have not been told that the police will be contacted. Second, many agencies measure investigative productivity according to the monetary value associated with the confession. This leads to another ethical issue in investigative interviewing, which is referred to as maximization. This practice refers to the process of estimating an approximate value for property stolen when there is no physical evidence to support the loss. The ethical problem here is that the total recovery value can be embellished through the manipulation of numbers (average dollar loss for each theft multiplied by the number of thefts). Consequently, an employee who is caught stealing on one occasion and admits to several previous thefts during the interview may face criminal charges for the entire (potentially inaccurate) amount.

In summary, drawing the line between ethical and unethical conduct can be difficult because the facts of each case are always different. The severity of the crime, supporting evidence, and the suspect's explanation are typically the factors that private investigators take into account when determining the interview strategy and whether or not to pursue criminal charges once the interview/interrogation has ended. Investigators must engage in open discourse about the choice of interview strategies with supervisors and colleagues. Further, when conducting interviews, security personnel should answer questions honestly and remain sensitive to the employee's circumstances. The choice of interview strategy should never be degrading or deceptive to the extent that specific promises about the outcome of the case are made to the suspect. In addition, company policies must dictate clearly the steps and criteria that should be considered when pursuing criminal action or restitution against any employee.

Table 9.1 illustrates a typology for understanding the types of ethical violations that may occur by retail security personnel. This typology table reflects its relative impact (e.g., the public, organization, and/or group). As the table shows, public misconduct consists of a larger variety of activities than group-related misconduct. Forms of group-related misconduct are less varied but can involve serious legal and ethical violations (i.e., sexual harassment). It is important to note that some forms of unethical conduct may consist of a com-

bination of two or more of these activities. Generally speaking, the ethical violations that involve interaction with the public are most likely to receive media
attention, while organization and work-group misconduct is more conspicu-
ous in nature. Racial and gender discrimination, disrespecting one's privacy,
and use of force violations are some of the most egregious forms of misconduct on the part of security personnel. Such ethical and legal violations can
occur with respect to investigations or in relation to other duties. For instance,
it is common for retail security to perform audits and inspections in addition
to investigation of theft and fraud. Retail security personnel may abuse their
power by engaging in quid pro quo harassment during inspections on operational controls. There are privacy infringements that can occur during the context of conducting integrity interviews and the post-interview/interrogation
process, such as revealing sensitive information to obtain a confession or discussing the details of an interview with individuals who do not have "a need
to know." Moreover, security personnel who perform unnecessary searches of
personal belongings of a shoplifter or another employee are violating that person's expectation of privacy; and therefore, they are acting unethically. Other
breaches of privacy may include the inappropriate use of closed-circuit television (see below).

Table 9.1 A Typology for Ethical Misconduct in Private Security Industry

	Public	Organization	Work-Group
Race and sex discrimination/harassment	✓	✓	✓
Privacy infringements	✓	✓	
Use of force violations	✓	✓	
Violations of apprehension policies	✓	✓	
Violations of interviewing protocols		✓	
Failure to investigate/audit reports	✓	✓	
Abuse of investigative equipment	✓	✓	
Time theft		✓	

Ethics and the Use of Closed-Circuit Television

In contrast to official law enforcement investigations, the private security
industry has benefited more from closed-circuit television technology (CCTV)
as an investigative tool. A recent major study examined the effects of CCTV on

crime reduction in the United States and Europe and found a "modest, but significant reduction" (16%) in crime overall (Welsh & Farrington, 2009). The impact of CCTV cameras on crime reduction was greatest for vehicle-related crimes in crime parks. This study, however, did not focus on crime reduction in public retail businesses. In general, most research on CCTV as a means of crime intervention focuses on areas such as transportation centers, public housing, amusement parks and malls as opposed to retail businesses. It is clear, however, that retail businesses benefit from CCTV cameras when there is sufficient manpower and training to operate them (Loveday & Gill, 2004).

The infusion of CCTV cameras into the field of private security has created a host of ethical issues for security managers and their staffs. In general, CCTV cameras serve two purposes—to conduct external and internal theft investigations and ensure the safety of employees and the public. Businesses that employ staff to monitor CCTV cameras typically do not provide these individuals with any formal training (Loveday & Gill, 2004; Waples, Gill, & Fisher, 2004). Hence, untrained and inexperienced investigators are often the most prone to abusing CCTV cameras during the course of their normal work schedules. Two serious forms of public-directed misconduct are racial profiling and sexual harassment. Racial profiling occurs when CCTV operators target minority citizens in public places and ignore non-minorities for the purpose of investigating criminal activity.

In addition to racial profiling for apprehension purposes, CCTV can be used to conduct inappropriate observations or surveillances of innocent shoppers or employees. The practice of "zooming" occurs when CCTV operators invade the privacy space of public citizens and employees through camera observation. What makes zooming such an insidious behavior is the fact that victims are not aware they are being stalked or harassed (albeit through video observation) while in a public business or retail establishment. Goold (2002) notes that the ethical dilemma of the "unobservable observer" can be partially rectified if the public was to be assured that the CCTV operators are well-trained and required to adhere to specific legal and ethical guidelines (p. 25).

However, it is unlikely that any formal policies regulating CCTV use will be enacted, at least in the near future. This is because these policies would be almost impossible to enforce. Therefore, CCTV camera operation poses unique ethical issues and that governance falls squarely on management staff to ensure the equipment is being used for its intended purpose. As technology has improved, corporate security managers are now capable of monitoring investigative teams as they operate CCTV cameras to ensure that equipment is being used for appropriate reasons. However, the process of monitoring CCTV camera use is time consuming and likely is not a priority of senior management.

As a result, the first-line supervisors who oversee private security teams are the individuals best positioned to ensure that CCTV camera equipment is used for its intended purposes.

Conclusion

The world of private security has progressed significantly in the last decade, which has caused many changes to policies affecting investigative operations. There are similarities and differences in the ways private security or retail investigations and public law enforcement conduct their business. Importantly, misconduct on the part of private security personnel is more likely to be litigated in civil courts as opposed criminal courts. This is largely due to the fact that there are state statutes (abuse of authority laws) that specifically apply to the conduct of governmental actors. As a result, private security misconduct almost always results in any one of several tort violations (i.e., false arrest, false imprisonment, intentional infliction of emotional distress) opposed to a federal or constitutional violation. As retail businesses scale down and re-allocate roles and responsibilities of their investigative staffs, private security professionals will need to ensure that they receive adequate training as it relates to investigation practices.

The duties of retail and private security personnel are also similar to public law enforcement agencies in some ways. One commonality deals with interviewing and interrogating suspects. Two of the ethical issues in regards to this practice are the choice of rationale strategy and the guard against false confessions. First, in contrast to police interviews and interrogations, a private security interviewer who seeks an admission from a suspect does not have to provide the suspect with his or her *Miranda* warning. Second, there are likely numerous instances whereby suspects falsely confess to private security interviewers for a variety of reasons. In fact, the potential for false confessions may be greater in the private security field due to the fact that the benefits (i.e., drawing unemployment) may outweigh any consequences associated with providing the confession.

Lastly, the technological movement has engendered new ethical dilemmas in regards to the use of CCTV camera systems. One of the limitations of the private security business is the absence of any state regulation or licensing requirements for retail investigative personnel, although bail bonds agencies and private security contractors are subject to state regulation. The lack of systematic oversight with regards to the use of CCTV cameras and other sensory-enhancing equipment creates the potential for ethical misconduct, particularly among entry-level investigative staff. As technology becomes a more pervasive investigative tool in the private security field, the potential for misconduct on the part of security staff will also likely increase.

Scenarios

1. You are a store investigator who observes a customer select a DVD player from one of the merchandise selection areas. As you observe the person from the sales floor you notice that the suspect has made eye contact with you on two occasions. You walk to an adjacent aisle to create distance, but when you regain position you are unable to find the suspect. Approximately 6 minutes later, you spot the suspect at the refund counter returning the item. What should you do?

2. You are a store investigator who has observed a customer shoplift a generator from a home improvement store. Upon approaching the suspect outside the store, he brandishes a knife as you attempt to apprehend him. What should you do?

3. You are monitoring the CCTV camera system with two other male investigators when you notice them zoom in on a young female shopper. One of them makes a sexist remark about the customer and there appears to be no legitimate reason for surveillance. What should you do?

4. You are a loss prevention manager who has just begun an interview with an employee suspected of stealing $100 from the cash register. You know there are previous shortages from registers in the employee's department, but you are unsure if she is responsible for those shortages. During the interview the employee admits to stealing the $100 from the register. You step outside the room to contact your supervisor and he/she advises you to tell the employee that if she does not confess, she will never see her kids again. What should you do?

5. You are conducting an investigative interview of a potential dishonest employee. When attempting to derive an estimated property loss, you ask the employee how many times have they stolen property. The employee replies, "Oh, I steal about $100 worth of stuff every week." You follow up by asking, "When was the first time you stole anything?" The employee responds, "Six months ago." Doing the math, you calculate 24 weeks for a total of $2400.00 in estimated stolen property. Checking the inventory report, you are unable to corroborate that amount in missing property. You present this information to the employee and they state, "I don't remember ever stealing that much." What should you do?

6. You are a store investigator conducting a store inspection/audit of cash counting procedures. You are aware the person responsible for the area has been formally reprimanded for maintaining the cash controls. During your audit, you notice minor errors that have caused small losses to your company. However, overall you note that the employee has made substantial improvement. What should you do?

7. You are conducting an interview/interrogation with an employee who is suspected of stealing $1,000 in merchandise from a business. You have firm evidence (CCTV video footage) of the thefts and your supervisor has informed you that after completing the interview you will need to contact the police to press charges against the employee. At the beginning the interview, the employee asks you whether the police will be called. What should you do?

8. One of the employees who is not a security officer at your place of business has asked you to go to lunch. What should you do?

9. While working with one of your colleagues one day you observe a shoplifter who has concealed a drill in his pants and is exiting the store. You have all of the necessary elements to make an apprehension. When you and your partner approach the suspect outside the store, he begins to run away. Your partner tackles the suspect and you handcuff him immediately. You notice the suspect attempt to bite your partner, so you hold him down to prevent the injury. While walking the suspect back to the security office, your partner pushes the suspect into the door and says, "Whoops, sorry." What should you do?

10. Because you are part of the security department, you do not have to use the time clock to punch in—your supervisor only requires that you sign-in and work 40 hours each week. Your supervisor has told you, however, that you are still subject to attendance policy and that all infractions will be documented by store management. One day you arrive 15 minutes late but no one has witnessed you arrive late. What should you do?

References

Aamodt, M.G., & Custer, H. (2006). Who can best catch a liar? A meta-analysis of individual differences in detecting deception. *The Forensic Examiner, 25,* 6–11.

Albrecht, S.W., Albrecht, C.O., Albrecht, C.C. & Zimbelman, M.F. (2016). *Fraud Examination,* 5th Edition. Boston: Cengage Learning.

Baum, Lawrence (2008). *American Courts: Process and Policy,* 6th Edition. USA: Houghton Mifflin.

Bond, C.F., & DePaulo, B.M. (2006). Accuracy of deception judgments. *Personality & Social Psychology Review*, 10, 214–234.

Cunningham, W.C., Strauchs, J.J. & Van Meter, C.W. *Private Security Trends: 1970 to 2000—The Hallcrest Report II*, Stoneham, Massachusetts: Butterworth-Heinemann, 1990.

Fay, J. J. (2006). *Contemporary security management* (2nd ed.). Burlington, MA: Butterworth-Heinemann.

Goold, B.J. (2002). Privacy rights and public spaces: CCTV and the problem of the "Unobservable Observer." Criminal Justice Ethics, Winter/Spring, 21–27.

Grannis, K. (2002). Retail fraud, shoplifting rates decrease, according to National Retail Survey. National Retail Federation. Retrieved September 2, 2010 at http://www.nrf.com/modules.php?name=News&op=viewlive& sp_id=945.

Hertig, C. A. (2008). Appendix A. In S. Davies & C. Hertig (Eds.), Security supervision and management: theory and practice of asset protection (pp. 120–122). Burlington, MA: Butterworth-Heinemann.

Kassin, S.M., & Wrightsman, L.S. (1985). Confession evidence. In S. Kassin & L. Wrightsman (Eds.), *The psychology of evidence and trial procedure.* (pp. 67–94). Beverly Hills, CA: Sage.

Kassin, S.M., Goldstein, C.C., & Savitsky, K. (2003). Behavioral confirmation in the interrogation room: On the dangers of presuming guilt. *Law and Human Behavior, 27*(2), 187–203.

Loveday, K., & Gill, M. (2004). Impact of monitored CCTV in a retail environment: What CCTV operators do and why. *Crime Prevention and Community Safety: An International Journal*, 6(3), 43–55.

McCrie, R. D. (2001). *Security operations management*. Woburn, MA: Butterworth-Heinemann.

Nemeth, C.P. *Private security and the investigative process.* (3rd ed.). Boca Raton: CRC Press.

Pawlowski, J. (2005). Stripped shopper sues Sam's Club. *Albuquerque Journal*, 22 April 2005.

Porter, S. & ten Brinke, L. (2008). The truth about lies: What works in detecting high-stakes deception? *Legal and Criminological Psychology*, 15, 57–75.

Trautman, N. (2008). Unethical acts by security officers. In S. Davies & C. Hertig (Eds.), *Security supervision and management: theory and practice of asset protection* (pp. 117–120). Burlington, MA: Butterworth-Heinemann.

Virgillo, A. (2010). Are we liars? Getting an admission at any cost. *Loss Prevention Magazine*. Retrieved September 15, 2010 at http://www.lossprevention magazine.com/ archives_view.html?id=2615.

Waples, S., Gill, M., & Fisher, P. (2009). Does CCTV displace crime? *Criminology and Criminal Justice*, 9(2), 207–224.

Welsh, B.C., & Farrington, D.P. (2009). Public area CCTV and crime prevention: An updated systematic review and meta-analysis.

Cases Cited

Gaines v. Nordstrom (D. Or., 2007).

10

Ethics and the Criminal Justice Supervisor

Chapter Objectives

- The student will understand the importance of leadership and ethics
- The student will learn about supervisory discretion and ethics
- The student will become aware of official misconduct and civil liability
- The student will gain information on abuse of authority laws
- The student will learn about sexual harassment and ethics
- The student will understand how supervisors influence on police, and correctional misconduct

Introduction

When Los Angeles police officers severely abused Rodney King in 1991, the American public was shocked to see that officials entrusted to protect and serve were capable of committing heinous crimes. Certainly this incident represents an extreme example of an ethics violation, but it is a violation of both criminal and civil law. The reality is that many ethics violations are not considered legal violations although ethical violations have the power to influence public opinion and the people who surround us in our social groups, family, and professional lives.

As a leader in the criminal justice field, a primary objective is to ensure that line officers act professionally and ethically at all times, particularly when they are not directly or indirectly supervised. Officers who behave unethically are a direct reflection of the supervisor's leadership qualities and the officer's commitment to follow rules. Most officers are highly ethical and do not pose a problem for their supervisor. This is partly a function of the screening process unique to the policing profession and the training that officers receive. However, the reality is that criminal justice actors are frequently faced with temptations and therefore they have potential to become complacent.

This chapter focuses on ethical issues that confront the criminal justice supervisor. It begins by providing some background on ethics and the two major commissions to investigate ethics violations in policing. Next, a discussion of the relationship between leadership and ethics is provided as it relates to general supervision in the criminal justice field. This approach is taken because leadership issues related to policing are similar to probation, parole and corrections. The third section focuses on common types of ethical violations in each of these fields. The final section ends with an overview of criminal and civil laws that are invoked when ethics violations transcend normative boundaries.

Commissions on Police Deviance

In the policing profession, there have been two major Commissions to investigate police corruption in our history—The Wickersham and Knapp Commissions. The 1929 Wickersham Commission was formed primarily to investigate violations of alcohol prohibition, and recommended more aggressive law enforcement to curtail the problem. The 1970 Knapp Commission was tasked to investigate widespread corruption within the New York Police Department. The investigation differentiated between minor forms of "grass-eater" corruption and major forms of "meat-eater" corruption, which relates to the amount of money an officer accepts in bribes. The Commission reported that minor forms of corruption were the most prevalent and mostly the result of police subculture and peer pressure. Serious corruption, on the other hand, was thought to be more predatory in nature and consisted of officers actively seeking out situations or individuals to exploit for financial gain.

Regardless of the type of criminal justice work performed, the potential for corruption and misconduct of officers is heightened when senior officers and supervisors do not conduct themselves with high levels of integrity. Conversely, when senior officers live by high ethical standards it is more likely that the officers who work for them will follow suit.

Leadership and Ethics

To begin, there is a difference between police *supervision* and *leadership*. Whereas supervision entails taking a reactive, approach to management, leadership is more proactive (More & Miller, 2007). The effects of an effective leader are immeasurable. Great leaders inspire, motivate, and instill high values in their employees, and ultimately impact the behavior of employees. Harrison (1996) has identified several critical elements of effective leaders:

1. Allowing the appropriate persons to make the necessary decisions.
2. Creating and facilitating an environment that breeds trust and openness.
3. Empowering subordinates to succeed, learn, and make decisions.
4. Creating and sticking to an organizational mission.

There is ample research on leadership theories and approaches with respect to criminal justice organizations. More and Miller (2007) identify three main theoretical approaches, but in reality these same theories can be applied to all types of criminal justice leadership roles. They are: (1) behavioral theories, (2) contingency theories, and (3) trait theories.

Behavioral theory focuses on the behavior of the supervisor to the extent that he or she is task-driven or empathetic to the needs of subordinates. Task-driven leaders thrive on structure, detail, and clear division of roles and responsibilities. The benefit of having a task-driven supervisor is that there is less likely to be a question as to the expectation or desired result. The drawback to task-driven leaders is that some employees work well independently and thus may feel uncomfortable working for leaders who do not give their employees adequate flexibility to make decisions. Conversely, leaders who have more empathy but provide less structure to employees may obtain higher levels of morale but lower levels of productivity, particularly for those employees who need direction and feedback. In the end, behavioral theory stresses the need to have a balanced approach that incorporates elements of structure and empowerment. The key for the supervisor is to determine the ideal combination of structure and empowerment to achieve the maximum benefit and desired goal for the employee and the organization.

Knowledge about the appropriate leadership strategy to use will have a positive impact on the employee, raise their morale, and reinforce high ethical standards. Contingency theory states that the leader must select the correct leadership style to match a particular problem or situation. Every situation that a leader confronts is different, but this does not mean that a leader should question the approach they have taken to deal with a particular circumstance. Moreover, there are many occasions when the benefits of having taken a particular approach will not become apparent until the respondent has had time to digest feedback and respond to the situation. The contingency model of leadership, created by Fred Fiedler (1967), emphasizes three factors: (1) position power, (2) structure of task, and (3) interpersonal relationships between a leader and his or her followers. In general, the greater the position power the leader holds, the more presence a leader will have with his or her constituents, thus minimizing the opportunity for occupational deviance and corruption. Fiedler enumerated specific traits that could be used to measure position power:

1. Ability to sanction and reward behavior.
2. Possesses official rank and status.
3. Has knowledge of the work performed, position, and the limitations (if any) to perform the specified work.
4. Is aware of possible alternatives that can be explored in order to accomplish the desired goal.

In addition to position power, a leader must also maintain a good interpersonal working relationship that is built on trust in order to create employee "buy-in." According to the contingency theory, this interpersonal relationship is key to the success of a leader because it is based on the respective personalities of the leader and follower. The more likely these personalities are to be similar, the more likely the two are going to get along and have a productive relationship. Likewise, disparate personality types can cause friction and a tendency for the subordinate to disrespect or be disloyal to the supervisor. For obvious reasons, there will inevitably be differences in personality types between officers and their supervisors. Particularly for new supervisors, the important factor to keep in mind is the need for communication so that some level of mutual trust can be established. For example, a young sergeant who has just been promoted may be viewed negatively by older subordinate officers because of lack of experience and not having "paid their dues." In turn, it is imperative that the new supervisor always retains a high level of respect toward his or her subordinates if he or she perceives that personality conflicts are detrimental to working relationships. In these cases, more structure and less emphasis on building interpersonal relationships is typically a more effective method to maintain officer morale and productivity that is built on high ethical values.

The trait theory of leadership holds that every leader possesses certain characteristics that allow them to be successful. According to this theory, leaders thrive on certain traits, such as the ability to present ideas, attain academic excellence, and the ability to work in a group. These all are qualities that represent "achievement" to subordinates. It should be noted that this theory also maintains that effective leaders do not have to possess many different types of traits to be effective, but that they have the capacity to influence others using their individual traits. Further, trait theory claims that successful leaders can have very different traits that work well in specific situations. For the criminal justice supervisor it is important to have a self-awareness of one's strengths and weaknesses in order to have a positive influence on subordinates. The more easily a supervisor can adapt to a situation or individual the more control he or she will have over their direct reports. For instance, a supervisor may be able to draw on personal experiences to explain to a subordinate about what to do in situation that involves an ethical dilemma. As a supervisor, you may explain to your subordinate that the public will occasionally attempt to persuade you to treat them favorably by offering you gifts, etc. You should explain how you deal with a gratuitous person and what the consequences for accepting those gifts have been in the past.

To some extent, the personal attributes of a supervisor directly impacts his or her ethical standards. The Importation Model holds that an employee's attitudes toward work are largely influenced by the individual characteristics of the employee (Cullen, Latessa, Kopache, Lombardo, & Burton, 1993). According to this perspective, a leader who maintains and cultivates high ethical standards in his or her employees may be less experienced and therefore less respected by subordinates. If the imported traits are not viewed favorably by direct reports there is the potential for authority to be compromised. However, the Environmental Model maintains that the employee's work habits are a function of the work environment rather than individual characteristics of an employee (Cullen, Link, & Wolfe, 1991). Moreover, a supervisor can have a profound impact on the officer's performance, self-concept, and the types of values and goals he or she establishes. The supervisor must be able to cultivate a work environment that fosters high ethical standards.

Maintaining an active leadership role with the officers helps alleviate much of the ambiguity that exists during the course of everyday tasks such as patrol, field visits, and community service. There has been a dramatic, positive change in the level of professionalism among law enforcement, corrections, and probation and parole personnel during the last few decades, largely a result of better hiring practices, training, and resources. The supervisor's job is to define and establish all of the criteria that are needed so that officers have clear direction about ethical expectations. The International Association of Chiefs of Police has established a model code of police ethics (see Figure 10.1).

Discretion

The decision-making authority of a criminal justice actor sets them apart from the vast majority of other occupations in that they have the power to arrest, detain, and incarcerate offenders. For instance, police officers have limited time to decide on a particular action: issue a warning, write a citation, or conduct an arrest. When officers must take immediate action without giving

Figure 10.1 1989 Police Code of Conduct

All law enforcement officers must be fully aware of the ethical responsibilities of their position and must strive constantly to live up to the highest possible standards of professional policing. The International Association of Chiefs of Police believes it important that police officers have clear advice and counsel available to assist them in performing their duties consistent with these standards, and has adopted the following ethical mandates as guidelines to meet these ends.

Primary Responsibilities of a Police Officer

A police officer acts as an official representative of government who is required and trusted to work within the law. The officer's powers and duties are conferred by statute. The fundamental duties of a police officer include serving the community, safeguarding lives and property, protecting the innocent, keeping the peace and ensuring the rights of all to liberty, equality and justice.

Performance of the Duties of a Police Officer

A police officer shall perform all duties impartially, without favor or affection or ill will and without regard to status, sex, race, religion, political belief or aspiration. All citizens will be treated equally with courtesy, consideration and dignity.

Officers will never allow personal feelings, animosities or friendships to influence official conduct. Laws will be enforced appropriately and courteously and, in carrying out their responsibilities, officers will strive to obtain maximum cooperation from the public. They will conduct themselves in appearance and department in such a manner as to inspire confidence and respect for the position of the public trust they hold.

Discretion

A police officer will use responsibly the discretion vested in his position and exercise it within the law. The principle of reasonableness will guide the officer's determinations, and the officer will consider all surrounding circumstances in determining whether any legal action shall be taken.

Consistent and wise use of discretion, based on professional policing competence, will do much to preserve good relationships and retain the confidence of the public. There can be difficulty in choosing between conflicting courses of action. It is important to remember that a timely word of advice rather than arrest—which may be correct in appropriate circumstances—can be a more effective means of achieving a desired end.

Use of Force

A police officer will never employ unnecessary force or violence and will use only such force in the discharge of duty as is reasonable in all circumstances.

The use of force should be used only with the greatest restraint and only after discussion, negotiation and persuasion have been found to be inappropriate or ineffective. While the use of force is occasionally unavoidable, every police officer will refrain from unnecessary infliction of pain or suffering and will never engage in cruel, degrading or inhumane treatment of any person.

Confidentiality

Whatever a police officer sees, hears, or learns of that is of a confidential nature, will be kept secret unless the performance of duty or legal provision requires otherwise. Members of the public have a right to security and privacy, and information obtained about them must not be improperly divulged.

Source: Reprinted from the Police Chief, 1990, p.18. Copyright held by the International Association of Chiefs of Police, 515 North Washington Street, Alexandria, VA 22314 USA. Further reproduction without express written permission from IACP is strictly prohibited.

Figure 10.1 1989 Police Code of Conduct, *continued*

Integrity

A police officer will not engage in acts of corruption or bribery, nor will an officer condone such acts by others. The public demands that the integrity of the police officers be above reproach. Police officers, must, therefore, avoid any conduct that might compromise integrity and thus undercut the public confidence in law enforcement agency. Officers will refuse to accept any gifts, presents, subscriptions, favors, gratuities, or promises that could be interpreted as seeking to cause the officer to refrain from performing official responsibilities honestly and within the law. Police officers must not receive private or special advantage from their official status. Respect from the public cannot be bought; it can only be earned and cultivated.

Cooperation with Other Officers and Agencies

Police officers will cooperate with all legally authorized agencies and their representatives in the pursuit of justice.

An officer or agency may be one among many organizations that may provide law enforcement services to a jurisdiction. It is imperative that a police officer assist colleagues fully and completely with respect and consideration at all times.

Personal/Professional Capabilities

Police officers will be responsible for their own standard of professional performance and will take every reasonable opportunity to enhance and improve their level of knowledge and competence that is essential for the efficient performance of duty. The acquisition of knowledge is a never-ending process of personal and professional development that should be pursued constantly.

Private Life

Police officers will behave in a manner that does not bring discredit to their agencies or themselves.

A police officer's character and conduct while off duty must always be exemplary, thus maintaining a position of respect in the community in which he or she lives and serves. The officer's personal behavior must be beyond reproach.

---

much time to deliberate on their options they have a greater risk of making the wrong decision. A routine traffic stop that appears relatively straightforward can quickly turn into a vehicle pursuit or shootout.

Police officers make decisions everyday that have ethical implications. For instance, a police officer decides on whether to issue a motorist a ticket or warning; a probation officer decides whether to revoke a probationer, and a correctional officer decides on whether to allow an inmate to violate minor rules such as the ability to make additional phone calls. The supervisor's failure to exercise discipline is a major contributor to low morale. Officers who perceive that their supervisor lacks the leadership skills to set high ethical standards may perceive the supervisor as being weak and easily manipulated. This lack of respect could lead to a "ripple effect" of ethical problems, such as failing to enforce laws, conduct patrols, or responding timely to low priority calls. This is commonly referred to as the slippery slope phenomenon (Sherman, 1985). The initial acceptance of gratuities, for instance, may be the first step toward more serious forms of graft on the part of police officers, such as accepting payoffs by drug dealers or vice-related crimes. In reality, the type of gratuity (or its value) may be the critical factor determining whether the acceptance of a gratuity is ethical, unethical, or illegal. But from a supervisor's perspective, addressing the situation promptly through documentation, discourse, and training are the keys to what ultimately creates an environment that thrives on positive morale and is intolerant of ethical violations.

It should be noted that there are many situations when criminal justice supervisors are authorized to discipline their subordinate officers but choose not to do so. Discretion as to when to enforce rules, therefore, is a critical factor that affects the integrity of the work group and the ethical standards of officers. On one hand, a police supervisor who formally reprimands subordinate officers too frequently can lead to poor morale. It is therefore advisable that police supervisors remain selective as to when to exercise formal discipline. A new police sergeant on patrol, for example, will receive formal and informal training from his peers. The new supervisor should remain open-minded about how veteran supervisors have dealt with misconduct in prior experience before making decisions about disciplining subordinates.

In contrast to negative discipline, the use of positive discipline on the part of the police supervisor "involves a systematic approach that is designed to instruct or guide employees in such a way that they become loyal, dedicated, responsible, and productive members of the organization" (More & Miller, 2007, p. 291). Positive discipline is the antidote to poor ethical standards. Supervisors who take the time to commend officers for a job well-done and reward them for accomplishing their goals will see higher levels of productivity, commitment, and morale. To some extent, criminal justice supervisors who use positive discipline can improve self-discipline in their officers. Good self-discipline and high self-esteem are important traits in officers and make them well-suited for law enforcement. But the reinforcement of self-discipline is critical to the vitality of the work group, and part of the supervisor's job is to provide appropriate feedback for officers that will allow them to improve self-confidence and discipline. Inevitably, ethics and productivity go hand in hand. One method that has been used by police supervisors to improve officer performance is the PRICE protocol, an acronym for pinpoint, record, involve, coach, and evaluate (Blanchard, 1989).

1. *Pinpoint*: Supervisors must constantly be aware of officer performance in order to identify signs of positive and negative performance.
2. *Record*: Supervisors must document performance issues and communicate those issues to the officer, as well as his or her supervisor.

3. *Involve*: Supervisors must assist the officer in developing a strategy to improve performance, within an appropriate timeline, and explain how the performance will be measured.
4. *Coach*: Supervisors should assess the officer's response to any coaching strategy and refine as needed or choose a different one.
5. *Evaluate*: Supervisors must evaluate and determine whether the goals identified have been achieved.

A supervisor who maintains consistent interaction with his or her officers has the best opportunity to gauge their performance and identify misconduct, if it exists. The following section provides a brief overview of various types of liability that a police supervisor must be aware of, and the types of police conduct that can serve as a basis for that liability.

Official Misconduct and Civil Liability

If a supervisor becomes aware that his or her officers are not exercising good judgment, the supervisor must immediately take action as opposed to overlooking minor infractions. The failure to do so may result in serious consequences such as civil liability. First, if a court finds that a supervisor's failure to discipline resulted in the officer's negligent conduct then the supervisor may be sued based on the theory of vicarious liability. This means that the supervisor and/or his agency are civilly liable for the actions of his or her subordinates even though he or she was not directly involved in the incident. Second, the supervisor can be disciplined by a higher ranking supervisor such as a lieutenant, captain, or chief for failing to take appropriate action against an officer who exercises poor decision-making skills.

In some ways, criminal justice managers have advantages to ensuring that subordinate officers remain accountable and compliant to rules. One of these sources is the criminal law itself. As long as police officers are carrying out their normal duties, they are authorized to break the law in some cases, and thus are protected by official or qualified immunity. There are important differences in the thresholds for liability in state and federal courts. For tort violations, the legal threshold is typically negligence or recklessness. Both of these terms describe a lower level of culpability than criminal culpability. Negligence or recklessness means that the officer did not specifically intend to commit a particular act, but that as a result of the officer's conduct it was foreseeable (based on court opinion) that such consequences would occur.

If an officer is sued in state court, he or she may invoke the defense of official immunity, meaning that the officer cannot be held liable for discretionary duties performed in good faith, as long as the officer was carrying out his or her normal job duties. The concept of good faith means that the officer "acted in the honest belief that the action taken or the decision was appropriate under the circumstances" (del Carmen, 2007, p. 528). In addition to the potential of being sued in state court, officers can also be held liable in federal court for constitutional violations or violations of federal law. The legal threshold of proof in federal court is determined largely by case law. Proof of liability in federal court is much more difficult to establish compared to standards of negligence or recklessness. The reason for this is that federal courts have typically interpreted constitutional and federal rights related to police misconduct narrowly in an effort to control the amount of litigation filed in federal courts and to defer to the opinions of state courts. In contrast to state tort violations, Title 42 of the U.S. Code, Section 1983 provides a remedy for plaintiffs to sue government officials who violate their federal or constitutional rights. These are typically referred to as "Section 1983 cases." In terms of police conduct, typical lawsuits arising under Section 1983 commonly involve allegations of unnecessary use of force (police pursuits, arrests, use of deadly/non-deadly force), right to due process (procedural or substantive due process), and equal protection of the law. It is also quite possible that an officer could be sued in state and federal court in the same case because the laws in both jurisdictions are frequently quite similar. There is no double jeopardy protection because state and federal courts are considered different jurisdictions.

Box 10.1 Dallas Officers Put On Leave

Public integrity unit investigating detention of tow truck driver

The Dallas Morning News (TX) — May 26, 2006

Two Dallas police officers accused of official oppression are now on administrative leave.

Police supervisors requested an investigation after a chain of events that they say began when Officer Michael Contreras argued recently with a tow truck employee after his car was towed. Police said the two officers ran a warrant check on the tow truck driver after Officer Contreras' car was towed.

The officers found that he had an outstanding warrant.

On May 21, Officer Contreras and Officer Edward Saenz went to the man's workplace and detained him, Dallas police Senior Cpl. Max Geron said.

Dallas police spokesman Rick Watson said the officers didn't take the man to jail and later released him.

"We're trying to determine what did they do to this individual," Lt. Watson said.

Officer Contreras was hired in 2003.

He has four commendations and no prior disciplinary action on his record.

Officer Saenz was hired in 1997. He has received at least 31 commendations and has been disciplined at least six times, including a written reprimand in December 2002 for false arrest.

Both officers were placed on administrative leave Monday. The department's public integrity unit will determine whether criminal charges are warranted.

Official oppression is a Class A misdemeanor punishable by up to a year in jail and a fine of up to $4,000.

Source: Holly Yan, "Dallas officers put on leave—Public integrity unit investigating detention of tow truck driver," *Dallas Morning News,* May 26, 2006.

Thinking Questions

1. If you were officer Saenz's supervisor, what action would you take based on this incident?
2. Do you think either officer should face criminal charges, civil liability, or only administrative consequences?
3. What is civil liability?
4. How does supervisory discretion have an effect on criminal justice ethics?

Abuse of Authority Laws

Official oppression and abuse of authority laws are found in each state's penal code. These laws apply specifically to the conduct of public officials as opposed to any citizen. Acts of official oppression may result in criminal or civil liability, but they mainly consist of laws applicable specifically to pubic officials. The following sections discuss the application of these laws to policing, probation and parole, and corrections with specific emphasis on the implications for criminal justice supervisors.

Box 10.2 Texas Penal Code

Title 8: Offenses Against Public Administration

Chapter 39. Abuse of Office

Sec. 39.02. ABUSE OF OFFICIAL CAPACITY.

(a) A public servant commits an offense if, with intent to obtain a benefit or with intent to harm or defraud another, he intentionally or knowingly:

> (1) violates a law relating to the public servant's office or employment; or

> (2) misuses government property, services, personnel, or any other thing of value belonging to the government that has come into the public servant's custody or possession by virtue of the public servant's office or employment.

(b) An offense under Subsection (a)(1) is a Class A misdemeanor.

(c) An offense under Subsection (a)(2) is:

> (1) a Class C misdemeanor if the value of the use of the thing misused is less than $20;

> (2) a Class B misdemeanor if the value of the use of the thing misused is $20 or more but less than $500;

> (3) a Class A misdemeanor if the value of the use of the thing misused is $500 or more but less than $1,500;

> (4) a state jail felony if the value of the use of the thing misused is $1,500 or more but less than $20,000;

> (5) a felony of the third degree if the value of the use of the thing misused is $20,000 or more but less than $100,000;

> (6) a felony of the second degree if the value of the use of the thing misused is $100,000 or more but less than $200,000; or

> (7) a felony of the first degree if the value of the use of the thing misused is $200,000 or more.

(d) A discount or award given for travel, such as frequent flyer miles, rental car or hotel discounts, or food coupons, are not things of value belonging to the government for purposes of this section due to the administrative difficulty and cost involved in recapturing the discount or award for a governmental entity.

(e) If separate transactions that violate Subsection (a)(2) are conducted pursuant to one scheme or continuing course of conduct, the conduct may be considered as one offense and the value of the use of the things misused in the transactions may be aggregated in determining the classification of the offense.

(f) The value of the use of a thing of value misused under Subsection (a)(2) may not exceed:

    (1) the fair market value of the thing at the time of the offense; or

    (2) if the fair market value of the thing cannot be ascertained, the cost of replacing the thing within a reasonable time after the offense.

Source: Texas Penal Code: Offenses Against Public Administration, Abuse of Office. Retrieved from http://www.statutes.legis.state.tx.us/docs/PE/htm/PE.39.htm, Oct. 2, 2010.

Police Misconduct

So the question you should ask is what happens when police supervisors do not uphold ethical standards for subordinates? Earlier in the chapter the term vicarious liability was mentioned. Ethical violations that go unpunished are likely to lead to more severe violations that have legal consequences for the supervisor and/or agency. In reality, there are numerous examples of situations that present ethical dilemmas for criminal justice supervisors. For instance, what begins as flirtatious conduct has the potential to become sexual harassment; and accepting a free cup of coffee may be the prelude to more serious forms of graft. Therefore, a commitment to discipline, supervision, and training of subordinates as to what represents "good ethics" is of the essence to criminal justice supervisors. In addition, recent cases have emerged that remind of us of the importance of sound administrative practices in shaping ethics, accountability, and transparency with the public. This section begins with a discussion of two ethical issues that police supervisors must deal with on a frequent basis: sexual harassment and the acceptance of gratuities. The section concludes with a discussion of the importance of management and oversight in cultivating an environment that promotes ethical behavior for criminal justice supervisors, officers, and other public officials.

Box 10.3 In the News

San Gabriel Valley Tribune (West Covina, CA) — October 19, 2009

EL MONTE — An El Monte police sergeant pleaded no contest to a charge of soliciting a prostitute more than a decade before he was named as defendant in a sexual harassment lawsuit filed against the city.

Al Tromp was charged in 1997 with the misdemeanor. After his no contest plea, a judge sentenced him to five days in jail and one year of probation, Los Angeles County District spokeswoman Jane Robison said.

Despite his conviction, he was allowed to keep his job with the police department.

Tromp, 52, is the central figure in a sexual harassment lawsuit filed against El Monte last week.

El Monte Police Officer Mechelle Marin alleges Tromp spoke into her breasts and made sexually derogatory statements while he supervised her.

Marin contends that she complained both verbally and in writing to supervisors, who failed to take corrective action.

Marin's lawyer said on Monday that the revelation of Tromp's prostitution conviction proves the department knowingly tolerated the sergeant's inappropriate behavior.

"This appears to be further evidence that Sgt. Tromp had a long-standing propensity to treat women as sexual objects," attorney Solomon E. Gresen said in a written statement. "One would think that the El Monte Police Department would have long ago recognized the need to rein in Sgt. Tromp's unlawful behavior."

El Monte Chief of Police Tom Armstrong denied that allegation.

Armstrong was not Chief in 1997 and said he is not comfortable commenting on any disciplinary actions that may have been taken against Tromp following the prostitution conviction.

However, he said the department acted quickly and responsibly when notified of Marin's complaints.

"We took action to immediately intervene to ensure the alleged behavior did not continue," Armstrong said. "An investigation began, and once that concluded, the allegation was reviewed and appropriate disciplinary action was taken based on what transpired.

"I'm confident we did the right thing."

News of Tromp's prostitution conviction comes just four days after another El Monte city employee was arrested on suspicion of soliciting a prostitute.

City Manager Jim Mussenden was arrested Thursday night in Pomona. He tendered his letter of resignation Saturday.

Court records indicate Tromp filed to have the conviction expunged from his record in 1998.

Both Tromp and Marin continue to work for the El Monte Police Department.

Source: "El Monte police sergeant accused in sexual harassment lawsuit has prostitution conviction," *San Gabriel Valley Tribune* [West Covina, CA], News, Oct. 19, 2009.

Sexual Harassment

Public administrators have the power to cultivate an environment where decision-making is based on sound ethical values. When ethical compromises occur, the person subjected to the harassment may be able to sue the harasser and his or her employer. The Fourth Circuit's decision in *Katz v. Dole* (1983) established two legal definitions of sexual harassment. One is quid pro quo, which is a form of "harassment in which a supervisor demands sexual consideration in exchange for job benefits" (*Katz v. Dole*, 1983, p. 1). The second form is called hostile environment (condition of work) harassment. A claim of sexual harassment can constitute a violation of Title VII of the Civil Rights Act of 1964 based on sexual discrimination. For example, if a police supervisor condones or directly engages in sexual harassment, then it becomes an illegal and discriminatory condition of employment that poisons the work environment. In such cases, the employer (police, probation/parole, or corrections department) may be held liable under a deep pockets theory of liability. In some cases, the courts may hold local municipalities vicariously liable for sexual harassment that occurs in the workplace if the supervisor is deemed to be at fault.

Accepting Gratuities

The acceptance of gratuities is a social norm in the criminal justice field. It is human nature for people to offer things as a sign of gratitude. However, the ethical dilemma for criminal justice supervisors concerns the motivation for such acts. For example, if a suspect kidnaps a child and police work diligently to find and recover the child safely, it would be natural for the parents to be grateful to the police for solving the crime. As a token of their appreciation, the parents may send the detective a case of select prime cut steaks. Many police ethics' protocols would forbid the detective from accepting the gift, but there is a difference between accepting a gratuity for services provided compared to an *expectation* that services will be rendered (Coleman, 2004). After all, such honest displays of appreciation are a form of positive discipline (rewards) that effects organizational behavior in a positive way.

One may assume that the acceptance of minor types of gratuities such as a cup of coffee would inevitably lead to serious forms of corruption. To be clear, there is no real evidence that such a relationship exists. We know, for instance, that most officers are not corrupt and that many officers have, at one point or another, accepted tokens of appreciation. However, for the criminal justice supervisor, the main concern is not if officers will become corrupt after having accepted gratuities. Coleman (2004) notes two reasons why police should not accept gratuities. He calls "the democratic ethos of policing" a public servant responsibility in where "public services should be available to all, [and] allowing a fee-for-service system for policing would be anti-democratic" (p. 36). In other words, those public establishments that provide police free meals or incentives are more likely to receive favorable treatment by the police. Consider the following scenario:

> Sergeant Jones decides to eat lunch at establishment A because (it is owned by a former police officer) and he knows he can eat there for free. He parks his patrol car in front of the restaurant, and engages in small talk with the wait staff after eating, which amounts to a 90 minute lunch. As a result of the sergeant's conduct his officers decide to eat there as well, on different shifts, following a similar routine.

Thinking Questions

1. What do you think the public's perception is toward the dining patterns of the sergeant and his officers?
2. What is the potential impact on the community of having increased officer presence at this establishment?

This type of scenario creates the impression that officers provide preferential treatment to some members of the community. As a result, citizens may develop negative perceptions toward criminal justice agencies based on the behavior of just a few. The power of the media to portray police officers in a positive or negative fashion is ubiquitous, and so police supervisors must understand the impact of the behavior on the community. Officers who accept gratuities from the public project an image that all police officers conform to a similar behavior pattern. In order for the police to improve public confidence they must be able to rely on the public for their support to address crime problems (Coleman, 2004).

Mismanagement of Criminal Justice Organizations

The shooting of Michael Brown in August of 2014 prompted waves of protest against the police department in Ferguson, Missouri. After a grand jury declined to indict Officer Darren Wilson, the officer who shot Mr. Brown, the Department of Justice initiated an independent investigation of the criminal justice system in Ferguson. The results of the DOJ's report highlighted numerous deficiencies in the way the Ferguson criminal justice system operated. For example, the report indicated that the municipal government did a poor job of collecting data on police-citizen encounters and use of force incidents. In addition, findings revealed that the courts kept warrants in file drawers instead of making them accessible through a computer database like most modern police departments (James & Ortellado, 2015, p.2). Other problems were noted by the DOJ such as the lack of transparency in police and court administration. For example, the report states:

> *The court's procedures and operations are ambiguous, are not written down, and are not transparent or even available to the public on the court's website or elsewhere.*
>
> *Further, Ferguson, unlike other [cities'] courts in the region, does not include any information about its operations on its website other than inaccurate instructions about how to make [a] payment.* (DOJ, 2015, p.45).

In summary, the DOJ concluded that the Ferguson police department and the municipal court system were deficient in the management of basic public services. Claims of racial discrimination against the Ferguson Criminal Justice System were fueled initially by the shooting of Mr. Brown but further supported by evidence showing that although African Americans made up 63% of the Ferguson population they accounted for 86% of the traffic stops (Appuzo, 2015). Data from the Missouri attorney general's office revealed that, once stopped, search rates of African Americans were double that of whites (Appuzo, 2015). Ferguson, like many other small sized American cities, generates a large share of its income through traffic fines. But the social and financial costs associated with failing to pay traffic fines are more burdensome for minorities due to repeated incarcerations for failing to pay the fines, which results in their inability to maintain employment.

The Ferguson case poses several ethical dilemmas for police and criminal justice supervisors. For example, many police chiefs are appointed by city councils that have a vested interest in ensuring that their municipalities remain financially stable. When fines generated through traffic and parking citations account for such a large portion of an overall city's general revenue, there is some pressure on police supervisors to ensure that officers are issuing citations regularly. In a study of the disbanding of police organizations, King (2014) found that one small town increased its average ticket revenue from $2,000 a year to nearly $10,000 (p. 683). Two theories have been used to explain the disbanding of police organizations—contingency and institutional. Contingency factors include the political, financial, social, and demographic factors that foster change in a police organization. Police agencies in "locales with declining populations and declining revenues are at an increased risk of being disbanded" (King, 2014, p. 685). More so than large organizations, small departments are more vulnerable to change because they lack the resources necessary to withstand political and public pressure (Bass, 1995). On the other hand, institutional forces consist of behaviors of criminal justice officials and their organizations. What begins as political pressure on the police department to issue more traffic citations or discontinue community outreach programs may lead to resentment from the community or local government leaders. These feelings of discontent can cause police supervisors to act unprofessionally or engage in more serious forms of graft or corruption. How do police supervisors balance the demands of local government without unfairly targeting citizens through aggressive ticketing practices? The lessons learned from Ferguson and other police department debacles underscore the importance of communication and transparency in city government. Police supervisors, like other city leaders, must advocate for policies that allow the public to access revenues and expenses so that there is no temptation to mislead the public. Such practices will also help ensure that the public does not perceive that its city government is being deceptive. Posting information on government websites, providing financial data on government operations to the media, and establishing long-term financial planning to effectively deal with revenue issues are some management strategies that will help reduce the propensity for misconduct. Even for small police organizations, the availability of technology makes communication easier and improves efficiency.

Probation and Parole Officer Misconduct

In Angleton, Texas, a former Brazoria County adult probation officer was indicted on misdemeanor and felony charges of official oppression in February, 2010 for tampering with a probationer's urine tests. While involved in a personal relationship with one of his female probationers, Jeffrey South had requested that the female probationer obtain marijuana for his personal use. South eventually entered a plea of guilt and agreed to serve a term of probation for the violations.

As in any sector of the criminal justice system, probation and parole officers have immense power when dealing with the public. Probation and parole officers have two main functions: (1) ensure that offenders do not threaten the safety of the community, and (2) provide adequate resources to rehabilitate offenders (Jones & Lurigio, 1997). At any given time, probation and parole officers may face a conflict about the extent to which they are able to provide adequate social services without compromising public safety. In such situations, probation and parole officers must put the need for community protection above the goal of providing effective rehabilitation.

Figure 10.1 shows the growing number of offenders under probation and parole supervision in the United States. It is clear that probation and parole supervisors have an immense responsibility when it comes to overseeing their officers. A report by the National Institute of Justice (2005) highlights some of the unique issues that probation and parole supervisors face in managing their staffs:

1. Probation and parole officers typically have high case loads of offenders who have committed more serious crimes than in the past.
2. Probation and parole officers receive less pay than many police officers.
3. The turnover rate of probation and parole officers is typically very high.
4. Career mobility and the lack of opportunity to advance one's career is relatively limited for probation officers.
5. Probation and parole officers experience high levels of stress due to pressures with deadlines and excess paperwork.

Figure 10.2 Offenders in Correctional Populations in the United States, by Type of Supervision

Adult correctional populations, 1980-2008

Source: Bureau of Justice Statistics, Correctional Surveys. Reprinted with permission.

As mentioned, the job of a probation and parole supervisor is to ensure that their officers provide the most effective supervision for their clients as possible without exposing the agency to undue risk or liability. Research on the types of liability that a probation officer and probation agency may be subjected to include (1) liability based on special relationship, (2) liability based on identifiable victims, (3) liability based on discretionary versus ministerial functions, and (4) liability based on the foreseeability of injury (Morgan, Belbot, & Clark, 1997).

As you learned previously in Chapter 8, Probation is used in lieu of incarceration and is much more common than parole in that it is used as a sanction for both misdemeanor and felony offenses. In either case, offenders must abide by specific court-ordered conditions. Parole, on the other hand, is granted by a parole board after an offender has served some period of confinement. A probation or parole officer may be held civilly or criminally liable for negligent supervision or their relationships with offenders. In addition, a third party who is injured as a result of the probation officer's conduct may also sue a probation officer and/or his or her agency. For instance, the failure to warn a victim when there is some foreseeable risk of harm may become the basis of a lawsuit against a probation officer. An exhaustive review of the types of liability that probation and parole officers face is beyond the scope of this chapter, but the following case reflects how a city can be held liable when it does not have sufficient policies relating to the supervision of probationers.

In *Benskin v. City of Fife* (2009), a Washington state appellate court faced the issue as to whether a "take charge" or "special relationship" existed between the city's probation department and the probationer, Mr. Kim, who was on probation for multiple convictions of driving while intoxicated. While on probation for these offenses, the defendant collided head-on with the victim's vehicle, causing her death. The court ruled that the probation officer and the department had a duty to supervise Kim and protect the public from foreseeable behavior. The conditions were that "Kim, a repeat DWI offender, provide proof of treatment, and essentially, refrain from driving" (p. 9). The Judge in charge of the probation department admitted that the "city's probation department [did] not have any written policies and procedures in place" (p. 7). A secondary issue involved the question of whether the city was entitled to immunity based on the supervision provided. The city argued it was entitled to quasi-judicial immunity because the probation officer exercised discretion to supervise Kim. Quasi-judicial immunity applies to probation and parole officers when they perform functions comparable to judges, such as enforcing conditions of probation or providing information to a parole board for parole determinations. In contrast, officers who perform administrative functions or supervisory functions are entitled to qualified immunity, meaning they are more vulnerable to civil liability. On summary judgment, the court ruled in favor of the plaintiff, holding that the judge performed supervisory duties similar to the probation officer and thus was not immune from suit. This case shows how a city can be vulnerable to litigation when there is a lack of sufficient policies and administrative oversight between the local courts and the probation agency.

Prison Culture and Correctional Supervisors

The prison culture is a direct reflection of correctional supervisors. When we hear the term "prison culture" we often think of the prison environment and compositional make-up of inmates inside a correctional facility. Further, we assume that prison culture is controlled entirely by inmates without considering the impact of correctional supervisors and staff on inmate behavior. For instance, correctional supervisors who are not actively involved in the day-to-day operations of running the facility may project an image to staff that they are "too good" to do real correctional officer work. In addition, when correctional officers disconnect from their staffs they may become complacent, increasing the potential for corruption between inmates and staff (Dobel, 2006).

There are high stakes consequences for the actions of correctional supervisors. In addition to managing staff and line officers, correctional supervisors set standards that ultimately impact the safety and well-being of inmates. The failure to adequately supervise, monitor, and uphold high ethical standards can lead to a failure to follow rules, which undermines the public's trust in the criminal justice system. Not every inmate escape or riot is a reflection of the quality of correctional supervision, but in many cases these incidents are symptoms of more entrenched organizational issues cultivated by correctional leaders.

Box 10.4 Ethics Panel Clears Corrections Official

He got state consultant to help with son's thesis

The Record (Hackensack, NJ) — October 18, 2003

In its first action, the newly revamped state ethics commission has ruled that Corrections Commissioner Devon Brown did not violate state law when he helped arrange for a department consultant to assist his son with his master's thesis. But the commission has put Brown and other state officials on notice that henceforth, they are prohibited from engaging in business transactions with their employees. The Executive Commission on Ethical Standards, in papers released Friday, said it had been investigating allegations that Brown used his official position to grant an unwarranted advantage to his son Mark, a student at Coppin State College in Baltimore. The nine-member panel found that Commissioner Brown had sought a recommendation last March from Stanley Repko, director of the Corrections Department's Office of Policy and Planning, for a statistician to work on his son's research project. Repko, the commission says, recommended Paul Gerrish, a Corrections Department consultant and former employee. Brown said he gave Gerrish his son's telephone number and advised Gerrish that he was acting only as an intermediary, according to statements both men gave to the commission. But a dispute developed over the fee for Gerrish's work, according to commission documents. Gerrish submitted a bill to Brown for $1,000, which allowed for a courtesy discount of $500 if the fee was paid within seven days, documents said. But the ethics commission says Commissioner Brown initially refused to pay Gerrish because he was not satisfied with the work. Brown eventually paid Gerrish $300, an amount not acceptable to Gerrish. In a statement, Commissioner Brown said he had strongly indicated to ethics officials from the start that the matter was between his son and Gerrish. "I regret very much that a seemingly innocent statistical project — a project that as a researcher I could have easily completed myself save for time constraints — could have engendered this kind of response," he said. "Essentially, this is a matter of a disagreement between two private parties about the quality of work produced, and the price paid for said work." In its ruling, the ethics commission said that ongoing business relationships between a supervisor and a subordinate are prohibited. But, the commission said, it never had addressed a case involving a one-time business arrangement.

Rita Strmensky, executive director of the ethics commission, said the panel will be issuing a state regulation prohibiting all such business arrangements.

In making its decision not to bring charges, the commission said there were several supervisory levels between Gerrish and Brown. It also said that Brown had no involvement in Gerrish's contract as a consultant.

Gerrish did not return phone calls placed to his home, and corrections officials refused to provide a phone number for Mark Brown.

The Brown decision was made at the ethics board's meeting on Tuesday. That meeting was the first for the board's new chairman, former Gov. Brendan Byrne, one of two new public members.

The board, which votes to approve or reject recommendations by its staff, has been criticized in the past because all of its seven appointees were members of Governor McGreevey's administration.

The board is still one of only four in the United States that does have a majority of public members. In addition, the board's fines scale, $100 to $500 per violation, has not changed since the panel was first formed in 1972.

Source: Randy Diamond, "Ethics panel clears corrections official—He got state consultant to help with son's thesis," *The Record* [Hackensack, NJ], October, 18, 2003, A04.

The Brown ethics case highlights the importance of discretion as a corrections supervisor.

Ethics clearly plays an important role for front-line officers, but as a supervisor the consequences can be even more significant. In this case, the Ethics Board cleared the Commissioner of any wrongdoing because no rules existed prohibiting "one-time" business transactions.

Ethical Pitfalls for Correctional Supervisors

Correctional supervisors must be aware of the constant challenges that exist in their organizations that impact their decisions. In dealing with these challenges, a primary concern for supervisors is to ensure that staff is held accountable for their actions. If preferential treatment or incompetence is tolerated, correctional supervisors will begin to lose control of correctional operations. Dobel (2006) has identified several "threats" in the correctional environment that supervisors must take into account. Some of these include:

- *Peer Culture*: This is the idea that things should be done "like they always have been." Newly promoted supervisors are likely to be heavily influenced by more experienced supervisors. Likewise, such a situation may create ethical dilemmas when actions taken are not conducive to the best interests of the organization, staff, and inmates. Communication is the key. Correctional supervisors must exercise good judgment and not be afraid to ask questions when things do not appear ethical or right.
- *Denial of Responsibility*: A good leader will never look for excuses when things go wrong. Instead, good leaders will look for solutions as opposed to "pointing the finger" at someone else.
- *Rigidity*: There may be a tendency for supervisors to shy away from dealing with conflict or performance issues with staff. Supervisors have a duty to confront difficult situations and exercise discretion in the application of rules when dealing with subordinates. If supervisors fail to make exceptions when extenuating circumstances exist they may be perceived as too rigid which can negatively affect morale and to some extent the integrity of staff.
- *Silence*: When correctional officers condone the abuse of power and use of force against inmates they compromise their integrity and create a dangerous environment for staff as well as inmates. Correctional supervisors must initiate prompt investigations when allegations arise and take the appropriate disciplinary action against all parties involved. In addition, they must be willing to discuss incidents as "lessons learned" so that the same mistakes are not repeated.

Conclusion

There is little debate that the meaning of the term "ethics" has evolved substantially over time. Criminal justice supervisors must have an understanding of the myriad of issues that affect ethical behavior—leadership, discretion, discipline, and wisdom are all important issues that affect the behavior of subordinates. Of critical importance is the need to ensure that subordinates remain accountable for their actions, yet supervisors must not be perceived as too overbearing by their subordinates. Creating an environment that builds morale, motivation, and respect is the task of leaders in the criminal justice field. Some of the leadership theories related to criminal justice supervision are behavioral, contingency, and trait. Each of these theories of leadership may be successfully employed in order to foster a high level of ethics and integrity among staff. When criminal justice leaders do not exercise good judgment in the application of rules, they open themselves and their organizations to liability claims. It is important for supervisors to know that there is rarely a situation where there are no signs of ethical misconduct before a serious violation occurs. Indeed, civil lawsuits may be filed against administrators in policing, probation and parole, and corrections, but most unethical misconduct never reaches the court system. When lawsuits do arise, plaintiffs will most likely attempt to prove that the supervisor and his or her agency was vicariously liable for the actions of subordinates because of the deep pockets (or higher payout potential) of government agencies. Plaintiffs may sue a government agency in state court based on a tort violation or they may file a federal lawsuit under section 1983, the Civil Rights Act of 1964, or any other federal law.

In the future, criminal justice supervisors will increasingly face challenges related to issues such as diversity in the workforce, technological advancements, and the constant threat of lawsuits. Criminal justice supervisors have the responsibility of ensuring that their staff is well-trained and that there is clear direction and accountability at all levels of the organization.

Scenarios

Police Supervisor

1. You have just been promoted to patrol sergeant. Two of your new officers suggest a great local hamburger place so you agree to have lunch with them. You are just getting to know the officers and want to make a good impression. In your prior position as a police detective and patrol officer, you al-

ways paid for your meals even when restaurant personnel offered freebies. You vowed when going through the police academy that you would always live by high ethical standards and as a police supervisor, you want to instill those same values in your officers. After finishing lunch, you notice that the two officers get up and speak to the restaurant manager who is standing behind the register briefly before leaving, but that neither officer paid for their meals. You approach the cash register. What should you do?

2. You are a new sergeant assigned to the property crimes division. Your lieutenant has informed you that investigative productivity is good in your unit and that there are several senior officers who you can learn from. Having been a detective prior to being promoted, you know how easy it is to get away with wasting time on the clock instead of performing assigned tasks. One of your senior officers (Jerry) says he is going to interview a potential witness of a burglary at around 2 p.m. You happen to get a call shortly thereafter that there was a vehicle break-in at a local park near a lake and you go to assist one of your new detectives at the scene. While driving to the scene, you see Jerry fishing from a nearby pier. It is about 3:00 p.m. What should you do?

3. You are a veteran patrol officer recently assigned to patrol a different area of a city. You notice that your new sergeant (Jim) is frequently unavailable for assistance on patrol stops and does not answer your calls when you have questions. One of your fellow officers informs you that the sergeant is dating one of the female officers on your shift and that he is most likely with the female officer somewhere. One day, Jim tells you that he will be "unavailable" for the rest of the afternoon and that if something comes up to give him a call. Later that day, a call comes in of a robbery in progress. You call Jim but no response. When you arrive at the crime scene, you notice that Jim has not responded to the incident. The lieutenant asks you where Jim is, or if you have heard from him. What should you do?

4. You are a police supervisor in a small town in charge of conducting background investigations. Your son's friend, Jake, is one of the applicants. Your son has told you in the past that he has heard from other people at school that Jake is a "bad apple" and that he has used drugs occasionally. Your job as police supervisor is to approve all of the background investigations, but when you review Jake's application you notice that he has mentioned that he has never used drugs in the past. What should you do?

Correctional Supervisor

5. You are a correctional supervisor (sergeant) at a prison facility. One your junior officers (Ted) informs you that Sam, a veteran correctional officer, approached him about a "gig" he is running in the prison that entails allowing inmates to obtain cell phones through contact visits. Sam tells Ted that he can profit too, up to $200 each week by "forgetting" to conduct pat down searches after contact visits. You know that Sam is well-respected by the inmates and other officers, and Sam has been a major reason why your prison facility is one of the safest ones in the state. What should you do?

6. A convicted child molester has been transferred to your facility from a local jail. Personally, you regard child molesters as the "worst of the worst." But knowing that child molesters have a high risk of being assaulted by other inmates, you tell one of your subordinates to place the inmate in administrative segregation. Another inmate later tells you that there are a couple correctional officers who want to see the inmate "get what he deserves" and that they intend to move him into general population next week when you are on vacation. The officers apparently intend to claim that moving the inmate was "an accident" but other inmates have planned to "rough up" the inmate when they have the opportunity. What should you do?

7. While working as a jail supervisor at a local correctional facility, you are monitoring the CCTV camera system one evening. You observe two inmates fighting in the recreation area. Before you can radio for assistance, two of your officers approach the inmates and diffuse the situation. Then you observe one of the officers punch the inmate while escorting him back to his cell. The officer in question is about to be promoted to sergeant. What action would you take?

8. You are a supervisor at a probation department. One of your old friends (Carl) from high school was just ordered to serve a sentence of probation for a DWI. One of your best friends (Ed), who is also a probation officer in the same agency, has been assigned as his probation officer. One day Carl runs into you at the agency while you are standing in Ed's office discussing another issue. Put in a precarious circumstance, what should you say? Later on that day, Ed tells you that Carl has failed a drug test—he came up positive for using marijuana. What should you do?

9. You are a probation supervisor at a large juvenile probation department. You notice that one of your officers regularly conducts field visits to homes of minority youth as opposed to non-minority youth. When you investigate

the matter further, you notice that the officer has filed for motions to revoke probation against 80% of the minority youth on probation but only 20% of the non-minority youth. On the other hand, the overall violation rate is more comparable (about 50/50 for these groups). While reading some of the officer's reports you notice that several non-minorities were not filed on for positive drug tests, but every minority was filed on by the officer. What would you do?

10. You are a probation supervisor working for a county probation department. While out playing pool one night with some fellow officers, you hear one of the officers make a comment that they don't document probation violations because it "causes too much paperwork." What would you do?

References

Appuzo, M. (March, 2015). Justice Department to Fault Ferguson Police, Seeing Racial Bias in Traffic Stops. Retrieved from: http://www.nytimes.com/2015/03/02/us/justice-department-report-to-fault-police-in-ferguson.html?_r=0.

Bass, J. (1995). Rural policing: Patterns and problems of micro departments. *The Justice Professional*, 9, 59–74.

Blanchard, K. (1989). A "PRICE" that makes sense. *Today's Office* (September).

Coleman, S. (1994). When police should say "No!" to gratuities. *Criminal Justice Ethics*, 23(1), 33–44.

Cullen, F.B., Link, J., & Wolfe, N. (1989). How satisfying is prison work? A comparative occupational approach." *Journal of Offender Counseling, Services, and Rehabilitation, 14*, 89–108.

Cullen, F.B., Latessa, R., Kapoche, L., Lombardo, L., & Burton, V. (1993). Prison wardens' job satisfaction. *The Prison Journal, 73*, 141–161.

del Carmen, R.V. (2007). *Criminal procedure: Law and practice*. Belmont, CA: Thompson/Wadsworth.

Department of Justice (March, 2015). Investigation of the Ferguson Police Department. Retrieved from: http://www.justice.gov/sites/default/files/opa/press-releases/attachments/2015/03/04/ferguson_police_department_report.pdf.

Dobel, J.P. (2006). Ethics and Values. In N. Campbell (Ed.), *Correctional leadership competencies for the 21st Century: Manager and supervisor levels*.

Fiedler, F.E. (1967) *A theory of leadership effectiveness*. New York: McGraw-Hill.

King, W. (2014). Organizational Failure and the Disbanding of Local Police Agencies. *Crime and Delinquency*, 60(5), p. 667–692.

James, B., & Ortellado, D. (March, 2015). DOJ report calls for transparency in Ferguson criminal justice system. Retrieved from: https://sunlightfoundation.com/blog/2015/03/10/doj-report-calls-for-transparency-in-ferguson-criminal-justice-system/.

Jones, M.E., & Lurigio, A.J. (1997). Ethical considerations in probation practice. *Perspectives, 20*(3), 26–32.

Harrison, S.L. (1996). Quality policing and the challenges for leadership." *The Police Chief,* 63(1).

More, H.W., & Miller, L.S. (2007). *Effective police supervision.* (5th ed.). Cincinnati, OH: Anderson/LexisNexis.

Morgan, K.D., Belbot, B.A., & Clark, J. (1997). Liability issues affecting probation and parole supervision. *Journal of Criminal Justice, 25*(3), 211–227.

National Institute of Justice. *Stress among Probation and Parole Officers and What Can Be Done About It.* Washington, DC: NIJ, 2005.

Sherman, L. (1985). Becoming bent: Moral careers of corrupt policeman. In F. Elliston & M. Feldberg, (Eds.), In *moral issues in police work* (250–267). Totowa, N.J.: Rowman & Littlefield.

Cases Cited

Benskin v. City of Fife, 2009 Wash. App. LEXIS 1768 (2009).
Katz v. Dole, 709 F.2d 251, 253 (4th Cir.1983).

11

Ethics and Fighting Terrorism

Chapter Objectives

- The students will learn a definition of terrorism
- The student will become aware of ethical issues in policing terrorism
- The student will learn about controversial Interrogation Practices applicable to terrorism
- The student will understand the ethical issues involved with use of Preventative Detention as a Tool for Fighting Terrorism
- The student will learn about the ethical dilemmas when prosecuting terrorists under federal law

Introduction

In April 2006, a veteran trooper in charge of managing the New Jersey's intelligence computer network accused a state police executive of tampering with classified information in order to show that the state's Office of Counter-Terrorism (OCT) had engaged in the racial profiling of Arab and Muslim citizens. The complaint alleged that a top ranking Lieutenant accessed protected documents on a "witch hunt" to destroy the integrity of the OCT. "Instead of working together in the state's fight against terrorism and counterterrorism, [the state police] have become competing entities in a struggle for political power, resources and jurisdiction" ("State police profiling," 2006, p. A03).

Particularly FBI + CIA

The War on Terror has created a new set of rules for law enforcement regarding the investigation of crime and the manner in which it is publicized. A common criticism of our law enforcement leading to the September 2001 attacks has centered on the lack of effective communication among local and federal agencies when sharing intelligence. Since the September attacks, the government's response has consisted of a series of legislative and judicial reforms that resulted in a loss of some constitutional protections for most citizens. With the erosion of civil liberties comes the potential for abuse, misconduct, and competition for power amongst law enforcement officials.

This chapter focuses on the ethical issues in fighting terrorism. Specifically, this chapter discusses the most salient issues surrounding the investigation and detention of suspected terrorists. Moreover, the emphasis is on the practical aspects of fighting terrorism as opposed to providing a review of different forms of terrorism or specific terrorist groups. Of all the criminal justice components, the law enforcement sector has endured the most scrutiny because it has the primary responsibility of investigating terrorist activity. A search of all the newspaper articles published in the United States beginning September 22, 2001 to present day (September, 2010) revealed 3,689 hits when using the key words "police, terrorism, and ethics." Conversely, a search using the terms "corrections, terrorism, and ethics revealed only 510 hits. In simple terms these results indicate that one is approximately 7 times more likely to see a newspaper article dealing with police, ethics and terrorism as opposed to corrections, ethics, and terrorism. However, scholars have debated the legal and ethical implications to the use of preventative detention as a means of controlling terrorists. Therefore, we also explore the ethical issues surrounding preventative detention of terrorists and discuss the circumstances in which it may be justified.

Defining Terrorism

What is terrorism? The U.S. Department of State defines terrorism as "premeditated, politically motivated violence perpetrated against noncombatant targets by subnational groups or clandestine agents" (U.S. Dept. of State, 2006). Definitions of terrorism, however, vary significantly because some view terrorists as acting in the interests of a particular nation. Broadly speaking there are two types of terrorism—domestic and international. They are distinguished based on where the group's operation originates. The Oklahoma City bombing is a notorious example of domestic terrorism because Timothy McVeigh, the main conspirator of the crime, was a citizen of the United States and the terrorist acts he committed were targeted on the United States. Conversely, international terrorism refers to acts of violence transpiring between two or more countries, such as in the case of the 9/11 attacks involving members of the al Qaeda terrorist group.

Ethical Issues in Policing Terrorism

Accusations that the police routinely engage in racial profiling (primarily involving African Americans) emerged well before the terrorist attacks of September 2001. However, in the aftermath of the attacks public approval toward the practice increased as it related to profiling males of "Arabic or Middle Eastern descent." The term racial profiling has been defined as "any police-initiated action that relies on the race, ethnicity, or national origin and not merely on the behavior of the individual" (Risse, 2007, p. 4). Risse (2007) maintains that profiling is most controversial when race is used as an information-carrier. The ethical dilemma that arises is whether the use of race is justifiable for investigative purposes. In order to justify the use of racial profiling we must consider the likelihood of success if it were to be used. This is an inherently subjective question, because it requires that we have some contextual information about the nature of the criminal activity and the suspects involved. In the case of ordinary street crimes there are official statistics indicating that many crimes are committed by young, African American males. This fact alone certainly does not make it ethical to conduct traffic stops, for instance, solely based on the fact that a motorist is African American. Very few terrorist incidents (domestic and international combined) have occurred in our country, but as American citizens we tend to be more fearful of a terrorist attack as opposed to being the victim of a street crime. The disparity between the fear of violent crime and the likelihood that one will be a victim of it is called the victimization paradox. This fear is at the base of the controversy surrounding the profiling of Middle Eastern males. Why are we so fearful of terrorists? The media gives us the impression that being a victim of a terrorist attack is imminent. Having said this, there are circumstances where one may argue that racial profiling may be ethical. Consider the example below.

Box 11.1 Speeder's Time in Jail Shows Local Terror Fight

Excerpt

Driving a friend's Mercedes-Benz, a 28-year-old man left Decatur early one morning two months ago and headed north on Interstate 69 en route to his home in the Chicago suburbs.

But that March 21 trip came to a halt about 2:45 a.m. near the DeKalb County line, when an officer with the Allen County Sheriff's Department clocked the man going more than 100 mph.

An ensuing search of the man's car — which turned up hidden compartments — and a computer search of his criminal history raised red flags.

Police charged the man with reckless driving, but the case surrounding Kefah Makamreh — once convicted in a wire fraud scheme where more than $1 million of stolen money was funneled to the Mideast and elsewhere — was far from a simple traffic arrest.

Instead, the case offered a brief glimpse into how local and federal law enforcement agencies operate in a region not considered the front lines of terrorism, where the federal government can conduct threat assessments on individuals who come in contact with police.

FBI officials based in Indiana say threat assessments for local law agencies have become common since 9/11. Part of that increase is attributed to the growing number of local officers trained to spot national security threats.

The Makamreh case also shows the steps prosecutors can take to detain suspects considered potential threats while such a review is conducted.

For Makamreh, who ended up spending more than a month in jail for a relatively minor offense, the case illustrated something else entirely.

"This was racial discrimination since day one," he said of his experience in Allen County.

The Arrest

There were no other cars around when Makamreh was pulled over for going 102 mph in a 70 mph zone, according to an Allen County Sheriff's Department report.

He was wearing a suit, had no luggage or other clothing, did not answer some questions the officer asked and had a book map of the United States with the pages for Tennessee and Texas folded, the report said. He also handed over expired documentation as identification.

When officers later searched the inside of Makamreh's car, they found multiple hidden compartments that, although empty, heightened officers' suspicions, Sheriff Ken Fries said.

According to Fries, such compartments can be used to hide drugs, guns or money.

In a phone interview after his release, Makamreh said he was on his way home from a legitimate business meeting when he was pulled over.

The only compartment in the car, he said, is used to store a first-aid kit and was built by the manufacturer.

He said he does not use or deal drugs and that he did not answer some of the officer's questions, such as why he was wearing a suit, because he thought they were strange.

Makamreh was arrested and charged with reckless driving and taken to the Allen County lockup.

Source: Jeff Wiehe, "Speeder's time in jail shows local terror fight," *The Journal Gazette,* Fort Wayne, IN, May 31, 2009. Reprinted with permission. View the article in its entirety at: http://www.journalgazette.net/article/20090531/LOCAL/305319925.

Ironically, there is little research available on the issue of police ethics training as it relates to counterterrorism. In a time of budgetary crisis, emphasis on the need for training to fighting terrorism and ensuring that civil liberties are protected is paramount. Local police departments, fire departments, and emergency personnel have revised their training requirements significantly since 9/11. The New York Police Department is a front-runner among law enforcement agencies in the development of training programs to address terrorism. It has deployed investigators to foreign countries such as Canada, Israel, Southeast Asia, and the Middle East to monitor extremists who may conduct another attack on New York City (Weissenstein, 2003). As of 2006, the Department of Justice has awarded 23 million to 31 regional training programs at the state and local levels focusing on a range of anti-terrorism issues, which includes training on how to respond appropriately to legal and ethical dilemmas. In addition to federal funding, state legislatures have also appropriated funding specifically for fighting terrorism. In 2003, Colorado pledged to devote $1 million a year for police ethics and terrorism training ("Rocky Mountain News," 2003, p. 22A).

The increase in funding opportunities for law enforcement agencies has led to the misuse of authority on the part of high-ranking state officials in charge of the dispersion of grant funding to law enforcement agencies. During 2003, a state ethics commission alleged that Michael O'Toole, a state official, had authorized the payment of $1,118,750 in discretionary grants to five law enforcement agencies that had not followed the required process for review of funding ("Ethics panel charges former state official," 2007, p. 1B). A short time after the grant monies were awarded, O'Toole joined a consulting firm that took a commission for securing the funding for the police agencies. The grants were for specialized training operations including anti-terrorism measures. According to the law, O'Toole could be fined up to $38,000 as a result of the violations. This story highlights the potential for abuse of discretion and power when funding is involved for law enforcement purposes. Given the high-priority status of fighting terrorism, it is likely that it will remain a magnet for federal grant monies for training in the years to come.

Interrogation Practices

Tragedy struck the city of Boston when on April 15, 2013, when a pair of bombs exploded at the Boston Marathon finish line killing three people and injuring 282 others. An intensive search ensued for Dzhokhar and Tamerlan Tsarnaev, the two brothers who were alleged to have carried out the terrorist attacks. Four days later, the public watched as law enforcement tracked down and apprehended Dzhokhar Tsarnaev, the lone survivor, in an abandoned boat in Watertown, MA. After the arrest occurred, the question became whether or not he should be read his *Miranda* rights as proscribed by *Miranda v. Arizona* (1966). At the press conference announcing the capture of Tsarnaev, the U.S. Attorney for Massachusetts, Carmen Ortiz, announced that the government could cite *New York v. Quarles (1984)* and the Public Safety Exception (PSE) to the *Miranda* requirement in cases of terrorism. In *New York v. Quarles* (1984), the Supreme Court created this exception to *Miranda*, which allows the admission of statements made to the police in order to ensure the safety of the public.

As a result of being unconscious due to a gunshot wound Tsarnaev was not immediately interrogated by police (Wright, 2013). Once he became alert and able to communicate, the FBI interrogated him for sixteen hours within a period of two days but did not provide him the *Miranda* warnings (Wright, 2013). "Mr. Tsarnaev wrote answers to questions in a notebook because he was unable to speak," claimed Tsarnaev's defense attorneys. "These notes reflect his attempt to respond to urgent questions as well as his poor functioning and limited cognitive ability" (Katersky, 2014, p. 2).

One ethical dilemma that this case presents is whether the police can interrogate a suspected terrorist under the PSE to *Miranda* days after the crime occurred. Should Tsarnaev have been read his *Miranda* warning? Or was there sufficient justification to warrant an exception to the rule based on gravity of the crime and the possibility that similar attacks might occur in the following days?

Only in two prior cases have U.S. Courts dealt with a situation similar to the interrogation of Dzhokhar Tsarnaev. On Christmas Day in 2009, Umar Farouk Abdulmutallab (the "Christmas Day Bomber") was arrested after a failed attempt to detonate a bomb on a flight from Amsterdam to London (Labott, et al. 2009). Abdulmutallab eventually confessed to the crime after approximately one hour of interrogation by the FBI. However, he was never given his *Miranda* warning. In a related event in 2010, Faisal Shahzad (the so-called "Times Square Bomber") confessed to a failed car bomb attack and provided the FBI with valuable intelligence and evidence (Wilson, 2010).

The decision to provide Abdulmutallab with his *Miranda* warning was met with criticism by conservatives who claimed that individuals involved in terrorist activity should not be tried in civilian courts but military courts, the latter of which affords defendants fewer due process protections.

In response to these criticisms, the Justice Department formulated a policy for handling unique interrogation situations such as this one. The result was the drafting of a DOJ policy applicable to interrogations involving suspected terrorists.

The FBI memo instructed agents to handle terrorism incidents in the following manner:

- If applicable, agents should ask any and all questions that are reasonably prompted by an immediate concern for the safety of the public or the arresting agents without advising the arrestee of his *Miranda* rights.
- After all applicable public safety questions have been exhausted, agents should advise the arrestee of his *Miranda* rights and seek a waiver of those rights before any further interrogation occurs. (DOJ Memorandum, 2010)

These recent developments in policing terrorism underscore the power of politics in shaping law enforcement practices. Further, it is important that police organizations ensure that the investigative policies they develop are consistent with established case law, state, and federal law. If policies are adopted that require officers to interrogate terrorist suspects based on exceptions to *Miranda*, officers must understand the limits of those exceptions so that they are not misinterpreted or applied in an inconsistent manner.

Interrogation Practices Abroad

The Federal Bureau of Investigation's 10-week training program in Quantico, Virginia, is the most prominent program for police ethics training, bringing in thousands of officers from local as well as international agencies. Much of the attention has been devoted to police interrogation practices and has indicated that such tactics are ineffective at obtaining reliable information from terrorist suspects (Williamson, 2006). While discussing abuse associated with interrogating suspected terrorist detainees, one may recall the Abu Ghraib prison incident. The question becomes whether torture inflicted on the detainees was either "*de jure* or *de facto*" (Addicott, 2007, p. 189). At the center of the conflict is the propriety of "stress and duress" interrogation practices. In a discussion regarding the use of controversial interrogation tactics on terrorist suspects, it is important to note the difference between the moral and legal definitions of the term "torture."

In 1984, the United Nations' Convention against Torture took a major step toward distinguishing between "torture" and lesser forms of abuse toward prisoners. The Convention against Torture specifically defined three factors that must be present in order for torture to exist in connection with interrogation practices:

1. The behavior must be based on an intentional act.
2. The act must be performed by a state agent.
3. The act must be performed in order to obtain a confession or information.

According to Article 3 of the Convention against Torture, it is unlawful to extradite an individual to another state or country where there are "substantial grounds" that the individual will be subjected to torture. This practice is frequently referred to as "rendition." An important case that dealt with this issue is *Bellout v. Ashcroft* (2004). In this case, the Appeals Court ruled that because Bellout was a member of the "Armed Islamic Group" (AIG), he constituted a threat to national security and therefore was not entitled to asylum. This case highlights the legal and ethical conflict arising in the application of the Convention against Torture's prohibition of torture and mistreatment of prisoners.

So much of what occurs in the context of enforcing national treaties and international laws falls to the responsibilities of states. As one might imagine, individual countries are less likely to police themselves, and as a result it is the court of public opinion that ultimately imposes meaningful checks and balances on interrogation practices. To illustrate the power of host countries to tailor investigative policies, the Lawyers in the Bush Justice Department's Office of Legal Counsel issued memorandums asserting that the President retained power to authorize torture even if it was unauthorized by treaty or statute ("License to torture," 2003, p. A19). The lawyers who drafted the memos—John Yoo and Jay Bybee—authorized the CIA to use waterboarding and sleep deprivation as interrogation tactics against terrorist suspects, but were eventually cleared in 2010 of any ethical misconduct by the Office of Professional Responsibility at the DOJ.

The use of torture to extract confessions from terrorists is probably the most controversial of all investigative measures. Even if we assume the use of torture is legal to obtain a confession from a terrorist or obtain intelligence, there is a great deal of skepticism about the reliability of that information. This is why such a practice is always unethical and should be abolished in its entirety.

Police-Corrections Partnerships

In 2007, the Immigration and Customs Enforcement launched a program called Secure Communities Initiative—a collaboration between federal and local law enforcement agencies to identify and deport criminal aliens. The program enables local correctional agencies to identify and track illegal immigrants once arrested and booked using biometrics-based immigration records. This information is then matched against DHS biometric records as well as FBI records to ensure that dangerous criminals are not released until their identities are determined. The program was originally intended to target major criminal activity, i.e., terrorist suspects and violence related to drugs and gangs. However, civil rights activists have claimed that, once arrested, arrestees are denied certain procedural safeguards such as the right to a probable cause hearing and detained them for mainly minor crimes instead of serious crimes for which the law was intended. Barry (2009) reported this mission statement from ICE relating to collaborative efforts from federal and local agencies in the fight against terrorism:

> Terrorism and criminal activity are most effectively combated through a multi-agency/multi-authority approach that encompasses federal, state, and local resources, skills and expertise. State and local law enforcement play a critical role in protecting our homeland security because they are often the first responders on the scene when there is an incident or attack against the United States. During the course of daily duties, they will often encounter foreign-born criminals and immigration violators who pose a threat to national security or public safety.

In the year 2010, Secure Communities Initiative was responsible for deporting a record of 392,000 criminal aliens; however, roughly 75–80% of those arrests were taken into custody for level 2 and 3 crimes instead of level 1 (major crimes including terrorism). Critics have alleged that this initiative creates distrust among illegal immigrant populations who may otherwise report crime to law enforcement. Unfortunately, one incident of poor decision-making can be detrimental to public trust in the police. As the federal government implements new policies to fight terrorism, local law enforcement agencies must have clear direction regarding the implementation of those policies.

Thinking Questions

1. The fear of politics and national security has led to federally-funded programs that rely on local jails and police agencies to operate them. How might these programs lead to net-widening in the criminal justice system?
2. What are the ethical issues associated with conducting an interrogation that is designed to elicit incriminating statements but those statements are not intended for use as evidence in a criminal prosecution?
3. If a criminal alien is detained for a minor crime and informs the police of his/her immigration status is it ethically permissible not to arrest the person?

Preventative Detention: A Tool to Fight Terrorism

Local jails and state prisons generally do not have specific policies governing the confinement of terrorist inmates. Prisoners are treated according to their risk level, which is determined by the type of crime committed, prior criminal history, and any unique circumstances (i.e., media attention) related to specific inmates. The most significant ethical issue related to the confinement of suspected terrorists is preventive detention. In a critical national-security speech in 2009, President Obama delineated five types of prisoners held at Guantanamo Bay. The President indicated that the group posing the greatest (moral or legal) dilemma entails those detainees whom the government is unable to prosecute or discharge and must remain in "prolonged detention." Albeit, there have been a significant number of defendants charged with terrorism-related crimes tried in Article III courts (or federal district courts). Ostensibly, the authority to designate a defendant an "enemy combatant" falls within the scope of the President's war powers. Notably, the Supreme Court has not ruled on the issue of the criteria for defining the "enemy combatant" status (see *Hamdi v. Rumsfeld* case below).

Issues regarding the constitutionality of preventive detention are grounded in procedural as opposed to substantive law. In large part, the question becomes: How dangerous must an individual be to justify preventative detention? This question consists of assessing the probability that the individual will engage in terrorism if they were to be released. In some cases, detainees have been released from the Guantanamo Bay prison only to become high ranking officials in the Taliban. Witness the case of Abdullah Ghulam Rasoul, whom the U.S. government deported to Afghanistan in 2007 and then became the operations commander of the Taliban for the south region. In addition, Said Ali al-Shihri, a Saudi Arabian, was deported to his country of citizenship and is allegedly the leader of an affiliate of al Qaeda in Yemen.

Two significant cases on the issue of preventative detention are *Hamdi v. Rumsfeld* (2004) and *Padilla v. Hanft* (denied cert., 2006). Yaser Esam Hamdi, an American citizen, was captured by U.S. forces in November 2001 and transported to Guantanamo Bay. The government justified his indefinite detention by reasoning that he was an "enemy combatant" and therefore not entitled to due process protections guaranteed by the Constitution. The Supreme Court ruled that Hamdi had the right to challenge his designation as an enemy combatant before a neutral decision-maker. The Court, however, did not specify what criteria should be used to determine "enemy combatant" status. Hamdi was eventually deported to Saudi Arabia and stripped of his American citizenship.

Padilla, also an American citizen, was taken into custody at the Chicago O'Hare airport based on suspicion of being a material witness to a planned al Qaeda attack on the United States. After arraignment, President Bush exercised his war powers to declare Padilla an enemy combatant. The question in this case was whether an American citizen can be detained indefinitely with-

[handwritten margin note, left side:] So it was Islamic extremists who pushed for this distinction. Taqiyya

out being granted access to counsel or having been formally charged of a crime. The Supreme Court declined to review his case on petition for certiorari; hence, there was no answer from the Court on the criteria for justifying indefinite detention. Padilla was eventually convicted in federal court of providing "material support" to a terrorist organization.

The Prosecution of Terrorists

Two models for assessing the ethicality of decision-making on the part of government attorneys are the "agency" and "public interest" approaches (Radack, 2009). The agency approach is based on a liberal view that unless a client's interests are illegal they are ethical. Further, this approach maintains that the agency's interests are paramount and that compromising ethical standards is necessary when laws cannot be readily applied to specific crime patterns. In an effort to validate the White House's War on Terror agenda, government lawyers invoked the agency approach in order prevent another terrorist strike against the United States ostensibly by charging defendants based on circumstantial, or in some cases, questionable evidence. In essence, the lawyer's loyalty is devoted primarily to the agency. In contrast, the public interest approach places greater weight on the attorney's obligations to protect the interests of innocent individuals and the judicial system. The attorney's primary objective is to serve the good of the community. For example, a government attorney who ascribes to the public interest approach is more likely to experience ethical dilemmas relating to the implementation of post-9/11 policies such as the Bush Administration's torture policies, the U.S. Patriot Act, and specific federal laws that have given the government more power to investigate and prosecute terrorists. Ethical issues related to prosecuting terrorists are inevitably tied to the application of procedural and substantive law to specific cases. The next section addresses federal anti-terrorism statutes and the discretion involved in the enforcement of terrorist activity.

Substantive Law and Prosecutorial Discretion

The reach of federal criminal laws applicable to terrorist activity is comparable to the criteria that are used to substantiate detention policies associated with the military commissions (Chesney, 2009). This section reviews major federal criminal statutes enacted since 9/11 to fight terrorism and the ethical issues associated with this legislation.

The U.S.A. Patriot Act

Congress passed this legislation as a response to the 9/11 attacks to loosen restrictions on federal power to investigate terrorism activity. Critics quickly responded that the government used the law to investigate criminal activity and more easily obtain a conviction against suspected terrorists. A few provisions of the Act—sections 206 (FISA), 213 (sneak-and-peak provision), and 215 (access to third-party business records) are particularly controversial. Sixteen of the original provisions were so contentious that a sunset was attached to the legislation making them inactive if Congress did not reauthorize the law. The issue, according to civil rights activists, is that there was insufficient judicial oversight of intelligence-gathering operations. As such, the U.S.A. Patriot Reauthorization Act of 2005 was passed in 2006 in which key provisions of the legislation were extended for another four years.

Section 206
The "roving wiretaps" provision of the Act allows the government, upon court order, to wiretap a particular suspect's conversations instead of monitoring a specific phone line.

Section 215
This section removed the limitations on the types of agencies and extended the scope of records to "any tangible items," including books, medical and psychiatric records, and financial documents. A controversial aspect of the law is that the entity in possession of the records is subject to a "gag" order, meaning that the agency must not disclose the fact that a court order has been served to obtain third-party records.

Section 213
This is the "sneak and peak" provision of the Act, which allows the government to conduct wiretap searches without providing notice to the subject of the court order for up to 90 days following the search.

The Patriot Act was a major piece of legislation enacted for terrorism investigations, but the critical question is whether such extensions of federal power have prevented terrorist attacks. Unfortunately, there is no way to assess this question empirically. The reason for this is that violations of privacy are rarely, if ever, disclosed to the public. The ethical question becomes whether the Patriot Act and similar laws (discussed below) have led to privacy infringements on innocent individuals who are not believed to be associated with terrorist activity, and whether such infringements can be justified to detect and prevent terrorist activity.

During the 1990s, Congress passed two "material support" statutes—18 U.S.C. §2339A (Violent Crime Control and Law Enforcement Act of 1994) and 18 U.S.C. §2339B (Antiterrorism and Effective Death Penalty Act of 1996). Under Section 2339A, a defendant may be prosecuted for providing "material support or resources" to a designated foreign terrorist group. Section 2339B criminalizes active membership in designated foreign terrorist groups, whereas 2339A makes it unlawful to provide financial support to specific crimes rather than terrorist groups. It does require, however, that the defendant was aware of the intended purposes of providing the support to carry out one or more specific criminal acts specified in the statute. In addition, more recent statutes have been enacted such as the Intelligence Reform and Terrorism Prevention Act of 1994 that prohibits engaging in combatant-style training from designated foreign terrorist organizations. This particular law was designed to target potentially dangerous individuals who are not members of terrorist groups.

Federal prosecutors can invoke conspiracy laws when they encounter evidentiary problems related to specific anti-terrorism statutes. Conspiracy law allows the prosecutor to interdict a terrorist plot prior to the act having been carried out; furthermore, as soon as it can be shown that the conspirator formed an agreement to commit a specific crime, or engages in overt action to further that offense, there is sufficient evidence to prove conspiracy. However, subjective determinations in the preemptive use of conspiracy law to target terrorist activity can create obstacles at trial. In general, the longer the government waits to intervene the more likely that evidence will accumulate and support a conviction at trial. Conversely, if the government intervenes too quickly there may be insufficient evidence to support a conviction.

An example of this dilemma arose in the case involving the Liberty City Seven, a "cult-like" religious group that allegedly conspired to blow up the Sears Tower, an FBI building, as well as other locations around the United States. The charges consisted of conspiracy and other weapons violations. At trial the government presented a wealth of video and auditory evidence—such as excerpts from a group ritual that consisted of vows to support al Qaeda, but it was unable to demonstrate that the defendants harbored firearms or detonateable devices to carry out the crime. The government finally secured convictions on 5 of the 7 original defendants after the first two trials ended in a mistrial. This case shows that the federal government has, in some cases, used its preemptive authority to interdict in suspected terrorist plots when the evidence needed to support a conviction is tenuous.

Two other federal laws frequently applied in terrorism cases are the Foreign Intelligence Surveillance Act (FISA) and the Classified Information Procedures Act (CIPA). In brief, the government has more flexibility to secure a FISA warrant because it is designed for "intelligence gathering purposes" as opposed to the more stringent probable cause standard required for a Title

III warrant. However, critics have argued that post-9/11 court rulings and the U.S. Patriot Act enable the government to employ FISA warrant evidentiary standards to cases that involve investigations that are unrelated to terrorism (Zabel & Benjamin, 2008). The other statute that raises ethical as well as legal dilemmas is CIPA. In applying CIPA to terrorism cases, judges struggle with the competing interests of the government to keep classified information secret and the need to provide the defendant with his or her right to use that information to protect their own interests or to obtain inculpatory information from the government.

Evidence of enforcement problems is reflected in the number of cases filed by the Justice Department following the September 11 attacks. A study conducted by a private research group at Syracuse University found that prosecutors had rejected approximately 35% of the referrals brought by the FBI and this number had increased to 91% by 2006 (Lichtblau, 2006, p. A1–9). In total the study found that of the approximately 6500 terrorism cases filed by the Justice Department since 9/11, only 1 in 5 have been convicted. Of those convicted, the median sentence for crimes classified as "international terrorism" was reported to be 20–28 days.

The previous section illustrates that federal prosecutors have immense discretion to prosecute terrorist-related activity. Problems surrounding the establishment of proof pose the greatest barrier to prosecutors in terrorism cases. To overcome these legal obstacles, prosecutors must invoke other laws, such as conspiracy, as a mechanism for prosecution. When to intervene, however, is a judgment call that challenges a prosecutors moral position on fighting crime (Miller, 2009). The agency and public interest approaches represent two sides of a continuum that ultimately influence the way terrorist cases are prosecuted.

Conclusion

The war on terrorism has created new legal strategies that raise significant ethical issues associated with the right to privacy and due process of law. The objective of post 9-11 legislation was to give the federal government more legal firepower to investigate the most insidious criminal acts. Although with good intent, new strategies have led to conflicts of interest, controversial policing tactics, and the erosion of basic civil rights. For instance, police agencies have been criticized for ethics violations by state ethics commissions regarding the allocation of federal grant moneys designed for counterterrorism training. Racial profiling remains a controversial tactic, although most

Americans support its use despite the many false positives that occur in routine police practice. Allegations of the most egregious acts of abuse on the part of U.S. soldiers of prisoners occurred at Guantanamo Bay, yet our government has justified the use of preventative detention for designated "unlawful enemy combatants." And finally, the U.S.A. Patriot Act has relaxed many of the Fourth Amendment protections normally afforded to suspects in traditional criminal investigations, yet measuring compliance is difficult to assess. As we move forward into the twenty-first century, more terrorist attacks are likely to occur. Criminal justice professionals must always question whether investigative or preventative strategies are ethical and morally justifiable.

Scenarios

1. You are a New York City police officer. A call has come into dispatch that two males in their late thirties, dark complected, were seen leaving an area in Times Square where a dirty bomb was discovered, undetonated, by the New York Police Department. No other information on their identity was given. About 15 minutes after the call came in, you observed two Middle-Eastern males in a rental car not far from the area. What action would you take?
2. You are an FBI agent executing a sneak-and-peak warrant to obtain financial records from a hospital on a suspected terrorist. As a courtesy, you notified the local police department to inform them that you would be conducting the search. One of the detectives in the department has contacted you and asked if you could look for some financial records in the hospital for a case he is working on. What would you do?
3. You are a CIA agent who has obtained classified information of secret prisons for terrorist suspects overseas that are illegal according to international law. Assume you have verified the information is true. As a condition of employment you signed a secrecy agreement. What would you do?
4. You are a local police officer dispatched to a call regarding a witness at a hotel who has overheard information regarding the planning of a terrorist attack. The witness stated that she heard a Middle-Eastern male talking on the phone on the balcony of the room adjacent to her room. When you arrive, you learn that the witness is an illegal immigrant. You are in a state that has just passed a law requiring you to arrest undocumented immigrants. What should you do?
5. You are a state police executive who conducts counter-terrorism training and certification for local police departments in your state. One of your for-

mer colleagues from a previous policing job has contacted you to inform you that he has obtained a grant to conduct additional training in his agency on counter-terrorism tactics. Performing the training will earn you a substantial stipend. There is no policy in your agency on the acceptance of grant monies from other law enforcement agencies. Officers from his agency, however, routinely attend your training program. What should you do?

6. You are a senior official for the Intelligence Division in a local police agency. The FBI also has a Counterterrorism Unit assigned to your region—both agencies are responsible for investigating terrorism. There has been tension between your agency and the FBI's Counterterrorism Unit in the past due to competition. Your agency learns that a certain imam (Muslim religious leader) may be able to provide your agency with valuable information regarding an al Qaeda bomb plot. The FBI has contacted you for information about the case, so you are aware that they have started an investigation as well. You want your agency to take credit for the arrest, but the evidence is largely circumstantial at this time. What would you do?

7. You are a prosecutor in possession of exculpatory evidence (evidence that would tend to show the defendant's innocence) in terrorism case. There is political pressure for you to obtain a conviction, and your supervisor has told you, "Don't let me down on this one." What would you do?

8. You are a prosecutor in a terrorism case. A key witness has agreed to provide information that will substantially increase the likelihood of convicting the defendant in your case. The information comes with a string attached—the key witness also faces charges of fraud and wants those charges dismissed in exchange for the information. Your supervisor has told you, "We need to bring this guy down." You have serious doubts, however, about the credibility of the key witness. What would you do?

9. You are a female intelligence officer working undercover on a terrorism investigation. Your suspect has made sexual advances toward you and you realize that in order to develop the investigation further you will need to have sex with the suspect. What would you do?

10. You are a local prosecutor in a state that does not have a law for threatening to kill someone. The state, however, has enacted a special anti-terrorism statute for prosecuting terrorists. School-related violence has reached epidemic levels in recent years, and as a result there is public pressure to more aggressively prosecute teenagers who have the potential of committing mass murder on school campuses. You have a case involving a 17-year-old accused threatening to bring a gun to school to kill a school liaison officer, and whose home, when checked by police, contained firearms, explosives,

and documents supporting white supremacy. Assess the ethical and practical issues involved in prosecuting the youth.

References

Addicott, J.F. (2007). *Terrorism law: Materials, cases, comments.* Tucson, AZ: Lawyers & Judges Publishing.

Barry, T. (2009, June 6). Secure communities elevates community insecurity. *Border Lines.* Retrieved from www.borderlinesblogspot.com/2009/06/secure-communities-elevates-community.html.

Chesney, R.M. (2009). Terrorism, criminal prosecution, and the preventative detention debate. *South Texas Law Review, 50,* 669–703.

Department of Justice (2010). Memorandum for the acting Deputy Attorney General. Retrieved from: http://www.justice.gov/sites/default/files/oip/legacy/2014/07/23/dag-memo-ciot.pdf.

Katersky, A. (2014, May 8). Boston Bombing Suspect 'Begged for Rest' During Questioning After Nearly Dying. Retrieved from: http://abcnews.go.com/Blotter/boston-bombing-suspect-begged-rest-questioning-dying/story?id=23640268.

Labott, E. (2009, December 29). Al Qaeda link investigated as clues emerge in foiled terror attack. Retrieved from: http://www.cnn.com/2009/CRIME/12/28/airline.terror.attempt/.

Lewis, A. (2005, Oct. 15). License to torture. *New York Times,* p. A19.

Lichtblau, E. (2006, September 4). Study finds sharp drop in the number of terrorism cases prosecuted. *New York Times,* A1–9.

Maddux, M. (2006, April 4). State police profiling dispute aired—Official allegedly manipulated data to discredit rival agency. *The Hackensack,* [New Jersey] p. A03.

Miller, S. (2009). *Terrorism and counter-terrorism: Ethics and liberal democracy.* Malden, MA: Blackwell Publishing.

Mitchell, M. (2006, April 4). State police profiling dispute aired—official allegedly manipulated data to discredit rival agency." *The Record* [Hackensack, NJ] p. A03.

Radack, J. (2006). Tortured legal ethics: The role of the government advisor in the war on terrorism, *Colorado Law Review, 77,* 1–41.

Risse, M. (2007). Racial profiling: A reply to two critics. *Criminal Justice Ethics,* Winter/Spring, 4–19.

Sanko, J.J. (2003, July 25). *Cops in pursuit of how to spend training funds.* Rocky Mountain News, p. 22A.

U.S. Department of State (2006). *Country reports on terrorism, 2005.* Retrieved October 1, 2010, from http://www.state.gov/s//ct/rls/crt.

Weissenstein, M. "NYPD Shifts Focus to Terrorism, Long Considered the Turf of Federal Agents," Associated Press, March 21, 2003.

Williamson, T. (2006). *Investigative interviewing: Rights, research and regulation.* Portland, OR: Willan Publishing.

Wilson, M. (2010, October 5). Shahzad Gets Life Term for Times Square Bombing Attempt, N.Y. TIMES, at A25, available at http://www.nytimes.com/2010/10/06/nyregion/06shahzad.html.

Wright, J. (2013). Applying Miranda's Public Safety Exception to Dzhokhar Tsarnaev: Restricting Criminal Procedure Rights by Expanding Judicial Exceptions. Columbia Law Review (Sidebar). Retrieved from: http://columbialawreview.org/boston-bombers-miranda-rights_wright/.

Zabel, R.B., & Benjamin, J.J. (2008). In pursuit of justice: Prosecuting terrorism cases in the federal courts, available at www.humanrightsfirst.info/pdf/080521-USLS-pursuit-justice.pdf.

Cases Cited

Bellout v. Ashcroft, 363 F.3d 975 (9th Cir. 2004).

Hamdi v. Rumsfeld, 542 U.S. 507 (2004).

Miranda v. Arizona, 384 U.S. 436 (1966).

New York v. Quarles, 467 U.S. 649 (1984).

Padilla v. Hanft, 547 U.S. 1062 (2006).

12

Ethics and Unique/Emerging Issues in Criminal Justice

Chapter Objectives

- The student will understand some of the unique issues facing the criminal justice system
- The student will learn how to approach unique criminal justice populations ethically
- The student will become aware of special populations in the criminal justice system
- The student will examine the effect of technology on criminal justice and ethics

Introduction

The preceding chapters in this text have helped you to understand the role that ethics play in the many possible career fields in criminal justice. The information in those chapters builds the foundation for ethical practice in the everyday work you may perform in criminal justice. Because of the nature of the criminal justice field, we often come into contact with people who have unique needs or challenges. As noted in many of the previous chapters how we handle situations reflects on our personal morals and ethics as well as the departments and agencies that we work for. For all members of the criminal justice community there is a call to treat people with fairness and equity, although this can and is sometimes difficult. In some cases, certain offenders or citizens are particularly demanding because of the negative notoriety and stigma they receive (sex offenders), or because much of what they experience is misunderstood (mental illness or mental retardation). This chapter will discuss some of the distinctive issues and special populations one will encounter working in the criminal justice field and some of the ethical conundrums that accompany working with these populations.

Mental Illness

According to a study done by the U.S. Department of Health and Human Services in 1999, one in five Americans has a diagnosable mental illness. According to Slate and Johnson (2008) there are generally no visible signs of mental illness and most individuals do not exhibit abnormal behavior that would be obvious to outsiders. It should also be noted that most of those who have a mental illness and are in crisis end up encountering and becoming involved with the criminal justice system. In fact, Slate, Buffington-Vollum and Johnson (2013) suggest that "[h]igh utilizers of mental health and public safety services are being targeted in a number of jurisdictions across the country."

This is due in part to the fact that state hospitals have been closing and continue to close. McGrew, Wright and Percosolido (1999) state that 54 state hospitals were closed from 1970 to 1997. Traditionally, individuals with mental health issues or mental illness would be treated at state funded treatment hospitals known as—state hospitals. In the closing of these type of facilities the patients then have to be transitioned back into the community through group homes or developmental centers. Unfortunately not all patients are a good fit for these facilities, slipping through the cracks (this can mean a variety of things although in many cases it means that they become homeless) or finding themselves in one of the only other government run institutions, jail or prison. Slate and Johnson (2008) call this trans-institutionalization, in which their mental health produced deviant behaviors have now been labeled criminal, placing them in the criminal justice machinery. What is also of concerns is the notion that criminal justice practitioners are not generally trained extensively on how to handle mentally ill individuals. The National Alliance on Mental Illness has designed specific strategies to reduce the criminalization of mental illness:

- Adopting programs such as the Memphis Police Crisis Intervention Team (CIT) program to train police officers who come into contact with people with severe mental illnesses in the community to recognize the signs and symptoms of these illnesses and to respond effectively and appropriately to people who are experiencing psychiatric crises.
- Supporting mechanisms to divert people with severe mental illnesses from arrest and incarceration into treatment before they are arrested and come into contact with correctional and court systems. In FY 2002, Congress appropriated $4 million for the federal Jail Diversion program at the Center for Mental Health Services (CMHS) authorized under P.L. 106-310 (Section 520g). NAMI urges full funding of $10 million for this program in FY 2003.

- Creating authority in state criminal codes for judges to divert non-violent offenders with severe mental illnesses away from incarceration into appropriate treatment. This includes authority for judges to defer entries of judgment pending completion of treatment programs and to dismiss charges and expunge the records of individuals who successfully complete treatment programs.
- Establishing specialty "mental health courts" to hear all cases involving individuals with severe mental illnesses charged with misdemeanors or non-violent felonies, with the purpose of diverting as many of these cases as possible away from criminal incarceration into appropriate mental health treatment and services. In 2000, Congress enacted and former President Clinton signed into law a bill (P.L. 106-515) authorizing grants to communities to establish demonstration mental health courts. In fiscal year (FY) 2002, Congress appropriated $4 million for these Courts. One of NAMI's priorities is to ensure that Congress appropriates full funding of $10 million for these Courts as part of the FY 2003 Commerce-Justice-State Appropriations bill. In 2003, $3 million was appropriated by Congress.
- Training probate, civil, and criminal court judges and other Court personnel about severe mental illnesses and legal issues affecting people with these illnesses.
- Creating specialized divisions or units within departments of parole and probation with specific responsibility for coordinating and administering services for people with severe mental illnesses who are on probation.
- Providing specialized training to parole officers about severe mental illnesses, the needs of people with these illnesses on probation, and treatment resources and benefits available to these individuals.

Therefore, because the criminal justice system has become a *de facto* mental health system learning how to manage offenders with a mental illness is essential, regardless of your career in criminal justice. For police officers, they generally have initial contact with the mentally ill individual. Traditional law enforcement models often encourage officers to issue commands and expect immediate compliance. In confrontations or situations with mentally ill persons, commands may or may not be understood. The individual might also feel scared or threatened and not act in a manner that is desired by the police officer. Slate and Johnson (2008) note that communication is essential in dealing with mentally ill offenders. There are a number of options that police could chase when dealing with a person with a mental illness which include: dealing with the situation informally, doing nothing at all, arrest, or civilly committing or involuntarily hospitalizing someone (although this is not always possible as facilities may have no open beds) (Cooper, McLearen, & Zapf, 2004). Box 12.1 examines the effect of training on one police department in the United States.

Box 12.1 Charleston Police Learn to Handle Mentally Ill Suspects

The Post and Courier (Charleston)

An angry man stands in front of a business, insulting and scaring customers as he yells about things and voices no one else can see or hear.

Someone calls 911.

It's the type of situation that has become a near-daily occurrence for Charleston police officers as the S.C. Department of Mental Health deals with multi-million-dollar cuts. The responding officers are typically faced with one of two options, neither of which will usually set well with the suspect: take the man to a hospital so he can get the treatment he needs, or take him to jail.

The worst mistake an officer can make in that situation is to be aggressive or impatient, according to Fred Riddle, director of Crisis Intervention Training and a former Richland County sheriff's deputy. Riddle travels the state to train officers on how to quickly recognize and safely respond to people with serious mental illness in crisis.

He told about 50 Charleston and Mount Pleasant police officers Friday that the key is to de-escalate the situation by keeping an open stance, standing a safe distance away, speaking calmly and asking simple questions that will help get their mind off what is aggravating them.

"Show some patience, have a good gift for gab and talk to these people," Riddle said. "Don't put your hand on your gun or play with your Taser."

He also cautioned officers against ridiculing the suspects, touching them or playing along with their hallucinations. Don't lie, he said.

"People with mental illness are not dumb, they're not stupid," he said. "They know what you're doing."

At the same time, an officer should never let his or her guard down, Riddle said. Doing so can lead to serious injury, or death, especially when dealing with someone who has a higher threshold for pain.

Officers said they considered the training crucial as more and more mentally ill patients walk the streets. Last month, a mentally ill man died after Greenville police officers who were called to have him committed used a Taser on him multiple times. Greenville police say the man tried to attack them.

Riddle said the gift of gab will not always work so police have to have a plan ahead of time in case physical force becomes necessary. Leaving the suspect alone isn't an option, he said.

"A police officer can't leave this individual in the streets of Charleston if he's a danger to himself and others," Riddle said.

Read more: http://www.thesunnews.com/2010/09/04/1674001/police-learn-to-handle-mentally.html#ixzz16hYDLLB3.

What is paramount in any interaction with the public and police is fair and ethical treatment. Through various training law enforcement officers can become aware of resources in how to deal with mentally ill citizens. Studies have shown that police officers have numerous encounters with persons with a mental illness. One study found that 92% of officers had experienced an encounter with a mentally ill individual within crisis in the past month (Borum, Deane, Steadman, & Morissey, 1998). Police officers are not the only criminal justice professionals who have interactions with mentally ill individuals.

Jail and prison personnel have interactions with mentally ill offenders on a daily basis. It has been estimated that 6% to 20% of the inmate population has a mental illness, regardless of whether or not it is diagnosed (Favier, 1998). More recent statistics point to even larger percentages of inmates suffering from mental health issues. James and Glaze (2006) found that approximately 45% of federal inmates, 56% of state offenders, and 64% of jail inmates are suffering from some sort of mental health problem. Jail personnel often receive offenders when they are in a heightened state of crisis, as they are dropped off there after being arrested. They may be unsure of the surroundings, as well as issues they may be having, if they are off of their medications. Additionally, it could be concluded that jails serve as a holding place for mentally ill offenders who might be headed for some type of state hospital or residential treatment facility. Jail correctional officers, unlike prison correctional officers, often deal with offenders in which they do not have a social history or classification report. As noted by McCullough (2006, p. 112), "One of the measures of the humanity of a prison is how well it treats its mentally ill inmates. It is both an ethical and a practical matter that they be protected, cared for and treated."

There are some practical ways that correctional personnel can ethically and effectively manage mentally ill inmates as outlined by McCullough (2006):

- Watch offender hygiene and eating habits closely—Supervision is more than counting and watching daily inmate activities. Noticing changes in specific inmates and letting caseworkers or treatment staff know might help an offender avoid a mental health crisis or violence towards themselves or others. Noticing small changes in demeanor or life habits can create a safer prison environment for everyone.

• Making sure they are appropriately dressed.
• Treating them like adults and expecting adult behavior in return.
• Ensuring that they are taking their medications—This is a critical issue for both the offenders and staff. If inmates refuse to take medications it is crucial that medical and treatment staff are made aware. It may also be helpful to let them know if the institution has a critical response team.

It is crucial that all staff in the correctional environment work together to create an environment where all inmates can feel safe. Making a commitment to being observant and sharing information with other departments is part of the ethical responsibility that should be carried out by all correctional personnel (as well as all criminal justice professionals). See Box 12.2 for an example of how Oregon is dealing with mentally ill clients in their criminal justice system.

Box 12.2 Mentally Ill Offenders

The Mentally Ill Offender Unit (MIO) provides supervision services for parole, probation and post-prison offenders who have been diagnosed with a severe and persistent mental illness. The unit works in partnership with a variety of community and statewide agencies that have mutual responsibility and interests in mental illness. The MIO Unit works with community treatment providers, the courts, Oregon Department of Corrections, police, Sheriff's Office/Jails, LPSCC, public defender, NAMI, Aging Services, mentors and mental health advocates and most community groups that work with this population. The collective objective of this project is to, enhance/preserve community safety, reduce legal/criminal recidivism and to reduce clinical/therapeutic recidivism.

The MIO Unit works to preserve public safety and divert probation and post prison offenders with severe mental illness/disabilities from incarceration and hospitalizations, into community based treatment/services and also to decrease/prevent further contacts with the criminal justice system.

Services

• Enhance public safety
• Improve availability of and access to comprehensive, individualized services, when and where they are most needed, to enable offenders with severe mental illness to maintain meaningful community membership and avoid inappropriate criminal justice involvement
• Improve access to appropriate services for people with severe mental illness who are at high risk of criminal justice involvement

- Identify specific needs of individuals with mental illness who are at risk of criminal justice involvement or, who have histories of criminal justice involvement, and match services to those needs
- Provide ongoing monitoring and surveillance
- Promote involvement in treatment
- Reduce mental health symptoms
- Reduce substance abuse and illicit drug use
- MIO Unit works to reduce inappropriate incarcerations of severely mentally disabled offenders and promote their well-being and related functioning
- Works to problem solve and improve MIO transition planning from Oregon Department of Corrections and county jails, as it relates to the special needs and problems presented by persons with severe mental disabilities
- Develop enhanced awareness of the consequences of behavior, the relapse process, and the importance of treatment
- Provide multi-problem, difficult to serve people the "structure" needed to:
  - Gain relative improvement in overall functioning
  - Gain adherence to medications
  - Develop acceptable social activities
  - Obtain pro-social and healthy living arrangements
  - Educate and provide information about resource availability to the offender's support network, family, advocates, mentors, etc.
- Reduce involvement in the criminal justice system
- Reduce jail admissions
- Reduce hospital admissions
- Reduce psychological crises
- Gain a decent quality of life outside of jails, prisons and hospitals
- Advocate for necessary resources for which the MIO is eligible
- Be an effective community partner while working to get each MIO to a relative state of recovery
- To supervise MIO within the community safely and effectively. Encourage compliance within their ability to do so
- Seeks to reduce the severity of psychiatric problems with the MIO as well as reducing inpatient psychiatric hospitalization days
- Reducing incidents of the mentally ill being victimized
- Reducing crime, recidivism, and incarceration

Mental illness and how we treat those with these conditions says a great deal about our society and the things that we value. The ethical treatment of individuals in the criminal justice system with mental health issues is paramount in any just society. As criminal justice agencies implement more training to their personnel, increase awareness of the issue, and hold employees accountable, we will come closer to reducing the criminalization of mental illness.

Thinking Questions

1. What are some strategies for reducing the criminalization of mental illness?
2. What are some strengths of the MIO?
3. What are some ways we can effectively manage mentally ill inmates?

Sex Offenders

The ethical treatment of sex offenders is not often discussed as they are often considered to be one of the most despised and hated offenders in the criminal justice system (McCullough, 2006). Many people believe that sex offenders should be punished to the extreme. One of the tensions of working with sex offenders in the criminal justice system is whether or not we are punishing or treating the offender. As noted by Levinson and D'Amato (2005) most correctional systems are attempting to combine punishment and treatment. It should also be noted that not all treatment that is given to sex offenders is voluntary. In some cases offenders are forced to take medication to decrease their sexual urges, such as Depo-Provera, also known as chemical castration. Some scholars argue that forced treatment will have limited results and that forced treatment of sex offenders is unethical and a violation of an individual's rights (Glaser, 2003). Others feel that sex offenders should have little to no rights as their type of offenses are hated and despised.

What is important to note is that people who are employed in the criminal justice field will encounter sex offenders, and should treat them ethically in the same manner that they would treat any other offender. Additionally, sex offender management cannot be seen as the responsibility of only one part of the criminal justice system. A comprehensive approach takes into account various components of the criminal justice system, including the following (Carter, Bumby, & Talbot, 2004):

*   Investigations of sex crimes;
*   Prosecution and sentencing decisions;
*   Assessment practices to inform decisions pre- and post-sentencing;
*   Prison-based and community-based interventions;
*   Supervision, tracking, and monitoring strategies; and
*   Public education and prevention efforts.

In 2008, the Center for Sex Offender Management published a report stating that the role of law enforcement was traditionally to investigate sex crimes and apprehend sex offenders. What has been taking place is a collaborative effort to manage sex offenders in the community by collaborating with many entities in a community.

> Beyond their initial investigation and apprehension functions, law enforcement officers play a significant part within the broader system of sex offender management, long after suspects are convicted and sentenced, and even after sex offenders have been discharged from the authority of corrections and supervision agencies. Some of the responsibilities have been added or expanded in recent years as a direct result of changes to state and federal sex offender-specific laws, whereas others build upon already established community policing strategies within and outside of the field of sex offender management. (Center for Sex Offender Management, 2008, p. 4)

Law enforcement officers must also not engage in noble cause corruption in the apprehension of sex offenders. If an officer believes or feels that a sex offender has perpetrated a crime, the officer must handle the investigation properly and not feel the need to engage in vigilante justice. Also, police and law enforcement have a duty to protect sex offenders from angry citizens who are out for revenge or seek to harm them. The news article below discusses how community anger can turn to violence towards sex offenders.

Box 12.3 Sex-Offender Project Stirs Anger: Wallingford House Riddled with BBs

The Seattle Times — November 12, 2004

A sign on the corner of Fifth Avenue Northeast and Northeast 51st Street in Seattle protests a proposal to turn the house, in the background, into a transitional residence for sex offenders. A large, hand-written sign nailed to a light pole at an intersection in Seattle's Wallingford neighborhood reads: Unlicensed House for 8 CONVICTED SEX OFFENDERS planned for THIS CORNER.

Under it is another sign posted by Seattle police, this one offering a $200 reward for information leading to the arrest of whoever shot at least 19 holes through windows on three sides of the house on the corner of Fifth Avenue Northeast and Northeast 51st Street. Local residents say the windows of the white, wood-frame house were riddled with BB shots sometime after the sex-offender signs went up Wednesday.

The signs and BB shots appeared a week after a highly charged community meeting where Wallingford residents angrily reacted to news that a faith-based group had signed a one-year lease on the property and planned to launch a pilot project for sex offenders at the site.

Christian-based Providence House has proposed turning the house into a self-help, transitional residence for five to eight Level 1, and possibly Level 2, sex offenders who have undergone treatment and are considered at low risk to reoffend. Such residences do not require licensing.

Since the Nov. 3 meeting, a couple hundred Wallingford residents have signed on to receive community e-mails about the proposal, determined to stop the project. The area has 125 kids under 18 living within a two-block radius of the house, said Aaron Burnett, a marketing executive who has lived in Wallingford for 10 years.

This morning, Providence House board members will meet privately with a core group of opponents. Everything, it seems, will be on the table for negotiation — including whether Providence House will go forward with leasing the house, said Burnett and Providence board member Jan Olson. The majority of Seattle's 4,055 registered sex offenders are considered Level 1 offenders. Level 1 sex offenders usually are first-time offenders who know their victims while Level 2 offenders generally have more than one victim, abuse for longer periods and are considered at moderate risk to reoffend. Level 3 offenders are at high risk to reoffend.

Olson said the board made a mistake by not giving the community adequate notice of its plans and vowed it wouldn't happen again. Although he said he understood residents' anger and emotion, the rudeness shown at the first meeting "was very disappointing." He said he expects today's meeting will be more productive.

" ... We have to look at whether or not it's an appropriate site," Olson said yesterday. "The Department of Corrections (DOC) has indicated they think it's an appropriate site, but the question that still needs to be answered is if this is the site for this pilot project."

Providence House was formed more than three years ago. Since then, board members have worked to develop a self-help model for sex offenders based on other 12-step recovery programs. Providence House's philosophy is to give offenders a place to live where they can be accountable to and for each other, Olson said.

(http://community.seattletimes.nwsource.com/archive/?date=20041112&slug=sex offenders12m)

Correctional staff also encounter sex offenders in their daily work lives. In a 1995 study by Weekes, Pelletier, and Beaudette, it was found that correctional officers perceived sex offenders as more dangerous, unpredictable, mysterious, aggressive, irrational, and afraid, as compared to non-sex offenders. Additionally, this study found that officers thought sex offenders had higher levels of mental illness and were far more "crazy" than non-sex offenders. Consequently, if officers see offenders in a negative way, it becomes easier to de-humanize them, demonize them and treat them differently or unethically. Prior to the Prison Rape Elimination Act of 2003 (PREA), it was not uncommon for officers to punish offenders by placing them with sexual predators (Eigenberg, 2002). This type of behavior is unethical. Sex offenders should be treated in the same manner as any other type of criminal. This can be challenging but criminal justice personnel are held to the highest standard.

HIV/AIDS

In part, due to the level of high risk behaviors that many offenders choose to engage in, criminal populations often have higher levels of HIV/AIDS than the general population. Inmates have the highest rate of infection among all institutional populations (Braithwaite, Braithwaite, & Poulson, 1999). In particular, correctional systems have unique challenges in attempting to stop the spread of HIV/AIDS. Offenders in most correctional settings are prohibited from engaging in sex with one another, although sexual intercourse does occur. While condoms can significantly decrease the spread of AIDS, handing these out in prison can be seen as condoning sexual contact and is a controversial issue. Box 12.4 is an overview of condom distribution in one part of America.

Box 12.4 Condoms In Jails: A Controversial Intervention

KPBS — April 19, 2010

CALIFORNIA — Health officials say the rate of HIV among people who are incarcerated is nearly seven times higher than the general population.

Distributing condoms to inmates is one way to prevent the spread of HIV, but that idea remains controversial.

In a downtown San Francisco jail, a guard checks on the cells that line the central corridor. This high-security facility is home to more than 800 inmates.

Inside the gym, there's a machine that distributes free condoms. It's the only condom machine inside a jail or prison in California. And it's one of only two jail condom distribution programs in the state.

San Francisco's long-time Sheriff Michael Hennessey says his program began in 1989, when AIDS was ravaging the city. Hennessey says he felt he needed to do something.

"So we started by printing up a little brochure, and when people would get out of jail, and pick up their property, we would give them the brochure, and we would scotch tape a condom to the brochure," Hennessey recalled. "And then after we'd done that for awhile, we thought probably the better thing would be to actually provide the condoms in the jail as a form of AIDS education."

Hennessey admits he had some reservations about it. He was concerned inmates could hide drugs in the condoms, or that sexual assaults would increase. His staff had some objections, too.

"They are the ones working the jails and they're very concerned about contraband of any kind," Hennessey pointed out. "There was certainly some homophobia, even though AIDS is not a gay disease, at the time it was viewed that way, back in the 80s."

However, after Hennessey talked with the wardens of some jail systems back east that handed out condoms, his fears went away.

In the beginning, inmates in the San Francisco jail could get a condom from a health educator. The machine came later.

Los Angeles became the second county in the state to offer a condom distribution program in its jails in 2001.

So far, no other county in the state has followed suit.

Captain Dan Pena runs the detention support division for the San Diego County Sheriff's Department. He oversees seven jails and nearly 5,200 inmates.

Pena says his department has no interest in handing out condoms.

"Primarily the reason for that, is sexual activity in jails or prisons is illegal; it's actually a felony," Pena said. "And because of that, we would not want to send a mixed message to the inmate population that knowing this is a crime, here's a condom. So that's our primary position."

Pena says San Diego County controls HIV in jails through education, and strict supervision of inmates. He says until there's evidence that handing out condoms in jail reduces the rate of HIV, the county won't change its approach.

San Francisco Sheriff Michael Hennessey thinks that's shortsighted. In fact, he thinks most sheriffs throughout California are wrong on this issue.

"They don't see the spreading of venereal diseases or HIV in their community a matter for law enforcement, whereas I do," Hennessey said. "And I see it also as people who run jails and prisons have an opportunity to educate people when they're in their custody."

Mary Sylla is the policy and advocacy director for the non-profit Center for Health Justice. She admits it's hard for most corrections officials to embrace condom distribution.

"It's a lot like syringe exchange, and you know, not very many communities in the nation have syringe exchange," Sylla said. "It takes a little bit of a shift in terms of thinking about public safety."

San Francisco County has studied the effects of its program. Officials say sexual activity in jail has not increased. There have been no reports of smuggling with condoms. Inmates report they have engaged in less high-risk behavior.

Based on San Francisco County's model, the state of California recently ended a one-year pilot program in Solano State prison. Some 2,000 inmates had access to a condom machine.

The state is currently evaluating the program. In the meantime, less than ten jails or prison systems nationwide distribute condoms.

(http://www.kpbs.org/news/2010/apr/19/condoms-jails-controversial-intervention/)

Practically speaking, employees in the criminal justice system must handle individuals with HIV/AIDS like any other offenders. Under HIPAA, offender medical history and records are considered protected health information which cannot be disclosed. Essentially, in many cases, personnel will have no idea the offender they are dealing with has HIV/AIDS unless the offender tells them or the information is obtained in violation of HIPAA. For officers and personnel dealing with offenders, it is generally considered to be good practice to always use universal precautions. Universal precautions involve treating all suspects or offenders as though they might have a communicable disease. Consequently, this would mean always wearing gloves when dealing with a situation that involves blood or making sure that a suspect did not have any sharp objects or needles on their person prior to searching them. Another way to ensure that you avoid putting yourself or others at risk for spreading any disease is to use common infection prevention techniques which are listed below:

1. Education and training for all staff and volunteers on a yearly basis.
2. Infection control measures, i.e., use of personal protective equipment, sanitation practices, and bagging and disposal of items contaminated with visible blood or other body fluids.
3. Ongoing support for staff and offenders on HIV/AIDS prevention HIV/AIDS among offenders has also become an issue as correctional systems seek out ways to end prison sexual violence. This issue will be covered in the next section of the chapter.

Thinking Questions

1. What are some comprehensive approaches to dealing with sex offenders?
2. What are universal precautions?
3. Name and discuss infection prevention techniques.

Prison Rape

The literature on prison rape is generally focused upon female inmates that are preyed upon by male correctional officers, or male inmates that are raped by other male inmates. Sexual abuse can take on multiple forms, including fondling of men and women during searches, correctional officers forcing themselves on male and female inmates allowing offenders to sexually assault and rape one another, and sex in exchange for drugs or other contraband. In a 2000 study by Struckman-Johnson and Struckman-Johnson they reported that 20% of all males are sexually abused while they are incarcerated. The sexual abuse of inmates has received increased attention, due to the Prison Rape Elimination Act of 2003, as well as campaigns to end prison rape led by Amnesty International and Just Detention International. The social science and psychological literature suggests that there are many ramifications that occur in response to prison rape including causing serious psychological and physical harm, harms to society by way of an increased propensity toward violence, and increasing costs of incarceration (Hensley, Castle, & Tewksbury, 2003). As a result of Congressional findings, the federal government created legislation to protect inmates as well as adopt national standards for correctional systems to follow. The purposes of the Prison Rape Elimination Act of 2003 are to:

1. establish a zero-tolerance policy for the incidence of prison rape in the United States;
2. make the prevention of prison rape a top priority in each prison system;
3. develop and implement national standards for the detection, prevention, reduction and punishment of prison rape;
4. increase the available data and information on the incidence of prison rape;
5. standardize the definitions used for collecting data on the incidence of prison rape;
6. increase the accountability of prison officials who fail to detect, prevent, reduce, and punish prison rape;
7. protect the Eighth Amendment rights of Federal, State, and local prisoners;
8. increase the efficiency and effectiveness of Federal expenditures through grant programs; and
9. reduce the costs that prison rape imposes on interstate commerce.

(42 U.S.C. 15602)

The legislation points out the many ramifications of the high incidence of prison rape. Table 12.1 outlines these failures noted by the Prison Rape Elimination Act.

Table 12.1 Ramifications of Prison Rape*

Financial Cost	Increases costs to run prison systems at the federal, state and local level
Violence	Directed at inmates Directed at staff
Heath Care Inside and Outside	Reduces effectiveness of disease prevention programs Increases incidence and spread of: tuberculosis, hepatitis B and C, HIV/AIDS, and other communicable diseases
Mental Health Expenditures	Substantially increases Post-Traumatic Stress Disorder, depression, suicide, and the exacerbation of existing mental health disorders among inmates
Social Costs	Increases recidivism Civil strife Violent crime Increases inter-racial tension and strife within prison and communities at large

* 42 U.S.C. 15601

The legislation is a response to the failure of state and federal prison systems to effectively create policies and punishments that reduce prison rape and protect inmates from brutalization.

Correctional agencies are now tasked with enforcing the Prison Rape Elimination Act through policy, practice, and changing prison culture. As noted previously in research by Eigenberg (2002), correctional staff often punished inmates by passing them off to a predator or by ignoring sexual behavior that occurred between offenders. Training correctional staff is a key component of ending prison rape. A two hour training course is offered by the National Institute of Corrections in which they try to train staff on the following objectives:

- Articulate the key components of the Prison Rape Elimination Act (PREA);
- Describe the understanding of the sexual abuse among male inmates, female inmates and staff and inmates;
- Describe how sexual behaviors impact the corrections system and security;

- Discuss the legal implications in the areas of staff sexual misconduct and inmate-inmate sexual assault;
- Demonstrate an understanding of the role, skills and duties of the first responder;
- Develop ways to effectively and appropriately respond when you first learn of an allegation of sexual abuse that may have occurred in your correctional facility;
- Identify the principles of investigation and the importance of a fair and timely investigative process;
- Practice the application of skills learned in the course;
- Discuss prevention strategies; and
- Articulate issues surrounding special population management.

Training must also be followed with effective policy changes. The state of Texas, has implemented an initiative called the Safe Prisons Program. According to TDCJ,

> The Safe Prisons Program Management Office provides administrative oversight to the Safe Prisons Program and technical support to the Unit Safe Prisons Program coordinators and executive administrative staff regarding in-prison sexual assaults. The agency has a "zero tolerance" policy for sexual assault. Safe Prisons Program, awareness training, and extortion awareness training, provides staff with an overview of the Safe Prisons Plan as well as information regarding how to help prevent extortion. Offender victims' representative training enhances the skills of staff who provide support services for offenders who have been victims of sexual assault. The Safe Prisons Program Management Office maintains a database of reported alleged sexual assaults and analyzes characteristics related to time, location and demographics of the participants. This office also provides statistics related to extortion, offender protection investigations, and allegations of sexual assaults, which help identify issues for further policy development. (TDCJ, 2010)

Prisons through training of staff, educating offenders, and effective policies and programs, can stop prison rape. Of additional paramount importance in understanding prison rape is that the ramifications of rape that occurs in prison go beyond prison walls or fences and become part of a greater society. If social costs occur as a result of prison rape, citizens and criminal justice agencies outside of institutional corrections will have to address these issues of increased violence, recidivism, and racial tension.

Thinking Questions

1. What is the Prison Rape Elimination Act of 2003?
2. What are some NIC training objectives?
3. What are some practical ways to prevent prison rape?

Conclusion

Criminal justice agencies and personnel have many challenges in their jobs. In addition to the daily ethical dilemmas they face, they must also deal with special population and emerging issues such as mentally ill offenders, sex offenders, HIV/AIDS, and prison rape.

References

Carter, M., Bumby, K., & Talbot, T. (2004). Promoting offender accountability and community safety through the Comprehensive Approach to Sex Offender Management. *Seton Hall Law Review*, 34, 1273–1297.

Center for Sex Offender Management (2008). Key Roles of Law Enforcement in Sex Offender Management. Washington D.C.: U.S. Department of Justice.

Eigenberg, H. (2002). Prison Staff and Male Rape. In *Prison Sex: Policy and Practice,* Christopher Hensley (ed.) Boulder, CO: Lynne Reiner Publishers.

Favier, K. (1998). *Health Care Management Issues in Corrections.* Lanham, MD: American Correctional Association.

Glaser, B. (2003). "Therapeutic jurisprudence: an ethical paradigm for therapists in sex offender treatment programs." *Western Criminology Review* 4:143–154.

James, D., & Glaze, D. (2006). *Mental Health Problems of Prisoners and Inmates.* Bureau of Justice Statistics.

Levinson, J., & D'Amato, D. (2005). An Ethical Paradigm for Sex Offender Treatment: Response to Glaser. *Western Criminological Review* 6, 145–153.

McGrew, J.H., Wright, E.R., & Pescosolido, B.A. (1999). Closing of a state hospital: An overview and framework for a case study. *The Journal of Behavioral Health Services & Research, 26*(3), 1999.

National Association on Mental Illness (2010). The criminalization of mental illness. Retrieved November 15, 2010, http://www.nami.org/Template.cfm?Section=Issue_Spotlights&Template=/TaggedPage/TaggedPageDisplay.cfm&TPLID=5&ContentID=21046.

Slate, R., & Johnson, W. (2008). *The criminalization of mental illness.* Durham, NC: Carolina Academic Press.

Slate, R., Buffington-Vollum, J. & Johnson, W. (2013). *The criminalization of mental illness. Second Edition.* Durham, NC: Carolina Academic Press.

Struckman-Johnson, C., & Struckman-Johnson, D. (2000). Sexual Coercion Rates in Seven Midwestern Prison Facilities for Men, *The Prison Journal* 80, 379–383.

Texas Department of Criminal Justice (2010). Safe Prisons Program Overview. Retrieved December 1, 2010, http://www.tdcj.state.tx.us/cid/cid_safe_prison_pgm.htm.

Weekes, J., Pelletier, G., & Beaudette, D. (1995). Correctional Officers: How Do They Perceive Sex Offenders? *International Journal of Offender Therapy and Comparative Criminology* 39, 55–61.

Additional Websites

http://www.wcsap.org/Advocacy/PDF/CONNECTIONS%20XI%202.pdf
http://www.csom.org/pubs/law_enforcement_key_roles.pdf
http://www.justdetention.org
http://www.amnesty.org
http://www.preatraining.org/information.php

13

Ethics and Forensic Science

Chapter Objectives

- The student will understand the various sources of professional standards in the field of forensic science
- The student will be able to identify the various professional associations and organizations in the field of forensic science
- The student will be familiar with "Strengthening Forensic Science in the United States: A Path Forward"
- The student will understand the need for scientific integrity and objectivity
- The student will understand that the primary role of a forensic scientist is truth-seeker
- The student will understand the difference between an expert and lay witness
- The student will understand the Federal Rules of Evidence which apply to the use of expert witnesses
- The student will understand the difference between the *Frye* and *Daubert* standards
- The student will understand the process used to qualify a expert witness
- The student will understand the difference between an expert witness and a court-appointed expert witness
- The student will understand the need for court-appointed experts
- The student will obtain helpful practice tips for testifying as an expert witness
- The student will understand the nature and extent of wrongful convictions

Introduction

The field of forensic science has grown significantly during the last two decades. Forensic science relies on the advances in science and technology to develop tools to solve crimes. These tools are designed to augment the more

307

traditional crime-solving techniques. The growth, popularity and attention to the role of forensic science in the criminal justice system has resulted in heightened expectations among the general public, jurors and criminal justice professionals who seem to expect that each and every case will be solved through the use of forensic science. While that is certainly not the case, the growth of media attention to the use of forensic techniques, infamous cases such as the O.J. Simpson murder trial and numerous television dramas such as *CSI* have contributed to modern perceptions and expectations.

Forensic Science Associations and Organizations

As any field evolves it must develop professional standards. Numerous professional organizations, associations and societies exist within the forensic science community. The largest of those organizations coalesce to form The Consortium of Forensic Science Organizations. The consortium was created in 2000 and includes the American Academy of Forensic Sciences (AAFS), ASCLD, ASCLD/LAB, IAI, NAME, and Forensic Quality Services (FQS) (NAS Report 2009, p. 74).

The American Academy of Forensic Sciences (AAFS) is one of the more prominent professional organizations in the field of forensic science. In existence for sixty-two years and with more than 6000 members worldwide, AAFS membership is constituted of both academics and practitioners in the various subfields of forensic science. The organization works toward professional development, encouraging research and establishing professional standards for its members. AAFS publishes the Journal of Forensic Sciences and operates the Forensic Science Education Programs Accreditation Commission.

Membership in the academy is voluntary and therefore not all forensic scientists are bound by its standards. The following excerpt in Box 13.1 contains the AAFS Code of Ethics and Conduct. As such, to avoid disciplinary action within the academy, its members must abide by these provisions.

Box 13.1 Article II. CODE OF ETHICS AND CONDUCT

SECTION 1 — THE CODE: As a means to promote the highest quality of professional and personal conduct of its members and affiliates, the following constitutes the Code of Ethics and Conduct which is endorsed by all members and affiliates of the American Academy of Forensic Sciences:

a. Every member and affiliate of the Academy shall refrain from exercising professional or personal conduct adverse to the best interests and objectives of the

Academy. The objectives stated in the Preamble to these bylaws include: promoting education for and research in the forensic sciences, encouraging the study, improving the practice, elevating the standards and advancing the cause of the forensic sciences.

b. No member or affiliate of the Academy shall materially misrepresent his or her education, training, experience, area of expertise, or membership status within the Academy.

c. No member or affiliate of the Academy shall materially misrepresent data or scientific principles upon which his or her conclusion or professional opinion is based.

d. No member or affiliate of the Academy shall issue public statements that appear to represent the position of the Academy without specific authority first obtained from the Board of Directors.

SECTION 2—MEMBER AND AFFILIATE LIABILITY: Any member or affiliate of the Academy who has violated any of the provisions of the Code of Ethics (Article II, Section 1) may be liable to censure, suspension or expulsion by action of the Board of Directors, as provided in Section 5h.

(www.aafs.org)

Other forensic science professional associations and/or organizations include the following:

American Academy of Forensic Sciences
American Board of Criminalistics
American Board of Forensic Anthropology
American Board of Forensic Odontology
American Board of Forensic Toxicology
American Society for Quality
American Society for Testing and Materials
American Society of Crime Laboratory Directors
American Society of Questioned Document Examiners
AOAC International
Association of Firearm & Tool Marks Examiners
Association of Forensic Quality Assurance Managers
California Association of Criminalistics
Canadian Society of Forensic Sciences
Council of Federal Forensic Crime Laboratory Directors
Forensic Science Society
International Association for Identification
International Association of Arson Investigators

International Association of Bloodstain Pattern Analysts
International Association of Coroners and Medical Examiners
International Association of Forensic Nurses
International Association of Forensic Toxicologists
Mid-Atlantic Association of Forensic Scientists
Midwestern Association of Forensic Scientists
National Association of Medical Examiners
National Center of Forensic Science
National Forensic Science Technology Center
New Jersey Association of Forensic Scientists
Northeastern Association of Forensic Scientists
Northwest Association of Forensic Scientists
Society of Forensic Toxicologists
Southern Association of Forensic Science
Southwestern Association of Forensic Scientists
Wisconsin Association for Identification

(NAS Report 2009, p. 76.)

Forensic scientists who are not members of professional organizations dedicated solely to forensic science may rely on accreditation standards, agency protocols and standard operating procedures (SOPs) within their agency or area of expertise. Forensic scientists may also be members of professional associations and therefore governed by standards of professional conduct and codes of ethics developed by organizations in their area of specialization. For example, the following fields have professional organizations and societies which have their own professional codes of conduct: anthropology, accounting, biological sciences, chemistry, physics, psychology, and psychiatry. As such, whether a forensic scientist functions on the scene, in the laboratory, or as a witness in court there are professional standards which must be respected. In the following chapter, we will examine the overarching ethical considerations which apply to any subfield of forensic science.

Professional Standards:
A Call for Action and Integration

The field of forensic science received significant attention in 2009 when the National Academy of Sciences released its report titled "Strengthening Forensic Science in the United States: A Path Forward." Congress charged the National Academy of Sciences to examine the field of forensic science in the United

States and present its findings and recommendations. This committee report emphasized, among other things, the following:

- The need for integrated governance in the field of forensic science
- The need for independence and scientific integrity among forensic science practitioners
- The need to establish a federal entity to oversee the evolution of the field of field of forensic science, promulgate professional standards and coordinate among the various dimensions of forensic science

In support of the recommendations, the committee acknowledged that the field of forensic science is significantly under-resourced and "is also hindered by its extreme disaggregation—marked by multiple types of practitioners with different levels of education and training and different professional cultures and standards for performance" (NAS Report 2009, p. 78). Noting the sheer breadth of the forensic science community and the variety of disciplines which are included in that community, the committee report strongly advocated for a "more central, strategic and integrated approach to forensic science at the national level" (NAS Report 2009, pp. 20–21). The call for a unifying force—a federal entity—to work towards stabilization of the field of forensic science certainly has advantages and disadvantages, however, it is encouraging that this discussion is occurring.

Following review of the mission and function of existing federal agencies which are in some manner involved in the field of forensic science, the committee concluded that no existing federal entity was sufficient to accomplish the task. The committee recommended that the new federal entity, National Institute of Forensic Science (NIFS) should have the following characteristics:

- It must have a culture that is strongly rooted in science, with strong ties to the national research and teaching communities, including federal laboratories.
- It must have strong ties to state and local forensic entities, as well as to the professional organizations within the forensic science community.
- It must not be in any way committed to the existing system, but should be informed by its experiences.
- It must not be part of a law enforcement agency.
- It must have the funding, independence, and sufficient prominence to raise the profile of the forensic science disciplines and push effectively for improvements.
- It must be led by persons who are skilled and experienced in developing and executing national strategies and plans for standard setting; manag-

ing accreditation and testing processes; and developing and implementing rulemaking, oversight, and sanctioning processes.

(NAS Report, pp. 80–81).

In light of the NAS report, the American Academy of Forensic Sciences published its response on September 4, 2009. The AAFS Board of Directors voted unanimously to support the recommendations set forth in the committee report and voted to adopt "seven principles to guide forensic science in the United States" (www.aafs.org). These principles are as follows:

1. All forensic science disciplines must have a strong scientific foundation.
2. All forensic science laboratories should be accredited.
3. All forensic scientists should be certified.
4. Forensic science terminology should be standardized.
5. Forensic scientists should be assiduously held to Codes of Ethics.
6. Existing forensic science professional entities should participate in government oversight of the field.
7. Attorneys and judges who work with forensic scientists and forensic science evidence should have a strong awareness and knowledge of the scientific method and forensic science disciplines.

Who Do I Work For? Scientific Integrity

A recurrent theme in the academic and professional discourse on professional standards and forensic science is the need for boundaries. Given the unique relationship among forensic scientists, law enforcement, prosecutors and defense attorneys, it is extremely important to recognize and honor the delineation between forensic science and the legal system. These boundaries are necessary to ensure the proper functioning of the legal system. While many forensic scientists are employed in state crime laboratories and work closely with law enforcement and prosecutors, the forensic scientist should always remain impartial, independent and objective. Failure to do so may jeopardize the integrity of the findings, recommendations of the forensic scientist, and presentation of the case in court.

Publications by most forensic science professional organizations and associations as well as the NAS committee report emphasize the need to maintain scientific integrity and professional distance. The NAS committee report specifically recommended that the " … federal entity that is established to govern the forensic science community cannot be principally beholden to law enforcement." This language illustrates the recognition that forensic scientists and criminalists must ultimately remain impartial.

The primary professional duty of a forensic science practitioner is to seek the truth. In order to effectively serve in this capacity, the forensic scientist has a professional duty to function first as a scientist. Throughout the process of scientific evaluation and analysis, the scientist should at all times maintain his or her independence and integrity. As such, the forensic scientist should not be expected to produce a particular result in a case but rather allow the science or technique to produce an objective and unbiased result.

The pressure to obtain a certain test result or to testify to certain findings can be significant. In many cases, there is considerable public and political pressure to identify a suspect, make an arrest and obtain a conviction. However, the forensic scientist should take care not to become part of the accusatory process or view themselves as a "crime-fighter." Rather, the forensic scientist should remain impartial and should function as an actor responsible for the independent examination and analysis of evidence.

While the forensic scientist may be employed by a state crime lab or police agency, the very nature of scientific integrity requires that the scientist remain objective and independent. This is often difficult or unpopular when confronted with the multitude of pressures which exist in the world of crimefighting. However, in order to maintain the integrity of the scientist, the process and any test results, maintaining these boundaries is critically important.

Thinking Questions

1. What are some characteristics of the NIFS?
2. Name and describe 5 forensic science associations and organizations.
3. What are some of the elements of the AAFS Code of Ethics?
4. What are some of the ethical challenges in developing national standards in forensics?

Professional Qualifications and Experience

The professional qualifications and experience of modern forensic scientists are extremely diverse. The field of forensic science is multidisciplinary and includes a vast number of subspecialties. In general, forensic science practitioners can be found in one of three venues: in the field, in the laboratory and in the courtroom. According to the NAS committee report, the forensic science community as it is currently conceptualized includes the following components and professionals:

1. Crime scene investigators
2. State and local crime laboratories
3. Medical Examiners
4. Private forensic crime laboratories
5. Law enforcement identification units
6. Resources such as registries and databases
7. Professional organizations
8. Prosecutors and defense attorneys
9. Quality system provides
10. Federal agencies

(NAS Report 2009, p. 55).

Given the diversity of the field it is understandable that there may be disaggregation of professional norms, values and standards.

Expert Witnesses and the Objectivity Requirement

Forensic science professionals often find themselves in court. Whether working as a crime scene investigator, a DNA analyst or a fingerprint examiner, all forensic scientist practitioners should prepare themselves for serving as a witness. In general, there are two types of witnesses: fact and expert. Fact witnesses are called to testify for the purpose of providing testimony about things that they have observed or otherwise have obtained knowledge. While forensic science practitioners are often relied upon as fact witnesses, they are also commonly called to testify as expert witnesses.

An expert is an individual who possesses certain knowledge in a particular field or area of expertise that would be helpful to the trier of fact (judge or jury). According to the Federal Rules of Evidence, individuals may be qualified as an expert witness based on their "knowledge, skill, experience, training, or education." While we generally believe experts are highly-educated individuals, other individuals may be extremely valuable as expert witnesses. Individuals do not necessarily need advanced education or an educational degree to serve as an expert witness. For example, a plumber may be an expert in the field of plumbing. While a particular educational degree is not required to be a plumber, this individual, by virtue of his or her training or experience, has certain knowledge that may be helpful in a case involving a busted pipe.

Rule 702 of the Federal Rules of Evidence states the following with regard to expert witnesses:

Rule 702. Testimony by Experts

If scientific, technical, or other specialized knowledge will assist the trier of fact to understand the evidence or to determine a fact in issue, a witness qualified as an expert by knowledge, skill, experience, training, or education, may testify thereto in the form of an opinion or otherwise, if (1) the testimony is based upon sufficient facts or data, (2) the testimony is the product of reliable principles and methods, and (3) the witness has applied the principles and methods reliably to the facts of the case.
(http://www.law.cornell.edu/rules/fre/ACRRule702.htm)

Some examples of expert witnesses include the following: scientists, social workers, physicians, therapists, law enforcement officers, DNA analysts, fingerprint examiners, plumbers, electricians, stamp collectors and many others. As one can see, there are many different individuals who may be qualified as an expert in a particular area. However, in order to be qualified to testify as an expert, the area (plumbing, DNA, tire impressions) about which the individual will testify must require "scientific, technical or specialized knowledge." In order to determine whether an area requires such knowledge, trial courts now utilize the *Daubert* test.

This test was developed by the United States Supreme Court in *Daubert v. Merrell Dow Pharmaceutical*, 509 U.S. 579 (1993). In the *Daubert* case, the Supreme Court held that prior to the admission of scientific testimony, the trial judge must determine that the evidence is both relevant and reliable. This places the trial judge in a position of having to make both a legal and scientific decision about potential expert testimony. The trial judge must be able to evaluate the proposed testimony or technique and make a determination regarding admission.

The *Daubert* standard is generally regarded as a more flexible standard than the previously-used *Frye* test. The *Frye* test required that prior to the admission of expert testimony, the proponent (party seeking admission of the expert testimony) must establish and the court must find that the technique or skill was "generally accepted as reliable in the relevant scientific community" (*Frye v. United States*, 1923). Rather than require proof that science or technology has attained "general acceptance" within a particular field, the *Daubert* standard provides an approach that requires the court to find that the proposed science, technology or technique is relevant and reliable. This avoids the inherent problems of establishing that a consensus exists regarding general acceptance.

In order to make the necessary determination under the *Daubert* standard, the Supreme Court set forth the following factors for trial judges to consider:

1. whether a theory or technique can be (and has been) tested;
2. whether the theory or technique has been subjected to peer review and publication;
3. the known or potential rate of error of a particular scientific technique;
4. the existence and maintenance of standards controlling the technique's operation; and
5. a scientific technique's degree of acceptance within a relevant scientific community.

Daubert v. Merrell Dow Pharmaceutical, Inc., 594 U.S. 579, 592–94 (1993).

These factors were developed in order to provide trial judges with guidance when they must make decisions regarding the admission of testimony by expert witnesses. Use of similar factors by trial courts also makes it more likely that consistent decisions will be made regarding the admission of certain types of expert testimony.

Qualification as an Expert Witness

In order to testify as an expert witness, an individual must first go through the process of "qualification." Qualification of an expert witness involves the use of *voir dire*. *Voir dire* is typically associated with the process of selecting a jury where jurors answer questions posed by the attorneys and occasionally by the court. These questions are designed to elicit information which may affect their ability to serve as a juror.

In the American legal system, *voir dire* is also used to establish or dispute the qualifications and expertise of a proposed expert witness. Therefore, *voir dire* refers to the process which is used to question a proposed expert. Most court rules require the calling party to disclose their intent to utilize a particular expert well in advance of trial. Procedures commonly require that the calling party give written notice of their intent to utilize an expert witness. This allows the opposing side to make arrangements for their own expert testimony if necessary and to engage in appropriate pre-trial discovery and research of the proposed expert. Such rules seek to ensure fair play when experts will be used. The side (plaintiff, state, or defense) who desires to offer the individual as an expert witness (the calling party) must present the individual in court for qualification. The calling party is allowed to question the individual first and should focus on establishing the (1) qualifications of the individual and (2) why expert testimony in this particular area is necessary. The calling party may (and should) ask questions regarding the education, training, experience or skills of the proposed expert. Generally speaking, the calling party will ask questions which will address those areas set forth in the factors outlined in the *Daubert* decision. Because these are the areas that the trial judge must evaluate, the calling party must establish that those factors have been satisfied.

Following questioning by the calling party, the proposed expert will be "tendered" as an expert witness. Tendering the proposed expert indicates to the court that the calling party has concluded questioning the witness and is requesting that the court accept the witness as an expert in the identified area. In some circumstances, the opposing side may accept the proposed expert without further questioning. However, these situations are rare. In the majority of cases, the opposing side will then question the proposed expert. In contested cases or in cases where the ultimate resolution of the important issues depend on the opinion of the expert, the opposing party may seek to discount or refute the qualifications of the individual in the hopes that the proposed expert will not be accepted as an expert witness in a particular area. Questioning by the opposing side may focus on the following areas:

- The qualifications of the expert;
- The relevance of the proposed testimony; and
- The reliability of the science, technique or area of expertise.

Following questioning by the opposing side, the trial court makes the final decision regarding the proposed expert. The expert is referred to as a "proposed expert" until the trial judge makes the final decision regarding expert status. The decision regarding qualification of an expert witness is within the "discretion of the court." In other words, the trial judge has the ultimate authority to determine, based on the evidence presented during *voir dire*, whether to qualify an individual as an expert witness. While the trial judge has the final decision-making authority with regard to admissibility of expert testimony, the jury will ultimately determine whether the expert testimony is helpful or credible. Once the court accepts the proposed expert, the expert may be called to testify as a witness at trial.

Expert Opinions

If an individual is qualified by the court as an expert witness, they may testify not only to those facts or circumstances that are within their personal knowledge but they make also give their expert opinion. The opinion of an expert witness is extremely important and can, in many cases, make the difference in the outcome of a case. Unlike lay witnesses (non-experts) jurors place significant weight on the value of expert testimony. An expert witness who is able to communicate clearly, educate the trier of fact on the issue requiring specialized knowledge and keep the information simple and direct will usually be well-regarded. In cases where a "battle of the experts" occurs, it is critically important to ensure that each side has a well-qualified individual testifying in that capacity. Due to the important role of expert witnesses in both civil and criminal cases, the Federal Rules of Evidence address issues associated with expert opinions. Federal Rules 703 and 705 are particularly important.

> ### Rule 703. Bases of Opinion Testimony by Experts
> The facts or data in the particular case upon which an expert bases an opinion or inference may be those perceived by or made known to the expert at or before the hearing. If of a type reasonably relied upon by experts in the particular field in forming opinions or inferences upon the subject, the facts or data need not be admissible in evidence in order for the opinion or inference to be admitted. Facts or data that are otherwise inadmissible shall not be disclosed to the jury by the proponent of the opinion or inference unless the court determines that their probative value in assisting the jury to evaluate the expert's opinion substantially outweighs their prejudicial effect.
> (http://www.law.cornell.edu/rules/fre/ACRRule703.htm)

A review of Rule 703 reveals that experts, unlike lay witnesses, are not required to limit their testimony to matters which are within their personal knowledge. Rather, there are a variety of acceptable bases for expert testimony. According to Federal Rule of Evidence 703, the opinion of an expert witness may be based on the following:

- Personal knowledge acquired prior to or during trial
- Secondhand information (including hearsay)
- Scholarly works and/or publications
- Evidence or testimony presented at trial

The Federal Rules of Evidence and state rules of evidence, which are similar in their expectations and requirements, appear to be quite flexible when it comes to acceptable bases for expert testimony. The most important consideration of any basis for expert testimony is that it be of a type " ... reasonably relied upon by experts in the particular field in forming opinions or inferences upon the subject..." (See Federal Rule of Evidence 703).

Most often, experts testify about their opinion without initially providing the underlying facts or data. However, if there are questions or concerns regarding the underlying basis of an expert opinion, the expert may be required to disclose the facts or data. Cross-examination about the underlying bases of an expert opinion is common. Federal Rule of Evidence 705 specifically addresses such situations.

Rule 705. Disclosure of Facts or Data Underlying Expert Opinion
The expert may testify in terms of opinion or inference and give reasons therefore without first testifying to the underlying facts or data, unless the court requires otherwise. The expert may in any event be required to disclose the underlying facts or data on cross-examination. (http://www.law.cornell.edu/rules/fre/ACRRule705.htm)

Court-Appointed Experts

In an effort to avoid cases where expert testimony is conflicting and confusing to the jury, the Federal Rules of Evidence allow the appointment of a court-appointed expert. Use of court-appointed experts is not common but rather is reserved for cases where expert testimony may be unduly complicated or confusing for the jury. The use of a neutral and objective court-appointed expert may avoid situations which render the trial nothing more than a "battle of the experts."

Federal Rule of Evidence 706 governs the use of court-appointed experts.

Rule 706. Court Appointed Experts
(a) Appointment.
The court may on its own motion or on the motion of any party enter an order to show cause why expert witnesses should not be appointed, and may request the parties to submit nominations. The court may appoint any expert witnesses agreed upon by the parties, and may appoint expert witnesses of its own selection. An expert witness shall not be appointed by the court unless the witness consents to act. A witness so appointed shall be informed of the witness' duties by the court in writing, a copy of which shall be filed with the clerk, or at a conference in which the parties shall have opportunity to participate. A witness so appointed shall advise the parties of the witness' findings, if any; the witness' deposition may be taken by any party; and the witness may be called to testify by the court or any party. The witness shall be subject to cross-examination by each party, including a party calling the witness.
(b) Compensation.
Expert witnesses so appointed are entitled to reasonable compensation in whatever sum the court may allow. The compensation thus

fixed is payable from funds which may be provided by law in criminal cases and civil actions and proceedings involving just compensation under the Fifth Amendment. In other civil actions and proceedings the compensation shall be paid by the parties in such proportion and at such time as the court directs, and thereafter charged in like manner as other costs.

(c) Disclosure of appointment.

In the exercise of its discretion, the court may authorize disclosure to the jury of the fact that the court appointed the expert witness.

(d) Parties' experts of own selection.

Nothing in this rule limits the parties in calling expert witnesses of their own selection.

(http://www.law.cornell.edu/rules/fre/ACRRule706.htm)

The following 10 facts reflect the essence of the appointment of court-appointed experts.

- Appointment is within the discretion of the court and does not limit the right of the parties to call their own expert witness.
- Court-appointed experts may be agreed upon by the parties or selected by the court.
- Parties in the case are allowed to voice their opinion regarding the expert, the qualifications of the expert or other matters which may affect the appointment.
- Court-appointed experts must agree to serve.
- Court-appointed experts must be notified in writing regarding their duties, role and expectations.
- Court-appointed experts must advise the court and the parties of their findings and opinion.
- Court-appointed experts may be required to participate in a pre-trial deposition or testify at trial.
- Court-appointed experts are subject to cross-examination by the parties.
- Court-appointed experts are entitled to compensation for their services.
- The amount of compensation is within the discretion of the court.

Whether serving as a court-appointed expert or an expert witness called by one side of a case, the primary function of the expert is to assist the trier of fact with an understanding of facts or issues which require specialized knowledge or skill. As such, the expert should not compromise his or her professional ethics in order to provide testimony which serves on side or the other. Rather, the expert should testify to an unbiased and objective professional opinion.

A few practice tips can be helpful to potential expert witnesses:

- Review all documents and files before rendering a professional opinion (do not give an opinion based solely on what is told to you by others).
- Review all documents and files before testifying. Refresh your memory before taking the stand.
- If you cannot remember, indicate that you cannot recall. It is far worse to attempt to "make it up as you go." A simple response "I cannot recall" is the best response.
- If you do not understand a question, simply indicate that you do not understand and ask for clarification. The lawyers can rephrase the question or simplify.
- Watch out for questions that ask you whether it is "possible" for this or that to have happened. Generally speaking, almost anything is "possible" and it is okay to admit that anything is possible. However, being possible does not make it likely or probable. Be sure to clarify when you respond to questions.
- Be sure you understand each and every assumption when asked to respond to a hypothetical situation.
- Keep your testimony simple, clear and concise. Remember, your job is to present an unbiased opinion which assists the judge or the jury.
- Do not overuse technical or scientific terms. If those terms are necessary, be sure to define them in layman's terms for the jury.
- Do not hesitate to answer questions about compensation. Most expert witnesses are compensated for their time and expertise. As such, it is not unethical to be paid for your services.
- Be open about the bases for your professional opinion. Be specific when testifying about how you arrived at your conclusions. Remember in your college algebra class when your instructor repeatedly told you to "show your work." The same principle applies when providing expert testimony. Be open about your methods and techniques.

Wrongful Convictions

Our collective concern about the integrity of forensic science or forensic scientists who are not respectful of professional ethics or boundaries is a result of an appreciation of the consequences of unethical, unprofessional or sloppy practices. For those who are convicted based on junk science, inaccurate techniques or biased testimony the results can be devastating. With the heightened

media attention given to cases involving wrongful convictions, society has become aware of the existence of these cases and their grave consequences.

Consider the sheer number of cases where an individual has been wrongfully
convicted. For example, The Center on Wrongful Convictions located at North-
western University has examined approximately 788 cases involving wrongful
convictions in the United States since the 1920s. Gross et al. (2005) identified 340
cases during the fifteen year period between 1989 and 2003 where individuals
were exonerated following wrongful conviction. The use of DNA resulted in the
exoneration of 40% of those individuals during that time period. According to The
Innocence Project at Benjamin N. Cordozo School of Law, 259 individuals have
been exonerated following wrongful conviction with the use of DNA technology.
While DNA has proven to be an invaluable tool in the efforts to exonerate individuals who are wrongfully convicted, the Innocence Project also identified "flawed
forensic science" as one of the five common themes which account for wrongful
convictions (http://www.innocenceproject.org). As such, the scientific tool that can
set a wrongfully-convicted person free can also result in their imprisonment.

Box 13.2 Crime Lab Woes Go Beyond Nassau

Newsday—December 19, 2010

Recent trouble at the Nassau County Police crime lab highlights a well-documented
but under-reported nationwide problem with the veracity and accuracy of police
"science."

In 2009, the National Academy of Science released the results of a congressionally
mandated study of forensic science. The committee found that forensic science is
plagued by the "absence of solid scientific research demonstrating the validity of
forensic methods"; a lack of research on human bias and error; labs governed by
law enforcement agencies instead of being independently run; a marked lack of adequate training and continuing education; nonadherence to rigorous performance
standards, and inadequate oversight.

This national study tells us that the problems in Nassau are hardly unique.

Perhaps because of television dramas like "CSI," forensic evidence is seen by the
public as well as by jurors as objective and conclusive. In truth, however, it is subjective and derived in many cases from the judgment of poorly educated technicians using subpar equipment and failing to diligently care for evidence.

Worse, the 2009 study found that much of what is touted as science is unsupported
by reasonable research in the specific field. Across the country, too many cases include questionable—and sometimes fraudulent—evidence.

The national report details problems in Houston, where several DNA experts employed by the lab alleged the DNA/serology unit was performing "grossly incompetent work" and producing deliberately misleading findings to help the prosecution.

In West Virginia, more than 100 convictions came into doubt and at least 10 were vacated because a crime lab employee falsified results. In 2008, a lab in Detroit had to be shut down because of false findings in 10 percent of a random sample of 200 murder cases.

These examples and the problems in Nassau taint every aspect of police forensics—from fingerprints to blood alcohol content, from ballistics to blood spatter, and from autopsies to child sex offense exams. The system is littered with poorly trained personnel, badly maintained equipment and unwarranted conclusions. We now have to add shoddy forensic practices to the list of systemic flaws that cause miscarriages of justice.

Criminal defense groups such as the National and New York Associations of Criminal Defense Lawyers have been at the forefront of the fight to improve standards for forensic labs. A number of improvements in the system are necessary.

First, "expert testimony" should be scrutinized initially by the prosecutors presenting the evidence. It is their responsibility to make sure that the forensic evidence they offer is credible. Next, the defense bar must do a better job at challenging forensics. Lawyers will prepare for weeks to cross examine an eye witness, but too often fail to ask a drug examiner any questions at all. Finally, judges must be the final gate keeper, excluding inadequate evidence. Just because witnesses calls themselves experts, doesn't mean they should be allowed to testify.

Next, we need legislation empowering a state agency with the ability to enforce national standards for methodology, education and accreditation. The group that issued the Nassau report is a private, not-for-profit organization that lacks real enforcement powers. Crime labs are not mandated to seek accreditation. We regulate everything from doctors to lawyers, from airline pilots to subway operators. Yet there is no regulatory body charged with overseeing and enforcing minimal standards for operation and staffing of police crime labs.

The curtain of "police science" is being pulled back, and we see not an all-knowing wizard but the flaws of a system in desperate need of an overhaul. Each failure potentially represents either the release of someone from whom society needs protection or an innocent person being unjustly imprisoned. We can and should be better.

Advances in forensic science technology, including properly trained lab personnel, will help law enforcement correctly identify perpetrators of crimes and thereby reduce the tragedy of wrongful convictions. Failing to act would be its own form of injustice.

(http://www.newsday.com/opinion/oped/crime-lab-woes-go-beyond-nassau-1.2550639)

Thinking Questions

1. What is an expert witness? What is the objectivity requirement?
2. What is the *Daubert* standard?
3. What are some of the differences in hired vs. court-appointed experts?
4. How have wrongful convictions created ethical issues in forensics?

Conclusion

The field of forensic science is extremely diverse. Unlike other professional fields such as medicine and law, attempts to create a uniform collection of standards, norms and ethics in the forensic science community are evolving. The NAS 2009 Report has artfully brought numerous issues regarding governance of the forensic science community to the forefront of the national discussion. Meaningful discussion coupled with a consistent commitment of resources will enable a system of integrated governance to be created and maintained.

Until integrated governance occurs, the field will continue to be influenced by the standards of conduct and rules of ethics promulgated by forensic science associations and organizations as well as a host of other professional associations for the various disciplines who participate in the world of forensic science. Additionally, forensic practitioners will be governed by accreditation standards, agency protocols and standard operating procedures in their labs or agencies. While the result is an extremely disaggregated network of professional norms, it becomes imperative that forensic science professionals strictly adhere to existing standards in order to ensure the most reliable result possible.

Scenarios

1. Assume that you are a crime scene investigator who works for a state police agency. Your supervisor, a lieutenant in Investigations, has just received a request for a team of CSIs to respond to a crime scene. Your lieutenant assigns you to lead the team and directs you to respond immediately. Your agency has been chasing a suspected serial killer for three years and the public is demanding an arrest. The suspect is currently in jail on a probation violation. As you leave to meet the team, your supervisor advises you to "get this guy no matter what it takes." How do you respond?

2. You are part of a forensic science planning team for the state legislature. The legislature is concerned about the fragmented approach to forensic science in your state and wants to explore ways to create a comprehensive and coordinated network of public and private forensic science providers. What are your recommendations for the legislature?

3. You are a DNA lab technician who works in a state crime laboratory. You recently completed analysis of several specimens from an ongoing rape investigation. A possible suspect is in jail charged with a minor offense. The local law enforcement agency is waiting on your report. The results of the DNA analysis are mixed. Two specimens match the suspect who is in jail,

but the other which is the more important, is inconclusive. You call the Chief of Police and attempt to explain the results, but he indicates that if two tests are a match, then we'll make the arrest. You are called to testify at trial as a DNA expert. What is your expert opinion?

4. You are a ballistics expert for a state law enforcement agency. You recently analyzed several bullet fragments collected from a possible murder scene. The local prosecutor contacts you daily to get an update on the testing. Once the testing is completed, the results are inconclusive. The fragments are so damaged you are unable to reach a conclusion. Once the prosecutor is advised of the results, she decides not to call you as a witness at trial. However, you later receive a subpoena from the defense. Are you required to testify? What will your testimony be in the case?

5. You are an independent document examiner. You testify in many cases and are willing to travel across the country, if necessary. A federal judge in a neighboring state has asked you to serve as a court-appointed expert witness in a income tax fraud case. You have a conflict with the dates of the trial and advise the court that you are unavailable during that week. The judge is not pleased and indicates that he will have you subpoenaed if you do not participate voluntarily. Is this appropriate? Why or why not?

6. You are a fingerprint examiner and are called as an expert witness by the prosecution in a homicide case. You have worked as an examiner for ten years. You have an undergraduate degree from an online university in philosophy and a master's degree in forensic science from a traditional graduate program. During *voir dire* to qualify you as an expert witness, the defense challenges your qualifications and argues that you lack a "scientific background." Is it likely that you will be able to testify as an expert in the field of fingerprint examination?

7. You are a forensic psychiatrist who often performs court-ordered evaluations to assess a defendant's competency to stand trial or sanity. You frequently testify as an expert witness in civil and criminal matters. You are hired by the prosecution to examine and evaluate a defendant in a capital case. You meet with the defendant two times and review his medical records. At trial you are asked to give your expert opinion regarding the defendant's mental health. What may you base your opinion on?

8. You are a social worker who works with abused and neglected children. You are assigned to child protective services in a county social services agency. You routinely testify in juvenile court cases about your observations and recommendations. During an adjudicatory hearing (trial), you are testifying on behalf of the county as an expert witness about removal of children from their home. You recommend that the children should be removed im-

mediately. You conducted a home study and interviewed the children's parents, grandparents, teachers and babysitters. You also found a diary excerpt from the mother's diary in the case file. All information in the mother's diary has been deemed inadmissible by the judge. However, it was this piece of evidence which most heavily influenced your recommendation. When you are asked about the basis for your recommendation may you testify about the diary excerpt?

References

Federal Rules of Evidence Rule 702
Federal Rules of Evidence Rule 703
Federal Rules of Evidence Rule 705
Federal Rules of Evidence Rule 706
Strengthening Forensic Science in the United States: A Path Forward. (2009). National Academy of Sciences. Washington, D.C.: The National Academies Press.

Cases Cited

Daubert v. Merrell Dow Pharmaceutical, 509 U.S. 579 (1993).
Frye v. United States, 293 F. 1013 (D.C. Cir. 1923).

Additional Websites

http://www.aafs.org
http://www.law.cornell.edu/rules/fre

About the Authors

The late **Kelly Cheeseman** was an Associate Professor of Criminal Justice at Messiah College. She received her Ph.D. in Criminal Justice from Sam Houston State University. Her research interests included female offenders, prison deviance, correctional officer stress and job satisfaction, institutional corrections, the death penalty, ethics and sexually deviant behavior. Kelly published articles in journals such as *The Journal of Criminal Justice, Journal of Criminal Justice Education, American Journal of Criminal Justice* and *Deviant Behavior*. She published a book entitled *Stress and the Correctional Officer* and was also a co-author of *The Death Penalty: Constitutional Issues, Commentaries, and Case Briefs*.

Claudia San Miguel is Associate Professor of Criminal Justice/Department Chair of the Department of Social Sciences at Texas A&M International University in Laredo, Texas. She is a co-author of *The Death Penalty: Constitutional Issues, Commentaries, and Case Briefs* and has also published in the area of intelligence-led policing strategies, anti-bully programs, youth violence, domestic violence, and community crime prevention. Dr. San Miguel is working on research involving the trafficking of women and children and has recently been awarded fellowships with the Department of Homeland Security to study the extant topics. She has also taught courses for the Department of State in Roswell, New Mexico on global human trafficking at the International Law Enforcement Academy.

Durant Frantzen is Associate Professor of Criminology at Texas A&M University–San Antonio. He is a co-author of *The Death Penalty: Constitutional Issues, Commentaries and Case Briefs*. Dr. Frantzen's recent research involves a grant funded evaluation of the Bexar County Specialty Courts. He also serves as a consultant to the Bexar County Sheriff's Department in the offender reentry programs division. His research has appeared in journals such as *Criminal Justice Review, Policing: An International Journal of Police Strategies and Management,* and *Criminal Justice Studies*.

Lisa S. Nored, J.D., Ph.D. is a Professor of Criminal Justice at the University of Southern Mississippi where she serves as Director of the School of Criminal Justice and the Mississippi Statistical Analysis Center. She earned undergraduate and graduate degrees in criminal justice, a law degree and the Ph.D. in Public Administration and Public Policy. Her research areas include juvenile justice, criminal justice policy and criminal law. Recent publications of her work appear in *American Journal of Criminal Justice, Journal of Police and Criminal Psychology* and *Criminal Justice Policy Review*.

Index